Chambers

JUNIOR *Illustrated* DICTIONARY

Revised and Updated

hachette INDIA

First published in 2024 by Hachette India
(Registered name: Hachette Book Publishing India Pvt. Ltd)
An Hachette UK company
www.hachetteindia.com

Chambers® is a registered trademark of Chambers Harrap Publishers Ltd,
an Hachette UK company

1

Cover Image Credits:
Shutterstock.com: Dinosaur, Bee, Rocket, Bug (Lady bird); **Pixabay.com:** Earth, Globe
Pexels.com: Xylophone, Lighthouse, Frog, Record, Mandrill, Guitar, Fish, Fungus, Astronaut, Loudspeaker, Skyscraper

The copyright details and credits for the photographs used in the book are on page 192.

ISBN 978-93-5731-390-2

Hachette Book Publishing India Pvt. Ltd
4th & 5th Floors, Corporate Centre
Plot No. 94, Sector 44, Gurugram – 122003, India

Typeset and design by Syed Salahuddin, Delhi

Printed and bound in India
by Manipal Technologies Limited

Contents

Introduction: About this dictionary	4
Your guide to the dictionary	6
Grammar guide and pronunciation notes	7
Word games	9
The dictionary	10

Picture topic pages

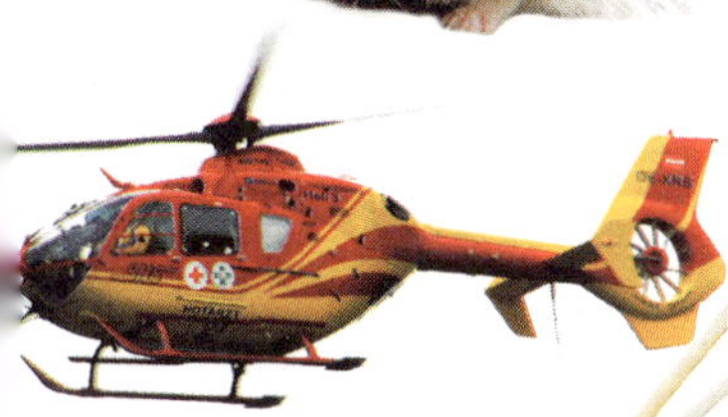

Aircraft	13
Bicycle	22–23
Birds	24
Cats	33
Castle	34
Dogs	54
Fish	65
Horses	82
Human body	83
Insects	87
Mammals	99
Musical instruments	105
Plants	120
Prehistoric animals	125
Reptiles	135
Shapes and colours	146
Ships and boats	148
Space	154
Trees	174
Zoos and wildlife parks	188

Spellcheck	189
Useful information	190
Countries and people	191
Image copyright information	192

About this dictionary

It has been estimated that if all the words of the English language (in all its varieties) could be collected into a single dictionary, there would be many millions of entries! Imagine how big it would be. But hardly the kind of dictionary the average user would require. So, needless to say, the headwords that appear in most dictionaries have been selected to meet the particular needs and interests of different groups of readers. That is why there is such a wide choice from 'mini' and 'pocket' dictionaries to 'concise' and big 'reference' dictionaries.

Children's dictionaries

Particularly important are the special dictionaries for children. For example, a 'first dictionary' designed for children who are just learning to read; a 'school dictionary' – an essential tool for the 11 years and older pupil; and a dictionary such as this Junior Illustrated Dictionary which has been specifically written and designed to meet the very special needs of children aged 9 upwards. These junior readers, who have started to read and write on their own, need a dictionary both as a reference and as an aid for checking spelling.

Choosing words carefully

The *Chambers Junior Illustrated Dictionary* provides a fresh and stimulating approach to the language based on a clear analysis of modern English and how it is used.

point

point points *noun*
1 the end of something sharp like a needle or a pencil.
2 a particular place or time. *At this point, she suddenly saw that everybody had left the room.*
3 a mark that somebody gets in a game or competition.
4 the purpose for doing something. *What's the point in taking your coat off if you're going straight out again?*

point points pointing pointed *verb*
if you point, you show where something is by using your finger.

pointed *adjective*
a pointed thing has a point at one end.

poison *noun*
a substance that will make you ill or kill you if it gets into your body.
poisonous *adjective*.

poke pokes poking poked *verb*
to poke somebody is to push something into them. *She poked me in my back with her finger.*

polar bear polar bears *noun*
a large, white bear that lives near the North Pole.

pole poles *noun*
1 a long, narrow, round piece of wood or metal. *a telegraph pole.* ◆ *a flag pole.*
2 a point at each end of the Earth that is farthest from the Equator. *the North Pole and the South Pole.*

police *noun*
those whose job is to protect people and make sure that everybody obeys the law.
policeman *noun*, **policewoman** *noun*, **police officer** *noun*.

polish polishes polishing polished *verb*
if you polish something, you rub it to make it shine. *David polishes his shoes.*
polish *noun*.

polite politer politest *adjective*
if you are polite, you behave well towards other people and think about how to make them feel comfortable. *It is polite to say "thank you" and "please".* ■ The opposite is **rude**.
politely *adverb*.

politics *noun*
all the activities to do with the government of a country.
political *adjective*.

pollen *noun*
a fine powder inside flowers that the wind or insects take to other flowers of the same kind so that they can produce seeds.

pollution *noun*
poisonous chemicals and other forms of dangerous dirt that cause damage to the air, water and environment.

pond ponds *noun*
a small area of water.

pony ponies *noun*
a small kind of horse.

pool pools *noun*
1 a small area of water.
2 a swimming pool.

poor poorer poorest *adjective*
1 a person who is poor has very little money. ■ The opposite is **rich**.
2 not good enough. *My spelling is very poor.*
3 unlucky or in a bad situation. *Poor John failed his driving test.* ● A word that sounds like **poor** is **pour**.

pop pops *noun*
1 modern, popular music.
2 a short, sharp sound like a small explosion.

poppy poppies *noun*
a plant with a large, bright flower.

popular *adjective*
liked by a lot of people. *a popular film.* ◆ *a popular girl.*
popularly *adverb*.

population populations *noun*
all the people who live in a particular area or country.

porcupine porcupines *noun*
an animal that has stiff hairs on its back, called quills.

pork *noun*
meat from a pig.

port ports *noun*
a place or town beside a large river or the sea where ships can stay and load and unload.

portable *adjective*
something that is portable is small enough or light enough to be carried around easily. *a portable computer.*

portion portions *noun*
an amount of food for one person. *a portion of chips.*

portrait portraits *noun*
a picture of a person.

122

position positions *noun*
1 the place where something is. *Can you check our position on the map?*
2 the way you are sitting, standing or lying down. *Get into a comfortable position.*

positive *adjective*
1 certain about something. *I'm positive I saw him.*
2 a positive number is higher than zero. ■ The opposite is **negative**.

possess possesses possessing possessed *verb*
if you possess something, you own it and it belongs to you. *Do you possess a TV?*

possible *adjective*
if something is possible, it can be done or it can happen. *Come as soon as possible.* ■ The opposite is **impossible**.
possibility *noun*, **possibly** *adverb*. *Is there the possibility of rain today?*

post posts *noun*
1 a long, thick, strong pole or piece of wood fixed in the ground. *a fence post.*
2 the system of sending letters and parcels from one place to another and delivering them to people's doors.

post posts posting posted *verb*
when you post a letter or a parcel, you send it through the post.

postcard postcards *noun*
a small piece of card, usually with a picture on one side, that you can use to send a short message to somebody. *They sent me a postcard with a cross drawn on it to show where their hotel is.*

postcode postcodes *noun*
a set of letters and numbers at the end of your address that tells the post office where you live. *My postcode is 110008.*

poster posters *noun*
a large picture, notice or advertisement that is put up on a wall.

post office post offices *noun*
1 a place where you can send letters and parcels and buy stamps.
2 the organization or group of people who collect, sort and deliver people's letters and parcels.

postpone postpones postponing postponed *verb*
if you postpone something, you put it off until later. *The race was postponed because of bad weather.*

pot pots *noun*
1 a round container. *a pot of tea.* ◆ *a paint pot.*
2 a container for plants to grow in made of plastic or clay.

potato potatoes *noun*
a white vegetable with a thin, brown skin that grows under the ground.

pottery *noun*
dishes and other objects made out of clay and then baked hard in a special oven called a kiln.

pouch pouches *noun*
1 a small bag.
2 a bag of skin that female kangaroos and some other female animals have on their stomach and which they use for carrying their babies in.

pounce pounces pouncing pounced *verb*
to pounce is to jump forward suddenly and catch hold of something. *The kitten pounced on the ball of wool.* ◆ *He pounced on the disk saying, "I thought I'd lost this!"*

pour pours pouring poured *verb*
when you pour a liquid, you tip a container such as a jug or bottle so that the liquid flows out. *Can you pour Granny another cup of tea?*

praise

poverty *noun*
people who live in poverty are very poor.

powder *noun*
tiny, dry grains that you get when you crush or grind something well.
powder *verb*.

power *noun*
1 the ability to do something. *Human beings have the power of speech.*
2 the force or strength of something. *The power of the wind brought the trees down.*
3 a person who has power can control what happens to a lot of people.

powerful *adjective*
a powerful person or thing has a lot of power. *a powerful king.* ◆ *a powerful engine.* ■ The opposite is **weak**.

practical *adjective*
1 to do with actually working or doing something rather than knowing or having ideas about it. *Do you have practical training in using computers?*
2 sensible, useful and likely to work. *a practical suggestion.* ◆ *He is a very practical man.*
practically *adverb*.
almost. *I've practically finished eating.*

practice *noun*
doing something again and again until you can do it well. *guitar practice.*

practise practises practising practised *verb*
if you practise something, you keep doing it until you can do it well. *Rachel practises her guitar playing for three hours everyday.*

praise praises praising praised *verb*
when you praise somebody, you say how well they have done something. *Everybody praised the brave firefighters.* ■ The opposite is **criticize**.

123

The *Chambers Junior Illustrated Dictionary* makes it a pleasure to learn about words.

Friendly and easy-to-use

This dictionary will help cultivate a genuine interest in all aspects of language. It is always friendly, simple and easy-to-use, helping readers develop skills that will enable them to become confident users of adult dictionaries and other alphabetical books of reference. A good dictionary should provide a wealth of information provided its usage is clear and accessible. In the pages that follow, we show young readers how to find their way around the dictionary and explore it. Among the many things they will explore and discover are: how to find a word; how words are spelt; the many different kinds of words; what words can do and what they mean; how words sometimes change for different purposes; and the complex relationship between words. And in no time they will discover that words are enjoyable (and that you can even have lots of fun and games with them, as we show on page 9).

Illustrations – integral and essential

This dictionary is not only a junior dictionary, it is also an illustrated dictionary – *Chambers Junior Illustrated Dictionary*. The colourful and fresh illustrations in this dictionary are not meant as decoration but are intended to work with the text. All are relevant and clarify definitions and, where they are labelled, further extend vocabulary. This is particularly true of the special topic pages and panels dealing with subjects such as bicycles, birds and castles, which are an important feature of this dictionary. So our advice to the young reader is: study the guide to the dictionary very carefully and find out about the dictionary's many special features. One will then be able to explore words, learn to understand them – and have fun with them.

The *Chambers Junior Illustrated Dictionary* is lively, authoritative and easy-to-use.

Your guide to the dictionary

How to find a word

All headwords (entries) in this dictionary are listed in the order of the alphabet. Words that begin with A are followed by those which begin with B, and so on until you reach Z. All the words under each letter of the alphabet are themselves in alphabetical order, so 'admit' follows 'admire', 'form' follows 'fork' and 'vampire' follows 'value'.

guide words
show first headword on the left-hand page and last headword on the right-hand page.

headword
all entries begin with a coloured headword showing how the word is spelt.

entry
a headword plus all its information, including any different definitions and related words.

alpha rule
helps you find the right letter section. The highlighted **b** shows that you are in the **b** section.

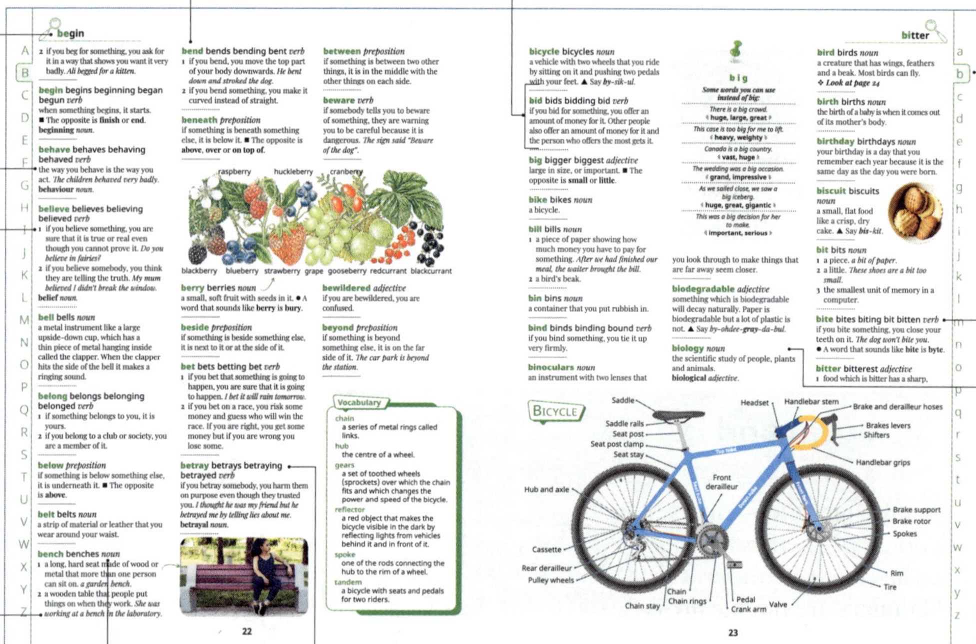

definition
what the word means.

different senses
some words have more than one meaning. Each different sense or definition is numbered.

example sentence
a sentence is used to make the meaning clearer.

verb tenses
show how the verb is written in the present continuous, present and past tenses.

related word
words belonging to the same word family.

changed form
indicates spelling changes when words are used in different ways. All plurals of nouns, verb inflections and the comparatives and superlatives of adjectives are shown.

part of speech
signals what a word does in a sentence. It shows whether the word is a noun, verb, adjective, adverb, conjunction or preposition (see page 8).

picture topic pages and panels
words and pictures are grouped by topic – birds, trees or space, for example. With their word boxes, these pages extend vocabulary and knowledge about the topic.

B b

new letter section
a big, coloured letter starts each section of the alphabet.

Useful features to help you explore words

thesaurus box

shows how one can vary and enrich one's vocabulary by choosing a different word with a similar meaning to express yourself. The *Chambers Junior Illustrated Dictionary* has thesaurus boxes for the following words: bad, big, eat, fast, good, happy, like, nice, piece, small.

happy

Some words you can use instead of happy:

I'm happy I've finished my homework.
content, pleased, glad

They are happy with their wedding presents.
delighted, pleased, thrilled

Christmas is a happy time of year.
merry, cheerful

small

Some words you can use instead of small:

All small animals look sweet.
baby, young

The writing is so small you need a magnifying glass to read it.
minute, tiny

Don't worry. It's only a small mistake.
unimportant, slight, minor

Centipedes have lots of small legs.
short

homophones

words which sound the same but have different meanings are marked with this sign ●

fair fairs *noun*
a place outside where rides, roundabouts and competitions are set up for people to have fun. ● A word that sounds like **fair** is **fare**.

pronunciation and rhyming words

words that are difficult or awkward to say have this sign ▲

fracture fractures *noun*
a break or crack in something, especially a bone. *Her arm is in a plaster because she has a fracture.* ▲ Say ***frak**-cher*. **fracture** *verb*.

opposites

the opposite meaning of some words is shown by this sign ■

fill fills filling filled *verb*
If you fill something, you put as much into it as it can hold. *Fiona filled the bottles with water.* ■ The opposite is **empty**.

spellcheck

the Spellcheck on page 189 lists many of the common words in the language. These are words that are not likely to be looked up for their meaning, but which may be difficult to spell. Also listed are some words in the dictionary which are difficult to spell – such as 'address', 'handkerchief' and 'jewellery'.

spelling tips

if you cannot find a word under one letter, it may be under another letter. For instance, the correct spelling for 'cangaroo is 'kangaroo'!

Spelling tip:

Some words that begin with a 'ca' sound are spelt with 'ka', for example 'kangaroo', 'karate'.

vocabulary boxes

many topic pages have a list of special words connected to the topic.

Vocabulary

broadleaf
trees with broad, flat leaves are deciduous.

deciduous
trees that shed their leaves in the autumn.

evergreen
conifers that keep their needle-like leaves in winter.

hardwood
the wood of slow-growing, broadleaf or deciduous trees. The wood is strong and used for making furniture.

heartwood
the oldest, hardest wood at the centre of the trunk.

first writings

at first, people would draw a picture of anything they wanted to record of – a woman, a horse, a bird for instance. The people of ancient Egypt could write quite complicated messages using these kinds of pictures. The people of ancient China also drew pictures of things they wanted us to know about. In time, these pictures became much simpler – just a few brush strokes known as 'characters'. Chinese is still written in characters.

About 3,000 years ago, a way of writing was developed which used signs for each sound in a word. Each letter stood for a sound. We call these letters alphabets. These are the 'bricks' we use to build our language.

Parts of Speech

noun: cheetah, antelope
The ***cheetah*** is chasing the ***antelope.***

noun
the 'name' of a person, place, thing or idea. ***Jim's video*** on ***justice*** and ***freedom*** was in his ***flat*** in ***Leeds.***

pronoun
stands in place of a noun.
He gave ***her*** a bar of soap. ***It*** was scented.

verb
a word expressing action or being. When he ***broke*** the window, he ***felt*** unhappy.

adjective
a word that describes a noun. It was a ***cold, frosty*** day so she wore a ***large, woollen*** hat.

adverb
gives more information about an adjective or another adverb. The ***very*** large horse galloped ***quickly*** around the course.

conjunction
a word that joins words or phrases. Jane ***and*** Dan went to work, ***but*** we stayed at home.

preposition
shows the relationship between one noun and another. The cat is sitting ***on*** the mat. The mouse is ***under*** the table.

interjection
a word that expresses a strong feeling. ***Ouch!*** That hurts. ***Oh!*** How nice.

verb: fit fits fitting fitted
*I **fitted** the jigsaw puzzle together.*

adjective: asleep
*The cat was **asleep** by the fire.*

adverb: upside-down
*The sloth is hanging **upside-down**.*

Pronunciation notes

Whenever you see this symbol '▲' in the dictionary a note will follow to help you pronounce a word properly. Sometimes, the word will be spelt out for you using these symbols, other times, it will be rhymed with a less difficult word. Pronouncing some words can seem hard but you will find it easier if you say the word out loud. Remember: practice makes perfect!

Get used to these sounds and soon you'll have no problems even with the longest, most complicated words!

Consonant sounds

Symbol used	*As in:*
p	**p**an
b	**b**ed
t	**t**ip
d	**d**ip
k	**c**ar, **k**ey
g	**g**et
f	**f**at
v	**v**an
th	**th**in and **th**ough
s/ss	**s**oup
z	**z**ero, bar**s**
sh	**sh**ip and plea**s**ure
h	**h**ot
ch	**ch**ips
j	**j**ump
m	**m**an
n	**n**o
ng	si**ng**
w	**w**et
l	**l**et
r	**r**ed
y	**y**et

Vowel sounds

Symbol used	*As in:*
i	b**i**t
e	b**e**d
a	m**a**t
o	d**o**g
u	c**u**t and p**u**ll
ee	s**ee**n, happ**y**
oo	f**oo**l, lum**i**nous
ar/ah	c**ar**, f**a**ther
or	f**our**, c**au**ght, p**aw**
ay/a+e	s**ay**, m**a**k**e**
y/ye	fl**y**, b**i**cycle
oy	b**oy**, p**oi**nt
oh/o+e	m**o**ment, b**oa**t
ow	c**ow**
ai	h**ai**r

Word games

Dictionaries need not be just for looking up words. You can have a lot of fun with them too. These word games will help you improve your wordpower. You can play them on your own or you could team up with your friends and have a wordpower competition.

Rhyming phrases

Think of a noun and then find an adjective that rhymes with it. We've started you off with a couple. How many pairs can you make?

fat/cat
green/bean

Guess what I am defining

1 living things so tiny that you cannot see them without a microscope.
2 a kind of dancing that tells a story.
3 a long hole in the ground that has been dug along the side of a road so that water can drain away.

Do you know the word – the plural – for more than one:

sheep, deer, child, goose, calf, mouse, man, foot, city, loaf?

Snakewords

This snake is made up of words that go together to make new words. What is the longest snakeword you can make?

Clockwise games

How many words can you find reading clockwise around this circle?

What's the word?

Look at these pictures and work out what they all have in common.

Tongue twisters

Try to say these tongue twisters ten times and very quickly:

Freddy thrush flies through a thick fog.
Red lorry, yellow lorry.
She sells sea shells by the sea shore.
The six Sheiks' sixth sheep's sick.
The Leith police dismisseth us.
Still the stinking steamer sank.

Which is the most difficult to say? Try to make up some tongue twisters of your own.

Can you match the opposites in this list?

deep	end
late	remember
hot	sad
careful	early
above	shallow
forget	narrow
happy	below
tall	careless
wide	cold
begin	short

Can you complete the following words?

butter...... (*clue:* an insect)
king......... (*clue:* a bird)
key........... (*clue:* as on a piano)
port......... (*clue:* be carried)
round...... (*clue:* the traffic)
sea.......... (*clue:* smell it)
sea.......... (*clue:* summer or autumn)
tight........ (*clue:* a circus act)
toad......... (*clue:* don't eat it)

Mark the odd one out

hat; bat; mat; dot; fat;
cleaner; kinder; fastest; bigger;
grunt; squeak; quack; ring; hiss;
bicycle; train; bus; toboggan;

Secret messages

An easy way to write a secret message is to write the words back to front. So instead of writing ELEPHANT you would write TNAHPELE.
Can you work out what this message says?

TEEM EM NI EHT TNARUATSER TA YADDIM.

Similar meaning

Can you match all the words with similar meanings?

harmful	chat
piece	find
discover	leave
even	damaging
begin	frightened
feel	touch
talk	start
angry	smooth
afraid	cross
go	bit

Answers on page 190

A a

abandon abandons abandoning abandoned *verb*
if you abandon somebody or something, you leave them behind. *The puppies had been abandoned by their mother.*

abbreviation abbreviations *noun*
a short way of writing a word or a group of words. *"Rd" is an abbreviation for "Road".*

ability abilities *noun*
if you have the ability to do something, you can do it. *Sarah has the ability to draw well.*

aboard *adverb, preposition*
if you are aboard a train, bus, ship or plane, you are on it or in it.

above *adverb, preposition*
higher than something. *My bedroom is above the kitchen. (preposition)* ◆ *Put the book on the shelf above. (adverb)*
■ The opposite is **below** or **beneath**.

abroad *adverb*
if you go abroad, you go to another country. *We went abroad for our summer holiday.*

absent *adjective*
if somebody is absent, they are not here. *Katie was absent from school yesterday.* ■ The opposite is **present**.

absorb absorbs absorbing absorbed *verb*
when a cloth or sponge absorbs water, it soaks it up.

accelerator accelerators *noun*
the pedal that you press with your foot to make a car go faster.

accent accents *noun*
1 the way that a person from a certain place speaks. *He spoke with a Yorkshire accent.*
2 a mark on a word that shows you how to pronounce it. *"Café" has an accent on the "e".*

accept accepts accepting accepted *verb*
1 if you accept something that somebody gives you, you take it. *She accepted the gift.*
2 if you accept an invitation to a party, you say that you will come.
■ The opposite is **refuse**.

accident accidents *noun*
something bad that happens without being planned. *Ella dropped the drinks. It was an accident.*
accidentally *adverb.*

accompany accompanies accompanying accompanied *verb*
if you accompany somebody, you go with them. *The teacher accompanied the children to the sports centre.*

account accounts *noun*
1 if you give an account of something, you describe what happened. *He wrote an account of the bank robbery in the local newspaper.*
2 an arrangement with a bank to keep and also withdraw your money.

accurate *adjective*
exactly right. *Is your watch accurate?*
▲ Say ***ak-yoo-rut***.

accuse accuses accusing accused *verb*
if you accuse somebody, you say that they have done something wrong. *The man was accused of stealing the money.*

ace aces *noun*
a playing-card with one symbol on it. *the ace of hearts.*

ache aches *noun*
a pain in your body that goes on hurting, such as earache. ▲ Rhymes with **take**.

achieve achieves achieving achieved *verb*
if you achieve something, you get it after trying very hard.

acid acids *noun*
a liquid that tastes sour such as lemon juice or vinegar. Some strong acids can burn your skin.

acid rain *noun*
rain that has chemicals in it from factories and cars. Acid rain damages trees, rivers and buildings.

acorn acorns *noun*
the nut that grows on an oak tree.

acrobat acrobats *noun*
a person who can do difficult and clever balancing tricks.

across *adverb, preposition*
if you walk across something such as a field, you walk from one side to the other.

act acts *noun*
1 one part of a play. *This play has three acts.*
2 something that you do. *an act of kindness.*

act acts acting acted *verb*
1 when you act, you do something. *She acted quickly to save the boy from drowning.*
2 if you act in a play or film, you play a part in it.

action actions *noun*
something that you do. *Frankie's fast actions saved the man's life.*

active *adjective*
if you are active, you are always busy and able to do lots of things.

activity activities *noun*
1 something that you do. *Playing football is his favourite activity.*
2 a lot of things happening and people doing things. *During the carnival there is a lot of activity on the streets.*

actor actors *noun*
a person who acts in a play or film.

add adds adding added *verb*
1 when you add numbers, you put them together to find an answer. *If you add 2 and 3, you get 5.* ■ The opposite is **subtract**.
2 if you add something to something else, you put the two things together. *She put coffee in a mug and added hot water and milk.*
addition *noun*.

address addresses *noun*
your address is the number or name of the building where you live, and the street and town where it is. *My address is 21 Morris Road, Southampton.*

adjective adjectives *noun*
a word that tells you what somebody or something is like. In the sentence "Tom has a new, red bike", "new" and "red" are adjectives.

admire admires admiring admired *verb*
if you admire somebody or something, you think they are very good. *Everyone admired Katie's painting.*

admit admits admitting admitted *verb*
if you admit something, you agree that you have done something. *Matthew admitted that he had broken the glass.*

adopt adopts adopting adopted *verb*
when somebody adopts a child, they take the child to live with them as part of their family.

adult adults *noun*
a person or an animal that is fully grown. *an adult bear.*

advance advances advancing advanced *verb*
when something advances, it moves forward. *The army advanced towards the enemy.*

advantage advantages *noun*
something that can help you to do better than other people. *In a game of basketball, it is an advantage to be tall.* ■ The opposite is **disadvantage**.

adventure adventures *noun*
something exciting that happens to you. *We got lost in the snow. It was a real adventure!*

adverb adverbs *noun*
a word that tells you more about a *verb, adjective* or another *adverb*. In the sentence "Ewen quickly opened the parcel", "quickly" is an adverb.

advertise advertises advertising advertised *verb*
if you advertise, you tell people about things that you are selling. *There is a poster to advertise a coach service.*

advertisement advertisements *noun*
information on a poster, in a newspaper or on the television that tells you about something to buy or something to do. ▲ Say ***ad-ver-tiss-ment***.

advice *noun*
if somebody gives you advice, they tell you what they think you should do.

advise advises advising advised *verb*
if you advise somebody, you tell them what you think they should do.

aerial aerials *noun*
a wire that sends out or receives radio or television signals. ▲ Say ***air-ee-al***.

aeroplane aeroplanes *noun*
a flying machine with wings and an engine.

aerosol aerosols *noun*
a can with liquid inside. You press a button to send out the liquid in a spray. ▲ Say ***air-o-sol***.

A B C D E F G H I J K L M N O P Q R S T U V W X Y Z

affect affects affecting affected *verb*
if something affects you, it makes you different in some way. *Smoking affects your health.*

affection *noun*
the feeling of loving or liking somebody. *Samantha shows great affection for her little sister Josephine.*
affectionate *adjective.*

afford affords affording afforded *verb*
if you can afford something, you have enough money to buy it. *I can't afford any more sweets this week.*

afraid *adjective*
if you are afraid, you think something bad will happen to you. *Are you afraid of the dark?*

afternoon afternoons *noun*
the part of the day between midday and evening. *I'm going swimming on Saturday afternoon.*

again *adverb*
if you do something again, you do it once more. *Tell me that story again.*

against *preposition*
1 if you play against somebody in a match, you are on the other side to them. *We played against a team from another school.*
2 next to, or touching something. *The ladder was against the wall.*
3 if you are against something, you do not agree with it. *I'm against testing drugs on animals.*

age ages *noun*
1 your age is how old you are.
2 a certain time in history. *Bronze Age.*

agree agrees agreeing agreed *verb*
if you agree with somebody, you think the same about something.
■ The opposite is **disagree**.
agreement *noun.*

agriculture *noun*
agriculture is keeping animals and growing plants for food.
agricultural *adjective.*

ahead *adverb*
in front of somebody or something. *We walked slowly, but the dog ran ahead.*

aim aims aiming aimed *verb*
1 if you aim at something, you point something such as an arrow at the thing you want to hit.
2 if you aim to do something, you try to do it. *We aimed to get home by 6 o'clock.*

air *noun*
the mixture of gases that we breathe.

aircraft aircraft *noun*
any machine that can fly. Aeroplanes and helicopters are aircraft. ❖ ***Look at page 13***

airport airports *noun*
a place where aeroplanes take off and land. *Heathrow is a very large airport near London.*

aisle aisles *noun*
a place where you can walk between rows of seats, such as in a theatre or a church. *The bride and groom walked down the aisle.* ▲ Say ***eye-l***.

alarm alarms *noun*
1 something such as a bell or a flashing light that warns you of something. *a burglar alarm.*
2 a sudden feeling of fear.

album albums *noun*
1 a book that you keep things such as photographs or stamps in.
2 a CD, tape or record with several different pieces of music on it.

alcohol *noun*
drinks such as wine and beer have alcohol in them. If people drink too much alcohol, they get drunk.
alcoholic *adjective. Wine and beer are alcoholic.*

alien aliens *noun*
a creature from another planet.
▲ Say ***ay-lee-en***.

alike *adjective*
if two things or people are alike, they are the same in some way. *The twins are not identical, but they are alike.*

alive *adjective*
a person, an animal or a plant that is alive is living now. *Plants need water to stay alive.* ■ The opposite is **dead**.

allergy allergies *noun*
an illness caused by something that does not normally make people ill. *Some people have an allergy to dust.*
allergic *adjective.*

alley alleys *noun*
a narrow path between buildings.

Aircraft

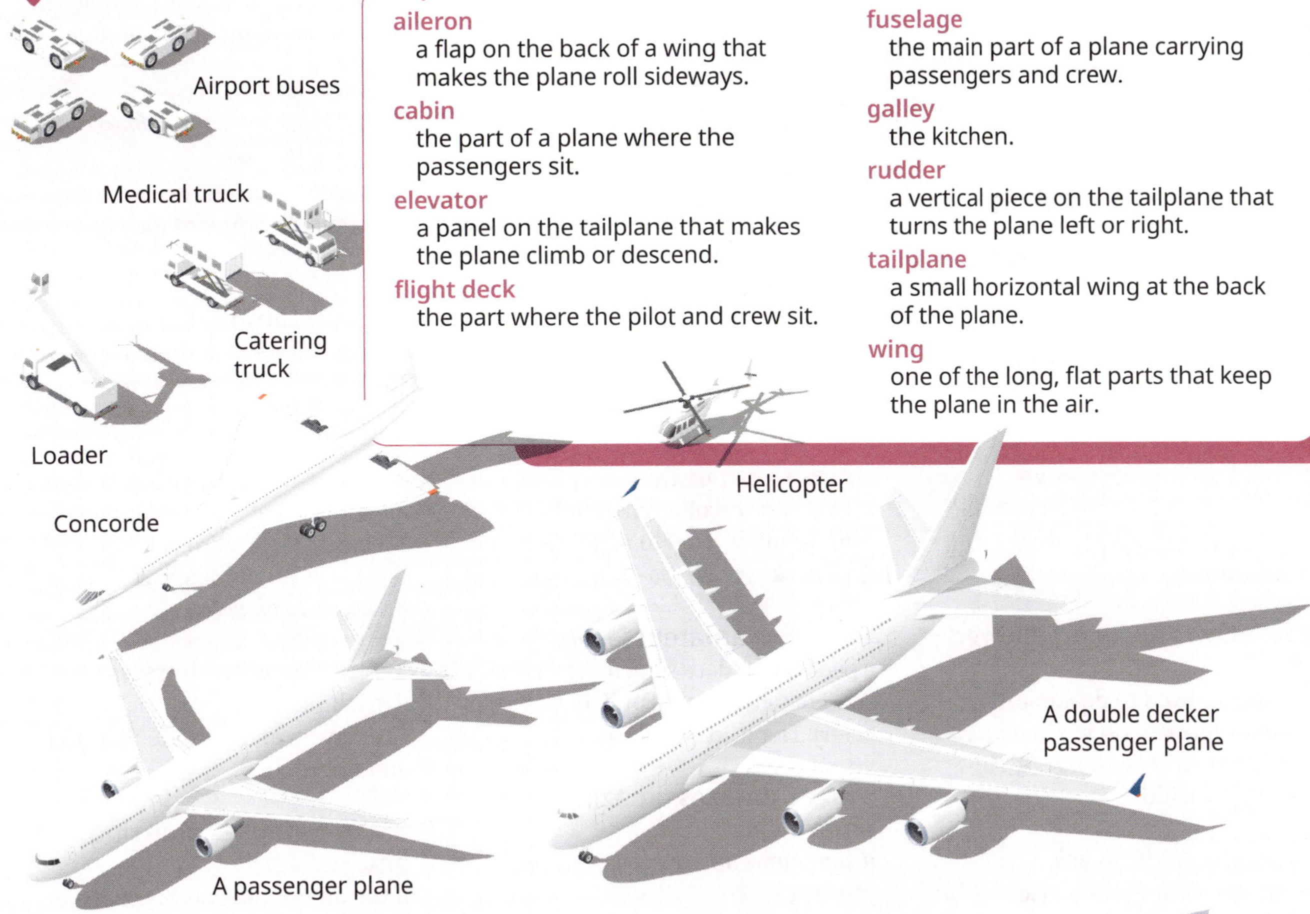

Vocabulary

aileron
a flap on the back of a wing that makes the plane roll sideways.

cabin
the part of a plane where the passengers sit.

elevator
a panel on the tailplane that makes the plane climb or descend.

flight deck
the part where the pilot and crew sit.

fuselage
the main part of a plane carrying passengers and crew.

galley
the kitchen.

rudder
a vertical piece on the tailplane that turns the plane left or right.

tailplane
a small horizontal wing at the back of the plane.

wing
one of the long, flat parts that keep the plane in the air.

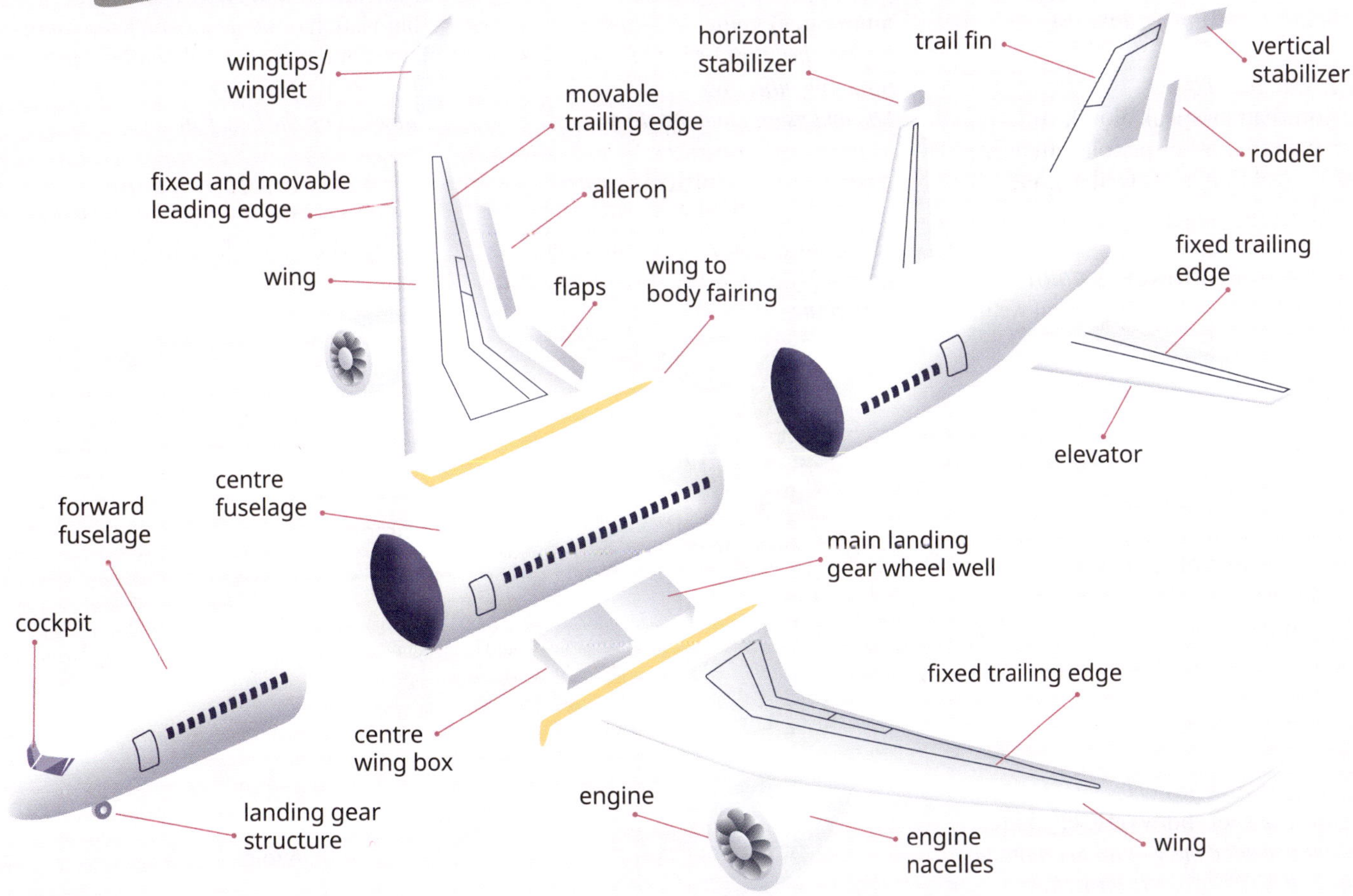

a b c d e f g h i j k l m n o p q r s t u v w x y z

A B C D E F G H I J K L M N O P Q R S T U V W X Y Z

alligator alligators *noun*
a large reptile similar to a crocodile but with shorter, wider jaws.
❖ ***Look above***

allow allows allowing allowed *verb*
if you are allowed to do something, somebody lets you do it. *I'm allowed to stay up later at weekends.* ■ The opposite is **forbid**.

alone *adjective, adverb*
by yourself, with nobody else. *Sophie walked home alone. (adverb)*

aloud *adverb*
if you read or speak aloud, you do it so that other people can hear.
● A word that sounds like **aloud** is **allowed**.

alphabet alphabets *noun*
all the letters from A to Z that we use to write words.
alphabetical *adjective*.

already *adverb*
before this time. *We ran to the bus stop but the bus had already gone.*

alter alters altering altered *verb*
if you alter something, you change it in some way. *My dad has altered his working hours so he can pick me up from school.*
alteration *noun*.

altogether *adverb*
counting everybody or everything. *My uncle gave me ₹5 and my aunt gave me ₹10, so I've got ₹15 altogether.*

aluminium *noun*
a light, silver-coloured metal. Aluminium is used to make cans and tin foil. ▲ Say *al-yoo-**min**-yum*.

amateur amateurs *noun*
a person who does something such as a sport because they enjoy it, but does not get paid for it. ▲ Say ***am**-at-ur*.

amaze amazes amazing amazed *verb*
if something amazes you, it surprises you very much.
amazement *noun*.
We watched the acrobat in amazement.
amazing *adjective*.
She told us an amazing story.

ambition ambitions *noun*
if you have an ambition to do something, you want to do it very much. *My ambition is to learn to fly an aeroplane.*

ambulance ambulances *noun*
a special van that takes people who are hurt or ill to the hospital.

among *preposition*
1 in the middle of. *The house stood among the trees.*
2 shared between two or more people. *She divided the sweets among the children.*

amount amounts *noun*
an amount of something is how much there is. *I get the same amount of pocket money as my friend.*

amphibian amphibians *noun*
an animal that lives on land but breeds in water. Frogs, toads and newts are amphibians. ▲ Say *am **fib**-ee-an*. ❖ ***Look below***

amplifier amplifiers *noun*
a machine that makes sounds louder. CD players and cassette players have amplifiers.

amuse amuses amusing amused *verb*
if you amuse somebody, you make them laugh or smile, or you keep them happy and busy. *The joke amused my sister.* ◆ *We played games to amuse ourselves on the long journey.*

ancestor ancestors *noun*
your ancestors are members of your family who lived a long time ago.

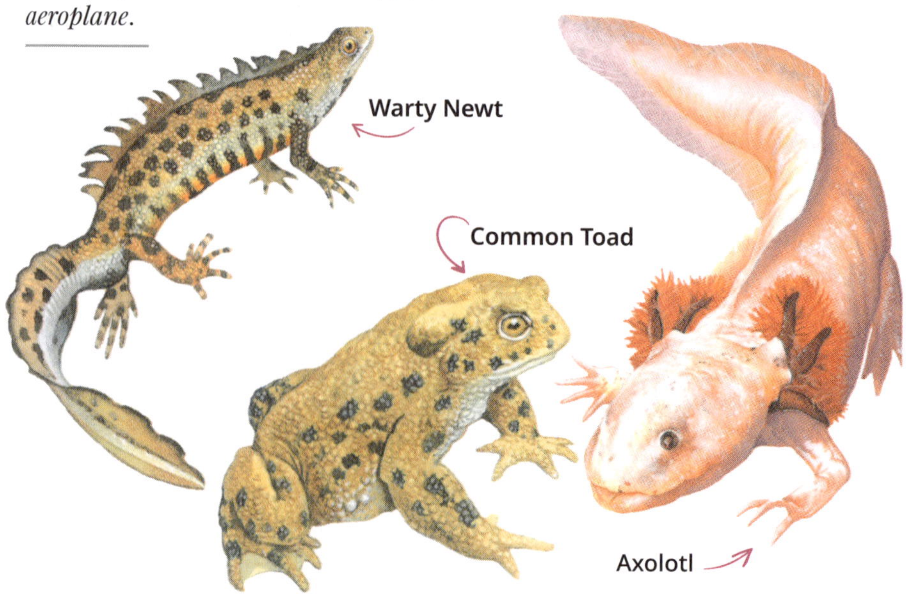

anchor anchors *noun*
a heavy, metal hook on a long chain that you drop into the water from a ship or boat to stop the ship or boat from floating away. ▲ Say ***ang-ker***.

ancient *adjective*
very old. *an ancient castle*.

anger *noun*
anger is the strong feeling you have when you think something is unfair.
angrily *adverb*.

angle angles *noun*
the corner where two lines meet.

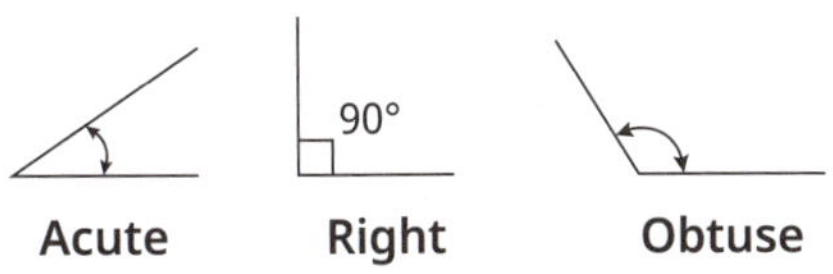

angry angrier angriest *adjective*
if you are angry, you feel anger.

animal animals *noun*
any living thing that is not a plant. Birds, fish, insects, frogs, snakes, rabbits and elephants are all animals.

ankle ankles *noun*
your ankle is the part of your leg where it joins your foot.

anniversary anniversaries *noun*
a day when you remember something special that happened on the same date in another year. *Today is my parents' 11th wedding anniversary*.

announce announces announcing announced *verb*
if you announce something, you say it in front of a lot of people. *Miss Burton announced to the class that she was leaving at the end of term*.

annoy annoys annoying annoyed *verb*
if you annoy somebody, you make them angry.
annoyance *noun*.

annual *adjective*
if something is annual, it happens once every year. *The town carnival is an annual event*.

answer answers answering answered *verb*
when you answer, you say something to somebody who has asked you a question or said something to you. *"What's the capital of France?" "Paris," she answered*.
▲ Say ***an-sur***.
answer *noun*.

ant ants *noun*
a tiny insect. Ants live in large groups called colonies.

antelope antelopes *noun*
an animal like a deer with horns and long legs that can run fast. Antelopes live in Africa and parts of Asia.

antenna antennas or antennae *noun*
1 a long, thin part on the head of an insect that it uses for feeling with.
2 an aerial.

anticlockwise *adjective, adverb*
if you turn anticlockwise, you move in the opposite direction to the hands on a clock. ■ The opposite is **clockwise**.

antique antiques *noun*
a thing that is very old and may be worth a lot of money. *My grandma collects antiques*. ▲ Say *an-**teek***.

antiseptic antiseptics *noun*
a cream or liquid that you put on a wound to keep it clean and germ-free.

antler antlers *noun*
one of two large horns that grow on the head of a male deer. The male deer, called a stag, loses its antlers every year and grows new ones.

anxious *adjective*
if you are anxious about something, you worry about it. *Mum was anxious because we were late home*. ▲ Say ***ank-shuss***.

ape apes *noun*
an animal like a big monkey with no tail. Gorillas, chimpanzees, orangutans and gibbons are all apes. ❖ ***Look below***

apologize apologizes apologizing apologized *verb*
if you apologize, you say you are sorry. *Billy apologized for being late*.
apology *noun*.

a b c d e f g h i j k l m n o p q r s t u v w x y z

apostrophe apostrophes *noun*
1 a mark that you use in writing to show that something belongs to somebody. *Lucy's book.* ◆ *my parent's house.*
2 a mark that you use in writing to show that a letter has been missed out. In the word "I'm", which is short for "I am", the apostrophe shows that the letter "a" has been missed out.
▲ Say *a-**poss**-trof-ee.*

apparatus *noun*
1 the pieces of equipment that you need to do a scientific experiment.
2 things such as bars and ropes that you use in gymnastics.

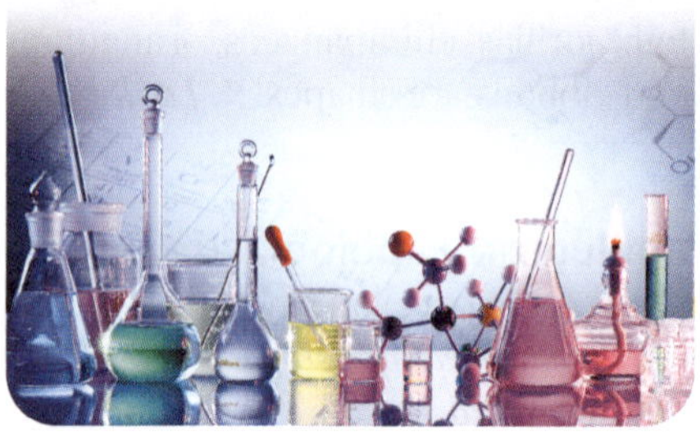

appear appears appearing appeared *verb*
1 if somebody or something appears, they come to a place where you can see them. *He appeared from behind a tree.* ■ The opposite is **disappear**.
2 if something appears to be a certain way, it seems to be that way. *A magnifying glass makes things appear bigger than they really are.*

appearance appearances *noun*
1 if you make an appearance, you come to a place where people can see you. *We all sat down when the teacher made a sudden appearance.*
2 your appearance is what you look like. *Having her hair cut really changed her appearance.*

appendix appendixes *noun*
your appendix is a small, closed tube inside your body. It is part of the long tube called the intestine that carries food out of your stomach.

appetite appetites *noun*
if you have an appetite, you are ready to eat something. *I hope you've got a big appetite because I've cooked a lot of food for dinner.*

applause *noun*
applause is when people clap their hands together to show that they liked something.

apple apples *noun*
a hard, round and green, red or yellow fruit that grows on a tree. Apples have seeds called pips inside.

apply applies applying applied *verb*
1 if something such as a rule applies to you, you must do what it says. *School rules apply to everyone in the school.*
2 if you apply for something such as a job, you write to somebody to ask for it.
application *noun.*

appointment appointments *noun*
a time that you have arranged to see somebody. *I have a doctor's appointment at 4 o'clock.*

appreciate appreciates appreciating appreciated *verb*
if you appreciate something, you are grateful for it. *I appreciate all your help.*
appreciation *noun.*

approach approaches approaching approached *verb*
if something approaches, it comes nearer to something/someone. *The train is approaching the station.*

approve approves approving approved *verb*
if you approve of something, you think it is good and right. *Mum doesn't approve of my new haircut.*

apricot apricots *noun*
a soft, round, orange-yellow fruit with a large kernel in the middle.

apron aprons *noun*
a piece of clothing that you wear over your clothes to keep them clean when you are cooking.

aquarium aquariums or aquaria *noun*
1 a glass tank where fish and other water animals are kept.
2 a building with lots of glass tanks where people can look at fish.

arch arches *noun*
a part of a bridge, building or wall that has a curved shape. Arches support buildings and let people, trains, boats, cars and other vehicles pass underneath.

archery *noun*
the sport of shooting with a bow and arrow. You shoot the arrow at a circular target.

architect architects *noun*
a person whose job is to design buildings. ▲ Say ***ar**-kee-tekt.*

area areas *noun*
1 a part of a country, a town or the world. *My uncle comes from this area.*
2 the size of a flat place. *If a room is 3 metres wide and 4 metres long, it has an area of 12 square metres.*
3 a place that you use for something special. *a play area.*

arena arenas *noun*
a place with rows of seats around it where you can watch sport or concerts.

argue argues arguing argued *verb*
if you argue with somebody, you speak in an angry way because you do not agree with them.
argument *noun*.

arithmetic *noun*
doing sums and working with numbers to find an answer.

arm arms *noun*
your arm is the part of your body between your shoulder and your hand.

armed *adjective*
if somebody is armed, they have a weapon, such as a sword or a gun and they are ready to fight.

armour *noun*
a suit of strong metal that soldiers used to wear to protect their bodies in battle.

arms *noun*
arms are guns, swords, bombs and other weapons used in fighting.

army armies *noun*
a large group of soldiers who are trained to fight on land in a war.

arrange arranges arranging arranged *verb*
1 if you arrange something such as a party, you plan it. *We are arranging a birthday party for my sister.*
2 if you arrange things such as flowers or your belongings, you set them out in a certain way or put them in order. *We arranged the books on the shelf in alphabetical order.*
arrangement *noun*.

arrest arrests arresting arrested *verb*
when the police arrest somebody, they catch them and accuse them of breaking the law.

arrive arrives arriving arrived *verb*
if you arrive somewhere, you get there. *She arrived at 3 o'clock.* ■ The opposite is **depart** or **leave**.
arrival *noun*.

arrow arrows *noun*
1 a thin stick with a sharp point at one end that you shoot from a bow.
2 a sign that points to tell you the way.

art *noun*
art is something beautiful that somebody has made, such as a painting or a statue.

artery arteries *noun*
an artery is one of the large tubes that carries blood from your heart to all parts of your body.

artificial *adjective*
if something is artificial, it is made by people and is not natural. *These are artificial flowers.*

artist artists *noun*
a person who draws or paints pictures or makes other beautiful things.

ash ashes *noun*
1 the grey powder that is left after something has been burnt.
2 a tree with grey bark that loses its leaves in winter.

ashamed *adjective*
if you are ashamed of something you have done, you are sorry and unhappy about it. *William was ashamed that he had told a lie.*

ask asks asking asked *verb*
1 if you ask a question, you say that you want to know something. *"What time is it?" she asked.*
2 if you ask for something, you tell somebody that you want it. *Tom asked for a bike for his birthday.*

asleep *adjective*
sleeping. *The cat was asleep by the fire.*
■ The opposite is **awake**.

assembly assemblies *noun*
a meeting of a big group of people for something special. *We have a school assembly every morning.*

assist assists assisting assisted *verb*
if you assist somebody, you help them.
assistance *noun*, **assistant** *noun*.

assorted *adjective*
if things such as sweets or biscuits are assorted, all different kinds are mixed together.

asthma *noun*
an illness that makes it difficult for a person to breathe. ▲ Say ***ass**-ma*.

astonish astonishes astonishing astonished *verb*
if something astonishes you, it surprises you very much. *She was astonished to hear the parrot talk.*

astronaut astronauts *noun*
a person who travels to space.

astronomy *noun*
the study of the Sun, Moon, planets and stars.

ate* past of eat.

* 'Past of' means 'past tense of'.

A B C D E F G H I J K L M N O P Q R S T U V W X Y Z

athlete athletes *noun*
a person who is good at sports such as running, jumping and throwing.

athletics *noun*
sports such as running, high jump, long jump and throwing.

atlas atlases *noun*
a book of maps.

atmosphere *noun*
1 the layer of gases that surrounds the Earth.
2 the feeling that a room or a place has. *The lounge had a warm, cosy atmosphere.*

atom atoms *noun*
a very tiny part of something. Everything is made of atoms. *Water is made of hydrogen and oxygen atoms.*

attach attaches attaching attached *verb*
if you attach something to something else, you join or fasten them together. *We attached the rope to a tree.*

attack attacks attacking attacked *verb*
if somebody attacks another person, they try to hurt them.
attack *noun.*

attempt attempts *noun*
a try. *After two attempts, I managed to get over the wall.*
attempt *verb.*

attention *noun*
if you pay attention to somebody, you listen to them or watch them carefully.

attic attics *noun*
a room or space under the roof of a house. *We keep our old toys in the attic.*

attract attracts attracting attracted *verb*
1 if somebody or something attracts you, you like them or find them interesting. *Katie was attracted to the red car.*
2 to attract also means to make somebody or something come nearer. *Magnets attract iron.*

attractive *adjective*
very nice to look at. *an attractive scarf.*

audience audiences *noun*
a group of people who are watching a play, film or concert. *At the end of the concert the audience applauded loudly.*

aunt aunts *noun*
your aunt is the sister of your mother or your father, or the wife of your uncle.

author authors *noun*
a person who writes stories or books.

autograph autographs *noun*
the signature of somebody famous.

automatic *adjective*
if a machine is automatic, it works by itself instead of a person doing the work. *A lot of trains have automatic doors.*

autumn autumns *noun*
the season of the year between summer and winter. *Leaves fall off the trees in autumn.*

available *adjective*
if something is available, you can have it. *The video is only available in America.*

avenue avenues *noun*
a street. Avenues are often wide with trees along both sides.

average *noun*
1 a usual or normal amount. *Ben's exam results were above average.*
2 in maths, to find the average of three numbers, 5, 9 and 10, add them up and divide by 3. $5 + 9 + 10 = 24$, and $24 \div 3 = 8$.

avoid avoids avoiding avoided *verb*
if you avoid something, you stay away from it. *The driver swerved to avoid the boy and his dog.*

awake *adjective*
if you are awake, you are not asleep.

award awards *noun*
a prize for something you have done well. *I won an award for swimming.*
award *verb.*

awful *adjective*
very bad. *This cake is stale. It tastes awful.*

awkward *adjective*
1 if you move in an awkward way, you are clumsy.
2 difficult or not convenient. *Our village is awkward to get to if you don't have a car.*

axe axes *noun*
a tool with a long handle and a sharp blade for cutting down trees and chopping wood.

B b

baboon baboons *noun*
a large monkey with a nose and mouth the same shape as a dog's.

a family of baboons

baby babies *noun*
a very young child.

babysitter babysitters *noun*
a person who looks after children when their parents are out.
babysit *verb.*

back backs *noun*
1 your back is the part of your body behind you, between your neck and your bottom.
2 the back of something is the opposite part to the front. *We keep our bikes at the back of the house.*

background backgrounds *noun*
the background is everything behind the main thing you are looking at. *This picture shows some camels with pyramids in the background.*

bacon *noun*
the meat from the back or sides of a pig which has been prepared over smoke or treated with salt.

bacteria *noun*
bacteria are living things so tiny that you cannot see them without a microscope. Bacteria live in air, soil, water, and inside people and animals, and some kinds can make you ill.

bad worse worst *adjective*
1 not good.
2 if you are bad at something, you cannot do it very well.
3 if food goes bad, it starts to smell or goes mouldy, so you cannot eat it.

badge badges *noun*
a piece of metal, plastic or other material with a picture or words on it. A badge is pinned or sewn to your clothes.

badger badgers *noun*
a wild animal with grey fur, and black and white stripes on its head. Badgers live in holes called 'sets' underground, and come out to feed at night.

badminton *noun*
a game in which players use racquet to hit a light object called a shuttlecock over a high net.

bad
Some words you can use instead of bad:

The weather was very bad last week.
unpleasant, nasty

You've been a bad girl.
naughty, disobedient

Sweets are bad for your teeth.
harmful, damaging

Is the pain bad?
severe

Her car is in bad condition.
poor

The food has gone bad.
rotten

bag bags *noun*
a thing that you use for carrying other things in.

bait *noun*
a piece of food that you fix to a hook or put in a trap to catch fish or animals.

bake bakes baking baked *verb*
when you bake food, you cook it in an oven. *I love the smell of freshly baked bread, don't you?*

balance balances balancing balanced *verb*
if you balance, you keep steady and do not fall over. *Connie balances on the box.*

balcony balconies *noun*
a platform joined to the wall of a building upstairs, with a wall or railing around it.

bald balder baldest *adjective*
someone who is bald has no hair on their head.

ball balls *noun*
1 a round thing that you use to play games. *a tennis ball.*
2 something made into a round shape. *a ball of wool.*
3 a very grand party where people dance.

ballet ballets *noun*
a kind of dancing that tells a story.
▲ Say ***bal**-ay.*

balloon balloons *noun*
a round bag made of rubber or other material and filled with air or gas so that it floats.

A B C D E F G H I J K L M N O P Q R S T U V W X Y Z

bamboo *noun*
a tropical plant with hollow stems, used to make things such as furniture.

ban bans banning banned *verb*
if somebody bans something, they say it is not allowed. *My parents have banned us from watching TV in the morning.*

banana bananas *noun*
a long, curved fruit with yellow skin. Bananas grow in hot countries.

band bands *noun*
1 a group of people who play music together.
2 a group of people who do something together. *a band of robbers.*
3 a narrow piece of material that goes around something. *Tennis players often wear wrist bands.*

bandage bandages *noun*
a long strip of material that can be wrapped around a part of your body that is injured in order to protect it.

bang bangs *noun*
a sudden and very loud noise.
bang *verb.*

bank banks *noun*
1 a building where people can keep their money safely.
2 the ground at the side of a river.

banner banners *noun*
a long piece of cloth with writing on it that people carry in a crowd or procession to show what they think about something. *The people in the crowd carried banners saying 'Stop animal experiments'.*

bar bars *noun*
1 a long, straight piece of metal.
2 a flat, solid piece of something. *a bar of soap.*
3 a place where you can buy and have a drink.
4 one of the short groups of notes that a piece of music can be divided into. When music is written down, the bars are shown by lines between the groups of notes.

barbecue barbecues *noun*
a kind of metal frame on which you can grill things like sausages or meat over hot charcoal outdoors. ▲ Say ***bar**-bi-kyoo.*

bare bare barest *adjective*
1 without any clothes on. *bare feet.*
2 a bare cupboard or shelf is empty.
● A word that sounds like **bare** is **bear**.

bargain bargains *noun*
a thing being sold which is much cheaper than you expected.

barge barges *noun*
a long boat with a flat bottom, used on canals and rivers.

bark barks barking barked *verb*
a loud noise that a dog makes.

bark *noun*
the rough outer covering of a tree's trunk and branches.

barley *noun*
a plant whose grain is used as food and for making beer.

barn barns *noun*
a large farm building for storing crops such as hay or keeping animals inside.

barrel barrels *noun*
a large container with curved sides that is used for storing liquids.

barrier barriers *noun*
a thing like a wall or fence that stops people or things getting past.

base bases *noun*
the base of a thing is the bottom part or the part that it stands on. *The lamp has a heavy metal base.*

baseball *noun*
a game played with a bat and a ball by two teams of nine players. Each player has to hit the ball and run around four points on the field before the ball is caught.

basement basements *noun*
a room or rooms below the ground floor in a building.

basic *adjective*
basic things are the important things that you cannot do without. *The one basic piece of equipment you need for football is a football goal net.*

basket baskets *noun*
a stiff bag made from cane or wire, for carrying things in.

basketball *noun*
a game played with a large ball by two teams of five players. The teams have to get the ball through a net fixed to a high metal ring at each end of the court.

bat bats *noun*
1 a small animal like a mouse with wings. Bats hunt for food at night.
2 a piece of wood or metal that you use for hitting the ball in sports such as baseball, cricket or table tennis.

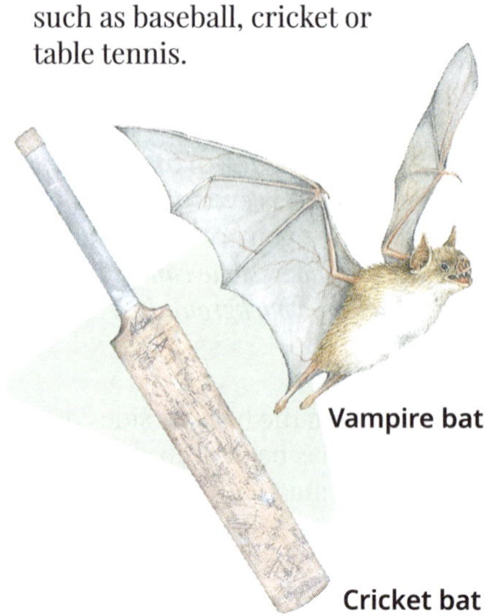

Vampire bat

Cricket bat

bat bats batting batted *verb*
when you bat, you have a turn at hitting the ball in games like cricket or baseball. *Jennifer batted the ball to Lucy.*

bath baths *noun*
1 a very large container for water that you get into to wash your whole body.
2 when you have a bath, you get into a bath and wash yourself.

battery batteries *noun*
a metal object that makes and stores electricity. You put batteries in things such as radios, cameras and torches to make them work.

battle battles *noun*
a fight between two armies.

bay bays *noun*
a part of the sea which has land curving around it on three sides.

beach beaches *noun*
the land beside the sea that is covered with sand or pebbles.

bead beads *noun*
a small, round piece of glass, wood or plastic with a hole through the middle. A piece of string can be threaded through the holes of lots of beads to make a necklace or a bracelet.

beak beaks *noun*
the hard, pointed part of a bird's mouth.

beam beams *noun*
1 a thick, strong piece of wood or metal that holds up a roof.
2 a line of bright light.

beam beams beaming beamed *verb*
if you are beaming, you have a big, happy smile on your face.

bean beans *noun*
a large seed that grows inside a pod. Sometimes you eat the whole pod and sometimes you eat the seed.
runner beans. ◆ *baked beans.*
● A word that sounds like **bean** is **been**.

bear bears *noun*
a big, wild animal with thick fur.
● A word that sounds like **bear** is **bare**.

bear bears bearing bore borne *verb*
1 if you cannot bear something, you cannot put up with it. *She couldn't bear the pain any longer.*
2 if you bear something, you carry or support it. *The cart bore a heavy load.*
● A word that sounds like **bear** is **bare**.

beard beards *noun*
the hair on a man's chin and face.

beast beasts *noun*
a wild animal.

beat beats beating beat beaten *verb*
1 if you beat somebody in a game or competition, you win.
2 to beat somebody or something means to hit them very hard again and again, especially with your hand or a stick.
3 if you beat eggs or cream, you stir them fast with a fork, spoon or whisk.
4 when your heart is beating, it is pushing the blood around your body regularly and keeping you alive.

beat beats *noun*
the regular rhythm of your heart or of a piece of music. *the beat of a drum.*

beautiful *adjective*
very lovely to look at, or listen to or smell. *a beautiful painting.* ■ The opposite is **ugly**.

beaver beavers *noun*
a furry animal with strong teeth and a flat tail. Beavers live by rivers or streams where they build homes called lodges.

become becomes becoming became *verb*
1 when one thing becomes another thing, it changes into it. *Caterpillars eventually become butterflies.*
2 when a person becomes something, they change to be it. *She became worried about her son when he didn't come home at the usual time.*

bed beds *noun*
1 the piece of furniture that you sleep on. The room where your bed is and where you sleep is called a bedroom.
2 the sea bed is the bottom of the sea.

bee bees *noun*
an insect with a yellow and black body that makes honey. ● A word that sounds like **bee** is **be**.

beef *noun*
the meat from a cow.

beer *noun*
an alcoholic drink made from grain.

beetle beetles *noun*
an insect with hard, shiny wings.
❖ *Look at page 87*

beetroot beetroots *noun*
a round, red vegetable that grows in the ground.

beg begs begging begged *verb*
1 if somebody begs, they ask people for money in the street.

A B C D E F G H I J K L M N O P Q R S T U V W X Y Z

2 if you beg for something, you ask for it in a way that shows you want it very badly. *Ali begged for a kitten.*

begin begins beginning began begun *verb*
when something begins, it starts. ■ The opposite is **finish** or **end**.
beginning *noun.*

behave behaves behaving behaved *verb*
the way you behave is the way you act. *The children behaved very badly.*
behaviour *noun.*

believe believes believing believed *verb*
1 if you believe something, you are sure that it is true or real even though you cannot prove it. *Do you believe in fairies?*
2 if you believe somebody, you think they are telling the truth. *My mum believed I didn't break the window.*
belief *noun.*

bell bells *noun*
a metal instrument like a large upside-down cup, which has a thin piece of metal hanging inside called the clapper. When the clapper hits the side of the bell it makes a ringing sound.

belong belongs belonging belonged *verb*
1 if something belongs to you, it is yours.
2 if you belong to a club or society, you are a member of it.

below *preposition*
if something is below something else, it is underneath it. ■ The opposite is **above**.

belt belts *noun*
a strip of material or leather that you wear around your waist.

bench benches *noun*
1 a long, hard seat made of wood or metal that more than one person can sit on. *a garden bench.*
2 a wooden table that people put things on when they work. *She was working at a bench in the laboratory.*

bend bends bending bent *verb*
1 if you bend, you move the top part of your body downwards. *He bent down and stroked the dog.*
2 if you bend something, you make it curved instead of straight.

beneath *preposition*
if something is beneath something else, it is below it. ■ The opposite is **above**, **over** or **on top of**.

berry berries *noun*
a small, soft fruit with seeds in it. ● A word that sounds like **berry** is **bury**.

beside *preposition*
if something is beside something else, it is next to it or at the side of it.

bet bets betting bet *verb*
1 if you bet that something is going to happen, you are sure that it is going to happen. *I bet it will rain tomorrow.*
2 if you bet on a race, you risk some money and guess who will win the race. If you are right, you get some money but if you are wrong you lose some.

betray betrays betraying betrayed *verb*
if you betray somebody, you harm them on purpose even though they trusted you. *I thought he was my friend but he betrayed me by telling lies about me.*
betrayal *noun.*

between *preposition*
if something is between two other things, it is in the middle with the other things on each side.

beware *verb*
if somebody tells you to beware of something, they are warning you to be careful because it is dangerous. *The sign said "Beware of the dog".*

bewildered *adjective*
if you are bewildered, you are confused.

beyond *preposition*
if something is beyond something else, it is on the far side of it. *The car park is beyond the station.*

Vocabulary

chain
a series of metal rings called links.

hub
the centre of a wheel.

gears
a set of toothed wheels (sprockets) over which the chain fits and which changes the power and speed of the bicycle.

reflector
a red object that makes the bicycle visible in the dark by reflecting lights from vehicles behind it and in front of it.

spoke
one of the rods connecting the hub to the rim of a wheel.

tandem
a bicycle with seats and pedals for two riders.

bicycle bicycles *noun*
a vehicle with two wheels that you ride by sitting on it and pushing two pedals with your feet. ▲ Say ***by*-*sik*-*ul*.**

bid bids bidding bid *verb*
if you bid for something, you offer an amount of money for it. Other people also offer an amount of money for it and the person who offers the most gets it.

big bigger biggest *adjective*
large in size, or important. ■ The opposite is **small** or **little**.

bike bikes *noun*
a bicycle.

bill bills *noun*
1 a piece of paper showing how much money you have to pay for something. *After we had finished our meal, the waiter brought the bill.*
2 a bird's beak.

bin bins *noun*
a container that you put rubbish in.

bind binds binding bound *verb*
if you bind something, you tie it up very firmly.

binoculars *noun*
an instrument with two lenses that you look through to make things that are far away seem closer.

big

Some words you can use instead of big:

There is a big crowd.
(**huge, large, great**)

This case is too big for me to lift.
(**heavy, weighty**)

Canada is a big country.
(**vast, huge**)

The wedding was a big occasion.
(**grand, impressive**)

As we sailed close, we saw a big iceberg.
(**huge, great, gigantic**)

This was a big decision for her to make.
(**important, serious**)

biodegradable *adjective*
something which is biodegradable will decay naturally. Paper is biodegradable but a lot of plastic is not. ▲ Say *by-ohdee-**gray**-da-bul.*

biology *noun*
the scientific study of people, plants and animals.
biological *adjective*.

bird birds *noun*
a creature that has wings, feathers and a beak. Most birds can fly.
❖ ***Look at page 24***

birth births *noun*
the birth of a baby is when it comes out of its mother's body.

birthday birthdays *noun*
your birthday is a day that you remember each year because it is the same day as the day you were born.

biscuit biscuits *noun*
a small, flat food like a crisp, dry cake. ▲ Say ***bis*-*kit*.**

bit bits *noun*
1 a piece. *a bit of paper.*
2 a little. *These shoes are a bit too small.*
3 the smallest unit of memory in a computer.

bite bites biting bit bitten *verb*
if you bite something, you close your teeth on it. *The dog won't bite you.*
● A word that sounds like **bite** is **byte**.

bitter bitterest *adjective*
1 food which is bitter has a sharp,

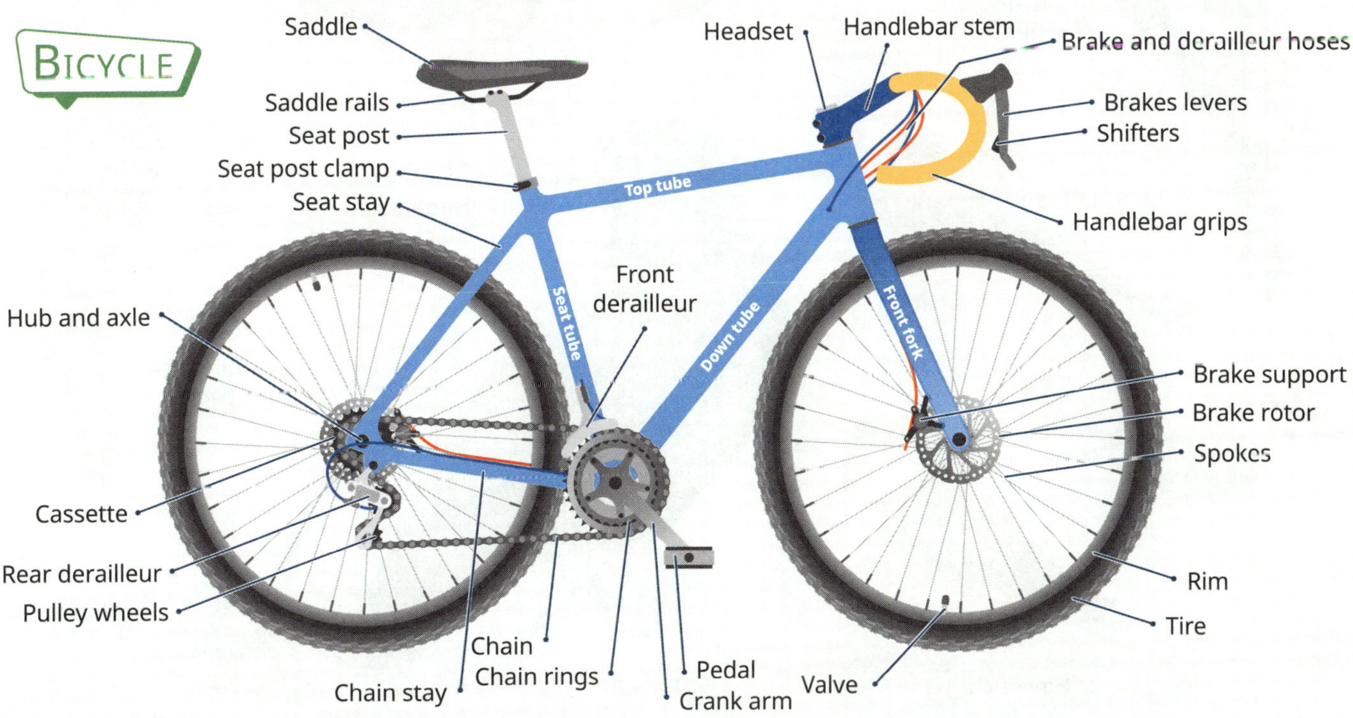

Birds

Vocabulary

barb
a hair-like branch from the shaft of a feather.

barbule
a tiny hook of hair branching from the barb of a feather.

bird of prey
a bird that kills other birds and small animals for food.

down
the small soft feathers beneath the outer feathers of water birds.

flipper
the arm-like limb that birds such as penguins use for swimming.

primary feather or **contour feather**
any one of the large feathers that covers a bird's wings, body or tail.

talon
a sharp, hooked claw on the feet of a bird of prey.

webbed feet
acquatic birds such as ducks and geese have a web of skin between their toes to help them swim.

nasty taste. *bitter medicine.* ■ The opposite is **sweet**.
2 if you are bitter about something, you go on being angry and upset about it a long time after it happened.
3 if the weather is bitter, it is very cold.

blackbird blackbirds *noun*
a bird that can often be seen in gardens. The female has brown feathers.

blackboard blackboards *noun*
a large, dark-coloured board that you write on with chalk.

blade blades *noun*
the sharp edge of a knife or sword.

blame blames blaming blamed *verb*
if you blame somebody for something, you say that it is their fault. *My brother blamed me for breaking his computer.*

blank blanker blankest *adjective*
if something is blank, it has nothing on it. *a blank sheet of paper.*

blanket blankets *noun*
a thick woollen cover for a bed.

blast blasts *noun*
an explosion. *One person was injured in the blast when the bomb went off.*

blaze blazes blazing blazed *verb*
when a fire blazes, it burns very strongly. *The forest fire blazed for more than a week.*

bleed bleeds bleeding bled *verb*
when a part of your body bleeds, blood flows out. *Mohammed cut his arm and it started bleeding.*

blew past of blow
● a word that sounds like **blew** is **blue**.

blind *adjective*
a person who is blind cannot see.

blind blinds *noun*
a roll of material that you pull down to cover a window.

blindfold blindfolds *noun*
a piece of material tied over somebody's eyes so that they cannot see.

blink blinks blinking blinked *verb*
when you blink, you shut both your eyes and open them again very quickly.

blister blisters *noun*
a small bubble of liquid just under your skin that you get if something has rubbed your skin a lot or if you get burned. *Rosamund's new shoes have given her two large blisters.*

blizzard blizzards *noun*
a snow storm with very strong winds.

block blocks *noun*
1 a thick piece of something solid, with flat sides. *a block of wood.*
2 a block of flats is a large building divided into flats. An office block is a large building divided into offices.

block blocks blocking blocked *verb*
if something blocks a place, it is in the way and nothing can get past. *A fallen tree blocked the road to the school.*

blond, blonde blonder blondest *adjective*
a person who is blond or blonde has light-coloured hair. We use the spelling **blond** for men and boys, and **blonde** for women and girls.

blood *noun*
the red liquid that flows all around your body through your arteries and veins.

bloom blooms blooming bloomed *verb*
when a plant blooms, its flowers come out. *Daffodils bloom in March.*

blossom *noun*
flowers on a tree. *Cherry blossom.*

blot blots *noun*
a drop of ink that has spilt on to something and left a mark.

blouse blouses *noun*
a piece of clothing like a shirt worn by a girl or woman.

blow blows blowing blew blown *verb*
1 if you blow, you breathe a lot of air out of your mouth at once. *He blew all nine candles out in one go.*
2 when you blow your nose, you breathe out through your nose very hard into a handkerchief.
3 if something blows somewhere, the wind is pushing it along. *Leaves were blowing about in the street.*
blow up something is blown up when it is destroyed with an explosion.

blow blows *noun*
a hard hit. *a blow to the head.*

blunt blunter bluntest *adjective*
1 a blunt knife does not cut very well because it is not sharp any more.
2 a blunt object has a rounded or flat end instead of a pointed one. *My pencil is blunt, I'll have to sharpen it.*
3 if you are blunt, you say exactly what you think even if it is not polite or kind.

blur blurs blurring blurred *verb*
when something blurs, you cannot see it clearly. *My eyes were so tired that the TV was beginning to blur.*

blush blushes blushing blushed *verb*
to become red in the face because you are embarrassed or ashamed.
blush *noun*.
A blush spread over his cheeks.

board boards *noun*
1 a flat piece of wood or stiff card with straight sides.
2 a blackboard.
● A word that sounds like **board** is **bored**.

boarding-school boarding-schools *noun*
a school where the pupils eat and sleep during the term.

boast boasts boasting boasted *verb*
if you boast about something you have or something you have done, you talk in a way that shows you are too proud of it. *John boasted that his parents had an expensive new car.*

boat boats *noun*
boats carry people and things across water. Some boats have engines, some have sails, and some you row by using oars or paddles. ❖ ***Look at page 148***

body bodies *noun*
1 all of the parts of a person or of an animal that can be seen or touched.
2 a dead person.

boil boils boiling boiled *verb*
1 when liquid boils, it gets so hot that bubbles appear on the surface and it starts to change into steam.
2 when you boil food, you cook it in boiling water. *boiled potatoes.*

boil boils *noun*
a big, painful spot on your skin.

bold bolder boldest *adjective*
a person who is bold is not afraid to do dangerous things.
boldness *noun*.

bolt bolts *noun*
1 a metal bar that slides across to lock a door or window.
2 a metal pin that screws into a metal nut to fasten things together.

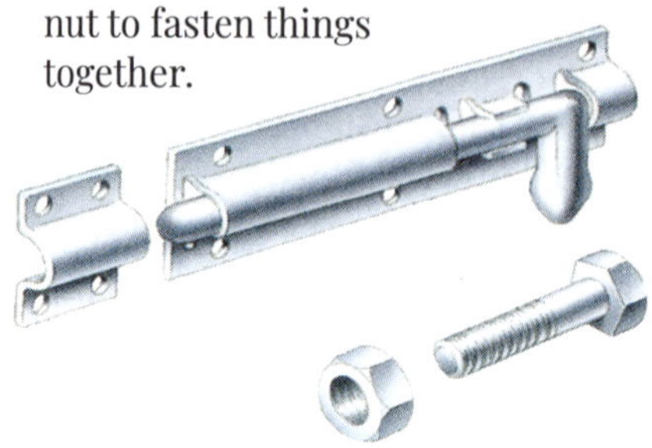

bolt bolts bolting bolted *verb*
1 when you bolt a door, you slide a bolt across it so that it cannot be opened.
2 when a person or an animal bolts, they suddenly run away. *The horse was frightened by the noise and bolted across the field.*

bomb bombs *noun*
a weapon containing chemicals that can be made to explode, damaging or destroying everything around it.

bone bones *noun*
a bone is one of the hard parts inside your body that make up your skeleton.

bonfire bonfires *noun*
a fire that is made outdoors to burn rubbish.

bonnet bonnets *noun*
1 the part of a car that covers the engine.
2 a kind of hat that is tied with strings under the chin.

book books *noun*
sheets of printed paper fastened together inside a cover.

book books booking booked *verb*
when you book something, you ask somebody to keep it for you. *My Mum phoned the restaurant to book a table for tomorrow evening.*

boomerang boomerangs *noun*
a curved stick that comes back to the person who throws it. The first people who lived in Australia, called Aboriginals, used the boomerang as a weapon for hunting.

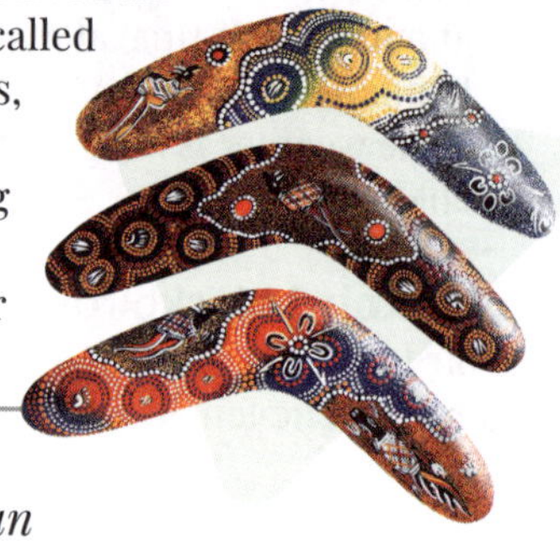

boot boots *noun*
1 a shoe that covers your foot and ankle, and sometimes part of your leg.
2 a space usually at the back of a car where you can put luggage.

border borders *noun*
1 the line that separates two countries.
2 a strip around the edge of something which is a different colour or has a different pattern.

bore bores boring bored *verb*
1 if something bores you, you are not interested in it.
2 if you bore into something, you make a hole in it using a drill. *The engineer bored a hole in the rock.*
boredom *noun*, **boring** *adjective*.

bore past of bear.

born *verb*
when a baby is born, it comes out of its mother's body.

borrow borrows borrowing borrowed *verb*
if you borrow something from somebody, they let you have it for a time and then you give it back. *I borrowed some books from the library.*
■ The opposite is **lend**.

boss bosses *noun*
the boss is the person who is in charge.

both *pronoun*
when something is true about two people or things, you can say it is true about both of them. *Both my sister and my aunt are called Mary.*

bother bothers bothering bothered *verb*
1 if something bothers you, it makes you feel worried or uncomfortable.
2 if you bother about something you care about it and take trouble with it.

bottle bottles *noun*
a tall container made of glass or plastic that liquid is kept in. *a milk bottle.*

bottom bottoms *noun*
1 the lowest part of something. ■ The opposite is **top**.
2 your bottom is the part of your body that you sit on.

bought past of buy
▲ Say ***bort***.

boulder boulders *noun*
a large, smooth rock.

bounce bounces bouncing bounced *verb*
when something bounces, it hits the ground or another hard surface and moves back up again. *In basketball, you have to bounce the ball.*

bound bounds bounding bounded *verb*
to bound is to move along by making big jumps. *The dogs were bounding in all directions.*

bound *adjective*
if something is bound to happen, it will definitely happen.

bound past of bind.

bouquet bouquets *noun*
a bunch of flowers. ▲ Say *boo-**kay***.

bow bows bowing bowed *verb*
if you bow, you bend your head or body forward. *Actors bow at the end of a play when people clap for them.* ▲ Rhymes with ***cow***.

bow bows *noun*
1 a long piece of wood with a string fastened at each end that is used to shoot arrows.
2 a knot with two loops.
3 a long, straight piece of wood with horse hair stretched along it and fastened at each end. A bow is used to play a musical instrument such as a violin or double bass.
▲ Rhymes with ***no***.

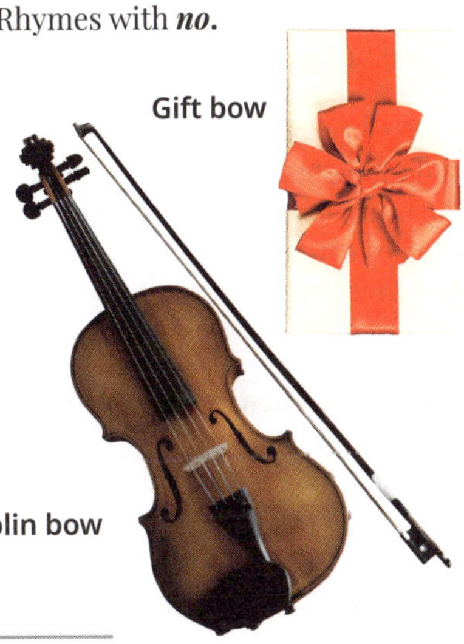

Gift bow

Violin bow

bowl bowls *noun*
a deep, round dish for food or liquids.

bowl bowls bowling bowled *verb*
when you bowl in a game like cricket, you throw the ball towards the person who is batting.

box boxes *noun*
a container, usually with a lid, that is used for packing or storing things.

box boxes boxing boxed *verb*
when people box, they fight with their fists in a sport called boxing.

boy boys *noun*
a male child. ● A word that sounds like **boy** is **buoy**.

brace braces *noun*
a piece of wire that a dentist can fit over your teeth to make them straighter.

bracelet bracelets *noun*
a piece of jewellery that you wear around your wrist.

braille *noun*
a form of writing made of patterns of raised dots that blind people can read by touching.

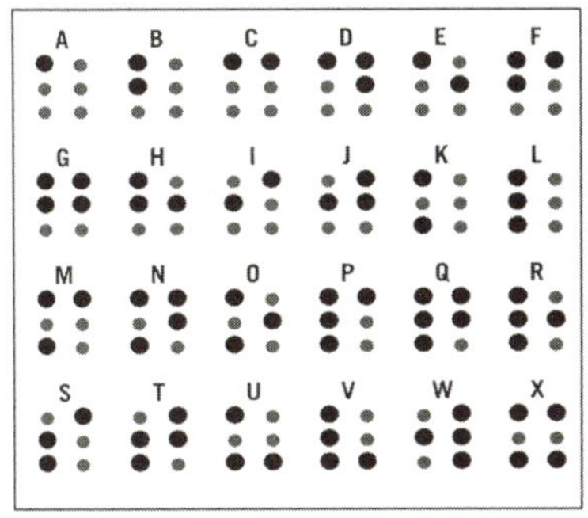

brain brains *noun*
the part inside your head that you use to think and that controls all the parts of your body.

brake brakes *noun*
the part of a bicycle or car which you use to make it go slower or stop. ● A word that sounds like **brake** is **break**.

brake brakes braking braked *verb*
when you brake, you make a bicycle or car go slower or stop by using the brake. ● A word that sounds like **brake** is **break**.

branch branches *noun*
a part of a tree that grows out from the trunk.

brass *noun*
a yellow metal made from copper and another metal called zinc. *This trumpet is made of brass.*

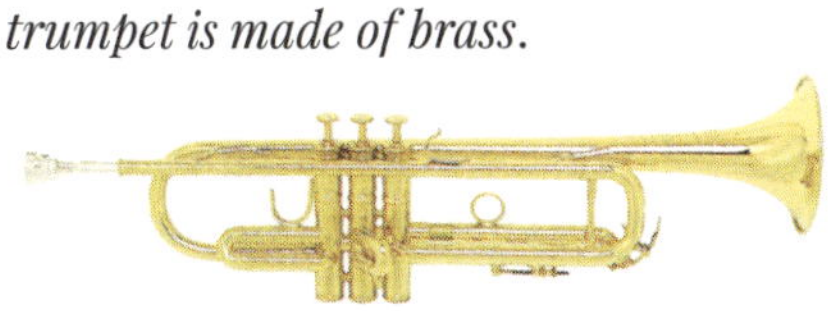

brave braver bravest *adjective*
if you are brave, you will do something frightening or dangerous without showing fear.

bread *noun*
a food made from flour, water and often yeast, and baked in an oven.

break breaks breaking broke broken *verb*
1 if you break something, you damage it so that it is in pieces or does not work any more. *I think I've broken the CD player.* ◆ *He broke the dish.*
2 if you break a promise, you do not do what you promised you would.
3 if you break the law, you do something that is not allowed by law.
● A word that sounds like **break** is **brake**.

break breaks *noun*
a short rest from work. *She's having a tea break.* ● A word that sounds like **break** is **brake**.

breakfast breakfasts *noun*
the first meal of the day.

breast breasts *noun*
a woman's breasts are the two round parts on the front of her chest that can make milk to feed a baby.

breath breaths *noun*
the air that goes in and out of your lungs through your nose or mouth when you breathe.

breathe breathes breathing breathed *verb*
when you breathe, you take air into your lungs through your nose or mouth and then let it out again.

breed breeds *noun*
one kind of an animal. *Spaniels and labradors are different breeds of dogs.*

breed breeds breeding bred *verb*
1 if you breed animals, you keep them in order to produce young ones.
2 when animals breed, they produce young ones.

breeze breezes *noun*
a gentle wind.

brick bricks *noun*
a block made out of baked clay that is used for building houses and walls.

bride brides *noun*
a woman on her wedding day.

bridegroom bridegrooms *noun*
a man on his wedding day.

bridesmaid bridesmaids *noun*
a girl or woman who helps the bride on her wedding day.

bridge bridges *noun*
something built over a river, railway line or road so that people and vehicles can travel from one side to the other.

Cantilever bridge

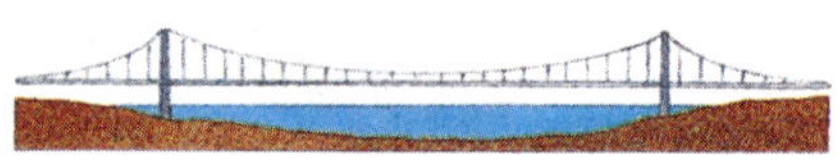

Suspension bridge

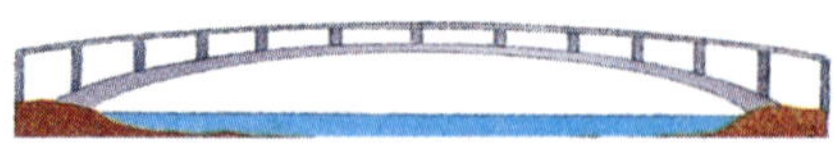

Arch bridge

brief briefer briefest *adjective*
something that is brief lasts only a short time. *We had a brief chat.*

bright brighter brightest *adjective*
1 a bright light shines very strongly. ■ The opposite is **dim**.
2 bright colours are clear and strong. ■ The opposite is **dull** or **dark**.
3 a bright person is clever. ■ The opposite is **stupid**.
▲ Say ***brite***.
brightness *noun*.

brilliant *adjective*
1 a brilliant person is very clever.
2 brilliant light is very bright.
3 very good. *We went to a brilliant disco last night.*

brim brims *noun*
1 if you fill a cup or glass to the brim, you fill it right up to the top.
2 the flat part that sticks out from the edge of a hat.

bristle bristles *noun*
1 a short, stiff hair on an animal.
2 bristles are the stiff hairs fastened to the handle of a brush.

brittle *adjective*
if something is brittle, it is hard but easy to break. *Eggshells are brittle.*

broad broader broadest *adjective*
wide. *a broad street.* ▲ Rhymes with ***cord***. ■ The opposite is **narrow**.

broadcast broadcasts broadcasting broadcast *verb*
when a radio or TV programme is broadcast, it is sent out so that you can hear it on the radio or see it on the TV.

broke broken past of break.

bronze *noun*
a brown metal made from a mixture of copper and tin. *All these ancient objects are made of bronze.*

brooch brooches *noun*
a piece of jewellery with a pin that you can fasten on to your clothes.
▲ Rhymes with ***coach***.

brook brooks *noun*
a small stream.

broom brooms *noun*
a brush with a long handle for sweeping.

broth *noun*
a clear, thin soup made by boiling meat, fish or vegetables.

brother brothers *noun*
a person's brother is a boy or man who has the same mother and father.

brow brows *noun*
1 a person's forehead.
2 the top of a hill.
▲ Rhymes with ***cow***.

bruise bruises *noun*
a dark mark on your skin where something has hit it or you have fallen over and banged it.

brush brushes *noun*
a set of bristles fastened to a handle. You use different sizes and shapes of brushes for different jobs like painting, cleaning your teeth or sweeping the floor.

brush brushes brushing brushed *verb*
if you brush something, you clean or tidy it with a brush. *Don't forget to brush your hair.*

bubble bubbles *noun*
a little ball of air or gas that you get in fizzy drinks or boiling water.

bucket buckets *noun*
a large container with a handle used for carrying liquid. *Ned filled a bucket with water and cleaned his bike.*

buckle buckles *noun*
a fastening on a belt or strap. *My belt has a silver buckle.*

bud buds *noun*
a part of a plant that opens up to become a flower or a leaf.

Buddhist Buddhists *noun*
a person who follows a religion started by a religious teacher called Buddha. ▲ Say ***buh**-dist.*

buffalo buffalo or buffaloes *noun*
a large kind of cow that has long, curved horns.

bug bugs *noun*
1 an insect.
2 an illness such as a cold or flu. *There's a nasty bug going around.*

build builds building built *verb*
when you build something, you make it by putting different parts together.

building buildings *noun*
any place which has walls and a roof, like a house, a shop or an office block.

bulb bulbs *noun*
1 the thick, round part of a plant such as a daffodil or tulip that is under the ground, from which the plant grows.
2 the round glass part of a lamp or light.

bull bulls *noun*
the male of the cattle family. Adult male elephants and whales are also called bulls.

bulldozer bulldozers *noun*
a tractor with a wide blade in front of it which is used to move earth or knock down buildings.

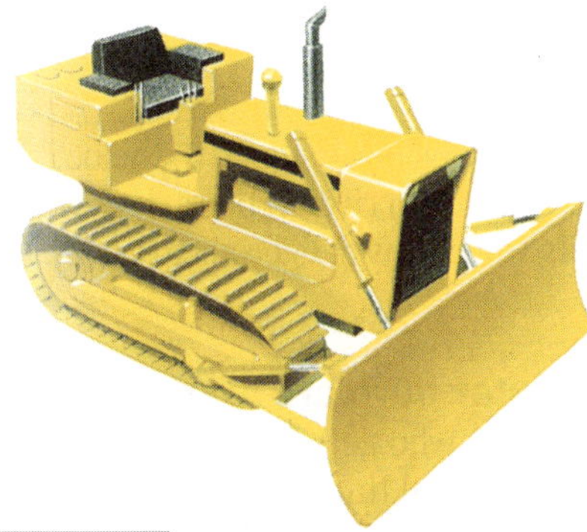

bullet bullets *noun*
a small piece of metal that is fired from a gun.

bully bullies *noun*
a person who hurts or frightens other weaker people.

bump bumps bumping bumped *verb*
if you bump into something, you hit it by accident. *I wasn't looking where I was going and I bumped into the wall.*

bump bumps *noun*
1 the sound that something makes when it hits something else. *She fell off the chair and landed on the floor with a loud bump.*
2 a round lump or swelling on a surface. *Dad has a bump on his head where he banged it on the ceiling.*
bumpy *adjective*.

bunch bunches *noun*
a group of things. *a bunch of flowers.* ◆ *a bunch of grapes.*

A B C D E F G H I J K L M N O P Q R S T U V W X Y Z

bundle bundles *noun*
a group of things tied together. *Katie tied the sticks into a bundle.*

bungalow bungalows *noun*
a low house that has only a ground floor.

bunkbeds *noun*
two beds, one above the other.

buoy buoys *noun*
a floating object fastened to the bottom of the sea or a river. A buoy shows a ship where it is dangerous to go.
▲ Say ***boy***.

burglar burglars *noun*
a person who gets into a house or shop to steal things.
burgle *verb*.

burglary burglaries *noun*
getting into a house or shop to steal things.

burn burns burning burnt or burned *verb*
1 if something is burning, it is on fire.
2 if you burn something, you damage it with fire or heat. *What's that smell? Have you burnt the potatoes?*

burn burns *noun*
a sore place on your skin, or a mark on something caused by fire or heat.

burrow burrows *noun*
a hole or tunnel under the ground where an animal lives. *Prairie dogs live in burrows.*

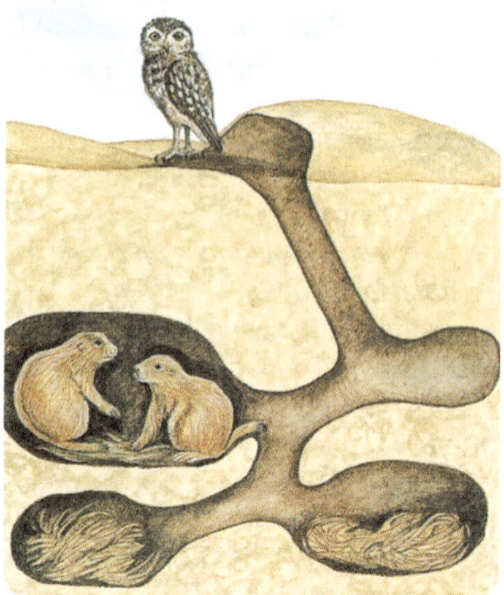

burst bursts bursting burst *verb*
when something bursts, it breaks open suddenly, especially because there is too much inside. *The little boy was crying because his balloon had burst.*

bury buries burying buried *verb*
when you bury something, you put it in a hole in the ground and cover it up. *Squirrels bury their nuts to store them for winter.* ▲ Say ***ber**-ee*. ● A word that sounds like **bury** is **berry**.

bus buses *noun*
a large vehicle that carries a lot of passengers by road.

A double decker bus

bush bushes *noun*
1 a large plant like a small tree with a lot of branches.
2 the bush is the wild part of the countryside in Australia or Africa.

business businesses *noun*
1 the work of making, buying or selling things. *The company does a lot of business with the United States.*
2 a company or shop that makes or sells things. *a hairdressing business.*
▲ Say ***biz**-niss*.

busy busier busiest *adjective*
1 if you are busy, you have a lot to do.
2 a place that is busy is full of people doing things. *a busy supermarket.*
▲ Say ***biz**-ee*.

butcher butchers *noun*
a person whose job is to sell meat.

butter *noun*
a yellow fat made from cream. You spread it on bread and use it in cooking.

butterfly butterflies *noun*
an insect with large, white or coloured wings and a thin body.
❖ ***Look below***

button buttons *noun*
1 a small object for fastening clothes.
2 a small thing that you press to make a machine work.

buy buys buying bought *verb*
when you buy something, you pay somebody money for it. ● Words that sound like **buy** are **by** and **bye**.

byte bytes *noun*
a unit of memory in a computer. One letter or one number takes up one byte. ● A word that sounds like **byte** is **bite**.

C c

cab cabs *noun*
1 a taxi.
2 the part of a lorry, train or bus where the driver sits.

cabbage cabbages *noun*
a large, round vegetable with green, white or dark-red leaves.

cabin cabins *noun*
1 a bedroom on a ship.
2 the part of a plane where the passengers travel.
3 a small house made of wood. *a log cabin in the forest.*

cable cables *noun*
1 a set of wires that carry electricity, television or radio signals. *an underwater telephone cable.*
2 a strong, thick wire or rope.

cable television *noun*
a way of sending television programmes using wires.

cactus cactuses or cacti *noun*
a plant with no leaves. Cactuses are covered in sharp spikes. Cactuses store water in their stems and grow in hot, dry places like deserts.

café cafés *noun*
a place where you can buy a drink and something to eat, and sit down to eat it. ▲ Say ***kaf-ay***

cage cages *noun*
a box or room with metal bars for keeping animals or birds in. *a hamster cage.* ◆ *a parrot cage.*

cake cakes *noun*
a sweet food that you make by mixing flour, butter, eggs and sugar, and baking it in the oven.

calculator calculators *noun*
a small machine for doing sums quickly. You work a calculator by pressing buttons with numbers on them.

calendar calendars *noun*
a list of all the days, weeks and months of one year.

calf calves *noun*
1 a young cow. Young elephants, whales and seals are also called calves.
2 the thick part at the back of your leg, between your knee and your ankle.

call calls calling called *verb*
1 if you call somebody, you shout to them. *"Dinner's ready," he called out.*
2 if you call somebody something, you give them that name. *She called the dog Spot.*
3 to call also means to go see somebody. *Did anyone call when we were out?*
call *noun.*

calm calmer calmest *adjective*
1 if you are calm, you are quiet and not afraid.
2 if the sea is calm, there are no big waves on it.
▲ Say ***kaam.***

camcorder camcorders *noun*
a camera that can take moving pictures and record sound.

camel camels *noun*
an animal with one or two humps on its back. Camels are used to carry people and things in the desert because they can travel for a long time without water.

camera cameras *noun*
a machine for taking photographs or making films.

camouflage camouflages camouflaging camouflaged *verb*
if somebody or something is camouflaged, you cannot see it because it is the same colour or shape as things around it. *This gecko is camouflaged by the ground it is sitting on.* ▲ Say ***kam-o-flaj.***
camouflage *noun.*

camp camps *noun*
a place where people live in tents or stay in tents on holiday.

camp camps camping camped *verb*
when you camp, you live in a tent or have a holiday in a tent.
go camping *We're going camping this summer in Scotland.*

can cans *noun*
a metal container for food, drink or paint. *a can of fizzy drink.*

canal canals *noun*
a long, narrow strip of water made for boats and barges to travel along.

A B C D E F G H I J K L M N O P Q R S T U V W X Y Z

cancel cancels cancelling cancelled *verb*
if you cancel something that you have planned, you stop it from happening. *We cancelled our trip because Mum was ill.*

cancer *noun*
a serious illness that makes some cells inside the body grow too fast and kill normal cells in the body.

candle candles *noun*
a stick made of wax with a string called a wick inside. You light the wick and the candle burns to give light.

cane canes *noun*
1 the hard, hollow stem of some plants such as sugar cane. You can make chairs and tables out of cane.
2 a long, thin stick, sometimes used as a walking stick.

cannon cannons *noun*
a big gun that fires heavy metal balls, or shells that explode.

canoe canoes *noun*
a light, thin boat that you move with a paddle. ▲ Say *kan-**oo***.

canopy canopies *noun*
1 a piece of material over a door or window that keeps the sun out.
2 a cover over something. *Tall trees form a canopy over the rainforest floor.*

canvas canvases *noun*
strong material that is used for making sails, tents or shoes.

canyon canyons *noun*
a deep, rocky valley. *In the United States, the Colorado river flows through the famous Grand Canyon.*

cap caps *noun*
1 a flat hat with a peak at the front. *a baseball cap.*
2 the top of a jar, bottle or pen.

cape capes *noun*
1 a piece of land that sticks out into the sea. *Cape Horn.* ◆ *Cape Canaveral.*
2 a loose coat with no sleeves that you wrap around your shoulders.

capital capitals *noun*
1 the most important city in a country from where the government usually operates. *Rome is the capital of Italy.*
2 a big letter in the alphabet. *The name Mark starts with a capital M.*

captain captains *noun*
1 the person in charge of a ship or an aircraft.
2 an officer in the army or navy.
3 the leader of a sports team. *a football captain.*

capture captures capturing captured *verb*
if you capture a person or an animal, you catch them and keep them in a place where they cannot escape. *The police captured the robbers.*

car cars *noun*
a machine with an engine and four wheels for travelling on the road. The driver uses the steering wheel to turn the car, and stops it by putting a foot on the brake.

caravan caravans *noun*
1 a vehicle that you can live in or use for holidays. Some caravans can be pulled along by a car.
2 a group of people, and animals, such as camels, that travel together.

card cards *noun*
1 stiff, thick paper.
2 a piece of stiff, thick paper with a picture and message on it. We send cards on birthdays and other special occasions.
3 one of a pack of 52 cards that you play games with. Each pack has four groups of cards called suits. These are hearts, diamonds, clubs and spades.

cardboard *noun*
very thick card. *It's made of cardboard.*

cardigan cardigans *noun*
a knitted jacket with buttons down the front.

care cares caring cared *verb*
1 if you care about somebody or something, you think they are important. *Jimmy cared for his puppy a great deal.*
2 if you care for somebody or something, you look after them.

care *noun*
if you do something with care, you try not to make a mistake or break something. *Wash the glasses with care.*

career careers *noun*
a job that you learn to do and then do for a long time. *a career in teaching.*

careful *adjective*
if you are careful, you think about what you are doing so that you do it safely and well. *Be careful when you cross the road.* ■ The opposite is **careless**.
carefully *adverb.*

careless *adjective*
if you are careless, you make mistakes because you are not thinking about what you are doing. ■ The opposite is **careful**.

carnival carnivals *noun*
a special time when people dress up in colourful clothes and sing, dance and play music as they move through the streets. *a dancer at a carnival.*

carpenter carpenters *noun*
a person who makes or mends wooden things such as chairs, tables or doors.

carpet carpets *noun*
a thick cover for the floor. Carpets are often made of wool.

carriage carriages *noun*
1 one of the separate parts of a train where the passengers travel.
2 an old-fashioned vehicle with wheels that is pulled by horses.

carrot carrots *noun*
a long, orange-coloured vegetable that grows under the ground.

carry carries carrying carried *verb*
when you carry something, you pick it up and take it to another place. *Tom carried the books upstairs.*

cart carts *noun*
a wooden vehicle with two or four wheels that is pulled by a horse or donkey.

carton cartons *noun*
a cardboard or plastic box for holding food or drink. *a carton of milk.*

cartoon cartoons *noun*
1 a film that uses drawings instead of real people or animals.
2 a drawing in a newspaper or magazine that is funny or makes a joke.

Spelling tip:
Some words that begin with a "ca" sound are spelt with "ka", for example kangaroo, karate.

cartwheel cartwheels *noun*
if you do a cartwheel, you put your hands on the ground and swing your legs over sideways in a complete circle, ending up standing on your feet again.

carve carves carving carved *verb*
1 if you carve wood or stone, you cut it to make a shape out of it.
2 if you carve cooked meat, you cut it into slices.

case cases *noun*
1 a bag that you carry things in when you go on holiday. *a suitcase.*
2 a container such as a pencil case.
3 a crime that the police are trying to solve. *The detective was working on a murder case.*

cash *noun*
money in coins and paper notes.

cassette cassettes *noun*
a plastic box with magnetic tape inside it which you can use to record and play music and other sounds. You can record and play moving pictures on a video cassette.

cast casts *noun*
1 all the actors in a play or film.
2 a hard plaster covering that holds a broken arm or leg in place while it is healing.

cast casts casting cast *verb*
1 if you cast something like a fishing line, you throw it.
2 if somebody in a story casts a spell, they use magic to trick somebody. *The wicked witch cast a spell on the prince and changed him into a frog.*

castle castles *noun*
a large building with thick, high walls. Castles were built long ago to keep the people who lived inside them safe from their enemies.
❖ ***Look at page 34***

casualty casualties *noun*
1 a person who is hurt or killed in an accident or a war. *There were three casualties in the road accident.*
2 a department in a hospital where people go for emergency treatment when they have an accident or suddenly become ill.

cat cats *noun*
a furry mammal with sharp claws. Small cats are kept as pets. Big cats such as lions and tigers live in the wild.

A B C D E F G H I J K L M N O P Q R S T U V W X Y Z

CASTLE

A First Century Wooden Castle

Stone Keep Castle, Dating from 1100

Concentric Castle, Dating from the 1290s

Vocabulary

bailey
the courtyard inside the walls.

battering ram
a heavy wooden pole that was rammed against an enemy castle wall or gate.

battlement
top of a castle wall with gaps through which people could fire on the enemy.

buttress
a pillar strengthening a wall.

drawbridge
a bridge over the moat that could be pulled up to stop the enemy getting into the castle.

dungeon
a prison under the castle.

keep
the main tower.

loophole
a slit in a wall for light, air or for shooting through.

mangonel
a machine for throwing stones.

moat
a ditch around the castle, usually filled with water.

portcullis
a grating that can be let down quickly to protect the gateway.

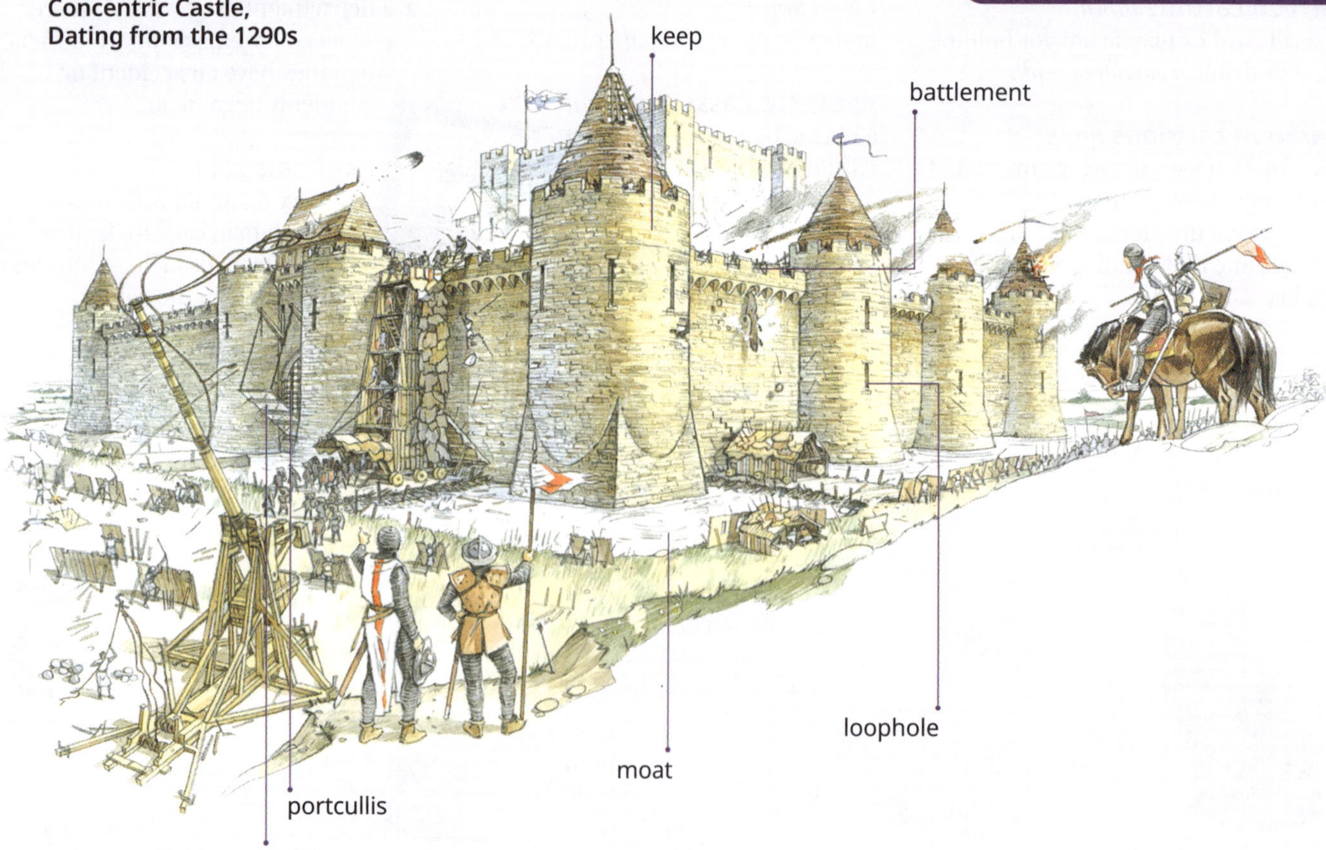

catalogue catalogues *noun*
1 a book listing all the things that a company or shop sells.
2 a list of all the books or other things in a library.

catapult catapults *noun*
a stick, shaped like a Y, with a piece of elastic stretched over it. You pull the elastic to shoot small stones.

catch catches catching caught *verb*
1 if you catch a ball, you take hold of it when it is moving.
2 if you catch a person or an animal, you stop them from running away.
3 if you catch a train or bus, you get on it to go somewhere.
4 if you catch an illness, you get it. *He caught a cold.*

caterpillar caterpillars *noun*
a small animal like a hairy worm that will turn into a butterfly or moth.

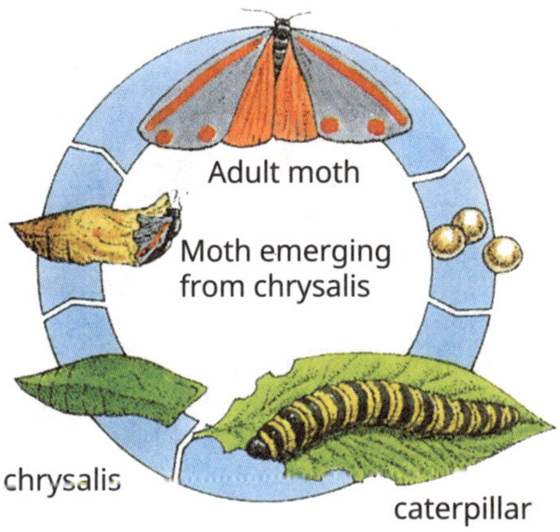

cathedral cathedrals *noun*
a large, important church. *St Paul's Cathedral is in London.*

cattle *noun*
cows and bulls. *a herd of cattle.*

caught past of catch.

cauliflower cauliflowers *noun*
a large, round white vegetable with green leaves on the outside.

cause causes causing caused *verb*
if you cause something, you make it happen. *Keep your dog on a lead or you'll cause an accident.*

cautious *adjective*
if you are cautious, you are very careful because of danger.

cave caves *noun*
a big hole under the ground, or in the side of a mountain or cliff.

CD CDs *noun*
a flat, round piece of plastic which can store music or information. CD is short for **compact disc**.

CD-ROM CD-ROMs *noun*
a disc that you use with a computer or a television to show words and pictures. CD-ROM is short for **compact disc read-only memory**.

ceiling ceilings *noun*
the top part of a room over your head. *The light is hanging from the ceiling.*

celebrate celebrates celebrating celebrated *verb*
when you celebrate something, you do something that you enjoy at a special time. *Let's have a party to celebrate your birthday.*
celebration *noun*.

celery *noun*
a vegetable with a white or pale green stem that you can eat raw or cooked.

cell cells *noun*
1 one of the tiny parts that make up all animals and plants. The human body contains millions of red blood cells.
2 a small room in a prison or police station where people are locked up.
● A word that sounds like **cell** is **sell**.

cellar cellars *noun*
a room under a building where you store things such as wine or coal.

cello cellos *noun*
a musical instrument like a big violin that you sit and hold between your knees. You play it by sliding a bow across the strings.
▲ Say *chell-oh*.
cellist *noun*.

cement *noun*
a grey powder that becomes hard like stone when you mix it with water and leave it to dry. Cement is used for building.

cemetery cemeteries *noun*
a place where dead people are buried.

centipede centipedes *noun*
a tiny animal like a worm but with many sets of legs.

central *adjective*
in the middle. *I live in central London.*

centre centres *noun*
1 the middle of something. *The table was in the centre of the room.*
2 a place where people go to do something special, such as a sports centre or a shopping centre.

century centuries *noun*
1 100 years.
2 a time of 100 years that we use in dates. *The 20th century is the time between 1900 and 1999.*

cereal cereals *noun*
cereals are plants such as rice and wheat that produce grain. We use the grain of cereal plants to make flour and bread. The cereal that you eat for breakfast is also made from cereals such as rice and wheat. ● A word that sounds like **cereal** is **serial**.

Rice Wheat Rye Oats Barley

ceremony ceremonies *noun*
the actions and words that are used at a special and important event such as a wedding.

certain *adjective*
1 if you are certain about something, you are sure it is true. *I'm certain I saw him yesterday.*
2 if something happens at a certain time, it happens then and not at other times. *The swimming pool is open all day at weekends, but only at certain times during the week.*

certificate certificates *noun*
an important piece of paper that shows that something is true. *birth certificate.*

chain chains *noun*
a chain is made from rings of metal joined together. *a bicycle chain.*

chair chairs *noun*
a seat with four legs and a back, for one person to sit on.

chalk chalks *noun*
1 soft, white rock.
2 a stick of soft, white or coloured material used for writing on a blackboard.
▲ Say ***chawk.***

challenge challenges challenging challenged *verb*
if you challenge somebody, you ask them to try to do something better than you. *Tom challenged Paul to a race.*

challenge challenges *noun*
if something is a challenge, it is difficult to do. *These sums are a real challenge!*

champion champions *noun*
a person who is the best at a sport or game. *Jazz is the champion.*

chance chances *noun*
1 a time when you can do something. *It was their last chance to escape.*
2 if there is a chance that something will happen, it might happen. *There's a chance it will rain today.*
by chance If something happens by chance, it happens without being planned.

change changes changing changed *verb*
1 when something changes, it becomes different. *Tadpoles change into frogs.*
2 if you change your clothes, you put on different ones. *Katie changed into her jeans.*

change changes *noun*
1 if there is a change in something, it is different now.
2 the money that you get back if you have paid too much for something.
3 coins like ₹1, 2, 5, 10 and 20. *Do you have change for the phone?*

channel channels *noun*
1 a narrow sea.
2 a television station. *Which channel is the programme on?*

chapter chapters *noun*
a part of a book.

character characters *noun*
1 the way a person or thing is. *She has a kind and loving character.*
2 a person in a play, film or book.

charge charges charging charged *verb*
1 if somebody charges you a certain amount of money for something, they are asking you to pay that amount. *He charged me ₹50 for the fruit.*
2 when the police charge somebody, they say that person has done something wrong.
3 if you charge at somebody or something, you run towards them very fast. *The bull charged at the fence.*
4 if you charge a battery, you pass an electric current through it to make it work. *She charged the battery in her mobile phone to keep it working.*

charge charges *noun*
the money that you have to pay for something. *There is a charge of ₹100 to get into the museum.*
in charge If you are in charge, you are the leader of a group of people. *The headteacher is in charge of the school.*

chariot chariots *noun*
a vehicle with two wheels pulled by a horse. Chariots were used in wars and races a long time ago.

charity charities *noun*
an organization which collects money to help people who need it.

chart charts *noun*
1 a drawing that shows important dates or numbers. *The chart shows how long different animals live.*
2 a map of the sea or the stars.

chase chases chasing chased *verb*
if you chase somebody, you run after them and try to catch them.

cheap cheaper cheapest *adjective*
something that is cheap does not cost a lot of money. ■ The opposite is **expensive** or **dear**.

cheat cheats cheating cheated *verb*
if somebody cheats, they do

something that is not fair, or that breaks the rules. *Play the game without cheating!*

check checks checking checked *verb*
when you check something, you look at it again to make sure that it is right. *Check your spellings in the dictionary.* ● A word that sounds like **check** is **cheque**.

check *noun*
a pattern of squares. ● A word that sounds like **check** is **cheque**.
checked *adjective.*
a checked shirt.

cheek cheeks *noun*
your cheeks are the soft parts on each side of your face.

cheerful *adjective*
if you are cheerful, you feel happy.
cheerfully *adverb.*

cheese cheeses *noun*
a white or yellow food made from milk. *Some cheese has a strong flavour.*

cheetah cheetahs *noun*
a large, wild cat that can run very fast

chef chefs *noun*
a person who cooks food in a restaurant.
▲ Say *sheff*.

chemical chemicals *noun*
a substance that is made by chemistry or used in chemistry.

chemist chemists *noun*
1 the chemist's is a shop where you can buy medicine and things such as soap and toothbrushes.
2 a person who prepares and sells medicines.
3 a scientist who works with chemicals.

chemistry *noun*
the scientific study of what substances are made of and how they work together.

cheque cheques *noun*
a piece of paper that people use to pay for things. When you pay by cheque, you write the price and sign your name on it. ● A word that sounds like **cheque** is **check**.

cherry cherries *noun*
a small, round, and red, yellow or black fruit. Cherries have a hard seed in the middle.

chess *noun*
a game that two people play with 16 chesspieces on a board with black and white squares.

chest chests *noun*
1 your chest is the front part of your body between your neck and your waist.
2 a big, strong box with a lid. *The pirates stored gold in a wooden chest.*

chew chews chewing chewed *verb*
when you chew food, you use your teeth to make it soft and to break it into smaller pieces.

chick chicks *noun*
a baby bird.

chicken chickens *noun*
a bird that people keep on farms for its eggs and meat.

chickenpox *noun*
an illness that gives you lots of itchy spots.

chief chiefs *noun*
the leader of a group of people.

child children *noun*
1 a young boy or girl.
2 a son or daughter. *They have two children.*

childhood *noun*
the time when you are a boy or girl, before you grow up. *He had a happy childhood.*

childish *adjective*
if you are childish, you are being silly and acting younger than your age.

chilli chillies *noun*
a small, red or green vegetable. Chillies have a very hot taste.

chilly chillier chilliest *adjective*
if you are chilly, you feel quite cold.

chime chimes chiming chimed *verb*
when a bell or a clock chimes, it makes a ringing sound. *The clock chimed midnight.*

chimney chimneys *noun*
a large pipe above a fire that lets smoke and gas go outside into the air.

chimpanzee chimpanzees *noun*
a small African ape. Chimpanzees are clever animals.

chin chins *noun*
your chin is the part of your face below your mouth.

china *noun*
things such as cups and jugs made from a kind of white clay. It breaks easily.

A B C D E F G H I J K L M N O P Q R S T U V W X Y Z

chip chips *noun*
1 a long, thin piece of fried potato.
2 a tiny piece of a material called silicon that has an electronic circuit on it. Chips are used in computers.
3 a small piece that has broken off something, or the gap that is left. *This plate has a small chip in it.*

chip chips chipping chipped *verb*
if you chip something, you accidentally break a small part off. *a chipped plate.*

chisel chisels *noun*
a long, thin tool with a sharp, flat edge at one end. You use it to cut wood or stone.

chocolate chocolates *noun*
1 sweet, brown food made from cocoa.
2 a sweet made of chocolate. *a box of chocolates.*

choice choices *noun*
1 all the things you can choose from. *There's a wide choice of books in the library.*
2 a person or thing that you choose.

choir choirs *noun*
a group of singers. ▲ Say ***kwire***.

choke chokes choking choked *verb*
if you choke, you cannot breathe because something is blocking your throat. *Tom choked on a fish bone.*

choose chooses choosing chose chosen *verb*
when you choose something, you take it because it is the thing you want.

chop chops chopping chopped *verb*
if you chop something, you cut it with a knife or an axe. *Ricky is chopping carrots with his mum.*

chord chords *noun*
a group of notes that you play at the same time in a piece of music.
▲ Say ***kord***. ● A word that sounds like **chord** is **cord**.

chorus choruses *noun*
the part of a song that you repeat at the end of each verse. ▲ Say ***kor-uss***.

chose chosen past of choose.

Christian Christians *noun*
a person who believes in and follows the teachings of Jesus Christ. *Italy is a Christian country.*
Christianity *noun*.

chrysalis chrysalises *noun*
a moth or a butterfly at the stage between a caterpillar and an adult, when it has a hard case around it.
▲ Say ***kriss-e-liss***. ❖ ***Look at page 35***.

chuckle chuckles chuckling chuckled *verb*
when you chuckle, you laugh quietly to yourself.

church churches *noun*
a building where Christians hold religious services.

cinema cinemas *noun*
a building where people go to watch films.

circle circles *noun*
1 a flat, round shape like a ring.
2 a part of a theatre or cinema where you sit upstairs.
circle *verb*.
The plane circled the airport.

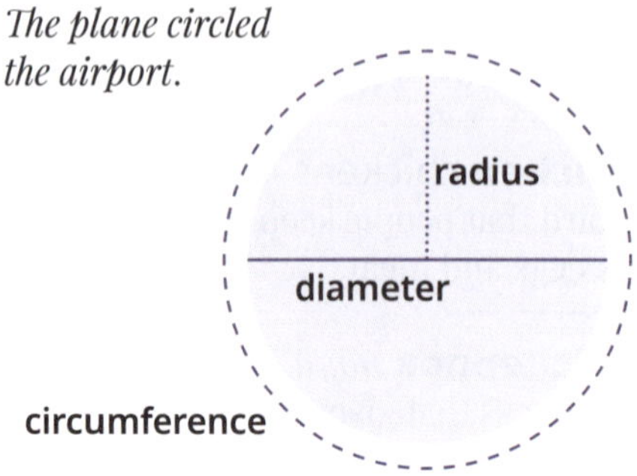

circuit circuits *noun*
1 a complete path that an electric current can flow around.
2 a path or road in the shape of a circle. *a motor racing circuit.*

circular *adjective*
round like a circle. *a circular table.*

circulation *noun*
the movement of blood around the body. Blood is pumped by the heart and travels in arteries and veins.

circumference circumferences *noun*
the distance around the edge of a circle. ❖ ***Look below***

circus circuses *noun*
a travelling show with people such as acrobats and clowns. A circus is held in a big, round tent.

city cities *noun*
a big and important town.

civilization civilizations *noun*
1 the way people live in a certain place and at a certain time. *We're learning about civilization in ancient Greece.*
2 living in a group with lots of laws and certain ways of doing things, not living wild in a forest.

claim claims claiming claimed *verb*
1 if you claim something, you say it is yours. *Nobody has claimed the watch I found.*
2 if you claim that something is true, you say it is true. *She claimed the dog had eaten her homework.*

clap claps clapping clapped *verb*
when you clap, you hit your hands together to make a noise. You clap to show you have enjoyed something.

clash clashes clashing clashed *verb*
1 when metal objects clash, they hit together making a loud, banging sound. *cymbals clash.*
2 if colours clash, they do not look good together. *Do you think red and orange clash?*

class classes *noun*
1 a group of people who learn together. *Sam and I are in the same class at school.*
2 a group of people, animals or things that are the same in some way.

classical *adjective*
in a style that has been used for a long time because people think it is good. *classical music.*

classroom classrooms *noun*
a room in a school where you have lessons.

claw claws *noun*
the long, sharp nails that an animal or bird has on its feet.

clay *noun*
sticky red or grey earth that becomes hard when it is dry. Clay is used to make pots and bricks.

clean cleaner cleanest *adjective*
something that is clean does not have any dirt or marks on it. *clean clothes.*

clean cleans cleaning cleaned *verb*
when you clean something, you make it clean. *Don't forget to clean your teeth.* ■ The opposite is **dirty**.

clear clearer clearest *adjective*
1 easy to see, hear or understand. *a clear photograph.*
2 easy to see through. Most glass is clear.
3 free from things that are blocking the way or covering something. *A clear sky does not have any clouds.*

clear clears clearing cleared *verb*
when you clear something, you take away things that you do not want or need. *We cleared the snow from the path.*

clever cleverer cleverest *adjective*
a person who is clever can learn and understand things quickly.

cliff cliffs *noun*
the high, steep side of a hill by the sea.

climate climates *noun*
the kind of weather that a place usually has. *India has a hot climate.*

climb climbs climbing climbed *verb*
when you climb something, you move up using your hands and feet. **climber** *noun*.

cling clings clinging clung *verb*
if you cling to somebody or something, you hold on to them very tightly. *I clung to my mum because I was afraid.*

clinic clinics *noun*
a place where you go to see a doctor.

clip clips *noun*
a small metal or plastic object used for holding things together. *a paper-clip.*

clip clips clipping clipped *verb*
if you clip something, such as a hedge or your fingernails, you cut small pieces off to make it neater.

cloak cloaks *noun*
a long, loose coat with no sleeves. *The king wore a velvet cloak.*

clock clocks *noun*
a machine that tells you the time.

clockwise *adjective, adverb*
if you turn clockwise, you move in the same direction as the hands on a clock. ■ The opposite is **anticlockwise**.

close closes closing closed *verb*
when you close something, you shut it. *He closed the drawer quietly.*
▲ Rhymes with **nose**. ■ The opposite is **open**.

close closer closest *adjective*
1 near, not remote. *I live close to school.*
2 if you are close to someone, you like them very much. *Richard and Raj are close friends.*
▲ Rhymes with **dose**.

cloth cloths *noun*
1 material made from something such as cotton or wool that we use to make clothes and other things.
2 a piece of material used for cleaning. *She wiped the table with a cloth.*

clothes *noun*
clothes are things such as jeans, skirts, jumpers and coats that you wear.

a b c d e f g h i j k l m n o p q r s t u v w x y z

cloud clouds *noun*
clouds are made of millions of drops of water which sometimes fall as rain. On a cloudy day, the sky is full of white or grey clouds.

clown clowns *noun*
a person in a circus who wears funny clothes and makes people laugh.

club clubs *noun*
a group of people who meet to do something that they are all interested in. *a swimming club.* ◆ *a chess club.*

clue clues *noun*
something that helps you find the answer to a puzzle or a mystery. *I can't guess who it is. Give me a clue.*

clump clumps *noun*
a group of plants growing together. *a clump of grass.*

clumsy clumsier clumsiest *adjective*
if somebody is clumsy, they often fall over and drop things.
clumsily *adverb.*

clung past of cling.

clutch clutches clutching clutched *verb*
if you clutch something, you hold it tightly. *The child clutched her mother's hand when they crossed the road.*

clutch clutches *noun*
the pedal in a car or other vehicle that you press when you change gear.

coach coaches *noun*
1 a bus that takes people on long journeys.
2 a person who teaches people a sport. *a tennis coach.*
3 a large carriage that is pulled along by horses.

Spelling tip:
Some words that begin with a 'co' sound are spelt with a 'ko', for example 'koala'.

coal *noun*
a hard, black substance that is dug out of the ground and burnt to give heat. Coal is made from plants that died millions of years ago.

coast coasts *noun*
the part of the land that is next to the sea. *a day trip to the coast.*

coat coats *noun*
1 you wear a coat on top of your other clothes to go out when it is cold.
2 the fur that an animal has is called a coat. *A leopard has a spotted coat.*

cobweb cobwebs *noun*
a net that a spider makes to catch insects.

cock cocks *noun*
1 a male bird.
2 a fully grown male chicken.

cockerel cockerels *noun*
a young male chicken.

cockpit cockpits *noun*
the front part of a plane where the pilot sits. The part of a racing car where the driver sits is also called a cockpit.

cocoa *noun*
1 a brown powder made from the beans of the cacao tree and used to make chocolate.
2 a drink made from cocoa powder mixed with hot milk.

Cocoa beans in cocoa pod

coconut coconuts *noun*
a large, round fruit with a hard, hairy brown shell. Inside there is a milky juice and sweet, white flesh that you can eat. Coconuts grow on palm trees in hot countries.

cocoon cocoons *noun*
a bundle of silky threads that some young insects make to cover themselves while they are developing into adults.

cod cod *noun*
a large sea fish that you can eat.

code codes *noun*
1 if you write something in code, you mix up the letters or change them into special signs. Only the people who know the code can read the message.
2 a group of letters or numbers that give information about something. *The postcode for this area of London is W1P 7AD.*
3 a collection of laws or rules. *The Highway Code.*

coffee *noun*
1 a brown powder made from the roasted and ground beans of the coffee tree. You use coffee to make drinks.
2 a hot drink that you make by mixing coffee powder with hot water.

coffin coffins *noun*
a box in which a dead person is buried.

cog cogs *noun*
1 a wheel with teeth around the edge. Cogs are used in machines to turn other things.
2 the teeth around the edge of the wheel are also called cogs.

coil coils *noun*
a thing that is twisted around into circles. *a coil of rope.*
coil *verb.*
The snake coiled around the branch.

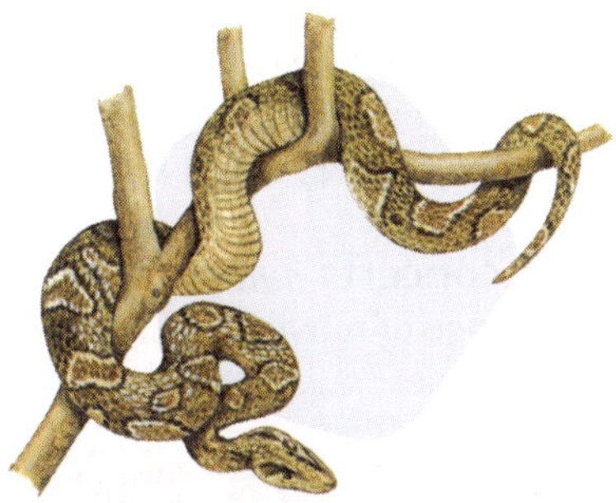

coin coins *noun*
a flat, usually round piece of metal that we use as money.

coincidence coincidences *noun*
a coincidence is when two things happen at the same time or in the same place by chance. ▲ Say *koh-**in**-si-denss.*

cold colder coldest *adjective*
1 not hot or warm. Ice and snow are cold.
2 unfriendly. *He gave me a cold look.*

cold colds *noun*
an illness that makes you sneeze and cough. *Lucy caught a cold.*

collage collages *noun*
a picture that you make by sticking lots of bits of material or paper on to a surface. ▲ Say ***kol**-arj.*

collapse collapses collapsing collapsed *verb*
1 if something collapses, it falls down suddenly. *The tent collapsed.*
2 if somebody collapses, they fall over because they are ill. *She collapsed in the street and was taken to hospital.*

collar collars *noun*
1 the part of a shirt or coat that goes around your neck.
2 a band that you put around the neck of a pet dog or cat.

collect collects collecting collected *verb*
1 when you collect things, you bring them together. *Please collect the dirty plates and put them in the sink.*
2 if you collect things such as stamps, you keep a lot of them because you like them. *I collect shells.*
3 when you collect somebody, you go and bring them back from somewhere. *Mum collects me from school.*
collection *noun.*
a stamp collection.

college colleges *noun*
a place where people go to study when they have left school.

collide collides colliding collided *verb*
if something collides with another thing, it crashes into it. *The bus collided with a lorry.*
collision *noun.*

colour colours *noun*
red, blue, yellow and green are colours.
colourful *adjective.*
❖ ***Look at page 146***

column columns *noun*
1 a tall piece of stone that holds up part of a building or stands on its own.
2 a long, thin strip of writing in a book or newspaper.

coma comas *noun*
if somebody is in a coma, they are in a very deep sleep and cannot wake up for a long time. People who have had a serious accident sometimes go into a coma.

comb combs *noun*
a flat piece of metal or plastic with teeth along one edge. You use it to make your hair tidy.
▲ Rhymes with **home**.
comb *verb.*

combine combines combining combined *verb*
when you combine things, you join or mix them together.
combination *noun.*

combine harvester combine harvesters *noun*
a large machine that is used on a farm. It cuts corn and collects the seeds.

comedy comedies *noun*
a funny play, film or TV programme.

comet comets *noun*
a thing in space that looks like a star with a tail and moves around the Sun.

comfortable *adjective*
if something is comfortable, it is nice to wear, sit in or lie on.
a comfortable bed.
comfortably *adverb.*

comic comics *noun*
1 a magazine that tells stories in pictures.
2 a person who tells jokes and makes people laugh.

comma commas *noun*
a mark (,) that you use in writing. You put commas between words in a list. *Katie, Tom, Lucy and I went to the park.*

command commands commanding commanded *verb*
if somebody commands you to do something, they tell you that you must do it. *He commanded the soldiers to march to the village.*

comment comments *noun*
if you make a comment about something, you say what you think about it.

a b c d e f g h i j k l m n o p q r s t u v w x y z

common *adjective*
1 if a thing is common, it exists in large numbers. *Robins and sparrows are common birds.*
2 something that happens often is common. *These days it is common for people to have computers at home.*
■ The opposite is **rare**.

communicate communicates communicating communicated *verb*
if you communicate with somebody, you talk or write to them. *Pilots communicate with the airport by radio.*

communications *noun*
communications are ways of sending information to people, or ways of moving from one place to another. Roads, railways and telephones are means of communication.

company companies *noun*
1 a group of people who work together to make or sell something.
2 being with others so that you are not alone. *My granny lives alone so she has a cat for company.*

compare compares comparing compared *verb*
when you compare two things, you look at them both together so that you can see in what ways they are the same or different. *When you have finished the sums, compare your answers with the ones in the back of the book.*
comparison *noun*.

compartment compartments *noun*
1 a small room in a train where people sit or sleep.
2 a part of a container. *My bag has separate compartments for my pencil case and hair brush.*

compass compasses *noun*
a compass helps walkers and sailors tell which direction they are going in. It has a magnetic needle that always points north.

compasses *noun*
a tool that you use for drawing circles. One arm has a sharp point and the other holds a pencil. You hold the pointed arm still and move the other around it. *a pair of compasses.*

competition competitions *noun*
a game or test that people try to win. *Sophie won first prize in the painting competition.*

complain complains complaining complained *verb*
if you complain about something, you say that you are not happy about it or that it makes you angry. *He complained about having to tidy his room.*
complaint *noun*.

complete *adjective*
1 if something is complete, it has no parts missing. *a complete pack of cards.*
2 in every way. *a complete surprise.*
completely *adverb*, **complete** *verb*.

complicated *adjective*
if something is complicated, it is difficult to do or understand. *The story had a very complicated plot.*

compliment compliments *noun*
if somebody pays you a compliment, they say something nice about you.

compose composes composing composed *verb*
to compose means to write music or poetry. *Beethoven composed nine symphonies.*
composer *noun*.

compulsory *adjective*
having to be done. *Studying maths is compulsory in all schools.*

computer computers *noun*
a machine that can solve problems quickly, store information or control other machines.

conceal conceals concealing concealed *verb*
if you conceal something, you hide it. *She concealed the box under the bed.*

concentrate concentrates concentrating concentrated *verb*
if you concentrate on something, you give all your attention to it. *Please be quiet, I can't concentrate on my book.*

concerned *adjective*
if you are concerned about something, you worry about it.

concert concerts *noun*
a performance of music to a big group of people.

conclusion conclusions *noun*
1 the end of something. *The story had a sad conclusion.*
2 if you come to a conclusion about something, you decide what happened and why it happened. *We came to the conclusion that she went home because she was very ill.*

concrete *noun*
a building material made from cement, sand and small stones mixed with water that goes hard when it dries.

condition conditions *noun*
1 how somebody or something is. *The car is old, but it's still in good condition.*
2 how things are around you. *The animals in the zoo lived in terrible conditions.*
3 something that you must do before you are allowed to do something else. *You can go out on the condition that you tidy your room first.*

conductor conductors *noun*
a person who stands in front of a group of musicians and controls how they play a piece of music.

cone cones *noun*
1 a solid shape that is pointed at the top and rounded at the bottom.
2 the hard fruit of a pine or fir tree.

confess confesses confessing confessed *verb*
if you confess something, you say that you have done something wrong. *Luke confessed that he had broken the fence.*
confession *noun*.

confidence *noun*
the feeling that you can do something well. *She climbed the tree with confidence.*
confident *adjective*.

confuse confuses confusing confused *verb*
1 if you confuse somebody, you mix up their ideas so that they cannot understand. *My sister tried to explain the rules of the game to me but she went too quickly and I got confused.*
2 if you confuse two things, you mix them up so that you cannot tell the difference between them. *I always confuse the words "there" and "their" because they sound the same.*
confusing *adjective*, **confusion** *noun*.

congratulate congratulates congratulating congratulated *verb*
when you congratulate somebody, you tell them that you are pleased about something they have done. *I congratulated Lucy on passing her dancing exam.*
congratulations *noun*.

conifer conifers *noun*
a tree with long, thin leaves called needles that stay green in winter. Conifers have hard brown fruit called cones. Pine trees are conifers.

conjunction conjunctions *noun*
a word that joins words or groups of words in a sentence. "And", "but" and "if" are conjunctions.

conker conkers *noun*
a hard, shiny brown fruit of the horse chestnut tree. ● A word that sounds like **conker** is **conquer**.

connect connects connecting connected *verb*
when you connect things, you join them together. *Ella and Neil connect the pieces to make a vehicle.*

conquer conquers conquering conquered *verb*
if an army conquers its enemies, it wins the war and takes control of them. ● A word that sounds like **conquer** is **conker**.
conqueror *noun*.

conscience consciences *noun*
your conscience is a feeling inside you that tells you about right and wrong. *Mazy didn't steal any sweets, so she has a clear conscience.*
▲ Say ***kon**-shunss*.

conscious *adjective*
if you are conscious, you are awake and you know what is happening around you. ▲ Say ***kon**-shuss*.
■ The opposite is **unconscious**.

consider considers considering considered *verb*
when you consider something, you think carefully about it. *We must consider what to do next.*

considerate *adjective*
if you are considerate, you think about other people's feelings and you are not selfish.

consist consists consisting consisted *verb*
if something consists of different things, it is made up of those things. *This cake consists of flour, eggs, butter and sugar.*

consonant consonants *noun*
any letter of the alphabet except a, e, i, o or u, which are vowels.

construct constructs constructing constructed *verb*
if you construct something, you build or put it together. *Tara is constructing a tractor.*

contact contacts contacting contacted *verb*
if you contact somebody, you write to them or telephone them.

contact *noun*
if two things make contact, they touch each other. *The spaceship made contact with the shuttle.*

contain contains containing contained *verb*
to contain something is to have something inside. *This tin contains coffee powder.*

container containers *noun*
a container is something that you put things in. Boxes, bottles and tins are containers.

content *adjective*
if you are content, you feel happy.
▲ Say *kon-**tent***.

A B C D E F G H I J K L M N O P Q R S T U V W X Y Z

contents *noun*
the contents of something are all the things inside. *Yasmin dropped her bag and all the contents fell on the floor.* ▲ Say ***kon**-tents.*

contest contests *noun*
a competition or game that people try to win. *a judo contest.*

continent continents *noun*
one of the seven big pieces of land in the world. The continents are: Africa, Asia, Europe, North America, South America, Oceania and Antarctica.

continue continues continuing continued *verb*
when you continue doing something, you keep on doing it. *We continued playing outside until it got dark.*

contract contracts *noun*
a written agreement between two people or groups. *an employment contract.*

control *noun*
if you have control over somebody or something, you can make them do what you want. *You should have more control over your dog and not let it run into the road like that.*
control *verb.*

convenient *adjective*
if something is convenient, it is easy to do or use. *The cinema is very convenient; it is just around the corner.* ■ The opposite is **inconvenient**.

conversation conversations *noun*
if you have a conversation with somebody, you talk to them. *Hugo and Toby are having a conversation.*

convince convinces convincing convinced *verb*
if somebody or something convinces you, they make you believe something.

cook cooks cooking cooked *verb*
when you cook food, you prepare and heat it, ready to eat.

cook cooks *noun*
a person who prepares and cooks food.

cooker cookers *noun*
a cooker is used to heat food. It has an oven inside for baking and roasting, and metal parts on the top that heat up for boiling and frying.

cool cooler coolest *adjective*
if something like water or the weather is cool, it is quite cold, but not very cold.

cool cools cooling cooled *verb*
when something cools, it becomes colder. *Take the cake out of the oven and leave it to cool.*

copper *noun*
a red-brown metal that is dug out of the ground. Copper wire is used to carry electricity.

copy copies copying copied *verb*
1 if you copy somebody, you try to do the same things or look the same as them. *Lucy copied her sister's way of talking.*
2 if you copy something, you write or draw something that is exactly the same as another thing. *The teacher asked us to copy the questions into our books for homework.*

copy copies *noun*
a thing that is made to look exactly the same as another thing.

coral *noun*
coral is found at the bottom of the sea. It is the skeletons of small sea creatures that are left when the animals have died. Most coral is pink, white or red.

cord cords *noun*
strong, thick string. ● A word that sounds like **cord** is **chord**.

core cores *noun*
1 the middle part of some kinds of fruit where the seeds are. *an apple core.*
2 the centre of the Earth. *The Earth's core is very hot.*

cork corks *noun*
1 the light bark of the cork oak tree. Cork is used to make things such as tiles and table mats.
2 a piece of cork is pushed into the top of a bottle to close it. You use a corkscrew to get a cork out of a bottle.

corn *noun*
plants such as wheat or oats that farmers grow for their seeds called grain. Corn can be made into flour.

corner corners *noun*
the place where two walls, roads or edges meet.

correct *adjective*
if something is correct, it is right and there are no mistakes. *Are all your spellings correct?*
correction *noun.*

corridor corridors *noun*
a long, narrow space inside or outside a building with rooms on each side of it.

cost costs *noun*
the amount of money that you must pay to buy something. *The cost of the cinema tickets was ₹350 each.*

cost costs costing cost *verb*
if something costs ₹5, you have to pay ₹5 to buy it. *How much did it cost?*

costume costumes *noun*
the clothes that actors wear or that people wear at special times. *They wore fancy dress costumes to the party.*

cosy cosier cosiest *adjective*
if a place is cosy, it is warm and comfortable.

cot cots *noun*
a small bed with high sides that a baby sleeps in.

cottage cottages *noun*
a small house in the country.

cotton *noun*
1 material that is made by weaving the soft white fibres of the cotton plant. *a cotton shirt.*
2 thread that people use for sewing.

cough coughs coughing coughed *verb*
when you cough, you make a sudden loud noise in your throat. *The smoke made me cough.*
cough *noun.*
I've got a bad cough. ▲ Say ***koff.***

council councils *noun*
a group of people who are chosen to plan and decide things for other people. *The town council is planning to build a new sports centre.*

count counts counting counted *verb*
1 when you count, you say numbers one after another in the right order. *I can count from one to a million!*
2 when you count things, you add them up to find out how many there are. *Can you count the spoons and see if we have enough?*

counter counters *noun*
1 a long, high table in a shop or bank between the people who work there and the people who want to buy things.
2 a small, round piece of plastic that you use in some games.

country countries *noun*
1 an area of land in the world with its own people and government. *France, Spain and Japan are countries.*
2 the land outside towns and cities.

county counties *noun*
one of the parts of Britain and Ireland that can make some rules for the people who live in it. *Lancashire and Dorset are counties in England.*

couple couples *noun*
1 two people who are together. *A young couple live next door.*
2 a few or more things. *a couple of oranges.*

courage *noun*
if you show courage, you are being brave.
courageous *adjective.*

course courses *noun*
1 an area of ground used for some games and sports. *Horses race on a race course.* ◆ *People play golf on a golf course.*
2 a set of lessons that you have when you learn something new. *My mum is doing a computing course.*
3 one of the parts of a meal. *We had chicken for the main course.*

court courts *noun*
1 a place where a group of people, called a jury, and a judge decide if a person has done something wrong and what their punishment should be.
2 a piece of ground where you can play a certain sport. *a tennis court.*
3 a place where a king or queen lives.

courtyard courtyards *noun*
an area surrounded by walls.

cousin cousins *noun*
your cousin is the child of your aunt or uncle.

cover covers *noun*
1 a thing that you put over another thing. *She got into bed and pulled the covers over her head.*
2 the outside of a book or magazine.

cover covers covering covered *verb*
1 to put something over something else to hide it or keep it warm.
2 when something covers another thing, it is all over it. *The grass was covered with snow.*

cow cows *noun*
a big female farm animal that gives us milk. Adult female whales, seals and elephants are also called cows.

coward cowards *noun*
a person who is easily frightened.

cowboy cowboys, cowgirl cowgirls *noun*
a person whose job is to look after cattle in the US.

crab crabs *noun*
a sea animal with a flat, hard shell and ten legs. The two front legs have big claws called pincers on the end.

crack cracks *noun*
1 a thin line on something where it has nearly broken. *This cup has a tiny crack in it.*
2 a sudden loud noise. *a crack of thunder.*

crack cracks cracking cracked *verb*
if something cracks, it has a thin split in it, but it does not break in pieces. *Hot water will crack the glasses.*

cracker crackers *noun*
1 a tube covered with coloured paper that has a small toy and a hat inside. It makes a loud bang when two people pull it apart.
2 a thin biscuit that you eat with cheese.

cradle cradles *noun*
a small, wooden bed for a baby.

craft crafts *noun*
work or a hobby where you make things carefully and cleverly with your hands. Pottery and wood carving are crafts.

crane cranes *noun*
1 a tall machine that lifts and moves heavy things.
2 a large water bird with a long neck and long legs.

crash crashes *noun*
1 an accident when something that is moving hits another thing. *a serious car crash.*
2 a loud noise like the sound of thunder. *There was a loud crash as he dropped the plates on the floor.*

crash crashes crashing crashed *verb*
when something crashes, it hits another thing very hard and makes a loud noise. *The car crashed into a wall.*

crate crates *noun*
a wooden or plastic box for carrying things in. *a crate of bananas.*

crater craters *noun*
1 a huge hole in the ground that is made by something like a bomb landing on it.
2 the hole at the top of a volcano where fire and hot, liquid rock called lava come out.

crawl crawls crawling crawled *verb*
when a baby crawls, it moves slowly along the ground on its hands and knees. When an insect crawls, it moves with its body close to the ground.

crayon crayons *noun*
a coloured pencil or wax stick that you draw and colour with.

creak creaks creaking creaked *verb*
if something like a door creaks, it makes a strange squeaking sound. *Don't step on that floorboard, it creaks.*

cream *noun*
the thick, pale yellow liquid on the top of milk. *Would you like cream?*

crease creases creasing creased *verb*
if you crease something, you put lots of untidy lines in it by crushing it, or not folding it carefully. *If you sit on your jacket you will crease it.*

create creates creating created *verb*
if you create something, you make something new.
creator *noun*, **creation** *noun*.

creature creatures *noun*
any animal, fish or bird. *Ants are very tiny creatures.*

creep creeps creeping crept *verb*
if something creeps along, it moves slowly and quietly. *The cat crept towards the birds.*

crescent crescents *noun*
1 the curved shape of a new moon.
2 a street that has a curved shape.

crew crews *noun*
all the people who work on a ship or an aeroplane.

cricket *noun*
1 a game played by two teams of 11 players with bats and a ball.
2 an insect like a grasshopper with wings and long legs that can jump quite high.

cried past of cry.

crime crimes *noun*
something that is against the law. *Murder is a very serious crime.*

criminal criminals *noun*
a person who does something that is against the law.

crisp crisper crispest *adjective*
if something such as a biscuit is crisp, it is hard and crunchy and easy to break.

crisp crisps *noun*
a very thin slice of potato that is fried in hot oil. *a bag of salted crisps.*

criticize criticizes criticizing criticized *verb*
if somebody criticizes you, they say you have done something badly or wrong. *Mrs Cobb criticized my handwriting for being untidy.* ■ The opposite is **praise**.

croak croaks croaking croaked *verb*
to croak is to make a deep rough sound like a frog makes. *"I've got a sore throat," she croaked.*

crocodile crocodiles *noun*
a large reptile with a long body and sharp teeth. Crocodiles live in freshwaters in some hot countries.

crooked *adjective*
not straight. *a crooked path through the trees.* ▲ Say ***krook**-id*.

crop crops *noun*
crops are plants that farmers grow as food. Wheat, rice and oats are all crops.

cross crosses *noun*
a mark like this + or this x.

cross crosses crossing crossed *verb*
when you cross something such as a road or a river, you go from one side to the other.

cross crosser crossest *adjective*
if you are cross, you are angry about something.

crouch crouches crouching crouched *verb*
when you crouch, you bend your knees so that your body is close to the ground. *Hugo crouched to look at the plant.*

crow crows *noun*
a big, black bird that makes a loud noise.

crow crows crowing crowed *verb*
to crow means to make a noise like a cock makes in the early morning.

crowd crowds *noun*
a lot of people together in one place. *There was a huge crowd at the football match.*

crowded *adjective*
if a place is crowded, it is full of people. *The swimming pool gets very crowded.*

crown crowns *noun*
a ring of precious metal and jewels that kings and queens wear on their heads.

cruel crueller cruellest *adjective*
a person who is cruel hurts people or animals on purpose.

cruise cruises *noun*
if you go on a cruise, you have a holiday on a ship that travels to different places.

crumb crumbs *noun*
a tiny piece of bread, cake or biscuit. *After the party, there were a lot of crumbs on the table.*

crunch crunches crunching crunched *verb*
if you crunch something hard and firm like a biscuit, you make a loud noise when you eat it. *She crunched a carrot.* **crunchy** *adjective*.

crush crushes crushing crushed *verb*
if you crush something, you press it hard so that you break or squash it.

crust crusts *noun*
1 the hard layer on the outside of a loaf of bread or pastry.
2 the Earth's crust is the thin outer layer.

crutch crutches *noun*
one or two long sticks that fit under your arms to help you walk if you have hurt your foot or leg.

cry cries crying cried *verb*
1 when you cry, you have tears falling from your eyes. *The baby is crying because he is hungry.*
2 to cry also means to shout or make a loud noise. *"Help!" she cried.*

crystal crystals *noun*
1 a hard kind of rock that looks like glass.
2 a small, hard piece of something such as salt or ice that has a regular shape.
▲ Say ***kriss**-tal*.

cub cubs *noun*
a young bear, lion, tiger, fox or wolf.

cube cubes *noun*
a solid shape with six square sides. *a cube of sugar.*

cuckoo cuckoos *noun*
a bird that makes a sound like its name. Cuckoos lay their eggs in the nests of other birds.

cucumber cucumbers *noun*
a long vegetable that is dark green on the outside and pale green inside. You can eat it raw in salads.

cuddle cuddles cuddling cuddled *verb*
when you cuddle somebody, you put your arms around them and hold them. *Dad cuddled the baby.*

cup cups *noun*
1 a small container with a handle. You drink liquids such as tea and coffee from a cup.
2 a metal container with two handles, that you can win as a prize. *He won a silver cup for coming first in the race.*

cupboard cupboards *noun*
a piece of furniture or a space in a wall with shelves and doors where you can keep things such as clothes or food. ▲ Say ***kub**-erd*.

cure cures curing cured *verb*
if something cures somebody, it makes their illness go away. **cure** *noun*.

curious *adjective*
if you are curious about something, you want to know more about it. *I was curious to know what the noise was.*

curl curls *noun*
a piece of hair in a curved shape.
curly *adjective.*
My sister has curly hair.

curl curls curling curled *verb*
if something curls or curls up, it bends into a curved shape. *The hedgehog curled up into a ball.*

currant currants *noun*
a small, dried grape. ● A word that sounds like **currant** is **current**.

current currents *noun*
1 air or water that is moving. *It is too dangerous to swim here because of the strong currents.*
2 electricity that is passing through a wire.
● A word that sounds like **current** is **currant**.

cursor cursors *noun*
a little sign on a computer screen that shows you where to type the next letter.

curtain curtains *noun*
curtains are pieces of cloth that you pull across a window or the front of the stage in a theatre to cover it.

curve curves *noun*
a line that bends smoothly. *The letter "S" has two curves in it.*

curved *adjective*
if something is curved, it has the shape of a curve.

cushion cushions *noun*
a bag filled with soft material that you put on a chair to make it more comfortable.

custom customs *noun*
something that people usually do. *It is a custom to give people presents on their birthday.*

customer customers *noun*
a person who buys something from a shop.

cut cuts cutting cut *verb*
1 you use scissors or a knife to cut things into pieces.
2 if you cut yourself, you hurt yourself by accident with something sharp. *Katie cut her hand on a piece of glass.*
cut *noun.*

cute cuter cutest *adjective*
if something like a kitten is cute, you like it because it looks pretty and sweet.

cutlery *noun*
knives, forks and spoons.

cycle cycles *noun*
a bicycle. *Jason rides his cycle to school.*

cycle cycles cycling cycled *verb*
when you cycle, you ride a bicycle. *Tom cycles to school every day.*
cyclist *noun.*

cylinder cylinders *noun*
a long, round shape like a tube or a can.

cymbals *noun*
two round metal plates that you use as a musical instrument. Cymbals make a loud clashing sound when you hit them together.

D d

daffodil daffodils *noun*
a bright-yellow, trumpet shaped flower that blooms in the spring.

dagger daggers *noun*
a short sword with one or two sharp edges.

daily *adjective, adverb*
every day.

dainty daintier daintiest *adjective*
small and neat. *We had some dainty little sandwiches with the crusts cut off.*

dairy dairies *noun*
a company that sells milk and other foods made from milk such as butter and cheese.

dairy *adjective*
dairy foods are milk, butter and cheese, and foods made from milk.

daisy daisies *noun*
a small flower with narrow, white petals around a yellow centre.

dam dams *noun*
a wall built across a river to hold back the water.

damage damages damaging damaged *verb*
if you damage something, you break it or harm it. *A car hit the wall and damaged it.* ▲ Say **dam**-*ij*
damage *noun.*

damp damper dampest *adjective*
a little wet.

dance dances dancing danced *verb*
when you dance, you move your body in time to music.
dance *noun.*

dandelion dandelions *noun*
a wild flower with a lot of bright-yellow petals.

danger dangers *noun*
1 if you are in danger, you are in a situation where something bad could happen to you. *The notice on the fence said: "Danger! Keep out!"*
2 something that might harm you. *Cigarettes are a danger to your health.*

dangerous *adjective*
something that is dangerous might harm you. *It's dangerous to go near the edge of the cliff.* ■ The opposite is **safe**.

dare dares daring dared *verb*
1 if you dare to do something, you are brave enough to do it even though it is dangerous. *Sonali wouldn't dare touch the angry swan.*
2 if you dare somebody, you ask them if they are brave enough to do something. *I dare you to walk along the top of that wall.*
dare *noun.*

dark darker darkest *adjective*
1 without any light. *Open the curtains. It's dark in here.* ■ The opposite is **light** or **bright**.
2 dark colours are nearer to black than to white. *Ricky is wearing a dark coloured T-shirt, Lucy's is light.* ■ The opposite is **light**, **pale** or **fair**.
darkness *noun.*

dart darts *noun*
a short arrow that you throw at a round target called a dartboard in a game called darts.

dart darts darting darted *verb*
if you dart somewhere, you run there very quickly and suddenly. *Dad darted into the shop and came out with ice creams for everybody.*

dash dashes dashing dashed *verb*
if you dash somewhere, you run there very quickly. *She put her umbrella up and dashed across the road.*

data *noun*
facts and information. Information stored in a computer is called data.
▲ Say ***day**-ta.*

date dates *noun*
1 the day, the month and sometimes the year when something happens. *What's the date today?*
2 a brown, sticky fruit with a seed inside. Dates grow on a type of palm tree.

daughter daughters *noun*
somebody's daughter is a girl or woman who is their child. ▲ Say ***dor**-ter.*

dawdle dawdles dawdling dawdled *verb*
if you dawdle, you walk very slowly, taking more time than you should.

dawn dawns *noun*
the beginning of the day when the Sun is just starting to come up.

day days *noun*
1 the time when it is light. ■ The opposite is **night**.
2 a measure of time. The 24 hours of a day start at midnight and end the next midnight.

daze *noun*
if you are in a daze, you cannot think clearly and you are confused. *He's hit his head and he's in a bit of a daze.*

dazzle dazzles dazzling dazzled *verb*
if a light dazzles you, it is very bright and shining straight in your eyes so that you cannot see.

dead *adjective*
no longer alive. *a dead bird.*

deaf *adjective*
a person who is deaf cannot hear very well or cannot hear at all.

dear dearer dearest *adjective*
1 something that is dear, costs a lot of money. ■ The opposite is **cheap**.
2 you write "dear" at the beginning of a letter, before the person's name.
● A word that sounds like **dear** is **deer**.

death deaths *noun*
the end of a person's or an animal's life, when they die.

debt debts *noun*
money that you owe somebody and have to pay them back. ▲ Say ***det**.*

decade decades *noun*
a measure of time. There are 10 years in a decade.

decay decays decaying decayed *verb*
when something decays, it goes bad or becomes rotten. *Eating sweets can make your teeth decay.*

deceive deceives deceiving deceived *verb*
if you deceive somebody, you trick them by making them believe something that is not true.

decide decides deciding decided *verb*
if you decide something, you make up your mind about what you are going to do. *I'm trying to decide what to buy my brother for his birthday.*

deciduous *adjective*
a deciduous tree loses its leaves in winter and gets new ones in spring.
▲ Say *dis-**id**-yoo-us.* ■ The opposite is **evergreen**.

decimal decimals *noun*
a fraction that you write as a number, with amounts less than one written after the dot, called a decimal point. 2.5 is a decimal. It is the same as $2\frac{1}{2}$.

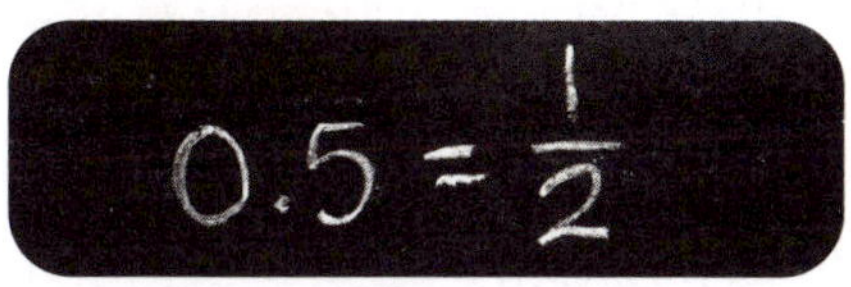

decimal *adjective*
a decimal system counts numbers in tens.

decision decisions *noun*
if you make a decision, you make up your mind about what you are going to do. *Have you made a decision yet?*

deck decks *noun*
a floor on a ship or bus.

declare declares declaring declared *verb*
if you declare something, you say something important to a lot of people. *I declare that the winner is Team A.*

decorate decorates decorating decorated *verb*
1 if you decorate something, you add things to it to make it look more beautiful. *Sam decorated the cake.*
2 if you decorate a room, you paint it or put wallpaper on the walls.
decoration *noun.*

decrease decreases decreasing decreased *verb*
if something decreases, it gets smaller or less. *The number of trees in the rainforests of South America has decreased over the last few years.* ■ The opposite is **increase**.

deep deeper deepest *adjective*
1 something that is deep goes a long way down from the top. *The river is very deep.* ■ The opposite is **shallow**.
2 a deep sleep is sleep that is hard to wake somebody from.
3 a deep voice is very low. *Men's voices are usually deeper than women's.*

deer deer *noun*
a wild animal that eats grass and can run very fast. Male deer (stags) have big horns called antlers on their head. ● A word that sounds like **deer** is **dear**.

defeat defeats defeating defeated *verb*
if you defeat somebody, you beat them in a game, competition or battle.
defeat *noun.*

defend defends defending defended *verb*
when you defend somebody or something, you protect them when somebody else is attacking them. *Jamie defended the goal.*
defence *noun.*

definite *adjective*
certain and not likely to change. *We haven't fixed a definite date for the trip.*
definitely *adverb.*
I'm definitely going to do my homework this evening.

defrost defrosts defrosting defrosted *verb*
to defrost is to unfreeze frozen food.

degree degrees *noun*
1 a measurement of temperature. Degree is sometimes written as °. *10°C is ten degrees Celsius.*
2 a measurement of angles. *A right angle is 90°.*
3 a qualification that you can get after you have studied at university.

delay delays delaying delayed *verb*
1 if you delay doing something, you put it off until later. *We had to delay our holiday for a week because my sister was very ill.*
2 to delay somebody is to make them late. *The bus was delayed for an hour because of the accident.*

delete deletes deleting deleted *verb*
if you delete something, you remove it from a piece of writing or from a computer's memory.

deliberate *adjective*
if something you do is deliberate, you do it on purpose.

delicate *adjective*
1 something that is delicate is small and lovely but it can be broken or damaged quite easily. *A spider's web is very delicate.*
2 a person who is delicate gets ill quite easily. *He's a delicate child.*

delicious *adjective*
food that is delicious tastes very nice.
▲ Say *dee-**lish**-us.*

delight delights delighting delighted *verb*
if something delights you, it makes you feel very pleased. *She was delighted with the beautiful present.*

deliver delivers delivering delivered *verb*
when you deliver something, you take it to the person it is supposed to go to. *A postman or postwoman delivers letters and parcels to your home.*

demand demands demanding demanded *verb*
if you demand something, you ask for it very strongly. *Dad demanded to know why I was so late getting home.*
demand *noun.*

demolish demolishes demolishing demolished *verb*
to demolish something is to destroy it completely. *The council is demolishing the old houses.*
demolition *noun.*

den dens *noun*
the home of a wild animal such as a lion or a bear.

dent dents denting dented *verb*
if you dent something that is made of metal, you damage it so that part of it is pushed in slightly instead of flat. *a dented tin.*

dentist dentists *noun*
a person whose job is to look after people's teeth.

deny denies denying denied *verb*
if you deny something, you say it is not true. *Tom denied taking the money.*

depart departs departing departed *verb*
if you depart, you leave. *The plane departs at 6.25 p.m.* ■ The opposite is **arrive**.
departure *noun.*

depend depends depending depended *verb*
1 if you depend on somebody or something, you need them. *The school depends on parents to raise money.*
2 if you depend on somebody, you trust them to do what they say they will. *I'm depending on you to help me.*
3 to depend also means to be decided by something. *Whether we have a picnic tomorrow depends on the weather.*
dependent *adjective.*
■ The opposite is **independent**.

depth depths *noun*
the depth of something is how deep it is. *What is the depth of the lake?*

deputy deputies *noun*
a person who does another person's job when that person is not there. *a deputy headteacher.*

descend descends descending descended *verb*
if something descends, it goes down. *We watched as the parachute slowly descended before landing.*
▲ Say *dee-**send***.

describe describes describing described *verb*
when you describe something, you say what it is like.

description *noun.*
The woman gave the police a description of the man she had seen.

desert deserts *noun*
an area where it is very dry and hardly any plants can grow. ▲ Say ***dez**-ert*.

deserted *adjective*
if a place is deserted, there is nobody there. *The house was deserted.*

deserve deserves deserving deserved *verb*
if you deserve something, it is fair that it should happen to you. *He trained very hard and he deserved to win the medal.*

design designs designing designed *verb*
if you design something, you decide what it will be like and then you draw it to show how it should be made.
▲ Say *dee-**zine***.

design designs *noun*
a pattern. *Each of these jumpers has a different design.* ▲ Say *dee-**zine***.

desire desires *noun*
a very strong wish for something. *She had a great desire to become an artist.*
desirable *adjective.*
worth having. *a desirable house.*

desk desks *noun*
a table that you sit at to write or read. Desks often have drawers.

despair despairs despairing despaired *verb*
if you despair, you feel no hope that something good will happen.

desperate *adjective*
if you are desperate, you are in a very bad situation and you will do almost anything to change it. *She was so desperate for food that she started begging on the streets.*

destination destinations *noun*
the place you are going to.

destroy destroys destroying destroyed *verb*
if you destroy something, you damage it or break it so badly that it cannot be mended. *Fire destroyed the house.*
destruction *noun.*
The storm caused a lot of destruction.

detail details *noun*
one of many small pieces of information about something. *I can give you some idea of what happened but I don't know all the details yet.*

detective detectives *noun*
a person who tries to find out who did a crime.

detergent *noun*
a powder or liquid that you use to clean clothes or dishes.

determined *adjective*
if you are determined to do something, you are going to do it and nothing can stop you. *Alex had trained very hard, he was determined to win the race.*

detest detests detesting detested *verb*
if you detest somebody or something, you hate them very much.

develop develops developing developed *verb*
when something develops, it changes as it grows. *Here we see a photograph developing.*
development *noun.*
the new housing development.

A B C D E F G H I J K L M N O P Q R S T U V W X Y Z

dew *noun*
small drops of water that form in the night on grass and plants. ● A word that sounds like **dew** is **due**.

diagonal *adjective*
a line that slants from one corner of something to the opposite corner.

diagram diagrams *noun*
a simple picture explaining something. *a diagram about plant growth.*

dial dials *noun*
the part of something such as a clock or speedometer that has numbers on it.

diameter diameters *noun*
a line drawn straight across a circle, through the centre.
❖ ***Look at page 38***

diamond diamonds *noun*
1 a very hard, clear, precious jewel.
2 a shape like a rectangle turned so that it is standing on one of its corners.

diary diaries *noun*
a book where you can write what has happened during the day or what you plan to do.

dice *noun*
small cubes with a different number of dots on each side. You use dice when you play some games. The word for one of the dice is a **die**.

dictionary dictionaries *noun*
a book that gives the meanings of words and how to spell them in the order of the alphabet. *If you don't understand a word, you look it up in a dictionary.*

die dies dying died *verb*
when a person, an animal or a plant dies, they come to the end of their life and stop living. ■ The opposite is **live**. ● A word that sounds like **die** is **dye**.
death *noun.*

diesel *noun*
a kind of oil that is used as fuel in bus and lorry engines. Some cars use diesel too. ▲ Say ***dee**-zel.*

diet diets *noun*
1 your diet is the food that you normally eat. *A healthy diet includes plenty of fresh fruit and vegetables.*
2 if you go on a diet, you eat only certain foods because you have an illness or because you are trying to lose weight.

different *adjective*
if something is different from another thing, it is not like it.
difference *noun.*
Can you tell the difference between these two horses?

difficult *adjective*
hard to do. ■ The opposite is **easy** or **simple**.
difficulty *noun.*

dig digs digging dug *verb*
if you dig, you use something such as a spade or fork to move earth or make a hole in the ground. Animals dig using their claws.

digest digests digesting digested *verb*
when you digest food, it passes through your body and gets broken up so that your body can use it to make energy.
digestion *noun.*

digit digits *noun*
1 one of the numbers from 0 to 9.
2 a finger or a toe.

dilute dilutes diluting diluted *verb*
when you dilute a liquid, you make it weaker by adding water.
dilution *noun.*

dim dimmer dimmest *adjective*
a dim light is not very strong or bright.

dinghy dinghies *noun*
a small, open boat that you row or sail.
▲ Say ***ding**-ee.*

dinner dinners *noun*
the main meal that you eat in the day, either in the evening or in the middle of the day.

dinosaur dinosaurs *noun*
a large reptile that lived millions of years ago and then became extinct.
❖ ***Look at page 125***

dip dips dipping dipped *verb*
1 if you dip something into a liquid, you put it in for a moment. *He dipped his brush into the paint.*
2 if something dips, it slopes down. *The road dipped suddenly after the bridge.* ■ The opposite is **rise**.

direct *adjective*
the direct way to go somewhere is by the shortest way and without stopping.

direct directs directing directed *verb*
1 if you direct somebody to a place, you tell them the way to go.
2 a person who directs a film or television programme tells the actors what to do.

direction directions *noun*
1 the way that something is pointing or moving. *Am I going in the right direction for the old castle?*
2 directions are instructions telling you how to do something.

dirt *noun*
mud, dust or marks on something.

dirty dirtier dirtiest *adjective*
covered with dirt or marks.
■ The opposite is **clean**.

disabled *adjective*
a disabled person has a part of their body that does not work properly.
disability *noun*.

disagree disagrees disagreeing disagreed *verb*
when people disagree, they do not think the same way about something. *My brother and I often disagree about what to watch on the TV.* ■ The opposite is **agree**.

disappear disappears disappearing disappeared *verb*
if something disappears, it goes out of sight. *We waved at the boat until it disappeared in the distance.* ■ The opposite is **appear**.
disappearance *noun*.

disappointed *adjective*
you feel disappointed when something you were looking forward to does not happen or when what happens is not as good as you hoped. *My parents were disappointed with my exam results.*
disappointment *noun*.

disaster disasters *noun*
a really terrible thing that happens. *An earthquake is a natural disaster.*

disc discs *noun*
a round, flat object.

discover discovers discovering discovered *verb*
if you discover something, you find out about it or see it for the first time. *We discovered a secret hiding place in the hollow trunk of a tree.*
discovery *noun*.

Word Builder

Dis - is a little word called a prefix that you can add to the beginning of certain words, often to change their meaning.

1 Not, or the opposite of disloyal, dishonest.
2 To do the opposite of disagree, dislike.

discuss discusses discussing discussed *verb*
if you discuss something, you talk about it with other people.
discussion *noun*.

disease diseases *noun*
an illness.

disguise disguises *noun*
something that you do to change the way you look so that other people do not know who you are.
▲Say *dis-**gize***.

disgust *noun*
a very strong feeling of not liking something that is really nasty or bad.
disgusting *adjective*.

dish dishes *noun*
a plate or a bowl used for cooking or for putting food on.

disk disks *noun*
a flat plastic case with a magnetic metal part inside that stores information from a computer.

dislike dislikes disliking disliked *verb*
if you dislike somebody or something, you do not like them.

distance distances *noun*
distance is how far apart two things are.
distant *adjective*.

distract distracts distracting distracted *verb*
if something distracts you, it takes your attention away from what you are doing. *I can't do my homework with the radio on because I get distracted by it.*
distraction *noun*.

disturb disturbs disturbing disturbed *verb*
if you disturb somebody, you stop them from doing something such as working or sleeping. *Don't disturb her, she's asleep.*
disturbance *noun*.

ditch ditches *noun*
a long hole in the ground that has been dug along the side of a road so that water can drain away.

dive dives diving dived *verb*
1 when you dive, you jump into water with your arms and head first.
2 to dive also means to go swimming underwater with special equipment that lets you breathe.
3 to dive is to go under water. *We watched the submarine dive.*
diver *noun*.

divide divides dividing divided *verb*
1 if you divide something, you separate it into smaller parts.
2 when you divide one number by another number, you see how many times the smaller number goes into the larger one. *8 divided by 2 is 4 (8 ÷ 2 = 4).* ■ The opposite is **multiply**.
division *noun*.
I am not very good at long division.

divorce divorces *noun*
the ending of a marriage.
divorce *verb*.
She divorced her husband.

dizzy dizzier dizziest *adjective*
if you feel dizzy, you feel as if everything is spinning around and you are going to fall over.

dock docks *noun*
a place where ships stop to load or unload goods or to get repaired.
dock *verb*.

doctor doctors *noun*
a person whose job is to help people who are ill to get better by giving them medicines or advice. We usually write "doctor" as "Dr" before a name.

document documents *noun*
a piece of paper with important information on it.

dog dogs *noun*
an animal that is often kept as a pet or for hunting or guarding things. A young dog is called a puppy.
❖ ***Look above***

doll dolls *noun*
a toy in the shape of a very small person.

dolphin dolphins *noun*
a mammal that lives in rivers or the sea but breathes air. Dolphins look like very large fish. ▲ Say ***dol**-fin.*

domino dominoes *noun*
dominoes are small, rectangular blocks of wood or plastic with different numbers of dots on them, used to play a game.

donation donations *noun*
an amount of money that you give, often to a charity.

donkey donkeys *noun*
an animal like a small horse but with longer ears.

door doors *noun*
a large piece of wood or glass that moves to open and close the way into a room, building or cupboard.

dose doses *noun*
an amount of medicine that you have to take at one time.

dot dots *noun*
a small, round spot. *a blue shirt with white dots.*

double *adjective*
twice as large or twice as many. *Natasha has double the number of bricks that Jazz has.* ▲ Say ***dub**-uhl.*

doubt doubts *noun*
if you have a doubt about something, you are not sure about it. *I don't have any doubt that our team will win.* ▲ Say ***dowt**.*

dough *noun*
a mixture of flour, water and other things that you cook to make bread, cakes or pastry. ▲ Say ***doh**.*

dove doves *noun*
a kind of pigeon. ▲ Say ***duv**.*

doze dozes dozing dozed *verb*
when you doze, you sleep very lightly and you can wake up easily. *Grandpa was dozing in his chair.*

dozen *noun*
twelve. *We made two dozen sandwiches for the party.* ▲ Say ***duz**-en.*

drag drags dragging dragged *verb*
if you drag something, you pull it

along the ground. *Freddie dragged his coat across the floor.*

dragon dragons *noun*
a very large animal in stories with a long body covered in scales. Dragons have wings and can breathe fire.

dragonfly dragonflies *noun*
an insect with a long, thin body and two sets of wings. Dragonflies live near ponds and rivers.

drain drains draining drained *verb*
1 when water drains away, it flows away slowly.
2 when you drain food, you pour away the water that it was cooked in. *Drain the pasta and serve with a sauce.*

drain drains *noun*
a pipe that carries water away.

drama dramas *noun*
1 a serious play.
2 an interesting or exciting thing that happens. *There was a great drama when Anya won the lottery.*

drank past of drink.

drastic *adjective*
severe or harsh.

draught draughts *noun*
cold air coming into a room because there is a slight gap between a window or door and the wall. ▲ Say ***draft.***
draughty *adjective.*

draw draws drawing drew drawn *verb*
1 when you draw, you use a pencil, pen or crayon to make a picture.
2 if you draw the curtains, you move them together by pulling.
3 if two teams of people draw in a game, both have the same score.
drawing *noun.*

drawer drawers *noun*
a wooden box that slides in and out of a piece of furniture.

dream dreams dreaming dreamt *or* dreamed *verb*
1 when you dream, you see pictures and hear sounds in your mind while you are sleeping. *I dreamt I could fly.*
2 when you dream of something, you think about how much you would love to do it. *She dreams of becoming a famous ballet dancer.*
dream *noun.*

dress dresses dressing dressed *verb*
when you dress you put on clothes.
■ The opposite is **undress**.

dress dresses *noun*
a piece of clothing that a woman or girl wears. A dress has a top part and a skirt joined together.

drew past of draw.

drift drifts drifting drifted *verb*
when something drifts, it is carried slowly along by the wind or by the movement of water. *She stopped the engine and let the boat drift.*

drill drills *noun*
a tool that is used for making holes.
drill *verb.*

drink drinks drinking drank drunk *verb*
when you drink, you take liquid into your mouth and swallow it.
drink *noun.*

drip drips dripping dripped *verb*
when liquid drips, it falls in drops. *Rain dripped off the roof.*

drive drives driving drove driven *verb*
when somebody drives, they control something such as a car or bus and make it go where they want.

drizzle *noun*
light rain in very small drops.

droop droops drooping drooped *verb*
when something droops, it hangs or bends down because it is weak or tired. *The flower drooped because it had no water.*

drop drops *noun*
a tiny amount of liquid. *a drop of water.*

drop drops dropping dropped *verb*
if you drop something, you let it fall. *I dropped the plate.*

drought droughts *noun*
a long period of time when there is no rain. ▲ Say ***drowt.***

drove past of drive.

drown drowns drowning drowned *verb*
if somebody drowns, they die because they cannot breathe under water.

drug drugs *noun*
1 a pill or medicine that a doctor gives you to treat an illness.
2 an illegal pill or chemical that someone takes.

drum drums *noun*
a musical instrument that you beat with a stick or your hands. A drum is made from a round frame with a piece of material stretched across it.
drummer *noun.*
Jed is a drummer in a band. ❖ ***Look at page 105***

drunk *adjective*
when somebody is drunk, they have drunk too much alcohol and cannot speak clearly or act sensibly.

drunk past of drink.

dry drier driest *adjective*
if something is dry, there is no water or liquid in it. ■ The opposite is **wet**.

dry **dries drying dried** *verb*
if you dry something, you make it dry. *Jordan is drying himself with a towel.*

duck **ducks** *noun*
a water bird with webbed feet and a flat, broad beak. A male duck is called a drake, and a young duck is called a duckling.

due *adjective*
when something is due at a particular time, it should happen at that time. *They are due to arrive at 10 o'clock.* ● A word that sounds like **due** is **dew**.

dug past of dig.

dull **duller dullest** *adjective*
1 a dull colour is not very bright.
2 a dull day is cloudy and the sun is not shining.
3 if something such as a film or book is dull, it is not interesting.
4 not sharp. *a dull ache.*

dumb *adjective*
1 completely unable to speak.
2 stupid.

dummy **dummies** *noun*
1 a model of a person that clothes can be put on. *I like the trousers on the dummy in the shop window.*
2 a rubber thing that a baby sucks.

dump **dumps dumping dumped** *verb*
if you dump something, you put it down quickly and carelessly. *My parents get cross when my sister just dumps her clothes on the floor.*

dune **dunes** *noun*
a low hill of sand by the sea or in a desert.

dungeon **dungeons** *noun*
an underground prison in a castle. ▲ Say ***dun**-jun.*

dusk *noun*
the time in the evening when it is nearly dark but not quite.

dust *noun*
dirt that is like powder. *The furniture was covered in dust.*
dusty *adjective.*

dustbin **dustbins** *noun*
a large container with a lid that you keep outside your house to put your rubbish in.

duty **duties** *noun*
a job that you have to do. *The dog belongs to my brother, so it's his duty to take it for walks.*

duvet **duvets** *noun*
a thick cover that keeps you warm in bed. Some duvets are filled with feathers. ▲ Say ***doo**-vay.*

dye **dyes** *noun*
a liquid that you soak cloth or your hair in to change its colour.
● A word that sounds like **dye** is **die**.
dye *verb.*

dyslexia *noun*
a learning difficulty that causes problems with reading and spelling.
▲ Say *dis-**lex**-ee-a.*

E e

eager *adjective*
if you are eager to do something, you want to do it very much. *Ben was eager to help with the cooking.*

eagle **eagles** *noun*
a large bird with a curved beak and broad wings. Eagles are called birds of prey because they catch and eat small animals and other birds.

ear **ears** *noun*
your ears are the part of your body that you hear with.

early **earlier earliest** *adjective, adverb*
1 near the beginning of a period of time. *Early cars had solid tyres. (adjective)*
2 before the usual time or the time that you are expected. *We went to the swimming pool early before it got crowded. (adverb)* ■ The opposite is **late**.

earn **earns earning earned** *verb*
if you earn money, you get money for work that you do. *Lauren sometimes earns extra pocket money by washing her mother's car.*

earring **earrings** *noun*
a piece of jewellery that you wear on your ear.

earth *noun*
1 the Earth is the planet that we live on. Our Earth moves around the Sun.
2 the ground that plants grow in.

earthquake **earthquakes** *noun*
an earthquake happens when part of

the ground suddenly begins to shake. Earthquakes happen when rocks beneath the surface of the Earth move.

easel easels *noun*
a stand for a blackboard or an artist's painting.

east *noun*
1 the direction from which the Sun rises in the morning.
2 the East is where countries such as China and Japan are.
east *adjective*, **eastern** *adjective*. *Norfolk is in eastern England.*

easy easier easiest *adjective*
not difficult. *These sums are easy!*
■ The opposite is **hard** or **difficult**.

eat eats eating ate eaten *verb*
when you eat something, you chew food in your mouth and swallow it.

echo echoes *noun*
an echo is the sound that comes back to you when you shout in a place such as a cave. ▲ Say *ek-oh*.

eclipse eclipses *noun*
1 an eclipse of the Sun is when the Moon comes between the Earth and the Sun so that you cannot see all the Sun's light (**a**).
2 an eclipse of the Moon is when the Earth comes between the Sun and the Moon so that you cannot see all the Moon's light (**b**).

edge edges *noun*
an edge is the end or side of something. *Don't stand on the edge of the cliff.*

education *noun*
education is teaching people to read, write and learn about all kinds of things in a school or college.

eat
Some words you can use instead of eat:

Robbits eat carrots.
nibble

Apples make a crunchy sound when you eat them.
chew, munch, bite

We ate at the new Italian restaurant.
dined

eel eels *noun*
a long, thin fish that lives in rivers or in the sea.

effect effects *noun*
an effect is a change that is caused by somebody or something. *The rubbish in the river had a bad effect on the fish.*

effort efforts *noun*
if you make an effort, you try hard to do something. *It takes a lot of effort to pull Angelina off the floor.*

egg eggs *noun*

1 birds, fish, some reptiles and some other animals lay eggs. The young of these animals live inside the eggs until they are ready to hatch.
2 a hen's egg with a hard shell that you can cook and eat.

elastic *noun*
a rubber material that stretches when you pull it. *elastic around the waist.*

elbow elbows *noun*
your elbow is the joint in the middle of your arm where it bends.

elderly *adjective*
rather old. *an elderly man.*

election elections *noun*
an election is when people choose who they want to be their leader by voting. *an election for a new president.*

electric *adjective*
a machine that is electric works by using electricity. *an electric cooker.*

electricity *noun*
the form of energy that travels along wires. Rubbing a balloon on hair creates a form of electricity called "static electricity".
electrical *adjective*.

electronic *adjective*
an electronic machine, such as a computer, uses a piece of material called a silicon chip that has a tiny electric circuit on it.

elephant elephants *noun*
a very big, grey animal with a long trunk and two long teeth called tusks. Elephants live in Africa and Asia. They eat grass, and parts of trees which they tear off with their trunks.

embarrassed *adjective*
if you are embarrassed, you feel shy or ashamed, and worried about what people think of you. *I was so embarrassed when I fell over and everyone laughed.*
embarrassment *noun*.

embroidery *noun*
sewing that you do with pretty colours and small stitches, to decorate cloth.
embroider *verb*.

embryo embryos *noun*
a tiny person or animal that has only just begun to develop inside its mother and has not been born yet. ▲ Say *em-bree-oh*.

emerald emeralds *noun*
a bright green jewel.

emergency emergencies *noun*
an emergency is when somebody is in danger and needs help immediately. *In an emergency, you should call 100.*

emotion emotions *noun*
a strong feeling such as love, anger or sadness. ▲ Say *ee-**moh**-shun*.

emperor emperors *noun*
a man who rules over a group of countries, called an empire.

employ employs employing employed *verb*
if you employ somebody, you pay them to work for you.

empress empresses *noun*
a woman who rules over a group of countries, called an empire.

empty *adjective*
if something is empty, there is nothing in it. *She drank all the milk and left the empty glass on the table.* ■ The opposite is **full**.

empty empties emptying emptied *verb*
if you empty something, you take out or throw away everything that is in it. *He emptied the jug of juice.* ■ The opposite is **fill**.

enchanted *adjective*
a place that is enchanted has been put under a magic spell. *The story is about an enchanted wood where the trees come to life.*

encourage encourages encouraging encouraged *verb*
if you encourage somebody, you make them feel that what they are doing is good and help them to go on doing it. *We encouraged my brother to swim a length of the pool.*
encouragement *noun*.

encyclopaedia encyclopaedias *noun*
a book that tells you about all kinds of facts and subjects from A to Z. ▲ Say *en-sye-kloh-**pee**-dee-a*.

end ends *noun*
1 the last part of something. *I'm almost at the end of my book.* ■ The opposite is **beginning** or **start**.
2 one of the short edges of something long. *They sat at opposite ends of the table.*

end ends ending ended *verb*
when something ends, it finishes. *What time does the film end?* ■ The opposite is **begin** or **start**.

enemy enemies *noun*
your enemy is a person who hates you or a person that you fight against.

energy *noun*
1 energy is the power that makes machines work and gives us heat and light. Electricity is one kind of energy.
2 your energy is the strength that your body has to do things. *You need a lot of energy to run 1,000 metres.*
energetic *adjective*.

engaged *adjective*
1 if two people are engaged, they have agreed to get married.
2 if a telephone number is engaged, you cannot talk to the person you want because they are already talking to somebody else.

engine engines *noun*
1 a machine that makes things move. *a car engine.*

2 the front part of a train that pulls it along.

enjoy enjoys enjoying enjoyed *verb*
if you enjoy something, you like doing it. *I enjoy playing football.*
enjoyable *adjective*, **enjoyment** *noun*.

enormous *adjective*
very, very big. *China is an enormous country.* ■ The opposite is **tiny**.

enough *adjective, adverb, noun*
if you have enough of something, you have as much as you need. *Have you had enough to eat?*

enter enters entering entered *verb*
1 if you enter a place, you go into it. *She entered the room quietly.*
2 if you enter a race or competition, you take part in it. *Did you enter the egg and spoon race?*

entertain entertains entertaining entertained *verb*
if you entertain somebody, you do things that they find interesting or amusing. *The clown entertained the crowd while the acrobats changed their costumes.*
entertainment *noun*.

enthusiasm *noun*
a strong feeling of liking something or wanting to do something. *The children were full of enthusiasm for the party.*
enthusiastic *adjective*.

entrance entrances *noun*
the way into a place. *I'll meet you at the entrance to the shop.* ■ The opposite is **exit**.

envelope envelopes *noun*
a folded paper cover for a letter or card. You write the address of the person you are writing to on the front of the envelope.

environment *noun*
the environment is the air, water, land, and all the plants and animals around us. *We must all try to protect the environment.*
environmental *adjective.*

envy envies envying envied *verb*
if you envy somebody, you wish you had the same things that they have. *I envied Bella because she had a new bike.*
envious *adjective.*

episode episodes *noun*
an episode is one part of a long story in a book, or on television or radio that you read, watch or listen to in several parts.

equal *adjective*
if things are equal, they are the same in size, amount or number. *The children had an equal number of sweets each.*
equally *adverb.*

equator *noun*
the equator is an imaginary line on maps that goes around the Earth at an equal distance between the North and South Poles. Countries near the equator are very hot.

equipment *noun*
all the things you need to do something. *sports equipment.* ◆ *kitchen equipment.*

error errors *noun*
a mistake.

erupt erupts erupting erupted *verb*
when a volcano erupts, it explodes and very hot liquid rock called lava shoots out of the top.
eruption *noun.*

escalator escalators *noun*
a staircase with moving steps.

escape escapes escaping escaped *verb*
when a person or an animal escapes, they get away from somebody or something. *The bird has escaped from its cage.*

especially *adverb*
most of all. *I like animals, especially cats and rabbits.*

essential *adjective*
if something is essential, it is absolutely necessary. *Warm clothes are essential in very cold weather.*

evaporate evaporates evaporating evaporated *verb*
when a liquid evaporates, it changes into a gas or vapour and seems to disappear. *Water evaporates when it is heated.*
evaporation *noun.*

even *adjective*
1 flat and smooth. an even floor. ■ The opposite is **uneven**.
2 even numbers can be divided exactly by two. *2, 4, 6 and 8 are even numbers.* ■ The opposite is **odd**.

evening evenings *noun*
the part of the day between afternoon and night. *The sun goes down in the evening.*

event events *noun*
something that happens, especially something important or unusual. *The school sports day is a big event.*

eventually *adverb*
after a very long time. *I waited for ages, then eventually the bus came.*

evergreen *adjective*
an evergreen tree does not lose its leaves in the winter. Pine trees are evergreen. ■ The opposite is **deciduous**.

evidence *noun*
proof of something that happened. *The paw marks were evidence that the cat had jumped on the table.*

evil *adjective*
a person who is evil is very bad and cruel. *an evil emperor.*

exact *adjective*
correct. *What is the exact time?*
exactly *adverb.*

exaggerate exaggerates exaggerating exaggerated *verb*
if you exaggerate, you pretend something is bigger, better or worse than it really is. *Tom was exaggerating when he said he saw a spider as big as a cat.*
exaggeration *noun.*

exam exams *noun*
a short word for examination. *a maths exam.* ◆ *a ballet exam.*

examination examinations *noun*
1 an important test that you are given to see how much you have learnt.
2 looking at somebody or something closely and carefully. *a medical examination.*

examine examines examining examined *verb*
if you examine something, you look at it closely and carefully. *Freddie examined the fossil with a magnifying glass.*

example examples *noun*
a thing that shows what other things of the same kind are like. *At the school open day, we showed our parents examples of our work.*

excellent *adjective*
something that is excellent is very good. *We had an excellent holiday.*

except *preposition*
but not. *We all went shopping except Peter who stayed at home.*
exception *noun.*

exchange exchanges exchanging exchanged *verb*
if you exchange something, you give one thing and get something else in return. *At the end of the holiday we exchanged addresses with our new friends.*

excited *adjective*
if you are excited, you are so happy that you cannot keep quiet or calm. *Freddie is so excited that he is jumping for joy!*
excitement *noun.*
exciting *adjective.*

exclaim exclaims exclaiming exclaimed *verb*
to exclaim means to say something in a loud voice because you are surprised or angry. *"What a mess!" she exclaimed.*
exclamation *noun.*
He gave an exclamation of surprise when he saw the huge present.

exclamation mark exclamation marks *noun*
a mark (!) that you use in writing. You put an exclamation mark to show that somebody is surprised or angry. *Oh no!*

excuse excuses *noun*
if you make an excuse, you try to explain why you did something wrong. *What's your excuse for being late this time?* ▲ Say *ex-**kyoos**.*

excuse excuses excusing excused *verb*
if you excuse somebody, you forgive them for something they did wrong. *I'll excuse you for forgetting your sports kit this time, but don't do it again.*
▲ Say *ex-**kyooz**.*

exercise exercises *noun*
1 exercise is something such as running or jumping that you do to keep your body strong and well. *The children are doing different kinds of exercise.*
2 an exercise is a piece of work that you do to help you learn something. *Our teacher asked us to finish exercise 2 for homework.*

exhausted *adjective*
very tired. *After running all the way up the hill, I was exhausted.*

exhibition exhibitions *noun*
a collection of things in a place such as a museum or gallery for people to come and look at. ▲ Say *ex-i-**bish**-un.*

exist exists existing existed *verb*
if something exists, you can find it in the real world now. *Do you think fairies really exist?*
existence *noun.*

exit exits *noun*
the way out of a building. *The exit is at the back of the cinema.* ■ The opposite is **entrance**.

expand expands expanding expanded *verb*
if something expands, it gets bigger. *When you blow air into a balloon it expands.*

expect expects expecting expected *verb*
if you expect something to happen, you think it will happen. *I expect they will be here soon.*

expedition expeditions *noun*
a long journey to find or do something special. *Robert Peary led an expedition to the South Pole.*

expensive *adjective*
something that is expensive costs a lot of money. ■ The opposite is **cheap**.

experience experiences *noun*
1 an experience is something that has happened to you. *What's the most frightening experience you've had?*
2 experience is knowing about something because you have done it for a long time. *I can cycle to school when I've had more experience of riding my bike on the road.*

experiment experiments *noun*
a test that you do to find out something. *We did an experiment to see which objects are acidic.*

expert experts *noun*
a person who knows a lot about something. *a computer expert.*

explain explains explaining explained *verb*
1 if you explain how to do something, you tell somebody about it so they can understand it. *My brother explained how to mend my bike.*
2 if you explain something that happened, you give reasons why it happened. *We explained that we were late because we had missed the bus.*
explanation *noun.*

explode explodes exploding exploded *verb*
if something such as a bomb explodes, it bursts suddenly with a very loud noise.
explosion *noun.*

explore explores exploring explored *verb*
when you explore, you look carefully around a place you have never seen before.
exploration *noun*.

express expresses expressing expressed *verb*
if you express what you think or feel, you show it in words or actions.

expression expressions *noun*
your expression is the look on your face that shows how you feel. *A smile is a happy expression.*

extensive *adjective*
covering a wide area. *an extensive park.*
extent *noun*.

extinct *adjective*
an animal or plant that is extinct does not exist now. *Dinosaurs became extinct millions of years ago.*
extinction *noun*.

extinguish extinguishes extinguishing extinguished *verb*
if you extinguish a fire, you put it out. *He extinguished the flames with a bucket of water.* ▲ Say *ex-**ting**-gwish*.

extra *adjective*
more than you usually have. *I took an extra jumper because I was cold.*

extraordinary *adjective*
very special or unusual. *I read an extraordinary story about a horse that could talk.*

extremely *adverb*
very. *Elephants are extremely big animals.*

eye eyes *noun*
your eyes are the part of your face that you use to see. In the middle of the eye is a hole called a pupil that lets light on to the lens behind. ● A word that sounds like **eye** is **I**.

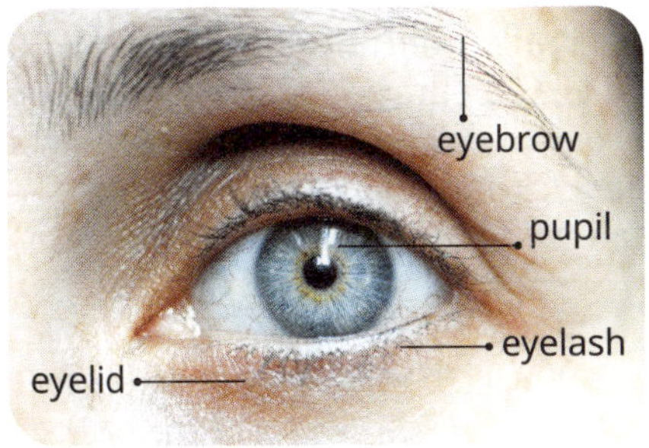

F f

fable fables *noun*
a story, usually about animal characters, that teaches you something.

face faces *noun*
your face is the front part of your head where your eyes, nose and mouth are.

fact facts *noun*
something that is known to be true and that you can prove.

factory factories *noun*
a building where people use machines to make things. *a car factory.*

fade fades fading faded *verb*
1 if something fades, it becomes paler so that you can no longer see it properly. *The ink on the document had faded so much that we could hardly read it.*
2 if a sound fades away, it slowly becomes quieter. *The music faded away until you couldn't hear it.*

fail fails failing failed *verb*
if you fail at something, you do not succeed in doing it. *She failed to get into the team because she had injured her knee.*
failure *noun*.

faint faints fainting fainted *verb*
if you faint, you become unconscious for a short time. *Sam fainted when he saw blood coming from the cut on his finger.*

faint fainter faintest *adjective*
something that is faint is not very strong or clear. *There is a faint smell of burning.*

fair fairer fairest *adjective*
1 a person who is fair has light-coloured hair and skin. ■ The opposite is **dark**.
2 something that is fair seems right or treats everybody the same. *It's not fair that I have to go to bed when Ben is allowed to stay up.* ■ The opposite is **unfair**.
● A word that sounds like **fair** is **fare**.

fair fairs *noun*
a place outside where rides and roundabouts and competitions are set up for people to have fun. ● A word that sounds like **fair** is **fare**.

fairy fairies *noun*
a magical creature in stories, like a very small person with wings.

faith *noun*
if you have faith in somebody, you trust them to do what they say.

faithful *adjective*
if you are faithful to somebody who trusts you, you do not do anything to hurt that person. *She's very faithful to her friends.*

fake fakes *noun*
a copy of something that looks like the real thing. *It's not a real diamond – it's just a fake.*

fall falls falling fell fallen *verb*
when something falls, it goes down or drops from a higher to a lower place. *Sam fell off the skateboard.*
fall *noun*.

false *adjective*
1 not true. *The man gave a false name to the police instead of his real name.*
2 not the real thing. *Tom is wearing a false beard and glasses.*

fame *noun*
being famous.

familiar *adjective*
if something is familiar to you, you know it well. *Her face was familiar but I couldn't remember her name.* ■ The opposite is **unfamiliar** or **strange**.

family families *noun*
1 a group of people made up of parents, grandparents and children. Aunts, uncles and cousins are also part of your family.
2 a group of animals or plants that are like each other in certain ways. *Polar bears are members of the bear family.*

famine famines *noun*
a time when there is not enough food for the people in a country to eat.
▲ Say ***fam**-in*.

famous *adjective*
known by lots of people. *a famous film star.*
▲ Say ***fay**-muss*.

fan fans *noun*
1 a machine with blades that turn around fast to keep a room cool in hot weather.

2 a flat object, often made of paper, that you wave in front of your face to keep you cool in hot weather.
3 a person who really admires somebody famous such as a singer or an actor, or who likes a certain sport very much. *football fans.*

fancy dress *noun*
clothes that you wear to a party that make you look like somebody or something different. *Jed's having a fancy dress party and I'm going to go as a gorilla. What are you wearing?*

fang fangs *noun*
a long, sharp, pointed tooth. Many animals that eat meat have fangs.

fantastic *adjective*
amazing or really good.

fare fares *noun*
the money that you pay to go on a bus, train or plane. ● A word that sounds like **fare** is **fair**.

farm farms *noun*
a place where people grow crops or keep animals to sell as food.
farmer *noun*.

fascinate fascinates fascinating fascinated *verb*
if something fascinates you, you feel very interested in it. *Snakes fascinate me.* ▲ Say ***fas**-in-ate*.
fascination *noun*, **fascinating** *adjective*.

fashion fashions *noun*
a way of dressing or behaving that is very popular for a time and that everyone wants to copy.

fast
Some words you can use instead of fast:

We caught a fast train to Edinburgh.
express, high speed

She's a very fast talker.
quick, rapid

The news spread fast.
quickly, swiftly, speedily, rapidly

fast faster fastest *adjective*
1 very quick. *She's a fast runner.*
2 if a watch is fast, it shows a time that is later than the real time. *My watch says five past two but it's five minutes fast, because it's only two o'clock.* ■ The opposite is **slow**.
fast *adverb*.

fast *verb*
a day or period of time when one does not eat food due to health or religious reasons.

fasten fastens fastening fastened *verb*
if you fasten something, you do it up or fix it firmly.

fat fatter fattest *adjective*
a person who is fat has a large, heavy body. *a fat pot-bellied pig.*
■ The opposite is **thin**.

fat fats *noun*
oil, butter or margarine that you can use to cook with.

father fathers *noun*
a man who has children.

fault faults *noun*
1 a thing that is wrong with a machine. *We had to take the camera back to the shop because it had a fault.*
2 if something bad is your fault, it happened because of you. *It's your fault we were late because you wouldn't get out of bed.*

favour favours *noun*
a kind and helpful thing that you

do for somebody. *Could you do me a favour and carry this box for me?*

favourite *adjective*
your favourite thing is the one you like best. *Jahaan is watching his favourite television programme.*

fax faxes *noun*
1 a machine which sends a picture or message along a telephone wire to another machine which prints it out.
2 a message or picture sent on a fax machine.

fear *noun*
the feeling that you have when you are afraid. *He has a fear of heights.*

feast feasts *noun*
a large, special meal for a lot of people.

feather feathers *noun*
one of the light, soft parts that cover a bird's body.

feeble feebler feeblest *adjective*
weak. *a feeble old man.*

feed feeds feeding fed *verb*
1 if you feed a person or an animal, you give them food. *We fed the ducks.*
2 when an animal feeds, it eats. *Cows and sheep feed on grass.*

feel feels feeling felt *verb*
1 when you feel something, you touch it and know what it is like against your skin. *Feel my bear – it's so soft.*
2 if you feel sad, happy or angry, you are that way at the moment. *I feel quite hungry.*

feeling feelings *noun*
a feeling is what you feel, like happiness, anger or worry.

feet plural of foot.

fell past of fall.

felt past of feel.

female *noun*
a female person or animal belongs to the sex that can have babies or lay eggs. Girls and women are female.
■ The opposite is **male**.

fence fences *noun*
a kind of wall made of wood or wire around a piece of land such as a garden or field. *a wooden fence.*

fern ferns *noun*
a plant that has leaves like feathers and no flowers.

ferocious *adjective*
fierce and violent. *The dog was ferocious and bit anybody who went near it.* ▲ Say *fer-**oh**-shuss.*

ferry ferries *noun*
a boat that carries passengers, cars and other vehicles across a river or a narrow bit of sea.

fertile *adjective*
fertile land is land where plants grow well.

festival festivals *noun*
a special day or a religious day that people have as a holiday so they can celebrate it. *During the festival of Chinese New Year, dragons dance to celebrate.*

fetch fetches fetching fetched *verb*
when you fetch something, you go to get it and bring it back. *Can you fetch me my coat from the hall, please?*

fever fevers *noun*
an illness that makes the temperature of your body higher than usual.

fibre fibres *noun*
a thread of wool, cotton or something similar that is used to make cloth.

fiction *noun*
stories that have been made up by somebody and are not about people that really exist. *The novels and stories of Dickens and Andersen are fiction.*

field fields *noun*
an area of land where farmers grow crops or keep animals.

fierce fiercer fiercest *adjective*
an animal that is fierce is angry and likely to attack you.

fight fights fighting fought *verb*
when people or animals fight, they attack and try to hurt each other. *Two boys were fighting in the playground.* **fight** *noun.*

figure figures *noun*
1 one of the signs that we use to write numbers, such as 1, 2 and 3.
2 the shape of a person. *I could just make out the figure of a tall man in the fog.*

file files *noun*
1 a box or cardboard cover for keeping papers in.
2 a set of information on a computer.
3 a tool with a rough surface that you use to make things smooth. *a nail file.*
single file a line of people or animals, one behind the other. *The children walked in single file into the school hall.*

a b c d e f g h i j k l m n o p q r s t u v w x y z

fill fills filling filled *verb*
if you fill something, you put as much into it as it can hold. *Fiona filled the bottles with water.* ■ The opposite is **empty**.

film films *noun*
1 a story in moving pictures that you watch in a cinema or on television.
2 a long, thin strip of plastic that you put in a camera for taking photographs. *I need a new film for my camera.*

fin fins *noun*
a fin is one of the thin, flat parts on a fish's body that help it to swim and balance.

final *adjective*
last. *The final episode of the TV series is on tonight.*
finally *adverb*.

find finds finding found *verb*
when you find something, you see it again after it has been lost or you did not know where it was. *I've found my old trainers. They were at the back of the cupboard.* ■ The opposite is **lose**.

fine finer finest *adjective*
1 healthy. *"How are you?" "I'm fine, thanks."*
2 bright and sunny. *We'll go to the beach if it's fine tomorrow.*
3 good enough. *There's nothing wrong with your work - it's fine.*
4 very thin. *You need a sharp pencil to draw a fine line.*
5 very good. *She's a fine athlete.*

fine fines *noun*
money that you have to pay as a punishment. *Mum had to pay a fine for parking on a double yellow line.*

finger fingers *noun*
your fingers are the long, thin parts at the end of your hands.

fingerprint fingerprints *noun*
the mark made by the tip of your finger showing the lines on your skin. *The police couldn't find any fingerprints because the thief had worn gloves.*

finish finishes finishing finished *verb*
when you finish something, you come to the end of it. ■ The opposite is **start** or **begin**.
finish *noun*.

fir firs *noun*
an evergreen tree with cones and leaves that are the shape of needles. ● A word that sounds like **fir** is **fur**.

fire fires *noun*
the hot, bright flames that come from something that is burning.

fire fires firing fired *verb*
1 to shoot bullets from a gun. *The thief fired at the policeman.*
2 to dismiss or sack somebody from their job. *Get out; you're fired!*

fire engine fire engines *noun*
a large lorry with hoses and ladders that fire-fighters travel in to get to a fire.

fire extinguisher fire extinguishers *noun*
a metal container full of chemicals or water that you use to put out a fire.

fire-fighter fire-fighters *noun*
a person whose job is to put out dangerous fires and to rescue people who are in danger.

fireplace fireplaces *noun*
a hole in a wall in a room beneath a chimney where you can light a fire.

fireworks *noun*
small objects containing chemicals that explode noisily and make brightly coloured sparks when you light them.

firm firmer firmest *adjective*
1 something that is firm is quite hard and does not change its shape when you press it. *Bananas are firm when they are green but get softer when they are ripe.*
2 if you are firm about something, you are sure and you are not going to change your mind. *We haven't made a firm decision yet about where we are going on holiday.*

firm firms *noun*
a business company. *Vatsala works for a large publishing firm.*

first aid *noun*
medical help or treatment that is given to a sick or hurt person before the doctor arrives.

fish fish or fishes *noun*
an animal that lives in water and breathes through gills. A fish has fins and a tail for swimming, and its body is covered in scales.
❖ ***Look at page 65***

fish fishes fishing fished *verb*
to fish is to try to catch fish. *My uncle taught us how to fish with a fishing-rod.*

fishmonger fishmongers *noun*
a person in a shop or market, who sells fresh fish to eat.

fist fists *noun*
you make a fist when you curl your fingers and thumb into your palm. *The boys were punching each other with their fists.*

Fish

Vocabulary

bony fish
one of the two main classes or groups of fish which includes all fish with bony skeletons.

cartilaginous fish
one of the two main classes or groups of fish in which the skeleton is made of tough, gristly cartilage instead of bone. Sharks belong to this class.

dorsal fin
the fin (designed to help a fish swim) on the back of a fish.

pelvic fin
the fin on the pelvis or "waist" of a fish.

pectoral fin
the fin on the "chest" or "breast" of a fish.

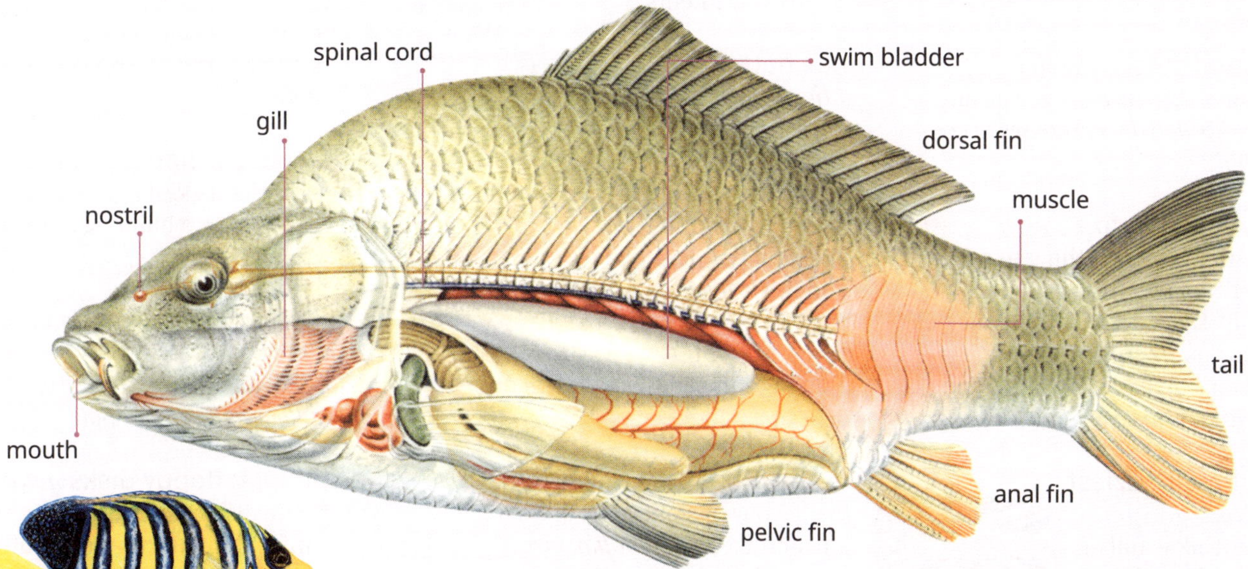

Regal Angelfish

Anthias

Striped Red Mullet

Tench

Anchovy

Sardine

Salmon

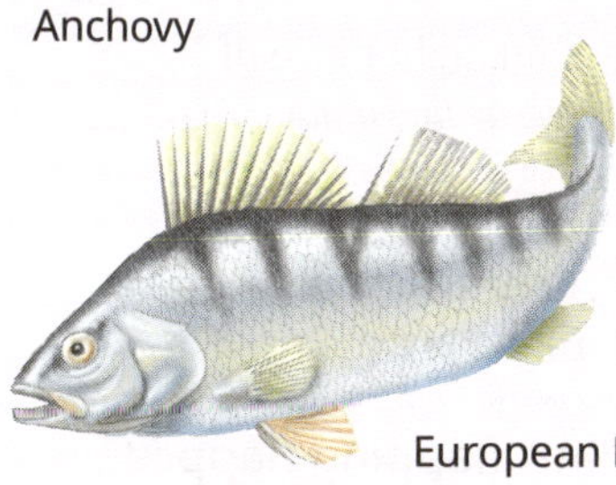
European Perch

Common Dace

Anglerfish

Common Carp

a b c d e f g h i j k l m n o p q r s t u v w x y z

A B C D E F G H I J K L M N O P Q R S T U V W X Y Z

fit fits fitting fitted *verb*
1 if something fits, it is the right size or shape. *These jeans don't fit me any more.*
2 if you fit things together, you join one thing to another. *I fitted the jigsaw puzzle together.*

fit fitter fittest *adjective*
if you are fit, your body is well and strong. *My dad does exercises to keep himself fit.*

fix fixes fixing fixed *verb*
1 when you fix something to another thing, you join the two things firmly. *She fixed the shelf to the wall.*
2 when you fix something that was broken, you make it useful again. *I've fixed your bike.*

fizzy fizzier fizziest *adjective*
a fizzy drink is full of small bubbles.

flag flags *noun*
a piece of cloth with a pattern on it, on the end of a pole. Each country has its own flag.

flake flakes *noun*
a small, thin, light piece of something. *a snowflake.*

flame flames *noun*
the hot, bright, burning gas that comes from a fire.

flap flaps flapping flapped *verb*
when a bird flaps its wings, it moves them up and down quickly.

flap flaps *noun*
a flat piece that hangs down to cover an opening. *a cat flap.*

flare flares *noun*
a bright flame or light used as a signal.

flash flashes *noun*
a sudden, bright light that lasts a short time. *a flash of lightning.*

flask flasks *noun*
1 a container with a lid for keeping hot drinks hot and cold drinks cold.
2 a glass container for liquids that is used for doing scientific experiments.

flat flatter flattest *adjective*
1 level and completely smooth and even, with no parts that are higher than the rest. *A table has a flat top.*
2 a flat tyre does not have enough air in it. *My bike has a flat tyre.*

flat flats *noun*
a set of rooms for living in, on one floor of a building.

flavour flavours *noun*
the flavour of something is what it tastes like. *different flavours of ice-cream.*

flea fleas *noun*
a tiny jumping insect with no wings. Fleas bite people and animals.

fleece fleeces *noun*
a sheep's coat of wool.

flesh *noun*
1 the soft part of your body that is under your skin, covering your bones.
2 the soft part of fruit or vegetables.

flew past of fly
● A word that sounds like **flew** is **flu**.

flight flights *noun*
1 a journey in a plane.
2 flying through the air. *Have you ever seen swans in flight?*
3 a flight of stairs is a set of stairs.

float floats floating floated *verb*
1 when something floats in a liquid, it stays on the top and does not sink. *an experiment to see what floats.*
2 when something floats in air, it moves along gently in the air without falling to the ground. *floating balloons.*

flock flocks *noun*
a group of animals of one kind. *a flock of sheep.* ◆ *a flock of geese.*

flood floods *noun*
a flood happens when a lot of water covers an area that is usually dry. Floods often happen when there has been a lot of rain. *The insurance will cover flood damage.* **flood** *verb.*

floodlight floodlights *noun*
very bright lights that light up a sports ground or a building at night.

floor floors *noun*
1 the flat part that you walk on inside a building.
2 a level of a building. *We live on the third floor of a block of flats.*

floppy disk floppy disks *noun*
a magnetic disk in a square case that stores information from a computer.

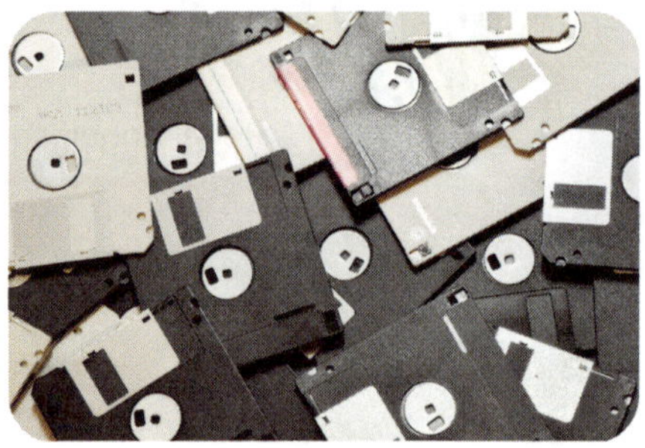

flour *noun*
white or brown powder that is made by grinding grains such as wheat. We use flour to make bread, cakes and pastry. ● A word that sounds like **flour** is **flower**.

flow flows flowing flowed *verb*
when a liquid flows, it moves smoothly along. *Rivers flow into the sea.* ◆ *The water flowed down the drain.*

flower flowers *noun*
the part of a plant at the end of the stem that has coloured or white petals. ● A word that sounds like **flower** is **flour**.

flown past of fly.

flu *noun*
an illness that gives you a high temperature and makes your body ache all over. Flu is short for **influenza**. ● A word that sounds like **flu** is **flew**.

fluffy fluffier fluffiest *adjective*
soft and light like wool or hair. *Baby chickens are fluffy.*

fluid fluids *noun*
a substance that flows. *Liquids and gases are fluids.*

fluorescent *adjective*
a fluorescent object glows in the dark when you shine a light on it. *Cyclists wear fluorescent strips so that car drivers can see them in the dark more easily.* ▲ Say *flor-**es**-ent*.

flush flushes flushing flushed *verb*
1 if you flush, your face goes red. *Thomas flushed with embarrassment.*
2 when you flush the toilet, you make a lot of water flow through it to clean it.

flute flutes *noun*
a musical instrument in the shape of a tube. You hold it sideways and play different notes by blowing across a hole near one end.

flutter flutters fluttering fluttered *verb*
when something flutters, it makes quick, light, flapping movements. *A moth was fluttering against the window.*

fly flies *noun*
a small insect with two wings.

fly flies flying flew flown *verb*
1 when something flies, it moves through the air. *A flock of geese was flying overhead.*
2 when you fly, you make a journey on a plane.

foal foals *noun*
a young horse.

foam *noun*
a mass of small air bubbles. *If you use washing-up liquid, you get a lot of foam.*

focus focuses focusing focused *verb*
when you focus a camera or a telescope, you move a part of it so that what you see through it is clear.

fog *noun*
a thick cloud near the ground that makes it difficult to see anything. **foggy** *adjective*.

foil *noun*
a very thin sheet of metal used to wrap food.

fold folds folding folded *verb*
when you fold something, you bend one part so that it covers another. *Fred folded his jumper before putting it in his suitcase.* ■ The opposite is **unfold**. **fold** *noun*.

follow follows following followed *verb*
1 if you follow somebody, you go along behind them. ■ The opposite is **lead**.
2 if one thing follows another, it comes after it. *Night always follows day.*

fond fonder fondest *adjective*
if you are fond of somebody, you like them very much and care about what happens to them.

food *noun*
all the things that people and animals can eat.

foolish *adjective*
very silly. ■ The opposite is **sensible**.

foot feet *noun*
the lowest part of the leg, below the ankle, on which people or animals stand.

football footballs *noun*
1 a game played by two teams who try to kick a ball into the other team's goal. The game is also called soccer.
2 the ball that you use to play football.

footprint footprints *noun*
the mark that the foot or the shoe leaves on a surface.

footstep footsteps *noun*
the sound that someone who is walking makes when each foot touches the ground. *I could hear footsteps coming up the path.*

forbid forbids forbidding forbade forbidden *verb*
if somebody forbids you to do something, they are telling you that you are not allowed to do it. *Our teacher has forbidden us to bring our pets to school.* ■ The opposite is **permit** or **allow**.

force forces forcing forced *verb*
1 if somebody forces you to do something, they make you do it. *He forced me to give him the money.*
2 if you force something somewhere, you use your strength to make it go there. *She tried to force a parcel through the letter box.*

force forces *noun*
power or strength. *A lot of trees were blown down by the force of the wind.*

forecast forecasts forecasting forecast or forecasted *verb*
if you forecast something, you say it is going to happen in the future. *She forecasts that the weather will become warmer at the weekend.*
forecast *noun*. *the weather forecast.*

A B C D E F G H I J K L M N O P Q R S T U V W X Y Z

forehead foreheads *noun*
your forehead is the part of your face above your eyes and below your hair.

foreign *adjective*
a person or thing that is foreign belongs to a country that is not your own. *Jane collects foreign stamps.*
▲ Say ***for**-en.*

forest forests *noun*
a very large group of trees.

forge forges forging forged *verb*
if somebody forges something, such as money, they make an exact copy of it in order to deceive people. *He was put in prison for forging passports to sell to criminals.* ▲ Say ***forj**.*
forgery *noun.*

forget forgets forgetting forgot forgotten *verb*
when you forget something, you do not remember it. *Don't forget your keys.*

forgive forgives forgiving forgave forgiven *verb*
when you forgive somebody, you do not mind any more about something bad they did to you. *Lily finally forgave me for losing her pen.*

fork forks *noun*
1 a tool with long, pointed parts called prongs at one end. You use a small fork for putting food in your mouth. Large forks are used for digging.
2 the place where something divides into two parts. *a fork in the road.*

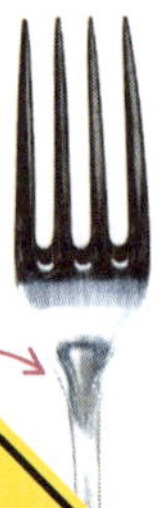

form forms *noun*
1 the shape of something. *a birthday cake in the form of a dog.*
2 a kind of something. *Gas and coal are forms of fuel.*
3 a printed paper with questions and spaces for you to write the answers.
4 a class in a school.

form forms forming formed *verb*
1 when things form a certain shape, they are arranged in that shape. *The chairs formed a half circle.*
2 when something forms, it starts to appear. *A crowd was forming outside the theatre.*

fortnight fortnights *noun*
two weeks. *a fortnight's holiday in Italy.*

fortress fortresses *noun*
a big, strong building such as a castle that can be defended against enemies.

fortune fortunes *noun*
1 good or bad luck.
2 a lot of money. *They won a fortune in the lottery.*

fossil fossils *noun*
what remains of a plant or animal that died millions of years ago and that has become part of a piece of rock.
fossilized *adjective.*

foster fosters fostering fostered *verb*
when somebody fosters a child, they take the child into their home and look after them for a while.

fought past of fight.

found past of find.

fountain fountains *noun*
a statue or object that sprays water up into the air.

fox foxes *noun*
a wild animal that looks like a small dog with red-brown fur and a long, thick tail.

fraction fractions *noun*
1 a part of a whole number. $\frac{1}{2}$ and $\frac{2}{5}$ are fractions.
2 a tiny part. *She opened the cage door a fraction but the hamster escaped.*

fracture fractures *noun*
a break or crack in something, especially a bone. *Her arm is in plaster because she has a fracture.*
▲ Say ***frak**-cher.*
fracture *verb.*

fragile *adjective*
something that is fragile can break easily. *Be careful not to drop that vase, it's quite fragile.* ▲ Say ***fraj**-ile.*

frame frames *noun*
1 an edge around something such as a picture or window.
2 the shape of something such as a building or vehicle that is built first out of metal or wood, so that the rest can be built over it. *An aeroplane has a strong steel frame.*
frame *verb.*
The pictures are being framed.

freckle freckles *noun*
a small brown spot on a person's skin.

free *adjective*
1 if you are free, you are able to do what you want or go where you want without anybody stopping you.
2 something that is free does not cost any money.
3 free also means not busy. *I'm busy now but I'll be free after supper.*
freedom *noun.*

freeze freezes freezing froze frozen *verb*
1 when water freezes, it gets so cold that it turns into ice.
2 when you freeze food, you make it very cold by storing it at a very low temperature so that it stays fresh for a long time.
freezing *adjective.*
● A word that sounds like **freeze** is **frieze**.

freezer freezers *noun*
a large metal chest or cupboard that freezes food so that it stays fresh for a long time.

freight *noun*
goods that a lorry, train, ship or plane is carrying. ▲ Rhymes with ***late***.

frequent *adjective*
something that is frequent happens or comes often. *There are frequent buses to the city centre from here.*

fresh fresher freshest *adjective*
1 food that is fresh has been made or picked recently and is not old or bad. *fresh eggs.* ◆ *fresh fruit.*
2 fresh air is air that is clean and good to breathe. *We went outside to get some fresh air.*
3 fresh water is water that is not salty.

fridge fridges *noun*
a kind of metal cupboard that is cold inside, where food can be kept fresh for a long time. Fridge is short for **refrigerator**.

friend friends *noun*
a person that you know well and like a lot. *Nathan, Lucas and Sam are best friends.*
friendship *noun*.

friendly friendlier friendliest *adjective*
a friendly person gets to know other people easily and acts like a friend towards them. *Erica is friendly with everybody.*

frieze friezes *noun*
a strip along the top of a wall that has coloured decorations or pictures on it. ● A word that sounds like **frieze** is **freeze**.

frighten frightens frightening frightened *verb*
if you frighten somebody, you make them feel afraid.
frightened *adjective*, **frightening** *adjective*.

frill frills *noun*
a strip of material with a lot of folds in it that is sewn on to the edge of something to decorate it. *a blouse with frills down the front.*
frilly *adverb*.

fringe fringes *noun*
1 a strip of hanging threads decorating the edge of something.
2 the front part of a person's hair that hangs down over their forehead.

frog frogs *noun*
a small animal with long, powerful back legs that it uses to jump. Frogs lay their eggs in water and these eggs develop into tadpoles.

front fronts *noun*
the part of something that faces forward or that you usually see first.
■ The opposite is **back** or **rear**.
in front of not behind. *There is a small garden in front of our house.*

frost *noun*
a layer of ice crystals like white powder that forms at night when the weather is very cold.
frosty *adjective*.

froth *noun*
a mass of small bubbles on the surface of a liquid.
frothy *adjective*.

frown frowns frowning frowned *verb*
when you frown, you pull your eyebrows down and make your forehead wrinkle, often because you are cross or worried. *He was frowning because he wasn't allowed to go to the football match.*

froze frozen past of freeze.

fruit fruits *noun*
the part of a plant that contains seeds or a stone. You can eat many kinds of fruit.

fry fries frying fried *verb*
when you fry food, you cook it in hot fat. You fry food in a frying-pan.

fuel fuels *noun*
something such as coal, wood, gas or petrol that we burn to make heat or power. *Cars and aeroplanes cannot run without fuel.*

full fuller fullest *adjective*
if something is full, there is so much inside it that there is no room for any more. *The bus was full of people.*
■ The opposite is **empty**.

full stop full stops *noun*
a dot (.) that you use in writing. You must always put a full stop at the end of a sentence.

fumes *noun*
smelly or poisonous smoke or gases that come from something that is burning or from chemicals. *petrol fumes.*

fun *noun*
when you have fun, you enjoy yourself.

fund funds *noun*
an amount of money that is going to be used for a special purpose. *The school is raising funds to build a new gym.*

funeral funerals *noun*
a ceremony in which a dead body is buried or burned.

fungus funguses or fungi *noun*
a kind of plant that is not green and does not have leaves or flowers. Fungi grow in damp, dark places. Mushrooms and toadstools are kinds of fungi.

funnel funnels *noun*
1 a tube that is wide at one end and narrow at the other. A funnel is used for pouring liquid into a narrow container such as a bottle.
2 a chimney on a ship.

funny funnier funniest *adjective*
1 if something is funny, it makes you laugh or smile. *a funny story.*
2 funny also means strange. *There was a funny smell coming from the kitchen.*

fur *noun*
the soft, thick hair that covers the body of many animals such as cats and hamsters. ● A word that sounds like **fur** is **fir**.
furry *adjective.*

furious *adjective*
very angry. *She was furious when she lost her keys.*

furniture *noun*
large things such as chairs, tables, beds and desks that people have in their homes and other buildings.

fuse fuses *noun*
a small piece of wire in electrical equipment that melts if too much electricity flows through it. Fuses prevent things from getting damaged and prevent fires from starting.

fuss *noun*
if you make a fuss about something, you keep being worried about it and talking about it although it is not very important. *What a lot of fuss you are making about nothing.*
fuss *verb.*

future *noun*
the time that has not happened yet. Nobody can be sure what will happen in the future. ■ The opposite is **past**.

G g

gadget gadgets *noun*
a tool that you use to do a special job.

gain gains gaining gained *verb*
1 to gain means to get or win something. *By the end of the game, our team had gained 10 points.*
2 to gain also means to get more of something. *The bicycle gained speed as it went down the hill.*

galaxy galaxies *noun*
a very large group of stars and planets in space. *The Earth is part of one galaxy.*

gale gales *noun*
a very strong wind. *Gales can blow down trees and damage buildings.*

galleon galleons *noun*
a big sailing ship that was used a long time ago. *a large galleon carrying treasure.*

gallery galleries *noun*
a place where you can go to look at paintings, sculptures or photographs.

gallop gallops galloping galloped *verb*
when a horse gallops, it runs very fast.

gamble gambles gambling gambled *verb*
when somebody gambles on something such as a horse race, they pay to choose a horse that they think will win. If that horse wins the race, that person will get their money back and win more money.

game games *noun*
a game is something that you play for fun. Games often have rules.

gang gangs *noun*
a group of people who do things together. *There was a big fight between the two gangs.*

gaol gaols *noun*
a prison. ▲ Say ***jail***.

gap gaps *noun*
a space between two things. *We climbed through the gap in the fence.*

garage garages *noun*
1 a building where somebody can keep their car.
2 a place that sells petrol or where people mend cars.

garden gardens *noun*
a piece of land near a house, where people grow flowers and vegetables.

garlic *noun*
a plant similar to a small onion with a very strong taste and smell. Garlic is used in cooking.

gas gases *noun*
a gas is something like air that is not liquid or solid and that you cannot see. Air is made of several gases mixed together. We use another kind of gas for cooking and heating.

gasp gasps gasping gasped *verb*
when you gasp, you take in a short, quick breath of air through your mouth. People gasp when they are surprised or hurt. *He was gasping for air when they pulled him out of the river.*

gate gates *noun*
a gate is a kind of door in a wall or fence. *a garden gate.*

gather gathers gathering gathered *verb*
1 if you gather things, you collect them. *We gathered wood for the camp fire.*
2 if people gather, they come together in a group. *The children gathered around the ice-cream van.*

gaze gazes gazing gazed *verb*
if you gaze at something, you look at it for a long time. *He stood on the shore gazing out to sea.*

gear gears *noun*
1 a set of wheels that work together in a car, bicycle or model to make it go faster or slower.
2 the special clothes or things that you need for something. *camping gear.*

geese plural of goose.

gem gems *noun*
a precious stone or jewel.

gene genes *noun*
genes are the tiny parts of the cells of plants and animals that control what they look like. Genes are passed from parents to children. ▲ Say ***jeen***.

general *adjective*
something that is general is to do with most people or things. *The general feeling is that exercise is good for you.*
generally *adverb.*

generation generations *noun*
all the people who were born at about the same time. *This photo shows three different generations of my family: my grandparents, my parents, my brother and I.*

generous *adjective*
if you are generous, you are kind and always ready to give money and other things. *a generous act.*
generosity *noun.*

genius geniuses *noun*
an unusually clever and intelligent person. ▲ Say ***jee**-nee-us*.

gentle gentler gentlest *adjective*
a gentle person is kind and careful, not rough. *Be gentle with the baby.*

genuine *adjective*
real, not fake. *Is this a genuine dinosaur fossil?* ▲ Say ***jen**-yoo-in*.

geography *noun*
the study of the countries of the world, and of things such as its mountains, rivers and people.

gerbil gerbils *noun*
a small, furry animal with long back legs. Some people keep gerbils in cages as pets.

germ germs *noun*
a very small living thing that can make you ill. *flu germs.*

ghost ghosts *noun*
the figure of a dead person that some people say they have seen.

giant giants *noun*
a very big, strong person in stories.

gift gifts *noun*
1 a present. *birthday gifts.*
2 if you have a gift for something, you are very good at it. *Harry has a gift for music.*

gigantic *adjective*
very, very big. *a gigantic mountain.*
▲ Say *jye-**gan**-tik*.

giggle giggles giggling giggled *verb*
if you giggle, you laugh in a silly way. *We couldn't stop giggling at our teacher's funny hat.*

gill gills *noun*
gills are the parts of a fish that it breathes through. A fish has a pair of gills, one on each side of its head.
❖ ***Look at page 65***

ginger *noun*
1 a plant with a strong, hot taste. You can use the root, or powder made from the root in cooking. *root ginger.*
2 an orange colour. *a ginger-haired boy.*

giraffe giraffes *noun*
a tall African animal with a very long neck. Giraffes feed on leaves and twigs from trees.

girl girls *noun*
a female child or a young woman.

a b c d e f g h i j k l m n o p q r s t u v w x y z

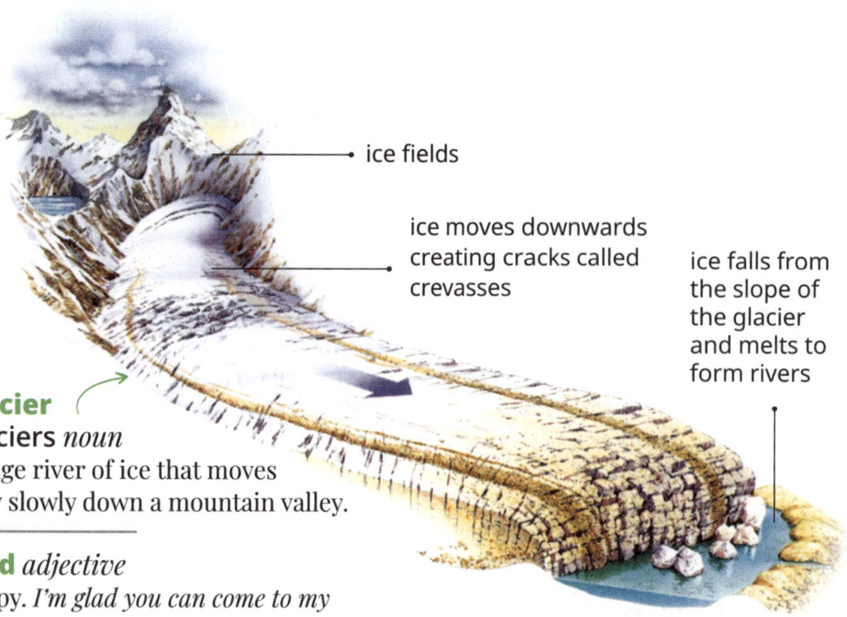

glacier glaciers *noun*
a huge river of ice that moves very slowly down a mountain valley.

glad *adjective*
happy. *I'm glad you can come to my birthday party.*

glance glances glancing glanced *verb*
if you glance at something, you look at it quickly. *She glanced at her watch.*

gland glands *noun*
one of the parts of your body that make the chemicals that your body needs. *Sweat glands produce sweat to help your body cool down when you are hot.*

glare glares glaring glared *verb*
If you glare at somebody, you look at them in an angry way.

glass glasses *noun*
1 glass is a hard material that you can see through and that breaks easily. Windows and bottles are made of glass. *A greenhouse is made of glass.*
2 a glass is a container that you drink from, made of glass.

glasses *noun*
glasses are two pieces of special glass, called lenses, in a frame. Some people wear glasses to help them see better. *She wears glasses to help her see more clearly.*

gleam gleams gleaming gleamed *verb*
to gleam means to shine with a soft light. *The lake gleamed in the moonlight.*

glide glides gliding glided *verb*
if something glides, it moves smoothly along. *The dancers glided gracefully around the floor.*

glider gliders *noun*
a very light aircraft that does not have an engine. Gliders fly by floating on currents of air.

glimpse glimpses glimpsing glimpsed *verb*
if you glimpse somebody or something, you only see them for a very short time. *We just glimpsed the rabbit as it ran into the wood.*

glitter glitters glittering glittered *verb*
if something glitters, it shines brightly with lots of flashes of light. *My ring glitters in the sunlight.*
glitter *noun*.

globe globes *noun*
a ball with a map of the world on it.

gloomy gloomier gloomiest *adjective*
1 if a room or a day is gloomy, it is dark and dull.
2 if you are gloomy, you feel sad.

glossy glossier glossiest *adjective*
shiny. *a dog with a glossy coat.*

glove gloves *noun*
a piece of clothing that you wear on your hand. *woollen gloves.*

glow glows glowing glowed *verb*
if something glows, it shines with a steady light. *The fire glowed in the dark.*

glue *noun*
a thick liquid that you use for sticking things together. *Sini and Sajni used glue to mend the broken pottery.*
glue *verb*.

gnat gnats *noun*
a small, flying insect that bites people. ▲ Say ***nat***.

gnaw gnaws gnawing gnawed *verb*
if you gnaw something hard, you keep biting it for a long time. *The dog was gnawing at a bone.*
▲ Say ***nor***.

gnome gnomes *noun*
a little old man in fairy stories who lives underground. Gnomes usually have long beards and pointed hats.
▲ Say ***nome***.

goal goals *noun*
1 a goal is the place where you have to make the ball go to score a point in games such as football or hockey.
2 a goal is also the point that you score when the ball goes into the goal.
3 a goal can also be something important that you want to do in your life. *My goal is to run the marathon in the Olympic Games.*

goat goats *noun*

an animal with horns and short, rough hair. A male goat is called a billy-goat, a female is a nanny-goat and a young goat is a kid. Goats are kept on farms for their milk.

gobble gobbles gobbling gobbled *verb*
if you gobble food, you eat it very quickly and greedily. *She gobbled up all the biscuits and cakes before anyone else could eat them.*

god gods *noun*
a being that people believe controls them and nature. Some people pray to many different gods. *Brahma, Vishnu and Shiva are the three main gods of the Hindu religion.*

goggles *noun*
special glasses that you wear to protect your eyes from water or dust. *He wears goggles when he's making models.*

go-kart go-karts *noun*
a small, low, open racing car. *go-kart racing.*

gold *noun*
a shiny, yellow metal that is used to make rings and other jewellery.

goldfish goldfish or goldfishes *noun*

a small, orange fish you keep as a pet.

golf *noun*
a game that you play by using long sticks called golf clubs to hit a ball into holes around a golf course.

gong gongs *noun*
a round piece of metal that you hit to make a loud noise.

good better best *adjective*
1 if something is good, people like it. *a good story.*
2 if you are good, you do as you are told.
3 if you are good at something, you can do it well. *Yasmin is good at spelling.*
4 if something is good for you, it makes you healthy. *Fruit is good for you.*

good

Some words you can use instead of good:

We need a good plumber to mend the broken pipes.
skilled, expert

He's a good pianist.
talented

The weather is good today.
marvellous

goods *noun*
things that can be bought and sold.

goose geese *noun*
a large bird with a long neck and webbed feet that lives near water. Some geese are wild but others are kept on farms for their eggs, meat and feathers. A male goose is called a gander, and a young goose is a gosling.

gorge gorges *noun*
a deep, narrow valley. *The river runs through the gorge.*

gorgeous *adjective*
very beautiful. *a gorgeous day.*
◆ *a gorgeous view of the sea.*
▲ Say ***gor**-juss.*

gorilla gorillas *noun*
a very big African ape with dark fur.

gorse *noun*
a prickly bush with yellow flowers.

government governments *noun*
a group of people who are in charge of a country. *In Britain, the prime minister is the head of the government.*
▲ Say ***guv**-er-ment.*

gown gowns *noun*
1 a long dress that women wear at special times. *a ball gown.*
2 a long, loose piece of clothing that judges and some lawyers wear.

grab grabs grabbing grabbed *verb*
if you grab something, you take it quickly and roughly. *The robber grabbed the money and ran away.*

graceful *adjective*
if somebody or something is graceful, they move in a beautiful way.

grade grades *noun*
a mark that a teacher gives you to show how good your work is. *I got grade A for my story and B for art.*

gradual *adjective*
if something is gradual, it happens slowly and steadily. *I'm making gradual progress at swimming.*
gradually *adverb.*

graffiti *noun*
writing and drawing on walls in public places. ▲ Say *gra-**fee**-tee.*

a b c d e f g h i j k l m n o p q r s t u v w x y z

A B C D E F G H I J K L M N O P Q R S T U V W X Y Z

grain grains *noun*
1 grain is the seeds of plants such as wheat and rice that we eat.
2 grains are tiny, hard bits of something such as salt, sugar or sand.

grand grander grandest *adjective*
big and important. *a grand country house.* ◆ *a grand party.*

grandchild grandchildren *noun*
a grandchild is the child of a person's son or daughter.

grandparent grandparents *noun*
your grandparents are the mother and father of your mother or father.

grape grapes *noun*
a small fruit, varying from green to black, that grows in bunches on a vine. Wine is made from grapes. Raisins are dried grapes.

grapefruit grapefruit *noun*
a large, round yellow fruit that is similar to an orange but not as sweet.

graph graphs *noun*
a diagram that shows how numbers and amounts compare with each other. *We drew a graph to show how much rain there was in each month of the year.*

grasp grasps grasping grasped *verb*
if you grasp something, you hold it tightly. *She grasped the child's hand as they crossed the road.*

grass grasses *noun*
the thin, green leaves that cover fields and lawns. *Sheep and cows eat grass.*
grassy *adjective.*

grasshopper grasshoppers *noun*
a jumping insect with strong back legs and two pairs of wings. Grasshoppers feed on plants.

grate grates grating grated *verb*
if you grate food, you rub it over a metal tool called a grater to shred it into very small pieces. *grated cheese.*
● A word that sounds like **grate** is **great**.

grateful *adjective*
if you feel grateful to somebody, you want to thank them because they have done something for you. *I was very grateful to her for finding my purse.* ■ The opposite is **ungrateful**.
gratefully *adverb.*

grave graves *noun*
a hole in the ground where a dead person is buried.

grave graver gravest *adjective*
very serious and important. *a grave mistake.* ◆ *a grave illness.*

gravel *noun*
small stones that are used to cover paths and roads.

gravity *noun*
the natural force that pulls everything down towards the Earth.

gravy *noun*
a sauce made from the juices that come out of meat when you cook it.

graze grazes grazing grazed *verb*
1 when animals graze, they move around eating grass. *The sheep were grazing in the field.*
2 if you graze your skin, you cut it slightly by scraping it against something. *When she fell over she grazed her knee quite badly.*

grease *noun*
thick oil or soft fat. *You will need very hot water to wash the grease off those dirty plates.*
greasy *adjective.*

great greater greatest *adjective*
1 very good. *a great film.*
2 very important. *a great king.*
3 very big. *a great crowd of people.*
● A word that sounds like **great** is **grate**.

greedy greedier greediest *adjective*
a person who is greedy wants more of something than they really need. *Don't be so greedy – leave some cake for your brother and sister.*

greenhouse greenhouses *noun*
a building made of glass, used for growing plants.

greet greets greeting greeted *verb*
when you greet somebody, you do something friendly when you meet them, such as saying "hello" or kissing. *They greeted each other by shaking hands.*

greeting greetings *noun*
words such as "hello", "good morning" or "Happy New Year" that you say when you meet somebody.

grew past of grow.

grief *noun*
great sadness. *She was filled with grief when her cat died.*

grill grills grilling grilled *verb*
if you grill food, you cook it on metal bars under or over strong heat. *the smell of grilled sausages.*
grill *noun.*

grin grins grinning grinned *verb*
if you grin, you have a big smile. *She grinned at me when I said hello.*
grin *noun*.

grind grinds grinding ground *verb*
if you grind something, you crush it into tiny pieces or into a powder. *grinding coffee beans*.

grip grips gripping gripped *verb*
if you grip something, you hold it very firmly. *She gripped the branch and swung from it*.

groan groans groaning groaned *verb*
if you groan, you make a long, deep sound because you are unhappy or in pain. *"My leg hurts," he groaned.*

groom grooms *noun*
1 a person who looks after horses.
2 a man on his wedding day.

groom grooms grooming groomed *verb*
if you groom an animal, you clean and brush it. *The children are grooming their horse before riding it*.

groove grooves *noun*
a long, thin line that is cut into a flat surface.

grope gropes groping groped *verb*
if you grope for something, you try to find it by feeling with your hands when you cannot see. *It was dark so she had to grope about for the door handle*.

ground grounds *noun*
1 the ground is what you walk on when you are outside. *We sat on the ground to eat our picnic*.
2 a piece of land that is used for something special. *a playground*.

ground past of grind.

group groups *noun*
1 a number of people or things that are together in one place. *A group of children stood near the ice-cream van*.
2 a group of musicians who play or sing together.

grow grows growing grew grown *verb*
1 when something grows, it gets bigger. *The puppies are growing very fast*.
2 if you grow something, you plant it so that it will develop. *Flora grew this plant from seed*.
3 to grow also means to become. *We are all growing older*.

growl growls growling growled *verb*
to growl is to make the low, rough noise that a dog or a bear makes when it is angry or frightened.
growl *noun*.

grown-up grown-ups *noun*
an adult. *Parents are grown-ups*.

growth *noun*
growing. *We measured the tree every month to check its growth*.

grumble grumbles grumbling grumbled *verb*
if you grumble, you complain about something in a cross way. *My sister often grumbles about having to do her homework*.

grunt grunts grunting grunted *verb*
to grunt is to make the short, deep, rough sound that a pig makes.

guarantee guarantees *noun*
1 a promise made by the makers of something, that they will mend or replace it if it goes wrong.
2 a promise that something will happen. *I want a guarantee that you will all behave yourselves*.
▲ Say *ga-ran-**tee***.
guarantee *verb*.

guard guards *noun*
a person who keeps somebody or something safe, or who stops people from escaping. *a Swiss guard*.

guard guards guarding guarded *verb*
if you guard somebody or something, you keep them safe, or stop them from escaping. *The house was guarded by two fierce dogs*.

guess guesses guessing guessed *verb*
when you guess, you try to give an answer to something when you do not really know if it is right. *Can you guess what's in the box?*
guess *noun*.
Have a guess at how much the birthday cake weighs.

guest guests *noun*
a person who is staying in your home because you have invited them. *We have guests staying with us this weekend*. ▲ Rhymes with ***best***.

guide guides guiding guided *verb*
if you guide somebody, you show them where to go or what to do. *Her job is to guide people around the city*.
▲ Rhymes with ***wide***.
guide *noun*.

guilty *adjective*
1 if you are guilty, you have done something wrong. ■ The opposite is **innocent**.
2 if you feel guilty, you feel sorry because you have done something wrong. *She felt guilty for being rude to her aunt*.

guinea pig guinea pigs *noun*
a small, furry animal with short ears and no tail. Some people keep guinea pigs as pets.

guitar guitars *noun*
a musical instrument with six strings that you play with your fingers.

gull gulls *noun*
a large, grey or white sea bird.

gulp gulps gulping gulped *verb*
if you gulp, you swallow something very quickly. *Katie gulped down the orange juice because she was thirsty.*

gum gums *noun*
1 your gums are the firm, pink flesh around your teeth.
2 a kind of glue.

gun guns *noun*
a weapon that shoots bullets. *He aimed the gun and fired two shots.*

gunpowder *noun*
powder that explodes. Gunpowder is used in guns and fireworks.

gutter gutters *noun*
an open pipe along the edge of a roof or a narrow ditch at the side of a road for carrying away rainwater.

gym gyms *noun*
a large room where you can do exercises, often using special equipment. Gym is short for **gymnasium** *noun*.

gymnast gymnasts *noun*
a person who does difficult and carefully controlled movements with their body in competitions. *an Olympic gymnast.*

gymnastics *noun*
1 exercises for your body.
2 a sport in which people do difficult and carefully controlled movements with their body in competitions.

H h

habit habits *noun*
something that you do often, usually without thinking about it. *Biting your nails is a bad habit.*

habitat habitats *noun*
the habitat of an animal or a plant is the kind of place where it lives. *This monkey's natural habitat is the jungle.*

hail *noun*
frozen rain falling as little balls of ice, called hailstones.

hair hairs *noun*
your hair is made up of lots of thin thread-like structures which grow on your head. Hair can also grow on other parts of your body. ● A word that sounds like **hair** is **hare**.

hairdresser hairdressers *noun*
a person whose job is to cut and arrange people's hair.

hairy hairier hairiest *adjective*
covered with hair. *The book is about a big, hairy monster.*

half halves *noun*
one of two equal parts of something. You can write half as ½. *Half of ten is five.* ◆ *Two halves make a whole.*

hall halls *noun*
1 the part just inside the door of a house or flat with doors leading to other rooms.
2 a large room or a building where events such as concerts and meetings take place. *a school hall.*

halt halts halting halted *verb*
when something halts, it stops. *The lorry halted at the traffic lights.*

halve halves halving halved *verb*
if you halve something, you divide it into two equal parts. *Halve the fruit and remove the stone.*

ham *noun*
meat from a pig's leg which has been treated with salt so it can be kept for a long time. *a ham and cheese sandwich.*

hamburger hamburgers *noun*
chopped beef pressed into a flat, round shape and eaten in a bread roll.

hammer hammers *noun*
a tool with a heavy part at one end that you use for hitting nails into things.

hammock hammocks *noun*
a bed made of strong cloth or pieces of rope which is hung at each end from something such as a tree or post.

hamster hamsters *noun*
a small animal that is often kept as a pet. It is similar to a large mouse with a very short tail. Hamsters can store food in pouches inside their cheeks.

hand hands *noun*
your hand is the part of your body at the end of your arm.

hand hands handing handed *verb*
if you hand something to somebody, you give it to them. *Hand me that book.*

handicap *noun*
something that makes it more difficult to do things. *Being tall can be a handicap in small cars.*

handkerchief handkerchiefs *noun*
a small square of cloth or paper tissue that you use for blowing your nose. ▲ *Say* ***hang**-ker-cheef.*

handle handles *noun*
1 the handle of something such as a cup or a bag is the part that you take in your hand to carry it or pick it up.
2 the handle of a door is the lever or knob that you move with your hand to open and close it.

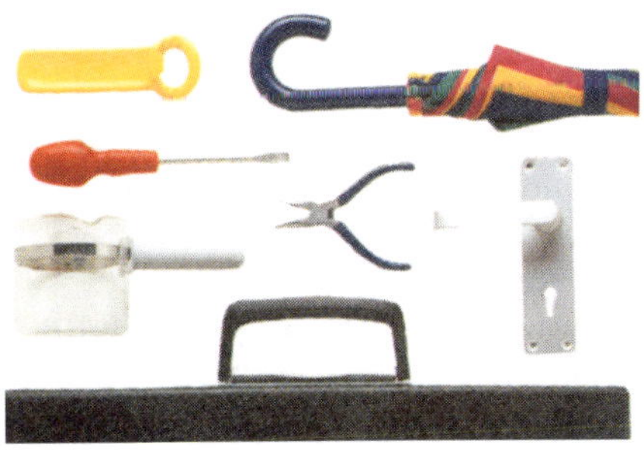

handlebar handlebars *noun*
the curved bar at the front of a bicycle or a motorbike that you use for steering.

handsome *adjective*
a man who is handsome has an attractive face.

handwriting *noun*
your handwriting is the way you write with a pen or pencil.

hang hangs hanging hung *verb*
if you hang something somewhere, you fix it from the top to something above it. *Hang your coat up in the wardrobe.*

hang-glider hang-gliders *noun*
a kind of large kite with a harness underneath which you fly through the air in the sport of hang-gliding.

happen happens happening happened *verb*
1 something that happens, occurs or takes place. *The accident happened because she was not paying attention.*
2 if you happen to do something, you do it by chance. *I happened to find your ball when I was in the garden.*

happy happier happiest *adjective*
if you are happy, you feel good because something nice has happened or because you are enjoying yourself. ■ The opposite is **unhappy** or **sad**.
happily *adverb*, **happiness** *noun*.

happy

Some words that you can use instead of happy:

I'm happy I've finished my homework.
contented, pleased, glad

They are happy with their wedding presents.
delighted, pleased, thrilled

Christmas is a happy time of year.
merry, cheerful

harbour harbours *noun*
an area of sea by the coast where ships can shelter.

hard harder hardest *adjective*
1 if something is hard, you cannot break, cut or bend it easily. *Stones, nuts and bolts are hard.* ■ The opposite is **soft**.
2 something that is hard to do is difficult. *a hard puzzle.* ■ The opposite is **easy**.

hard harder hardest *adverb*
hard means a lot. *Sarita works hard.*

hard disk hard disks *noun*
the part inside a computer where a large amount of information is stored.

harden hardens hardening hardened *verb*
when something hardens, it becomes hard. *Hold the pieces together until the glue has hardened.* ■ The opposite is **soften**.

hare hares *noun*
an animal that looks like a large rabbit with long ears and long legs. ● A word that sounds like **hare** is **hair**.

harm harms harming harmed *verb*
1 if you harm somebody, you hurt them. *The dog won't harm you.*
2 if you harm something, you damage it.

harmful *adjective*
if something is harmful, it could hurt you or make you ill. *Looking straight at the sun is harmful to your eyes.* ■ The opposite is **harmless**.

harmless *adjective*
if something is harmless, it will not hurt you. *Our dog is harmless – she wouldn't bite anybody.* ■ The opposite is **harmful**.

harmony harmonies *noun*
a group of musical notes that sound nice when you hear them together.

harness harnesses *noun*
1 a set of straps and metal parts that go around a horse's head or body so that you can control it.

a b c d e f g h i j k l m n o p q r s t u v w x y z

2 a set of straps for fastening something such as a parachute to a person's body.

harp harps *noun*
a musical instrument. It has a large frame with strings which you play (pluck) with your fingers.
harpist *noun*.

harsh harsher harshest *adjective*
1 if somebody behaves in a harsh way, they are cruel or unkind. *That was a very harsh punishment.*
2 a harsh winter is very cold and difficult.
3 harsh sounds are loud and unpleasant. *a harsh voice.*

harvest harvests *noun*
the time when farmers pick or cut their crops because they are ripe.

hat hats *noun*
a covering that you wear on your head.

hatch hatches hatching hatched *verb*
when a baby bird or other animal hatches, it breaks out of its egg.

hatchet hatchets *noun*
a small axe.

hate hates hating hated *verb*
if you hate somebody or something, you have a very strong feeling of not liking them. *I hate getting up early in the morning.* ■ The opposite is **love**.

haunted *adjective*
if a place is haunted, there is supposed to be a ghost there. *a haunted house.*
▲ Say ***horn**-ted*.

hawk hawks *noun*
a large bird with a curved beak and strong claws that eats other birds and small animals.

hay *noun*
grass that has been cut and dried and is used to feed horses and cattle in the winter months.

hazard hazards *noun*
a danger or risk. *Patches of oil on the sea from leaking tankers are a hazard to sea birds and fish.*
hazardous *adjective*.

head heads *noun*
1 your head is the top part of you, where your hair and face are.
2 the person who is in charge of a group. *the head of a large company.*

headache headaches *noun*
a pain in your head.

headlight headlights *noun*
headlights are the bright lights on the front of a car or other vehicle.

headline headlines *noun*
words in larger print at the top of a story in a newspaper.

headphones *noun*
small speakers that fit on your ears and that are joined together by a band over the top of your head. Headphones let you hear music and other sounds without other people hearing them.

headquarters *noun*
the building where the people in charge of in an organization work. *The company's headquarters are in Paris.*

headteacher headteachers *noun*
the teacher who is in charge of a school.

heal heals healing healed *verb*
if something heals, it gets better after being ill or injured. *I hurt my ankle two weeks ago but it's healed now.* ● A word that sounds like **heal** is **heel**.

health *noun*
your health is how well you are. If your health is bad, you are ill. If your health is good, you are well. ▲ Say ***helth***.

healthy healthier healthiest *adjective*
1 if you are healthy, you are well and fit.
2 something that is healthy is good for you and helps you to stay well. *Fresh fruit and vegetables are healthy foods.*
▲ Say ***helth**-ee*. ■ The opposite is **unhealthy**.

heap heaps *noun*
a large, untidy pile of things. *She left her clothes in a heap on the floor.*

hear hears hearing heard *verb*
when you hear a sound, you notice it through your ears. ● A word that sounds like **hear** is **here**.

heart hearts *noun*
your heart is the part of you, inside your chest, that pumps the blood around your body. ▲ Say ***hart***.

heat *noun*
warmth. *I can feel the heat from the sun on my skin.*

heat heats heating heated *verb*
if you heat something, you make it hot. *He heated some water to make coffee.*

heave heaves heaving heaved *verb*
if you heave something somewhere, you use a lot of energy to lift, push or pull it. *Ben and Joe heaved the rope together.*

heavy heavier heaviest *adjective*
something that is heavy weighs a lot. *The suitcase was too heavy for me to lift.* ■ The opposite is **light**.

hedge hedges *noun*
a line of bushes or small trees growing close together at the edge of a garden, road or field.

hedgehog hedgehogs *noun*
a small, brown animal with sharp spikes, called spines, all over its back. Hedgehogs come out to feed on insects at night and curl up into a ball to protect themselves when they are in danger. ❖ ***Look at page 155***

heel heels *noun*
1 your heel is the back part of your foot.
2 the part of a shoe or boot that is under the back part of your foot.
● A word that sounds like **heel** is **heal**.

height heights *noun*
the height of something is how high it is from the bottom to the top. *The height of the tree is six metres.*
▲ Rhymes with ***kite***.

held past of hold.

helicopter helicopters *noun*
an aircraft without wings that is kept in the air by long blades attached to its roof, which turn round very fast.

helmet helmets *noun*
a hard hat that protects your head.

help helps helping helped *verb*
if you help somebody, you make it easier for them to do something. *Sam helped me with my maths homework.*
help *noun*.

helpful *adjective*
1 if you are helpful, you do what you can to help other people.
2 something that is helpful is useful. *Thank you for your helpful advice.*

helpless *adjective*
if you are helpless, you cannot look after yourself. *A baby is completely helpless when it is born.*

hem hems *noun*
the edge of a piece of material that is folded over and sewn to make it neat.

hen hens *noun*
1 a female chicken that lays eggs that we eat.
2 any female bird.

herb herbs *noun*
a plant that we use to give flavour to food or to make medicines. *Marjoram, rosemary and mint are all herbs.*

herd herds *noun*
a large group of animals of one kind that live together. *Elephants live in herds.*

hero heroes *noun*
1 a person who is very brave or very good.
2 the main male character in a book, play or film.

heroine heroines *noun*
1 a woman who is very brave or very good.
2 the main female character in a book, play or film.
▲ Say ***herr-oh-in***.

heron herons *noun*
a large, grey bird with long legs and a long neck. Herons live near water and eat fish.

hesitate hesitates hesitating hesitated *verb*
if you hesitate, you stop for a short time before you do something, often because you are not sure what to do. *She hesitated before answering me.*
hesitation noun.

hexagon hexagons *noun*
a flat shape with six sides. ❖ ***Look at page 146***
hexagonal *adjective*.

hibernate hibernates hibernating hibernated *verb*
when an animal hibernates, it stays in a deep sleep all through the winter. *Bears, dormice and hedgehogs hibernate.*
hibernation *noun*.

hiccup hiccups *noun*
a sudden, short breath in and a noise that sounds like "hic", that you cannot help making. You sometimes get hiccups when you eat or drink too quickly.
hiccup *verb*.

hide hides hiding hid hidden *verb*
1 if you hide, you go where nobody can find you. *You hide, and I'll come and look for you.*
2 if you hide something, you put it where nobody can find it. *She hid the present under the bed.*

hieroglyphics *noun*
a kind of writing that uses pictures instead of letters and words. Hieroglyphics were used in ancient Egypt. ▲ Say ***hye-row-glif-iks***.

high higher highest *adjective*
1 something that is high goes up a long way from the bottom to the top. *a high wall.*
2 high also means a long way above the ground. *We were high up in the mountains.* ■ The opposite is **low**.

hijack hijacks hijacking hijacked *verb*
if somebody hijacks a plane or ship, they take control of it by threatening the passengers and crew and then try to make it go where they want it to.
hijacker *noun*.

a b c d e f g h i j k l m n o p q r s t u v w x y z

hill hills *noun*
an area of land that is higher than the land around it.
hilly *adjective*.

hind *adjective*
an animal's hind legs are its back legs.

Hindu Hindus *noun*
a person who follows a religion called Hinduism. Hindus worship several different gods and believe that after you die you are born again.
Hinduism *noun*.

hinge hinges *noun*
a piece of metal that fixes a door to its frame at one side, so that it can open and close.

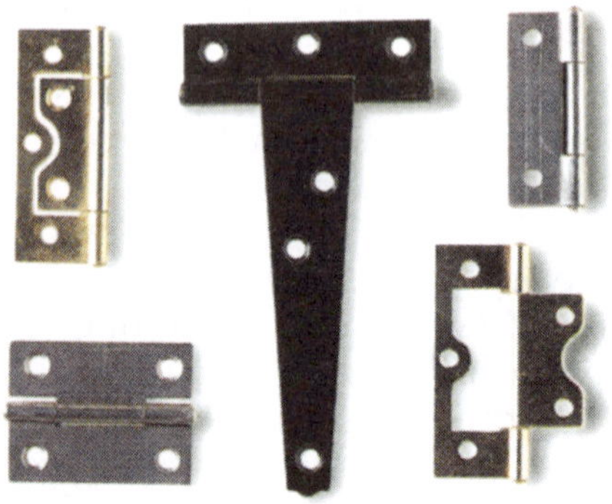

hint hints hinting hinted *verb*
when you hint, you let somebody know something without actually saying it. *Ben hinted that he wanted a new bike.*
hint *noun*.

hip hips *noun*
your hips are at the side of your body between your waist and the top of your legs.

hippopotamus hippopotamuses *noun*
a large animal with a thick skin and very short legs. Hippopotamuses live by lakes and rivers in Africa. A hippopotamus is sometimes called a **hippo** for short.

hire hires hiring hired *verb*
if you hire something, you pay to have it for a certain time. *We'll hire a boat for the afternoon and go out on the lake.*

hiss hisses hissing hissed *verb*
if something hisses, it makes a sound that is like saying a very long "s". *Snakes hiss when they are angry.*

history *noun*
the study of things that happened in the past. *At school we are learning about the history of our town.*
historical *adjective*.

hit hits hitting hit *verb*
when you hit something, you touch it quickly and with force. *I hit the ball with the bat.*

hive hives *noun*
a special box for bees to live in and where you can collect their honey.

hoarse hoarser hoarsest *adjective*
if you are hoarse, your voice sounds rough. *He yelled at the top of his voice all through the match until he was hoarse.* ● A word that sounds like **hoarse** is **horse**.

hobble hobbles hobbling hobbled *verb*
if you hobble, you walk with difficulty because your feet hurt. *He was hobbling along slowly because his feet were covered in blisters.*

hobby hobbies *noun*
something that you enjoy doing in your spare time. *My hobbies are swimming, reading and collecting shells.*

hockey *noun*
a game played outdoors by two teams of eleven players who try to get a hard ball into a goal by hitting it with a long, curved stick.

hold holds holding held *verb*
1 if you hold something, you have it in your hand or hands. *Can you please hold the baby?*
2 if a container holds a certain amount, it can have that amount in it but no more. *The bottle holds a litre of water.*

hole holes *noun*
a gap or space in something. *These jeans have a hole in the knee.* ● A word that sounds like **hole** is **whole**.

holiday holidays *noun*
a time when you do not have to go to school or work. *How long are the summer holidays?* ◆ *Heather is going to Mexico for her holiday.*

hollow *adjective*
something that is hollow has an empty space inside it. *Chocolate eggs are hollow.* ■ The opposite is **solid**.

holly *noun*
an evergreen tree that has red berries and leaves with sharp points.

hologram holograms *noun*
a three-dimensional image made by laser beams.

holy holier holiest *adjective*
something that is holy is very special because it is to do with religion. *Monks and nuns are holy people.*

home homes *noun*
your home is the place where you live. *When does Max get home from school?*

homework *noun*
work for school done at home.

honest *adjective*
if you are honest, you tell the truth and people can trust you. ▲ Say ***on-est***. ■ The opposite is **dishonest**.
honesty *noun*.

honey *noun*
a sweet, sticky food that is made by bees. ▲ Rhymes with ***funny***.

honeymoon honeymoons *noun*
a holiday that a couple takes when they have just got married.

hood hoods *noun*
a part of a coat or jacket that you can pull over your head.

hoof hooves or hoofs *noun*
the hard covering on the foot of some animals such as a horse or deer.

hook hooks *noun*
a curved piece of metal or plastic that is used for hanging things on or for holding or fastening things. *There is a hook on the back of the door for hanging your coat on.* ◆ *A fish-hook is tied to the end of a fishing-line for catching fish.*

hoop hoops *noun*
a large ring made of wood, metal or plastic.

hoot hoots hooting hooted *verb*
1 to hoot is to make the long "oo" sound that an owl makes.
2 when drivers hoot, they make a loud noise with a car horn. *The driver hooted impatiently at the car in front.*

hop hops hopping hopped *verb*
1 if you hop, you jump on one leg.
2 when an animal or insect hops, it moves along by jumping. *The frog hopped away.*

hope hopes hoping hoped *verb*
if you hope something will happen, you want it to happen and you think it probably will. *I hope you will be able to come to my party.*
hope *noun*, **hopeless** *adjective.*
He's hopeless at diving.

hopeful *adjective*
if you are hopeful, you think that what you want will probably happen. *The police are hopeful that they will soon be able to solve the crime.*

horizon horizons *noun*
the line in the far distance where the land or the sea seems to meet the sky.
▲ Say *hor-**eye**-zon.*

horizontal *adjective*
something that is horizontal goes from side to side, parallel to the ground, not up and down. *The top of the table is horizontal to the floor.*
■ The opposite is **vertical**.
horizontally *adverb.*
The smoke spread out horizontally over the town.

horn horns *noun*
1 horns are the hard, pointed, bony parts that grow out of the head of some animals such as cows and goats.
2 a horn is a brass musical instrument that you blow into to make sounds.
3 a horn is also an instrument in a car or other vehicle that the driver uses to make a loud noise as a warning.

horrible *adjective*
terrible, or very unpleasant. *What a horrible thing to say!*
horribly *adverb.*

horror *noun*
1 a feeling that you get when you are very shocked and upset at something terrible. *We were filled with horror at the news of the famine in Africa.*
2 a horror story is a story that is meant to frighten you.

horse horses *noun*
a large animal with a long tail and a mane. People ride horses or use them to pull carts or carriages. A female horse is called a mare, a male horse is a stallion and a young horse is a foal. ● A word that sounds like **horse** is **hoarse**.

horse chestnut *noun*
a large tree that produces a large nut called a conker.

hose hoses *noun*
a long, plastic pipe that is used for spraying water. *You can use a hose to water the garden or clean a car.*

hospital hospitals *noun*
a building where people who are ill or injured are looked after by doctors and nurses.

host hosts *noun*
a person who invites guests and looks after them when they come.

hostage hostages *noun*
a person who is held prisoner by somebody who threatens to hurt or kill the prisoner if they do not get what they want.

hot hotter hottest *adjective*
1 something that is hot has a high temperature. *Careful! Those chips are hot!* ■ The opposite is **cold**.
2 hot foods have a strong taste and make your mouth feel as if it is burning when you eat them. *Chillies are hot.*

hotel hotels *noun*
a building with bedrooms where people pay to stay for a few nights.

hour hours *noun*
a period of 60 minutes. There are 24 hours in a day. ▲ Rhymes with ***tower***. ● A word that sounds like **hour** is **our**.

HORSES

Vocabulary

aids
the signals a rider gives to tell the horse what to do.

bit
the metal or rubber device attached to the bridle and placed in the horse's mouth.

bridle
the part of saddle that is placed over a horse's head and to which the bit and reins are attached.

colt
a male foal.

filly
a female foal.

gait
the pace of a horse: walk, trot, canter, gallop.

house houses *noun*
a building where people live.

hover hovers hovering hovered *verb*
if something hovers, it stays in one place in the air. *A rescue helicopter hovered over the boat.*

hovercraft hovercrafts *noun*
a vehicle that can move over land and water. A hovercraft floats on a cushion of air as it travels along.

howl howls howling howled *verb*
when an animal howls, it makes a long, loud crying sound. *Wolves were howling in the distance.*

hug hugs hugging hugged *verb*
when you hug somebody, you put your arms around them and hold them tight.
hug *noun.*

huge *adjective*
very, very big. ■ The opposite is **tiny**.

hum hums humming hummed *verb*
when you hum, you make a singing sound with your lips closed. *He was humming a tune while he worked.*

human humans *noun*
a person. *A lot of animals are afraid of humans.* ❖ ***Look at page 83***

humid *adjective*
humid weather is hot, sticky and damp. ▲ Say ***hyoo-mid.***

humour *noun*
the ability to make people laugh or to see when something is funny. *She has a good sense of humour.* ▲ Say ***hyoo-mer.***
humorous adjective.

hump humps *noun*
1 a large, round lump, on a camel's back, for example.
2 a bump in the road.

hung past of hang.

hungry hungrier hungriest *adjective*
if you are hungry, you want to eat.
hunger *noun.*

hunt hunts hunting hunted *verb*
1 to hunt is to chase and catch wild animals to kill them, either to eat or as a sport.
2 if you hunt for something, you look everywhere for it. *I've been hunting for my watch all morning.*
hunt *noun.*

hurl hurls hurling hurled *verb*
if you hurl something, you throw it as far and as hard as you can. *She hurled the stone at the wall.*

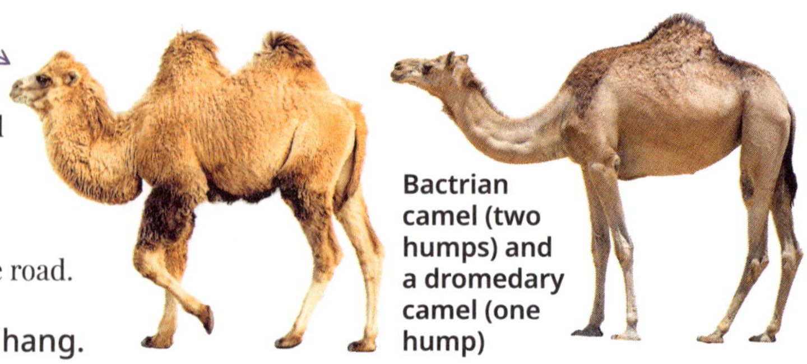

Bactrian camel (two humps) and a dromedary camel (one hump)

Human Body

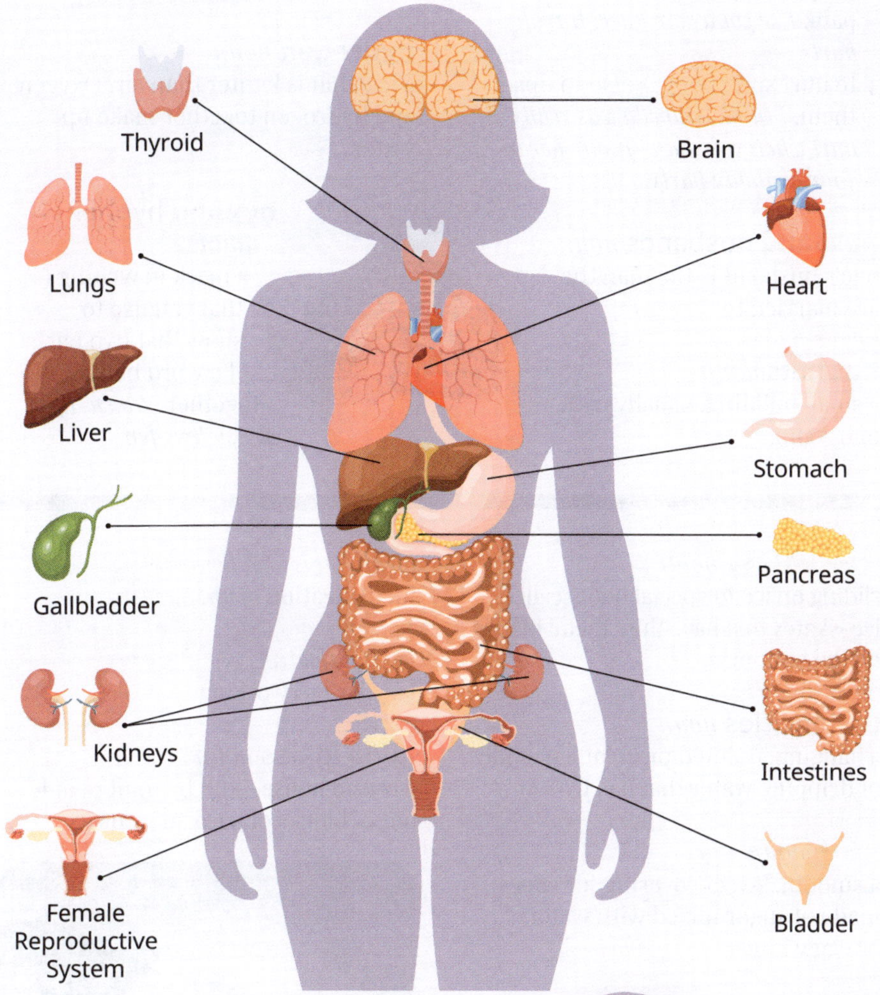

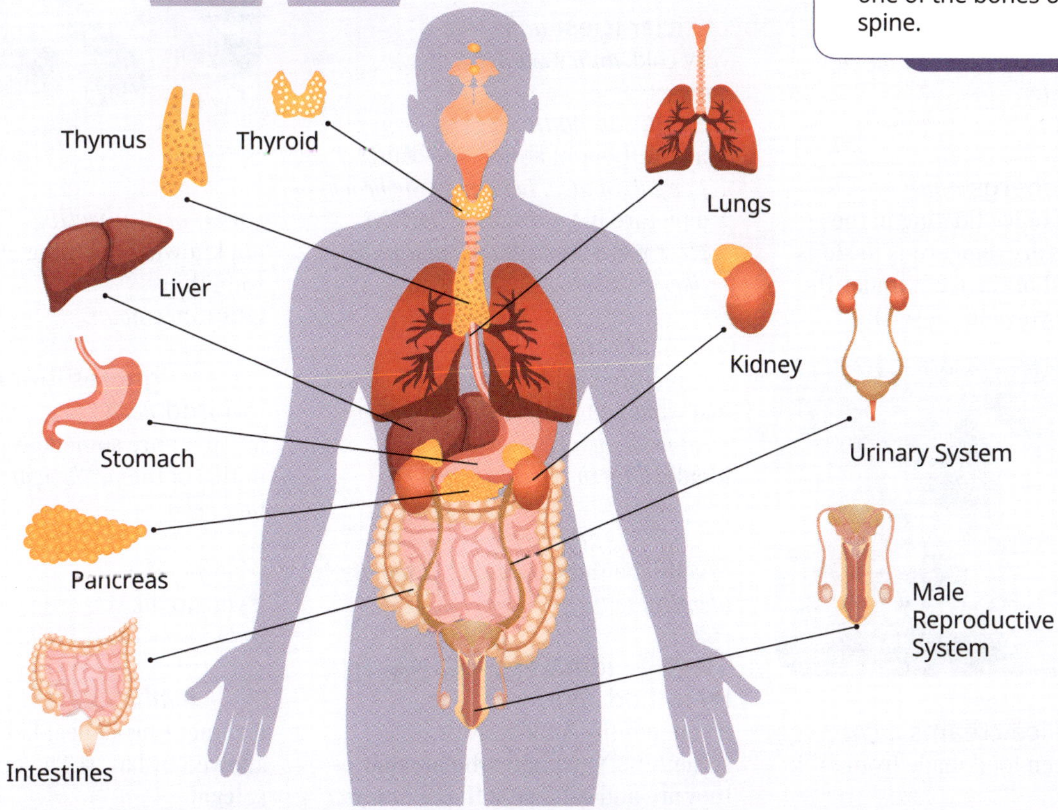

Vocabulary

cornea
the clear, bowl-shaped tissue over the coloured part of the eye through which light enters.

iris
the coloured part of the eye is a thin tissue in front of the lens.

pupil
the black hole in the iris controls the amount of light entering the eye.

retina
tissue at the back of the eye that, like film, is sensitive to light and receives images of things seen.

sclera
the tough white tissue that is the eye's framework. At the front of the eye it becomes the clear cornea.

shin
the front part of the leg below the knee.

vertebra, vertebrae
one of the bones of the spine.

A B C D E F G H I J K L M N O P Q R S T U V W X Y Z

hurricane hurricanes *noun*
a powerful storm with winds that are strong enough to blow down trees or damage roofs.

hurry hurries hurrying hurried *verb*
if you hurry, you try to get somewhere or do something as quickly as possible. *You'd better hurry or you'll miss the match.*
hurry *noun*.

hurt hurts hurting hurt *verb*
1 if you hurt yourself, you cause pain to a part of your body. *Did you hurt yourself when you fell over?*
2 if a part of your body hurts, it feels pain. *I've got a sore knee. It really hurts.*
3 to hurt somebody is also to upset them. *I think Arabella was really hurt when you didn't invite her to your birthday party.*

husband husbands *noun*
one's husband is the man they are married to.

hut huts *noun*
a small building, usually with one room.

hutch hutches *noun*
a wooden and wire cage for a rabbit.

hydrogen *noun*
a gas that is lighter than air. Oxygen and hydrogen together make up water.

hyphen hyphens *noun*
a mark in writing (-) that you use to show that two parts of a word belong together. *grown-up*.
▲ Say ***hye**-fen*.

I i

ice *noun*
frozen water. *There was ice on the pond last winter.*
icy *adjective*.

iceberg icebergs *noun*
a huge piece of ice floating in the sea. Icebergs are dangerous to ships because most of the ice is under the water where you cannot see it.

ice-cream ice-creams *noun*
a sweet, frozen food made from milk or cream.

ice-skating *noun*
sliding on ice in special boots called ice-skates that have thin, metal blades on the bottom.

icicle icicles *noun*
a hanging, pointed piece of ice made of dripping water that has frozen.

icing *noun*
a smooth, sweet covering for cakes, made of sugar mixed with water or egg whites.

icy icier iciest *adjective*
very cold. *an icy wind*.

idea ideas *noun*
1 a new thought about something. *I've got an idea. Let's go to the beach!*
2 a picture in your mind. *The film gives you a good idea of what India is like.*

ideal *adjective*
if something is ideal, it is perfect and just what you want. *The weather was ideal for a picnic.*
ideally *adverb*.

identical *adjective*
exactly the same. *Ben and Jason are identical twins.*

identify identifies identifying identified *verb*
if you identify somebody or something, you know who or what they are and can name them. *Can you identify this wild flower?*
identification *noun*.

idle *adjective*
lazy, or not working.

igloo igloos *noun*
a round house, built by Inuit people out of blocks of hard snow or ice.

ignorant *adjective*
not knowing anything about something.
ignorance *noun*.

ignore ignores ignoring ignored *verb*
if you ignore somebody, you take no notice of them. *She ignored me when I said hello.*

ill *adjective*
if you are ill, you are not well. *I didn't go to school today because I was ill.*

illegal *adjective*
if something is illegal, it is not allowed by law. ■ The opposite is **legal**.

illness illnesses *noun*
something such as measles or a cold that makes you feel unwell.

illusion illusions *noun*
something that you think you can see, but that is not really there.

illustration illustrations *noun*
a picture in a book or magazine. *This dictionary has lots of illustrations.*

image images *noun*
1 a picture on paper, on a screen or in a mirror. *A ghostly image appeared in the mirror.*
2 a picture in your mind. *I have an image of how I want to look when I'm a grown-up.*

imaginary *adjective*
something that is imaginary is not real and exists only in your mind. *I read a story about a boy who had an imaginary friend.* ▲ Say *i-**maj**-in-ar-ee.*

imagination *noun*
your imagination is your ability to think of new ideas or create pictures in your mind. *Use your imagination and draw whatever you like.*
imaginative *adjective.*

imagine imagines imagining imagined *verb*
when you imagine something, you create a picture of it in your mind. *Can you imagine living in a cave like the people in the Stone Age?*

imitate imitates imitating imitated *verb*
if you imitate somebody, you copy the way they talk or act. *The mime artist started to imitate my actions.*
imitation *noun.*
It is not a real Christmas tree, but a plastic imitation.

immediately *adverb*
now. *The ambulance arrived immediately after we telephoned.*

immune *adjective*
if you are immune to a disease, you cannot catch it. *The doctor said that I should be immune to measles because I've already had it.*
immunize *verb.*

impatient *adjective*
if you are impatient, you do not like waiting for things. *I get very impatient waiting for the bus.* ■ The opposite is **patient**.
impatience *noun.*

important *adjective*
1 if something is important, it matters a lot. *It is important to look both ways before you cross the road.*
2 a person who is important has a lot of power. *The king is an important man.*
importance *noun.*

impossible *adjective*
if something is impossible, you cannot do it, or it cannot happen. *You can't walk on water - it's impossible.*
■ The opposite is **possible**.

impress impresses impressing impressed *verb*
if you impress somebody, they think that what you have done is very good. *Her drawings impressed me.*

impression impressions *noun*
1 thoughts and feelings that you have about somebody or something. *My first impressions of the new school were that it was very large and noisy.*
2 if you make an impression on somebody, they remember what you are like and what you have done. *The ballet dancer made a great impression on all of us.*

impressive *adjective*
if something is impressive, people admire it, especially because it is very good or very big. *an impressive castle.*

improve improves improving improved *verb*
if something improves, it gets better. *With practice my spelling will improve.*
improvement *noun.*

include includes including included *verb*
to include is to have somebody or something as part of a group or as part of the whole thing. *Sushant was pleased to be included in the football team.*

increase increases increasing increased *verb*
if something increases, it gets bigger in size or amount. *The number of cars on the roads has increased.*
■ The opposite is **decrease**.
increase *noun.*

incredible *adjective*
if something is incredible, it is difficult to believe. *an incredible story.*

incubator incubators *noun*
1 a container where babies who are born early are kept until they grow bigger and stronger.
2 a container where eggs are kept warm until they hatch.

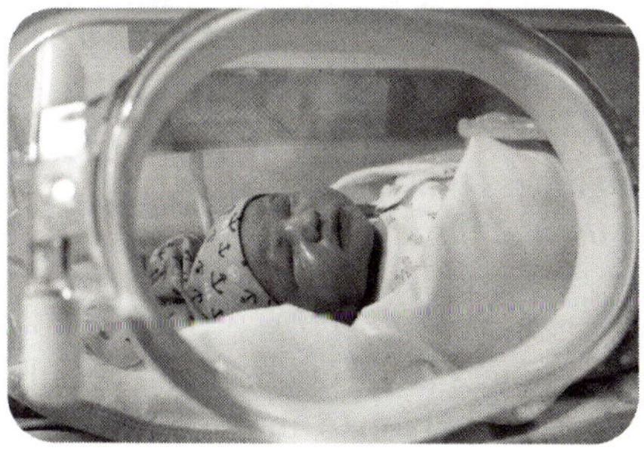

independent *adjective*
if you are independent, you do not want or need help from other people.
■ The opposite is **dependent**.
independence *noun.*

index indexes *noun*
a list of words from A to Z at the end of a book. The index tells you what things are in the book and where they are.

indigestion *noun*
an uncomfortable feeling that you have in your stomach when you have eaten too much or eaten the wrong food. *If you eat those apples before they are ripe, you'll get indigestion.*

a b c d e f g h i j k l m n o p q r s t u v w x y z

A B C D E F G H I J K L M N O P Q R S T U V W X Y Z

individual *adjective*
to do with one person or thing, not a whole group. *individual flowers.*

individual individuals *noun*
one person. *Every individual is different.*

indoors *adverb*
inside a building. *We went indoors when it started to rain.* ■ The opposite is **outdoors**.

industry industries *noun*
the work of making things in factories. *the car industry.*
industrial *adjective. an industrial area.*

infant infants *noun*
a baby or young child.

infection infections *noun*
an illness that is caused by germs. *a throat infection.*

infectious *adjective*
if an illness is infectious, it goes easily from one person to another. *Measles is a very infectious disease.*

inflate inflates inflating inflated *verb*
if you inflate something such as a balloon or a tyre, you blow it up with air or gas.
inflatable *adjective.*

influence *noun*
if somebody or something has an influence over you, they have a certain effect on you so that you change the way you think or behave. *My parents don't like me playing with Daniel because they say he is a bad influence on me.*
influence *verb,* **influential** *adjective.*

inform informs informing informed *verb*
if you inform somebody about something, you tell them about it. *The teacher informed us that there would be a history test next week.*

information *noun*
the facts about something. *This dictionary gives you information about words and how to spell them.*

ingredient ingredients *noun*
ingredients are all the things that you put in when you make something. *The ingredients for making a cake are butter, sugar, flour and eggs.*

inhabitant inhabitants *noun*
the inhabitants of a place are the people or animals that live there. *The inhabitants of the island are mainly fishermen and their families.*
inhabit *verb.*

initial initials *noun*
the first letters of each of your names. *Tom Jackson's initials are T.J.*

injection injections *noun*
if a doctor or nurse gives you an injection, they put medicine into your body through a special needle.
inject *verb.*

injure injures injuring injured *verb*
if you injure yourself, you hurt a part of your body. *He injured his leg playing football.*
injury *noun.*

ink inks *noun*
a coloured liquid that is used for writing or printing. *The words on this page were printed with ink.*

inland *adjective, adverb*
towards the middle of a country, away from the sea. *an inland lake.*

inner *adjective*
1 in the middle of a place. *He lives in inner London.*
2 inside something. *A bicycle tyre has an inner tube.* ■ The opposite is **outer**.

innocent *adjective*
if you are innocent, you have not done anything wrong. *The police have accused him of stealing the money but he says he is innocent.* ■ The opposite is **guilty**.
innocence *noun.*

inquire inquires inquiring inquired *verb*
if you inquire about something, you ask about it. *We inquired about the timings of the trains to Hull.*
inquiry *noun. an official inquiry into the disaster.*

insect insects *noun*
a small creature with six legs and a body that is divided into three sections. Many insects have wings. *Ants, grasshoppers and butterflies are insects.* ❖ ***Look at page 87***

insert inserts inserting inserted *verb*
if you insert a thing into something else, you put it inside it. *She inserted the key into the lock and opened the door.*

insist insists insisting insisted *verb*
if you insist on doing something, you say very firmly that you want to do it so that no one can stop you. *Eleanor insisted on wearing her new trainers.* **insistence** *noun.*

INSECTS

Wasp

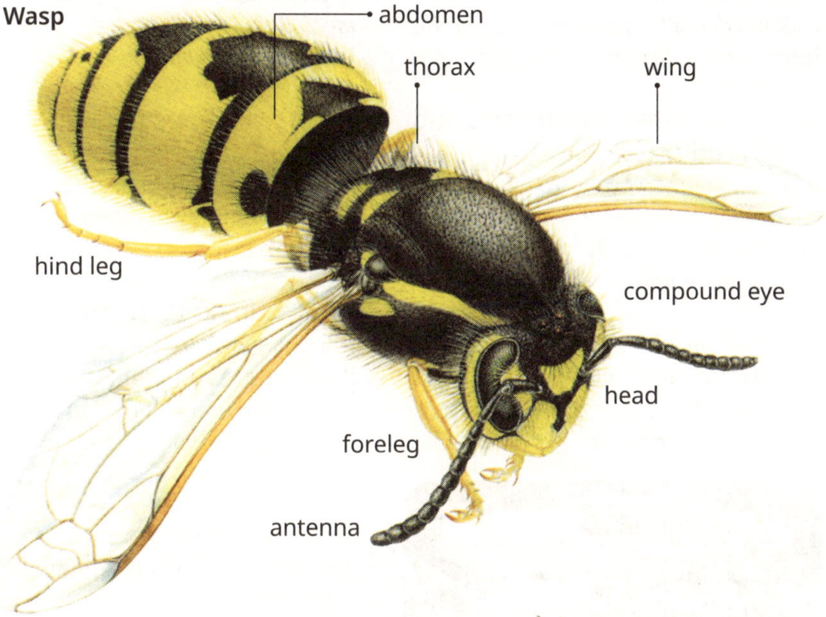

Vocabulary

abdomen
the rear part of an insect's body containing the stomach.

compound eye
an insect's eye is formed of thousands of six-sided lenses.

entomology
the study of insects. A person who studies insects is called an entomologist.

exoskeleton
the strong, hard outer "skin" of an insect that is a kind of skeleton. Insects have no framework of bones inside them.

metamorphosis
the dramatic changes that take place when an insect develops from an egg into an adult as when a caterpillar turns into a butterfly.

thorax
the middle part of an insect's body.

Cockchafer

Grasshopper

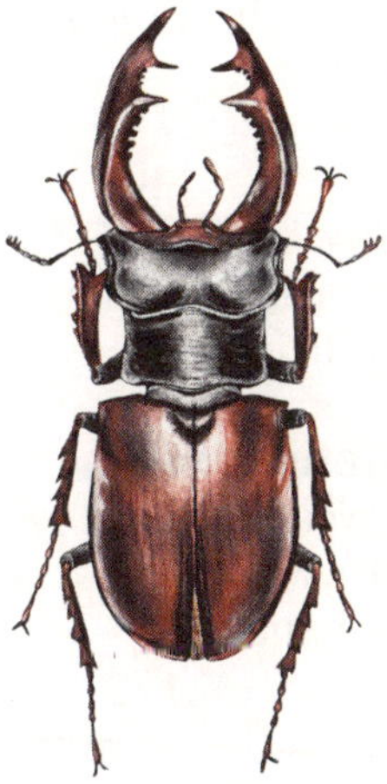
Stag beetle

Leaf insect

European mantis

Africanized honeybee

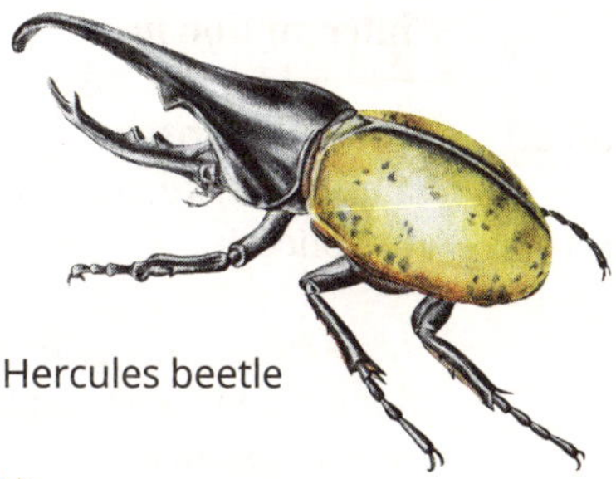
Hercules beetle

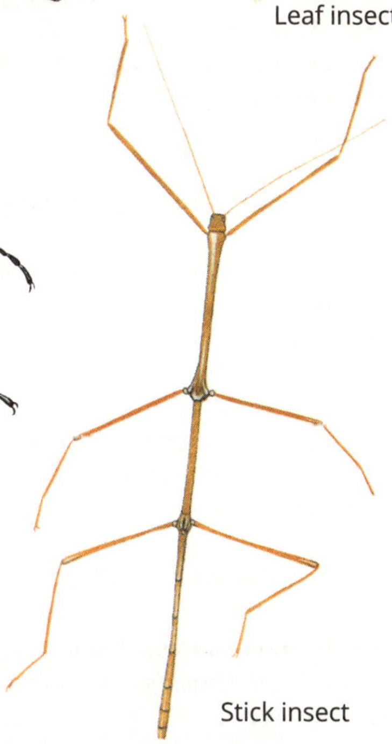
Stick insect

Dung beetle

Colorado potato beetle

Fire ant

inspect inspects inspecting inspected *verb*
to look at something carefully.
inspection *noun*.

instant *adjective*
if something is instant, it happens very quickly, or you can make it very quickly. *instant coffee.*

instead *adverb*
in the place of somebody or something else. *I don't like ice-cream. May I have fruit instead?*

instinct instincts *noun*
something that makes people and animals do things without having to think or learn about them. *Birds build their nests by instinct.*

instructions *noun*
words that tell you how to do something. *She gave us instructions on how to look after the puppies.*

instrument instruments *noun*
1 a thing that is used for doing a special job. *A telescope is an instrument for looking at things such as stars.*
2 a musical instrument is something that you play to make music. *Recorders and pianos are instruments.* ❖ ***Look at page 105***

insulate insulates insulating insulated *verb*
to cover something with a material so that electricity cannot pass through it.

insult insults insulting insulted *verb*
if somebody insults you, they upset you by saying nasty or rude things to you.
insult *noun*.

intelligent *adjective*
a person who is intelligent is able to learn and understand things quickly.
intelligence *noun*.

intend intends intending intended *verb*
if you intend to do something, you plan to do it. *What do you intend to do now?*
intention *noun*.

interest interests interesting interested *verb*
if something interests you, you like it and want to know more about it. *Football doesn't interest my gran at all.*
interesting *adjective*.

interfere interferes interfering interfered *verb*
if you interfere, you try to do something for somebody when they do not want your help.
interference *noun*.

interior *noun*
the interior of something is the part inside it. *The interior of the car was red and black in colour.*

international *adjective*
if something is international, it has to do with more than one country. *an international football match.*

interrupt interrupts interrupting interrupted *verb*
if you interrupt somebody, you stop them while they are saying or doing something. *Please don't interrupt me.*
interruption *noun*.

interval intervals *noun*
a break between two parts of a play or concert.

interview interviews *noun*
a meeting when you answer questions about yourself. *a job interview.*

intestine intestines *noun*
your intestine is the long tube inside your body that carries food from your stomach. ❖ ***Look at page 83***

introduce introduces introducing introduced *verb*
if you introduce two people who have never met before, you tell them each other's names so they can get to know one another. *Tim introduced me to Bob.*
introduction *noun*.

invade invades invading invaded *verb*
when an army invades, it goes into another country to attack it.
invasion *noun*.

invent invents inventing invented *verb*
if you invent something, you make something that has never been made or thought of before.
invention *noun*.

inventor inventors *noun*
a person who invents something.

investigate investigates investigating investigated *verb*
when you investigate something, you try to find out all about it. *The police investigated the theft.*
investigation *noun*.

invisible *adjective*
if something is invisible, you cannot see it. ■ The opposite is **visible**.

invitation invitations *noun*
if somebody has given you an invitation, they have written or spoken to you to ask you to go somewhere.

invite invites inviting invited *verb*
if you invite somebody, you ask them to come to your home, to a party or a meal.

involve involves involving involved *verb*
1 if you are involved in something, you take part in it. *Are you involved in the school play?*
2 if something is involved in an activity, it is part of it. *Tennis involves a lot of skill.*

iron *noun*
1 iron is a strong, hard metal that is found in rocks. Iron is used for making tools, gates and other things.
2 an iron is an electrical tool that you use to make clothes smooth.
▲ Say ***eye-un***

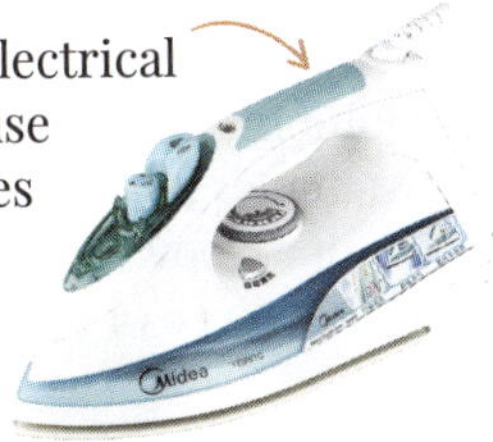

irritate
irritates irritating irritated *verb*
if something irritates you, it annoys you.
irritation *noun*.

Islam *noun*
the religion that Muslims follow.

island islands *noun*
a piece of land with water all around it. ▲ Say ***eye-land.***

itch itches itching itched *verb*
when a part of your body itches, you have a feeling on your skin that you want to scratch it.
itch *noun*, **itchy** *adjective*.

ivy ivies *noun*
a plant with shiny, pointed leaves that stay green in winter. Ivy climbs up walls and trees.

J j

jack jacks *noun*
the playing-card that comes between the ten and the queen and has a picture of a young man on it.

jacket jackets *noun*
a short coat.

jagged *adjective*
something that is jagged has a lot of sharp points along the edges. *a jagged piece of broken glass.*

jaguar jaguars *noun*
a wild cat that has brown and yellow fur with black spots. Jaguars live in North and South America.

jail jails *noun*
a prison.

jam *noun*
1 a food made by cooking fruit with sugar. *Billie loves strawberry jam on toast.*
2 a traffic jam is a large number of vehicles unable to move.

jam jams jamming jammed *verb*
if something jams, it cannot move. *The paper has jammed in the printer.*

jar jars *noun*
a glass container for jam or other foods. *a jar of pickles.*

jaw jaws *noun*
your jaws are the two large bones in your mouth that hold your teeth. Your jaws move up and down when you speak and eat.

jealous *adjective*
if you are jealous, you want what somebody else has and it makes you angry and unhappy. *Joe was jealous of his little sister because she always seemed to get what she wanted.*
▲ Say ***jel-uss.***
jealousy *noun*.

jeans *noun*
trousers made from thick, strong, cotton material called denim.
● A word that sounds like **jeans** is **genes**.

jelly jellies *noun*
a clear, slightly wobbly food with a fruit flavour. *At Amanda's party, we had orange jelly and ice-cream.*

jellyfish jellyfish or jellyfishes *noun*
a sea animal that has a clear, round body and long tentacles that sting.

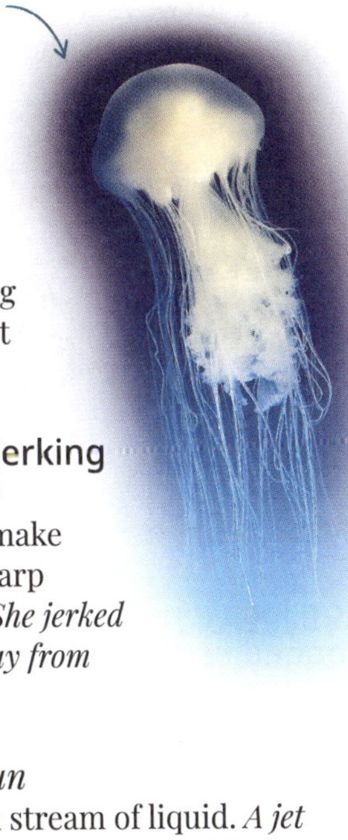

jerk jerks jerking jerked *verb*
to jerk is to make a sudden, sharp movement. *She jerked her hand away from the flame.*

jet jets *noun*
1 a fast, thin stream of liquid. *A jet of water was coming out of the burst pipe.*
2 a fast plane with an engine that sucks air in and then forces it out at the back.

Jew Jews *noun*
a person who belongs to the race of people who in ancient times lived in Israel, or a person who follows the religion called Judaism.
Jewish *adjective*.

A B C D E F G H I J K L M N O P Q R S T U V W X Y Z

jewel jewels *noun*
a beautiful and valuable stone such as a diamond, ruby or emerald.

jewellery *noun*
rings, bracelets, necklaces, brooches and other things that people wear to decorate their bodies. Jewellery is often made of valuable metals such as gold or silver, and jewels such as diamonds or rubies.

jigsaw jigsaws *noun*
a puzzle made up of a lot of small pieces of wood or thick card that fit together to make a picture.

job jobs *noun*
1 the work that a person does to get money. *My mum is looking for a job at the moment.*
2 a piece of work that you have to do. *My sister and I were given the job of washing the car.*

jockey jockeys *noun*
a person who rides a horse in races.

jog jogs jogging jogged *verb*
if you jog, you run quite slowly, for exercise.

join joins joining joined *verb*
1 when you join things, you put or fix them together. *I joined the pieces of the jigsaw puzzle.*
2 if you join a group, you become a member of it. *Maria has joined the school band.*

joint joints *noun*
1 a joint is part of your body where two bones are joined together, such as your elbow or knee.
2 a large piece of meat with a bone in it.

joke jokes *noun*
something that somebody says or does to make people laugh.

journalist journalists *noun*
a person who writes news and stories for newspapers. ▲ Say ***jer**-na-list.*
journalism *noun.*

journey journeys *noun*
when you go on a journey, you travel from one place to another. *It's a three-hour journey by car from here to the coast.* ▲ Say ***jer**-nee.*

joy *noun*
a feeling of great happiness. ■ The opposite is **sorrow**.
joyful *adjective.*

Judaism *noun*
the religion of the Jews.

judge judges *noun*
1 a judge is the person who controls what happens in a court of law and decides what a guilty person's punishment should be.
2 a person who decides who is the winner in a competition.

judo *noun*
a sport from Japan in which two people try to throw each other down using various special movements.

jug jugs *noun*
a container with a handle and a shaped part at the top that is used for pouring liquids.

juggle juggles juggling juggled *verb*
if you juggle, you throw several things into the air and catch them, one after another, so there is more than one thing in the air at once. *The man is juggling.*
juggler *noun.*

juice juices *noun*
the liquid from fruit, vegetables or meat. *orange juice.* ◆ *carrot juice.*
juicy *adjective.*

jump jumps jumping jumped *verb*
when you jump, you push your body quickly and suddenly up into the air.
jump *noun.*

jumper jumpers *noun*
a piece of knitted clothing that covers your arms and the top part of your body.

junction junctions *noun*
a place where roads or railway lines meet. ▲ Say ***junk**-shun.*

jungle jungles *noun*
a thick forest in a tropical country.

junior *adjective*
younger. ■ The opposite is **senior**.

jury juries *noun*
a group of 12 ordinary people in a court of law who have to decide whether the person on trial is guilty or innocent.

justice *noun*
a way of treating people that is both fair and right.

K k

kaleidoscope kaleidoscopes *noun*
a tube that you look through and see lots of coloured patterns in as you turn it. ▲ Say *ka-**lie**-do-scope.*

kangaroo kangaroos *noun*
a wild animal that lives in Australia. It has strong back legs and moves by making long jumps. A female kangaroo has a kind of pocket called a pouch at the front where she keeps her baby.

karate *noun*
a sport from Japan in which two people fight with their hands and feet using special movements.
▲ Say *ka-**rah**-tee.*

keen keener keenest *adjective*
if you are keen on something, you like it very much. *Joe is keen on football.*

kennel kennels *noun*
a small house for a dog.

kerb kerbs *noun*
the edge of a pavement next to a road. *They stood on the kerb waiting to cross the road.*

kettle kettles *noun*
a container with a handle and a spout, that is used for heating water. *Put the kettle on and make some tea.*

key keys *noun*
1 a piece of metal that is shaped so that when you turn it, it locks or unlocks something such as a door or padlock.
2 the keys of a piano are the parts that you press when you play to make different musical notes.
3 the keys of a computer are the parts with letters and numbers that you press when you work at the computer.
4 the key to a map is a list that tells you what the symbols on the map mean.

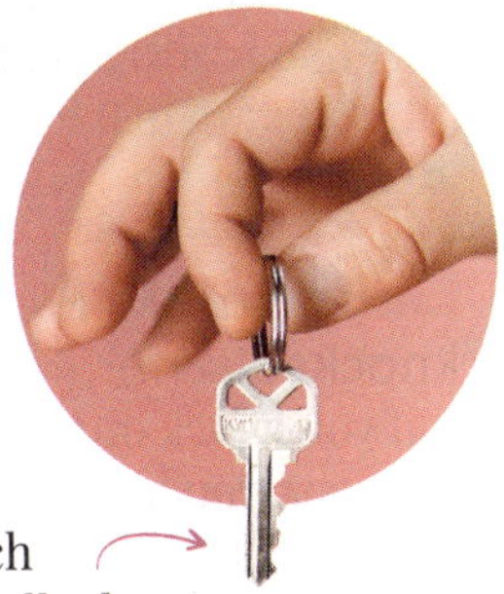

keyboard keyboards *noun*
1 the part of the computer with buttons, called keys, that have letters and numbers on them.
2 the row of keys on a piano or other musical instrument.
3 an electronic keyboard makes musical sounds.

kick kicks kicking kicked *verb*
if you kick something, you hit it with your foot. *Ben kicked the ball.*

kid kids *noun*
1 a young goat.
2 a child.

kidnap kidnaps kidnapping kidnapped *verb*
when somebody kidnaps another person, they take them away and hide them so that their family or friends will have to pay money to free them.

kidney kidneys *noun*
your kidneys are the two parts inside your body that help to clean your blood.

kill kills killing killed *verb*
to kill somebody or something means to make them die.

kind kinder kindest *adjective*
a person who is kind is friendly and gentle and likes to help other people.
■ The opposite is **unkind**.

kind kinds *noun*
a sort or type. *There are thousands of different kinds of insects.*

king kings *noun*
a king is a man who leads his people and belongs to a royal family.

kingfisher kingfishers *noun*
a bird with bright-blue and orange feathers that lives near rivers and streams and eats fish.

kiss kisses kissing kissed *verb*
when you kiss somebody, you touch them with your lips in a friendly way.
kiss *noun.*

kit kits *noun*
1 all the clothes and things that you need to do something. *a football kit.* ◆ *a tool kit.*
2 a set of pieces that you put together to make something. *a model ship kit.*

kitchen kitchens *noun*
a room where food is kept and cooked.

kite kites *noun*
a toy that you fly in the wind. It is made of a light frame covered with paper or cloth, attached to a long piece of string.

kitten kittens *noun*
a very young cat.

knee knees *noun*
your knees are the parts in the middle of your legs where they bend. *He fell over and grazed his knee.* ▲ Say ***nee.***

kneel kneels kneeling knelt *verb*
when you kneel, you go down on your knees. ▲ Say ***neel.***

knew past of know.
● A word that sounds like **knew** is **new**.

knife knives *noun*
a knife is a tool for cutting. It has a handle and a long, sharp piece of metal called a blade. ▲ Say ***nife.***

knight knights *noun*
a soldier who wore armour and rode a horse hundreds of years ago. Knights fought in battles for their king or queen. ● A word that sounds like **knight** is **night**.

knit knits knitting knitted *verb*
when you knit, you use wool and two long needles to make clothes. *My grandmother knitted this jumper for me.* ▲ Say ***nit.***

knob knobs *noun*
1 a round handle that you use to open a door or a drawer.
2 a knob is also a button that you turn or press to make a machine work.
▲ Say ***nob.***

knock knocks knocking knocked *verb*
1 if you knock on something such as a door, you hit it hard so that people will hear you.
2 if you knock something over, you hit it so that it falls. *I knocked over the vase and it broke.* ▲ Say ***nok.***

knot knots *noun*
a place where a piece of string, thread or rope is tied. *Can you undo this knot?* ● A word that sounds like **knot** is **not**.

know knows knowing knew known *verb*
1 if you know something, you have it in your mind and you are sure that it is true because you have learnt it. *Do you know what the capital of Peru is?*
2 if you know somebody, you have met them before. *I know her because she is in my class.* ● A word that sounds like **know** is **no**.

knowledge *noun*
what you know and understand about something. *She has a good knowledge of computers.* ▲ Say ***nol-ij.***

knuckle knuckles *noun*
your knuckles are the bony parts where your fingers join your hands, and the bony parts in the middle of your fingers where they bend.
▲ Say ***nuk-ul.***

koala koalas *noun*
an animal that looks like a small bear with thick, grey fur. It lives in trees in Australia, and feeds on their leaves and bark. A female koala has a kind of pocket called a pouch at the front where she keeps her baby.

Ll

lace *noun*
thin, delicate material with a pretty pattern of tiny holes in it. *a pair of lace gloves.*

laces *noun*
pieces of cord or string that you use to fasten shoes or boots.

ladybird ladybirds *noun*
a small, round beetle. Ladybirds are usually red with black spots on their wings.

laid past of lay.

label labels *noun*
a small piece of paper fixed to something that gives you information about it. *different types of labels.*

laboratory laboratories *noun*
a room where scientists work and do experiments using special equipment. ▲ Say *la-**bor**-a-tree.*

lack *noun*
if there is a lack of something, it is missing or there is not enough of it. *The lack of rain meant that the crops did not grow properly.*

ladder ladders *noun*
two long, metal or wooden poles with bars, called rungs, between them that you can use to climb up or down.

ladle ladles *noun*
a big, deep spoon with a long handle, used for serving soup.

lain past of lie.
● A word that sounds like **lain** is **lane**.

lake lakes *noun*
a large area of water with land all around it.

lamb lambs *noun*
1 a young sheep.
2 meat from a young sheep.

lame *adjective*
if a person or an animal is lame, they cannot walk properly because one of their legs has been hurt. *The dog was lame in one leg after it was hit by a car.*

lamp lamps *noun*
an object that uses electricity, gas or oil to give light.

land lands *noun*
1 the solid, dry part of the world that is not covered by sea. *The sailors were glad to be on land again after spending three months at sea.*
2 a country. *He told the children tales of the foreign lands he had visited.*

land lands landing landed *verb*
when a plane lands, it comes down to the ground and stops. ■ The opposite is **take off**.

lane lanes *noun*
1 a narrow road.
2 part of a main road or motorway that is wide enough for one car at a time. *Drivers should always signal before they change lanes.* ● A word that sounds like **lane** is **lain**.

language languages *noun*
the words that people use to talk and write to each other. *These books are written in different languages.*
▲ Say ***lang**-gwij*.

lantern lanterns *noun*
a light inside a glass and metal case that you can carry.

lap laps *noun*
1 your lap is the top half of your legs when you are sitting down. *His little grandson was sitting on his lap.*
2 one journey around a race track.

laptop laptops *noun*
a small computer that you can open and use on your lap.

large larger largest *adjective*
big in size or amount.
■ The opposite is **small** or **little**.

larva larvae *noun*
an insect after it has come out of an egg but before it has become an adult.

laser lasers *noun*
a machine that produces a very powerful beam of light. People use laser beams for many different things such as surgery.

lasso lassos *noun*
a piece of rope with a large loop at one end that you can make bigger or smaller. Cowboys use lassos to catch cattle.
▲ Say *lass-**oo***.

late later latest *adjective, adverb*
if you are late, you come after the time that you were supposed to. *I was late for the dentist because I missed the bus.* ■ The opposite is **early**.

lather *noun*
a lot of small bubbles that you make when you mix water with soap or washing powder. ▲ Say ***lah**-ther*.

laugh laughs laughing laughed *verb*
when you laugh, you make sounds that show that you find something funny. ▲ Say ***larf***.

laughter *noun*
the sound of somebody laughing.
▲ Say ***larf**-ter*.

launch launches launching launched *verb*
1 when somebody launches a ship or boat, they make it go into the water.
2 when a rocket or missile is launched, it is sent up into the sky.

launderette launderettes *noun*
a place where you can take your dirty washing and wash and dry it in a machine yourself.

lava *noun*
hot, liquid rock that flows from a volcano when it erupts.

lavatory lavatories *noun*
a toilet. ▲ Say ***lav**-a-tree*.

law laws *noun*
a rule or a set of rules made by the government, that everybody in a country has to obey. *Stealing is against the law.*

lawn lawns *noun*
an area of short grass in a garden or park.

lawyer lawyers *noun*
a person whose job is to advise people about the law and sometimes to speak for them in a court of law. ▲ Say ***loy**-er*.

lay lays laying laid *verb*
1 if you lay something down, you put it down carefully.
2 when you lay a table, you put knives, forks, spoons and other things on it, ready for a meal.
3 when a hen lays an egg, it produces it.

lay past of lie.

layer layers *noun*
a flat piece of something that lies between two other pieces of it or that lies on the top. *A sandwich usually has three layers, two slices of bread and the filling in between – this one has seven.*

lazy lazier laziest *adjective*
somebody who is lazy does not want to work or do very much. *She gets a lift to school every morning because she's too lazy to walk.*
laziness *noun*.

lead leads leading led *verb*
1 if you lead somebody, you go in front of them to show them the way. *Follow me and I'll lead you to the church.* ■ The opposite is **follow**.
2 if you lead a group of people, you are in charge of them. *The general led his troops to the battle.*
3 if you are leading in a race or game, you are winning at the time *John was leading for most of the race.*
▲ Say ***leed***.
leader *noun*.

A B C D E F G H I J K L M N O P Q R S T U V W X Y Z

lead leads *noun*
a long, thin piece of leather or a chain that you attach to a dog's collar to stop it from running away. ▲ Say ***leed***.

lead *noun*
a soft, heavy, grey metal. ▲ Rhymes with ***bed***. ● A word that sounds like **lead** is **led**.

leaf leaves *noun*
leaves are the thin, flat parts of a plant that grow from the stem or from branches or twigs. Leaves are usually green.

leaflet leaflets *noun*
a piece of paper with information or advertisements printed on it.

leak leaks leaking leaked *verb*
if something leaks, liquid or gas escapes from it through a crack or hole. *The washing machine is leaking and there's water all over the floor.*

lean leans leaning leant or leaned *verb*
1 if you lean against something, you rest against it so that part of your weight is on it. *She leant against the wall.*
2 if you lean somewhere, you bend your body in that direction. *Raj leant across the table to talk to me.*

leap leaps leaping leapt or leaped *verb*
if you leap, you jump high or a long way. *The dog leapt over the fence.*
leap *noun*.

leap year leap years *noun*
a year that has an extra day, the 29th February, so that the year has 366 days instead of 365. Leap years happen once every four years.

learn learns learning learnt or learned *verb*
when you learn something, you find out about it or how to do it. *I am learning to play the piano.*

leather *noun*
a strong material made from an animal's skin. Leather is used to make things such as shoes and bags.

leave leaves leaving left *verb*
1 when you leave, you go away from somewhere. ■ The opposite is **arrive**.
2 when you leave something, you let it stay where it is. *I left my hat and coat at Jo's house.*

led past of lead.

left *noun, adjective, adverb*
when you write the word "left", the "l" is to the left of the "e". *Carla writes with her left hand.* ■ The opposite is **right**.

leg legs *noun*
1 your legs are the two long parts of your body that you use for walking.
2 the legs of a table or chair are the long, narrow parts that stand on the floor and support the top part.

legal *adjective*
if something is legal, the law says you can do it. ▲ Say ***lee**-gul*. ■ The opposite is **illegal**.

legend legends *noun*
a story from long ago, that may or may not be true. *Do you know the legend of King Arthur?* ▲ Say ***lej**-end*.

leisure *noun*
a time when you do not have to work and you can do what you enjoy.
▲ Say ***lesh**-er*.

lemon lemons *noun*
a bright-yellow fruit with sour juice.

lend lends lending lent *verb*
if you lend something to somebody, you let them have it for a while and then they give it back to you. *Can you lend me a pen?* ■ The opposite is **borrow**.

length *noun*
the length of something is how long it is. *My desk is two metres in length.*
lengthen *verb*.
to make or become longer.

lens lenses *noun*
a curved piece of glass or transparent plastic used in a camera, a pair of glasses, a telescope, or something similar to help you see more clearly.

lent past of lend.

leopard leopards *noun*
a wild cat that has yellow fur with black spots. Leopards live in Africa and Asia. ▲ Say ***lep**-erd*.

leotard leotards *noun*
a tight piece of clothing that covers you from your shoulders to your thighs, made of material that stretches. Dancers wear leotards.
▲ Say ***lee**-o-tard*.

lesson lessons *noun*
a period of time when you are taught something by a teacher.

let lets letting let *verb*
if you let somebody do something, you do not stop them from doing it. *Will you let me stroke your dog?*

letter letters *noun*
1 one of the signs that we use to write words, such as a, b and c.
2 a written message that you send or receive by post.

lettuce lettuces *noun*
a plant with large, green leaves that we eat raw in salads. ▲ Say ***let**-iss*.

level *adjective*
flat and not sloping. *The table keeps shaking because the floor isn't level.*

lever levers *noun*
1 a long bar that you put under something heavy at one end so that you can lift the heavy object by pushing on the bar at the other end.
2 a long handle like a stick that you use to make a machine work.
▲ Say ***lee**-ver.*

liar liars *noun*
a person who tells lies.

library libraries *noun*
a building or room that has books, tapes, CDs and videos for people to borrow.

licence licences *noun*
an official piece of paper that gives you permission to do something. *a driving licence.* ▲ Say ***lie**-sens.*

lick licks licking licked *verb*
if you lick something, you move your tongue over it. *The girl licked her lollipop.*

lid lids *noun*
a cover for a box, pot, tin or jar.

lie lies lying lied *verb*
if you lie, you say something that you know is not true.
lie *noun.*

lie lies lying lay lain *verb*
when you lie down, you rest your body in a flat position, for example on the floor or on a bed.

life lives *noun*
a person's or an animal's life is the time they are alive, until they die. *I'll remember today for the rest of my life.*

lifeboat lifeboats *noun*
a boat that is used for rescuing people who are in danger at sea.

lift lifts lifting lifted *verb*
if you lift something, you pick it up or raise it. *I can't lift this case – it's too heavy.*

lift lifts *noun*
1 a machine like a large box that carries people or goods up and down between floors in a building.
2 if somebody gives you a lift, they take you somewhere in their car. *Can you give me a lift home from the party?*

light lights *noun*
1 light is the bright rays that come from the Sun, the Moon, or from a lamp, that lets you see things.
2 a light is a thing that produces light. *Can you turn on the light?*

light lighter lightest *adjective*
1 something that is light does not weigh very much and you can pick it up easily. *A feather is light.* ■ The opposite is **heavy**.
2 light also means not dark. *My room is very light because it has two big windows.*
3 light also means pale in colour. *light green.* ■ The opposite is **dark**.

light lights lighting lit *verb*
if you light something, you make it start burning. *Mum lit the candles on the birthday cake.*

lighthouse lighthouses *noun*
a tower with a very bright light on top that flashes to warn ships that they are near rocks or to show them the safe way to go.

lightning *noun*
a flash of very bright light that you see in the sky when there is a storm.

like likes liking liked *verb*
1 if you like somebody or something, you think they are nice.
2 if you like doing something, you enjoy it. *I like swimming more than any other sport.* ■ The opposite is **dislike**.

like

Some words you can use instead of like:

I like fire-fighters because they help people.
admire, respect

I would like an ice-cream.
enjoy, want

He's a vet because he likes animals.
fond of, loves

like *preposition*
very similar to somebody or something. *Jahaan looks just like his dad.* ■ The opposite is **unlike**.

likely likelier likeliest *adjective*
if something is likely, it is probably going to happen. ■ The opposite is **unlikely**.

limb limbs *noun*
an arm or a leg. ▲ Rhymes with ***him***.

lime limes *noun*
a fruit similar to a lemon, with green skin and sour juice.

limit limits *noun*
the largest amount of something that is allowed. *The speed limit on this road is 80 kilometres per hour.*

limp limps limping limped *verb*
if a person or an animal limps, they walk in an uneven way because one of their legs or feet has been hurt.

line lines *noun*
1 a long, thin mark on something. *Draw a line under the title of your story.*
2 a number of people or things next to each other or one behind the other. *There was a long line of people queuing to get into the film.*
3 a long piece of rope or string. *My father is hanging the washing on the line to dry.*

link links *noun*
1 a ring in a chain.
2 a connection between things or people. *The police believe there is a link between the two crimes.*

lion lions *noun*
a large wild cat that has light-brown fur and lives in parts of Africa and Asia. The male lion has a large mane. A female lion is called a lioness and a young lion is a cub.

lip lips *noun*
your lips are the two soft parts that form the edges of your mouth.

liquid liquids *noun*
water or anything else that flows like water. ■ The opposite is **solid**.
liquid *adjective*.

list lists *noun*
a line of things that are written down one under the other. *a shopping list.*
list *verb*.

listen listens listening listened *verb*
when you listen, you pay attention to sounds so you can hear them. *Listen carefully to the instructions.*

lit past of light.

litter *noun*
1 rubbish such as bits of paper and cans that are thrown away on the street or in a public place instead of being put in a bin.
2 a group of baby animals that are born at the same time to one mother. *Our cat had a litter of four kittens.*

little *adjective*
1 small in size. ■ The opposite is **big** or **large**.
2 a little child is a young child. *I loved drawing when I was little.*
3 small in amount. *There's only a little bit of cake left.*

live lives living lived *verb*
1 to live means to be alive. ■ The opposite is **die**.
2 if you live somewhere, that is where your home is. *I live with my granny.*
▲ Rhymes with ***give***.

live *adjective*
1 a live animal is alive. *Have you ever seen a real, live crocodile?* ■ The opposite is **dead**.
2 a live TV or radio programme is being broadcast as it is happening.
▲ Rhymes with ***five***.

lively livelier liveliest *adjective*
full of energy or excitement. *The old man is lively for his age.*

liver livers *noun*
your liver is the large part inside your body that helps to clean your blood and digest your food.

living *noun*
when you do something for a living, you earn money by doing it. *She earned her living as a journalist.*

lizard lizards *noun*
a reptile with four very short legs, rough skin and a long tail.

load loads *noun*
something that is being carried somewhere. *The donkey carried a very heavy load of wood.*

load loads loading loaded *verb*
1 if you load a car or other vehicle, you put a lot of things into it to take somewhere. *The men loaded the furniture into the lorry.* ■ The opposite is **unload**.
2 if you load a gun, you put bullets in it. *Soldiers can load their guns quickly.*
3 if you load a camera, you put a film in it. *Have you loaded the film?*
4 if you load a computer, you put information or a program into it.

loaf loaves *noun*
bread that is cooked in one piece and then cut up into slices.

loan loans *noun*
money or something else that somebody lends you and that you have to pay or give back later.

lobster lobsters *noun*
a sea animal with a hard shell, eight legs and two large claws in front. Lobsters can be eaten.

local *adjective*
close to where you live. *We go to the local school.*
locally *adverb*.

lock locks *noun*
an object that fastens a door or lid so that you cannot open it without a key.

lock locks locking locked *verb*
if you lock something such as a door, you fasten it with a key. *Remember to lock your bike.* ■ The opposite is **unlock**.

locomotive locomotives *noun*
a railway engine.

loft lofts *noun*
a space under the roof of a house where you can store things.

log logs *noun*
a piece of a thick branch cut from a tree. *We need some logs to put on the fire.*

lonely lonelier loneliest *adjective*
if you are lonely, you are sad because you are on your own or because you do not have any friends. *Patsy feels lonely in her new school.*

long longer longest *adjective*
1 far between one end and the other. *a long bridge.*
2 for more time than usual. *The film was very long and we got bored.*
■ The opposite is **short**.

long longs longing longed *verb*
if you long for something, you want it very much. *She longed to have a pony of her own.*

look looks looking looked *verb*
1 when you look at something, you use your eyes to see it.
2 if somebody or something looks a certain way, they seem that way to you. *You look tired.*
3 if you look for something, you try to find it.
4 if you look after somebody or something, you take care of them. *Dad looked after us when Mum was ill.*

loop loops *noun*
a circle made in a piece of string, rope, thread or wire.

loose looser loosest *adjective*
1 not fixed firmly in place. *a loose tooth.*
2 too big to fit properly. *My trousers are loose.* ■ The opposite is **tight**.

lorry lorries *noun*
a large motor vehicle that is used for carrying goods by road.

lose loses losing lost *verb*
1 if you lose something, you do not know where to find it.
2 if you lose a competition, game or fight, you do not win it.
3 if you have lost weight, you now weigh less than you did before. *My dad is on a diet; he is trying to lose weight.*

loss losses *noun*
the loss of something is not having it any more. *Emily felt sad about the loss of her necklace because her gran had given it to her.*

lottery lotteries *noun*
a game in which you choose some numbers, or buy tickets with numbers on them, and if they are the right ones, you win a prize.

loud louder loudest *adjective*
something that is loud makes a lot of noise. *loud music.* ■ The opposite is **quiet** or **soft**.
loudness *noun*.

loudspeaker loudspeakers *noun*
a piece of equipment that makes sounds louder. When a singer sings into a microphone, the audience can hear his or her voice through loudspeakers.

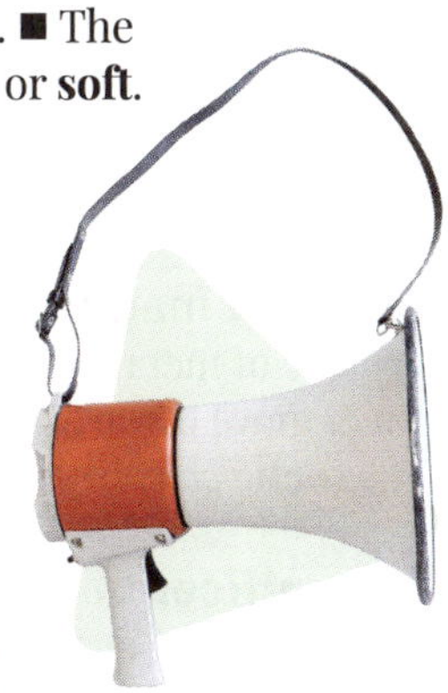

love loves *noun*
a very strong feeling of liking somebody or something. ■ The opposite is **hate**.

lovely lovelier loveliest *adjective*
beautiful, or very pleasant. *The park looks lovely in the spring when all the trees are in blossom.*

low lower lowest *adjective*
1 not very far from the ground. *There was a low wall between the houses.*
2 deep in sound. *He has a very low voice.* ■ The opposite is **high**.

lower lowers lowering lowered *verb*
if you lower something, you bring it slowly down. *They lowered the flag.* ■ The opposite is **raise**.

loyal *adjective*
if you are loyal to somebody, you always support them. *She is a loyal friend.* ■ The opposite is **disloyal**.
loyally *adverb*.

luck *noun*
1 luck is when something happens by chance instead of when you plan it or make it happen. *There is no skill needed to play this game. It's just luck whether you win or not.*
2 luck is also good things that happen to you by chance. *Wish me luck for my piano exam!*

lucky luckier luckiest *adjective*
if you are lucky, you have good things happening to you by chance. *What is your lucky number?* ■ The opposite is **unlucky**.

luggage *noun*
all the bags, cases and boxes that you take with you when you are travelling. *Have you packed your luggage yet?* ▲ Say **lug-ij**.

luminous *adjective*
something that is luminous glows in the dark. *My watch has luminous hands.*

lump lumps *noun*
1 a solid bit of something. *a lump of cheese.* ◆ *This sauce has lumps in it.*
2 a swelling. *I've got a lump on my head where I banged it.*
lumpy *adjective*.

lunch lunches *noun*
a meal that you eat in the middle of the day.

lung lungs *noun*
your lungs are the two parts like bags inside your chest that fill up when you breathe in and then empty again when you breathe out.

luxury luxuries *noun*
something that is expensive and very nice to have, but that you do not need. *Mum says we can't afford the luxury of a holiday this year.* ▲ Say **luk-sher-ee**.
luxurious *adjective*.

A B C D E F G H I J K L M N O P Q R S T U V W X Y Z

M m

machine machines *noun*
a thing with parts that move to do work or to make something. We use machines in the home to help us sew, cook and clean. A washing machine cleans our clothes and a machine called a vacuum cleaner sucks up dirt from carpets.
machinery *noun*.

mad madder maddest *adjective*
1 a person who is mad has an illness in their mind.
2 mad also means very silly. *You're mad if you jump off this wall.*

madness *noun*
ill in your mind.

magazine magazines *noun*
a thin book with pictures, stories and information about things in it. Magazines come out every week or every month.

maggot maggots *noun*
a creature that looks like a worm and grows up to become a fly. People use maggots to catch fish.

magic *noun*
1 a power that makes strange and wonderful things happen. *The witch made the frog disappear by magic.*
2 the skill of doing clever tricks, such as making things disappear.
magic *adjective.*
a magic spell.

magical *adjective*
1 produced by magic. *A magical hat that makes you disappear.*
2 strange or very exciting. *a magical fireworks display.*

magician magicians *noun*
a person who can do magic tricks.

magnet magnets *noun*
a piece of metal that makes iron or steel move towards it.
magnetic *adjective.*

magnificent *adjective*
very beautiful or grand. *a magnificent view.*

magnify magnifies magnifying magnified *verb*
when you magnify something, you make it look bigger. *We magnified the insect under the microscope.*

magnifying glass *noun*
a special piece of glass called a lens that can make things look bigger.

mail *noun*
letters, postcards and parcels that you send by post. ● A word that sounds like **mail** is **male**.

main *adjective*
most important. *the main entrance to the church.*

major *adjective*
large, important or serious. *Paris is a major city.* ◆ *Cancer is a major illness.*
■ The opposite is **minor**.

major *noun*
an officer in the army.

make makes making made *verb*
1 if you make something, you put things together so that you have a new thing. *Mandy is making a cake.*
2 to cause something to happen. *The balloon made a loud bang when it burst.*
3 to do something. *I made a mistake.*
4 if you make somebody do something, you force them to do it. *Dad makes me go to bed at 9 o'clock.*

make-up *noun*
special powders, paints and creams that people put on their faces. Face powder and lipstick are kinds of make-up.

male males *adjective*
a person or animal that belongs to the sex that cannot have babies or lay eggs. Boys and men are male.
■ The opposite is **female**. ● A word that sounds like **male** is **mail**.

malt *noun*
malt is made from a grain called barley that has been dried. Malt is used to make whisky, beer and vinegar.

mammal mammals *noun*
animals that give birth to their young and do not lay eggs. They also feed their young with milk. People, horses and whales are all mammals. ❖ ***Look at page 99***

man men *noun*
a grown-up male person.

manage manages managing managed *verb*
1 if you manage to do something difficult, you do it well. *Those sums were hard, but I managed to do them.*
2 if you manage people at work, you tell them what to do.

manager managers *noun*
a person whose job is to run or control such things as a bank, a shop or a hotel.

mane manes *noun*
the long hair on the neck of a horse or a male lion.

manner manners *noun*
1 the way that you do something. *She smiled in a friendly manner.*
2 Your manners are the way you behave when you are eating or talking to other people. *It's bad manners to talk with your mouth full.*

map maps *noun*
a drawing that shows you what a place looks like from above. Maps show things such as roads, mountains and rivers. *Will you draw me a map of how to get to your house?*

marathon marathons *noun*
a race when people have to run a very long way. A marathon is 42 km (26 miles) long.

marble *noun*
a kind of very hard stone that can be polished until it is shiny. Marble is used to make statues and buildings.

marbles *noun*
small, coloured glass balls that you use in some games.

march marches marching marched *verb*
when you march, you walk like a soldier with regular steps.
march *noun.*

margarine *noun*
a soft, yellow fat that looks like butter, but is not made from milk.

margin margins *noun*
a space around the writing or printing on a page.

mark marks *noun*
1 a spot, stain or line on something that spoils it. *Your shoes have left a dirty mark on the carpet.*
2 Marks are numbers or letters that your teacher gives you to show how good your work is. *Ben got the highest marks in the class.*
mark *verb.*

market markets *noun*
a place, usually in the open air, with lots of little shops called stalls, where you can buy things such as fruit and vegetables or clothes.

marmalade *noun*
a jam made from oranges or lemons.

marriage marriages *noun*
1 the special ceremony or legal relationship when a couple becomes husband or wife to someone.
2 the time a couple live together as husband or wife to someone. *Grandma and Granddad have had a long and happy marriage.*

marry marries marrying married *verb*
to become husband or wife to someone.

marsh marshes *noun*
an area of land that is soft and wet.

A B C D E F G H I J K L M N O P Q R S T U V W X Y Z

marsupial marsupials *noun*
a mammal, the female of which has a pouch for carrying her young. Kangaroos and koalas are marsupials.

Different types of marsupials

marvellous *adjective*
very good, wonderful. *We had a marvellous day at the seaside.* ◆ *What a marvellous idea!*

mascot mascots *noun*
a toy or doll that people keep because they think it will bring them good luck.

mask masks *noun*
something you wear on your face to hide it or to protect it. Doctors in a hospital wear masks so that they do not breathe germs over patients.

mass masses *noun*
1 a large number of people or things. *There were masses of people at the football match.*
2 a large amount of something solid, *a mass of rock.*
3 a mass is a service in some Christian churches.

massacre massacres *noun*
the violent killing of a lot of people.

massive *adjective*
very big, strong and heavy. *massive castle walls.*

mast masts *noun*
a tall pole that holds a flag or the sails on a boat.

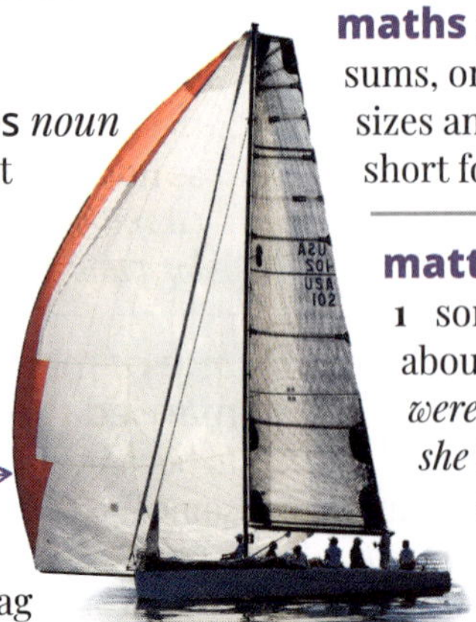

mat mats *noun*
1 a small carpet. *Please wipe your feet on the doormat.*
2 a piece of wood or material that you put on the table under a plate. *Put the hot dishes on a table-mat.*

match matches matching matched *verb*
if two things match, they are the same colour, shape or pattern, or they look good together. *Jazz's hat matches her scarf.*

match matches *noun*
1 a small, thin stick of wood or thick card that makes fire when you rub it against something rough. *He struck a match and lit the bonfire.*
2 a game that is played between two teams or two players. *a football match.* ◆ *a tennis match.*

mate mates *noun*
1 a friend. *Joe was playing cricket with his mates.*
2 one of two animals that have come together to have young ones. *Most birds choose a mate in the spring.*
mate *verb.*

material materials *noun*
1 things that you use to make other things with. Glass, wood and stone are materials that we use to build houses.
2 a cloth that we use to make things such as clothes. *Jack bought material to make new curtains.*

maternal *adjective*
to do with being a mother. *Mothers have maternal feelings.*

maths *noun*
sums, or working with shapes, sizes and measurements. Maths is short for mathematics.

matter *noun*
1 something that you must talk about or do. *Mum said there were some important matters she had to see to.*
2 a problem or difficulty. *What's the matter with your computer?*
3 a thing that you can see or touch. *The world is made of matter.*

matter matters mattering mattered *verb*
if something matters, it is important. *Ben has lost my ruler, but it doesn't matter because I have got another one.*

mattress mattresses *noun*
the thick part of the bed that you lie on.

mature *adjective*
if you are mature, you are grown-up, or you behave in a grown-up way.

maximum *noun*
the most you can have of something. *Yasmin got 98 marks out of a maximum of a 100.*
maximum *adjective.*
What's the maximum speed of this car?
■ The opposite is **minimum**.

mayor mayors *noun*
a person who is in charge of the council or government of a town or city.

maze mazes *noun*
a kind of puzzle made out of hedges or paths. You go into the maze at one end and have to find your way out.

meadow meadows *noun*
a field of grass. Wild flowers often grow in meadows. ▲ Say ***med**-oh*.

meal meals *noun*
the food that you eat at certain times of the day. Breakfast, lunch, tea, dinner and supper are all meals.

mean *adjective*
somebody who is mean does not like giving things or spending money. *She's really mean – she ate all those sweets and didn't give us any.*

mean means meaning meant *verb*
1 if you ask what something means, you want somebody to explain it so that you can understand it. *What does this word mean?*
2 if you mean to do something, you plan and want to do it. *I meant to tidy my room, but I forgot.*
meaning *noun*.

meanwhile *adverb*
if something happens meanwhile, it happens at the same time as something else, or before something else happens. *I'm getting a new bike next week, meanwhile I'll have to borrow my sister's bike.*

measles *noun*
an illness that gives you little red spots all over your skin. *Jim wasn't at school today because he has measles.*

measure measures measuring measured *verb*
when you measure something, you find out how big, tall, long, wide or heavy it is. *Angelina is being measured by Marianne.*
measurement *noun*.

meat *noun*
the part of an animal that we eat.

mechanical *adjective*
if something is mechanical, it is done, made or works by a machine. *a mechanical clock.*

medal medals *noun*
a kind of badge that somebody gives you when you win something or when you do something very brave or special. *She won a gold medal in the swimming contest.*

meddle meddles meddling meddled *verb*
if you meddle with something, you touch or move it when you have been told not to. *The teacher told us not to meddle with the computer.*

media *noun*
newspapers, radio and television.

medicine medicines *noun*
the tablets, liquid and drugs a doctor gives you when you are ill to make you feel better.

medium *adjective*
not large or small but a size in between. *Do you want a small, medium or large T-shirt?*

meet meets meeting met *verb*
when you meet somebody, you go to the same place at the same time as them. *Meet me at the gym at 3 o'clock.*
meeting *noun*.

melody melodies *noun*
a tune that you sing or play on a musical instrument.

melon melons *noun*
a big, round, yellow or green fruit with lots of seeds inside.

melt melts melting melted *verb*
when something melts, it changes into a liquid. *Flora's ice-cream is beginning to melt in the sunshine.*

member members *noun*
a person who belongs to something such as a club or a sports team. *Ben is a member of the school football team.*

memorize memorizes memorizing memorized *verb*
to memorize is to learn something so that you can remember it exactly. *Have you memorized all the names of the players in the team?*

memory memories *noun*
1 being able to remember things. *It is easy to learn spellings, if you have a good memory.*
2 your memories are the things that happened to you a long time ago and that you can still remember. *My grandmother has lots of happy memories of her childhood.*
3 the part of a computer where it stores information.

men plural of man.

mend mends mending mended *verb*
when you mend something that is broken, you make it useful again. *Katie is mending her bike.*

mental *adjective*
if something is mental, it is in your mind or you do it in your mind. *mental arithmetic.*

mention mentions mentioning mentioned *verb*
if you mention something, you say a little bit about it. *Did Ben mention where they were going?*

menu menus *noun*
1 a list of things that you can eat in a café or restaurant.
2 a list on a computer that tells you what you can do.

mercury *noun*
a metal that has a silver colour and is usually liquid. Mercury is used in thermometers.

mercy *noun*
if you show mercy to somebody, you do not hurt them or punish them.

mermaid mermaids *noun*
a sea creature in stories that has the head and body of a woman and the tail of a fish.

merry merrier merriest *adjective*
happy and full of fun. *Merry Christmas!*

mess *noun*
things are a mess when they are dirty or not where they belong. *Your bedroom is in a mess – please tidy it up!* ■ The opposite is **neat**.
messy *adjective*.

message messages *noun*
words that you say or write when the person you want to speak to is not there. *Tom isn't in. Leave a message for him.*

messenger messengers *noun*
a person who brings a message. *We sent a messenger to get help.*

met past of meet.

metal metals *noun*
a hard material that is used for making things such as cars and aeroplanes. Metal goes soft or liquid when it is heated. Silver, iron and copper are different kinds of metals.

meteor meteors *noun*
a piece of rock or metal that travels in space and burns when it nears the Earth.

meteorite meteorites *noun*
a piece of rock or metal from space that has landed on the Earth.

meter meters *noun*
an instrument that measures how much gas, electricity or water has been used. *a gas meter.* ◆ *a parking meter.*

method methods *noun*
a way of doing something. Baking, frying and boiling are methods of cooking.

metre metres *noun*
a measure of length. There are 100 centimetres in a metre. The short way of writing metre is 'm'.

metric *adjective*
metres, litres and kilograms are all part of the metric system.

mice plural of mouse.

microphone microphones *noun*
an instrument that is used to record sound or to make sounds louder than they really are. *She sang with a microphone.*

microscope microscopes *noun*
an instrument that makes very small things look much bigger. *We looked at the insect under the microscope.*

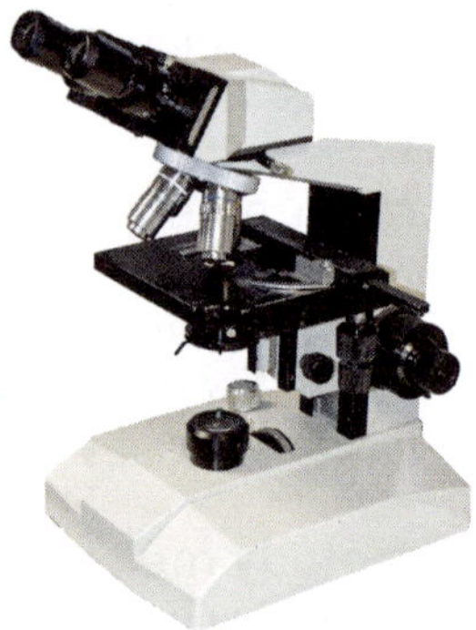

microwave oven microwave ovens *noun*
a kind of oven that cooks food very quickly using waves called electromagnetic waves.

midday *noun*
twelve o'clock in the middle of the day. ■ The opposite is **midnight**.

middle *noun*
the part of something that is not near the outside edges. *There is a vase of flowers in the middle of the table.*

midnight *noun*
twelve o'clock in the middle of the night. ■ The opposite is **midday** or **noon**.

migrate migrates migrating migrated *verb*
when birds and animals migrate, they move to another country for part of the year so that they can find food. Some British birds migrate to Africa for the winter.
migration *noun*.

milk *noun*
the white liquid that mothers and female mammals make in their bodies to feed their babies. People drink the milk that cows make.
milky *adjective*.

mill mills *noun*
1 a building where a machine grinds grain into flour.
2 a factory for making things such as steel, paper, or materials such as wool or cotton.
3 a small tool that grinds or crushes things. *a pepper mill.*

millionaire millionaires *noun*
a very rich person who has more than a million pounds or dollars, or 10 lakh rupees.

mime mimes miming mimed *verb*
if you mime something, you use actions but you do not speak. *Tom mimed blowing up a balloon and we had to guess what he was doing.*

mind minds *noun*
your mind is the part of you that thinks, feels, learns and remembers things.

mind minds minding minded *verb*
1 if you mind something, you feel unhappy or angry about it. *"Do you mind if I borrow your bike?" "No. I don't."*
2 to mind also means to be careful of something. *Mind the steps!*

mine mines *noun*
a place where people dig under the ground to get things such as coal, gold or diamonds. *a saltmine.*

mineral minerals *noun*
minerals are things such as coal, gold, salt or oil that are found in rocks or under the ground.

miniature miniatures *noun*
a very small copy of something much bigger.
miniature *adjective*.
miniature furniture. ▲ Say **min-i-cher**.

minimum *noun*
the smallest amount you can have of something. *We need a minimum of four people to play this game.*
minimum *adjective*.
Eighteen is the minimum age for driving. ■ The opposite is **maximum**.

minister ministers *noun*
1 a person who holds services in a church.
2 an important person in the government. *the Minister of Education.*

minor *adjective*
not very serious or important. *a minor injury.* ■ The opposite is **major**.

mint *noun*
1 a plant called a herb. It is used to add flavour to things such as meat, toothpaste and sweets. *mint chocolate.*
2 a sweet with a strong mint flavour. *peppermints.*
3 the place where coins are made.

minus *noun, preposition*
1 you use the minus sign (-) to show that you have taken one number away from another. *Seven minus four is three (7 – 4 = 3).*
2 minus also means below zero. *The temperature was minus ten degrees.*

minute minutes *noun*
a measure of time. There are 60 seconds in a minute and 60 minutes in an hour. ▲ Say ***min**-it.*

minute *adjective*
very, very small. *a minute insect.* ▲ Say ***my**-nyoot.*

miracle miracles *noun*
a wonderful thing that happens that seems impossible and that you cannot explain. *It would be a miracle if pigs could fly.* ▲ *Say **mir**-i-kul.*

mirror mirror *noun*
a piece of special glass that you can see yourself in. Mirrors reflect light.

mischief *noun*
naughty or annoying behaviour. **mischievous** *adjective. Mike played a mischievous trick on his uncle.*

miserable *adjective*
if you are miserable, you feel very unhappy or sad. *Katie is miserable because she can't go on holiday.*

miss misses missing missed *verb*
1 if you miss a ball, you do not hit or catch it.
2 if you miss a bus or a train, you are not there in time to catch it.
3 if you miss somebody, you are sad because they are not there. *I really missed my friend when he moved houses.*

mist mists *noun*
a low cloud of tiny drops of water that is difficult to see through. *In the early morning, the fields were covered in mist.*

mistake mistakes *noun*
something that you do wrong. *I only made one spelling mistake.*

mix mixes mixing mixed *verb*
1 when you mix things, you stir them or put them together so that sometimes they make something new. *If you mix blue and red paint, you get purple.* ◆ *Oil and water do not mix.*
2 when people mix, they come together and talk to each other. *I mix with lots of different people at school.*

mixture mixtures *noun*
something that is made when two or more things are mixed together. *Butter, flour and sugar go into this cake mixture.*

moan moans moaning moaned *verb*
1 if you moan, you keep talking in a cross way about something that you do not like. *He was moaning about having to tidy his room.*
2 when a person or an animal moans, they make a low, sad sound because they are in pain or unhappy. *The dog was moaning because it was shut in the car.*

mobile *adjective*
if something is mobile, it can move or you can move it easily. *a mobile phone.*

mock mocks mocking mocked *verb*
if you mock somebody or something, you make fun of them.

model models *noun*
1 a small copy of something. *a model ship.*
2 a person who sits or stands so that an artist can draw them.
3 a person who wears new clothes so that people can see what the clothes look like before they buy them.

modern *adjective*
new or happening now. *We live in a modern house.*

modest *adjective*
if you are modest, you do not boast about how good or clever you are.

moist *adjective*
damp or a little wet. *The ground was moist after the rain.*
moisten *verb.*

moisture *noun*
small drops of water on something or in the air.

mole moles *noun*
a small animal with dark fur that lives under the ground and digs tunnels with its strong claws. Where moles have been digging they leave piles of earth called molehills.

moment moments *noun*
a very short time. *I'll be back in a moment.*

money *noun*
the coins and notes that we use to buy things with.

mongrel mongrels *noun*
a dog whose mother and father are of different breeds.

monk monks *noun*
monks are a group of men who obey rules and live and pray together in a building called a monastery because of the religion they believe in.

monkey monkeys *noun*
an animal with long arms and legs and a long tail that lives mainly in trees in hot countries.

monster monsters *noun*
a big, frightening creature that you read about in stories.

month months *noun*
a measure of time. There are twelve months in a year. *January is the first month of the year.*
monthly *adjective, adverb.*
a monthly magazine.

monument monuments *noun*
a large statue or building that people have made to remember an important person or event. *Nelson's Column is a famous monument in London.*

mood moods *noun*
the way that you feel at different times. *Ben was in an angry mood today, but Katie was in a cheerful mood.*

moon moons *noun*
the Moon is a small satellite that travels around the Earth once every four weeks. You can often see it in the sky at night.

mop mops *noun*
a mop is a tool with a long handle for washing floors. It is made of sponge or bundles of cloth.

moor moors *noun*
an open area, often covered with grass and a spiky, low-growing plant called heather.

morning mornings *noun*
the early part of the day before midday. *What time do you get up in the morning?*

mosque mosques *noun*
a building where Muslims go to pray.
▲ Say ***mosk***.

mosquito mosquitoes *noun*
a small, flying insect that lives in hot, wet places. Female mosquitoes bite people and animals. People can get a serious illness called malaria from mosquito bites.
▲ Say *mos-**kee**-toe*.

moss mosses *noun*
a soft, green plant that grows like a carpet on trees and damp ground.

moth moths *noun*
an insect that looks like a butterfly but that usually flies around at night.

Buff ermine moth

Cinnabar moth

Common emperor moth

mother mothers *noun*
a woman who has children.

motion *noun*
movement or the way of moving. *The motion of the boat on the rough sea made him feel sick.*

motor motors *noun*
the part inside a machine that makes it move or work. Fridges and washing machines have electric motors.

motorbike motorbikes *noun*
a kind of bicycle with an engine.

motorway motorways *noun*
a long, wide road where cars, lorries and coaches can go fast. You cannot walk or ride a bike along a motorway.

mould moulds *noun*
1 the green or grey fungus that grows on food that has gone bad. *This cheese is covered in mould.*
2 a container for making things into a certain shape. *a jelly mould in the shape of a mouse.*

mountain mountains *noun*
a very high piece of ground. The highest mountain in the world is Mount Everest.

mouse mice *noun*
1 a small furry animal with sharp teeth and a long tail. Mice are rodents.
2 a small instrument on your desk that you use to make the cursor on your computer screen move.

moustache moustaches *noun*
hair that grows above a man's top lip.
▲ Say *mus-**tash***.

mouth mouths *noun*
1 the part of your face that you open and close to talk and eat.
2 the mouth of a cave is the way into it.
3 the mouth of a river is the place where it enters the sea.

move moves moving moved *verb*
1 when you move, you go from one place to another. *Don't move, I want to take your photograph.*
2 if you move something, you put it in another place. *We moved the piano into the sitting room.*
movement *noun.*

mow mows mowing mowed *verb*
when you mow grass, you cut it with a machine called a lawnmower.
▲ Rhymes with ***low***.

Musical instruments

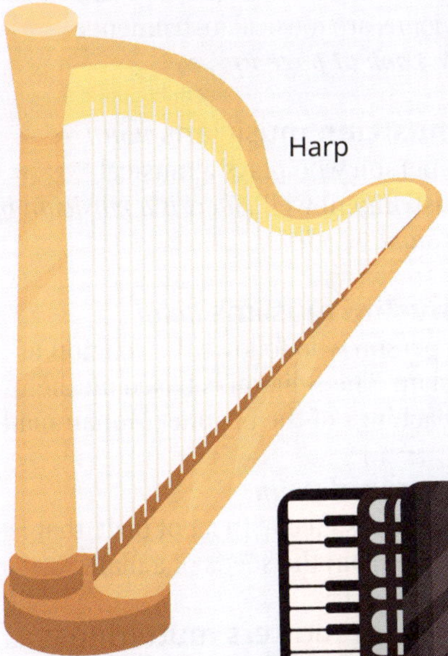
Harp

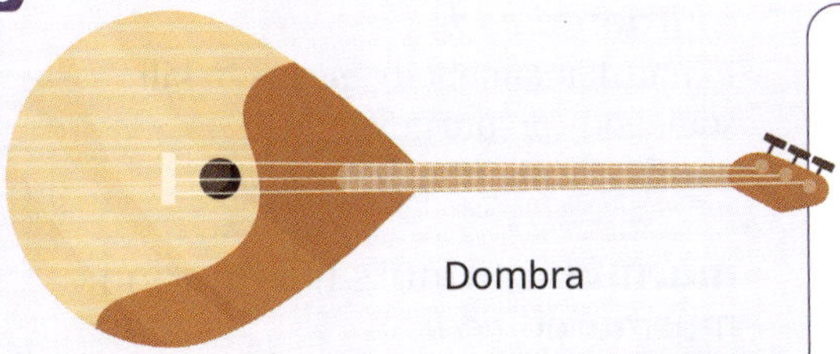
Dombra

Melodica

Accordian

Drum

Violin

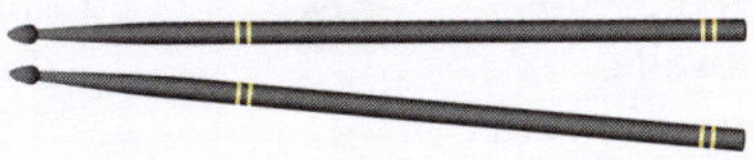
Drumsticks

Guitar

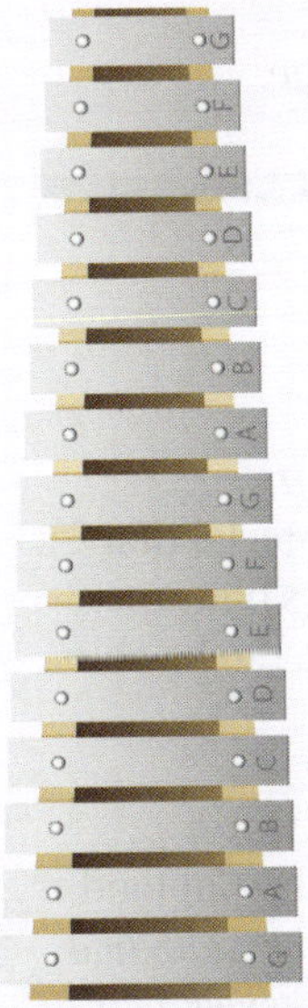
Xylophone

Snare drum

Maracas

Half moon tambourine

Vocabulary

brass
metal wind instruments that you play by making your lips vibrate. Horns, trumpets and trombones are brass instruments.

keyboard
instruments with keys that you press to make notes. Pianos, harpsichords, organs and synthesizers are keyboard instruments.

percussion
instruments that are struck to produce a sound. Cymbals and drums are percussion instruments.

strings
instruments with tightly stretched strings that you pluck or stroke with a bow. Cellos, guitars and violins are string instruments.

wind instruments
they work by making a column of air vibrate inside a tube.

woodwind
wind instruments with holes along the tube that change the note.

A B C D E F G H I J K L M N O P Q R S T U V W X Y Z

mud *noun*
soft, wet earth. *After playing football, Tom was covered in mud.*
muddy *adjective.*

muddle muddles muddling muddled *verb*
1 if you muddle things, you make them untidy. *Don't muddle up my clothes!*
2 if somebody muddles you, they mix things up so that you cannot understand them. *My teacher muddles me when she asks so many questions.*
muddle *noun.*

mug mugs *noun*
a big, tall cup that you use without a saucer. *a mug of hot coffee.*

multiply multiplies multiplying multiplied *verb*
when you multiply a number, you add the number to itself several times. Four multiplied by three is twelve (4 + 4 + 4 = 12, or 4 x 3 = 12). ■ The opposite is **divide**.
multiplication *noun.*

munch munches munching munched *verb*
when you munch something hard, you bite and chew it in a noisy way. *Ben was munching an apple.*

murder murders murdering murdered *verb*
to murder somebody means to kill somebody on purpose.
murder *noun,* **murderer** *noun.*

murmur murmurs murmuring murmured *verb*
if you murmur, you say something softly and quietly.
murmur *noun.*

muscle muscles *noun*
your muscles are the parts inside your body that stretch so that you can bend and move. Muscles are attached to your bones.
muscular *noun.*

museum museums *noun*
a building where lots of interesting things are kept for people to look at. *We saw a model of a dinosaur at the museum.*

mushroom mushrooms *noun*
a small plant without leaves that looks like a tiny umbrella. People eat some kinds of mushrooms, though some are poisonous. A mushroom is a fungus.

music *noun*
the sounds that come from somebody singing or playing a musical instrument, like a piano, flute or guitar.
musical *adjective.*

musical instrument musical instruments *noun*
something that you play to make music. Violins are musical instruments.
❖ ***Look at page 105***

musician musicians *noun*
a person who plays a musical instrument well. *Sheri is a musician in a band.*

muslim muslims *noun*
a person who follows the religion of Islam. The religion is based on the teachings of the prophet Muhammad.

mustard *noun*
a yellow sauce with a hot taste that is made from the seeds of a plant.

mutter mutters muttering muttered *verb*
if you mutter, you speak in a quiet and angry way. *"I don't want to go home," she muttered.*

muzzle muzzles *noun*
1 the nose and mouth of an animal such as a dog or a fox.
2 something that you can put over a dog's mouth to stop it from biting.

mystery mysteries *noun*
something strange that has happened and that you cannot explain.

myth myths *noun*
1 a very old story with a special meaning. *Greek myths are about gods and goddesses.*
2 a story that is not true.

N n

nail nails *noun*
1 a thin piece of metal with one pointed end and a flat end, like a very large pin. *She's hammering a nail into the wall to hang the picture on.*
2 your nails are the hard part at the end of your fingers and toes.

naked *adjective*
with no clothes on. ▲ Say ***nay-kid.***

name names *noun*
the word we use to call somebody or something. *The dog's name is Scooby.*

nap naps *noun*
a short sleep.

nappy nappies *noun*
a thick piece of soft material that you put around a baby's bottom when they are too young to be able to go to the toilet.

narrator narrators *noun*
a person who tells a story out loud or explains to somebody. *Anupama was the narrator for the school play.*
▲ Say *na-**rate**-or.*

narrow narrower narrowest *adjective*
if something is narrow, it is thin and does not measure very much from one side to the other.
■ The opposite is **broad** or **wide**.
narrowness *noun*.

nasty nastier nastiest *adjective*
1 horrible or not nice. *a nasty smell.*
2 unkind or cruel. *He was really nasty to me.*
nastily *adverb*, **nastiness** *noun*.

nation nations *noun*
a country with its own laws and government. The people of a nation share the same history and language.

national *adjective*
to do with the whole of a nation or the people in a nation. *the national news.*

natural *adjective*
if something is natural, it is made by nature and not by human beings. *the natural beauty of the Scottish mountains.* ■ The opposite is **artificial**.
naturally *adverb*.

nature *noun*
animals, plants and all the things that are not made by human beings. ▲ Say ***nay**-cher*.

naughty naughtier naughtiest *adjective*
if you are naughty, you have behaved badly or done something you should not have done. *"You naughty girl, stop hitting your brother!"* ▲ Say ***nor**-tee*.

navigate navigates navigating navigated *verb*
if you navigate a ship or aircraft, you find out and say which way to go.

navy navies *noun*
the ships and the sailors that are used to defend a country or fight an enemy.

near nearer nearest *adjective, preposition*
close by or a short distance from something or somebody. *Where's the nearest underground station?* ◆ *In the picture, I'm standing near the statue.*
■ The opposite is **far**.

nearly *adverb*
almost but not quite. *She nearly won.*

neat neater neatest *adjective*
clean and tidy with everything in its proper place. ■ The opposite is **messy**.

necessary *adjective*
if something is necessary, it is needed or has to happen. *It is necessary to have a passport when you go abroad.*
necessarily *adverb*.

neck necks *noun*
the part of a person or animal that joins their head to their body. *The giraffe has a very long neck.*

necklace necklaces *noun*
a piece of jewellery such as a chain that you wear around your neck.

nectar *noun*
a sweet liquid in flowers that insects collect and that bees make into honey.

need needs needing needed *verb*
if you need something, you have to have it in order to live or to do a job. *People and animals need air and water or they die.* ◆ *I need some more green thread to finish my embroidery.*

needle needles *noun*
1 a thin, pointed piece of metal with a hole at one end for thread that is used for sewing.
2 a long, thin stick used for knitting.
3 a long, thin leaf on a pine tree.
4 a short tube with a thin, sharp point at one end that doctors use to give injections.

negative *adjective*
1 meaning "no". *She gave a negative answer.*
2 A negative number is less than zero. *-20.* ■ The opposite is **positive**

negative *noun*
film from a camera from which photographs are printed.

neglect neglects neglecting neglected *verb*
1 if you neglect something or somebody, you do not look after them and give them the time and attention they need. *He neglected the garden.*
2 to fail to do something. *He neglected to answer the letter.*

neighbour neighbours *noun*
a person who lives near or next to you. *We have very friendly neighbours.* ▲ Say ***nay**-ber*.

neighbourhood neighbourhoods *noun*
the area where you live. *I've lived in this neighbourhood all my life.* ▲ Say ***nay**-ber-hood*.

nephew nephews *noun*
the son of your brother or sister.
▲ Say ***nef**-yoo*.

nerve nerves *noun*
1 your nerves are the long, thin parts inside your body that link your brain to other parts of your body. They carry the messages to and from your brain that make your body move and feel.
2 it may be used to refer to someone's ability to be brave and calm when something is difficult or frightening.

nervous *adjective*
1 worried about something that is going to happen. *I'm nervous about the test.*
2 easily frightened. *a nervous horse.*
■ The opposite is **calm**.

nest nests *noun*
a home made by birds, squirrels, wasps and other animals for their babies.

net nets *noun*
material made of thread, string or rope joined with knots so as to leave small holes between.

netball *noun*
a game played by two teams of seven players who have to try to get a ball through a big, round net at each end of the court.

nettle nettles *noun*
a wild plant with hairy leaves that sting you if you touch them.

network networks *noun*
1 a system of things that are connected at many different points. *the railway network.*
2 a company or group of companies that broadcast the same radio or television programmes.

never *adverb*
at no time ever in the past or the future. *He is a beautiful horse but he has never won a race.*

new newer newest *adjective*
1 if something is new, it has only just been made, or you have only just bought it. *I got some new games for my birthday.*
2 different from somebody or something you knew before. *We've got a new head teacher.* ■ The opposite is **old**.

news *noun*
information about what is going on or has just happened.

newspaper newspapers *noun*
sheets of folded paper that have news stories and pictures and other information printed on them.

newt newts *noun*
a small amphibian with short legs and a long tail that lays its eggs in water.

nib nibs *noun*
the pointed part of a pen that touches the paper when you write.

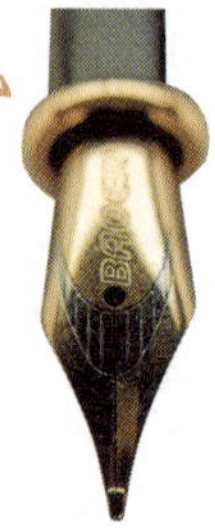

nibble nibbles nibbling nibbled *verb*
if you nibble, you eat something slowly, taking very small bites of it.

nice

Some words you can use instead of nice:

We had a nice supper.
delicious, tasty

The nice woman next door.
kind, friendly, likeable

We had a nice time on our holiday.
enjoyable, pleasant, wonderful

What nice weather we are having.
good, fine, beautiful, mild

nice nicer nicest *adjective*
1 if you think something is nice, you like it or enjoy it.
2 kind and easy to like. *a nice person.*

nickname nicknames *noun*
a short or special name that people call you instead of your real name.

niece nieces *noun*
the daughter of your brother or sister. ▲ Say ***nees***.

night nights *noun*
the time when it is dark and most people are asleep. ■ The opposite is **day**. ● A word that sounds like **night** is **knight**.

nightmare nightmares *noun*
a frightening dream.

nocturnal *adjective*
awake and active mostly at night rather than during the day. *The owl is a nocturnal creature.*

nod nods nodding nodded *verb*
when you nod, you move your head up and down to show you agree with something or to say "yes".

noise noises *noun*
1 a sound. *I heard a strange noise.*
2 sounds that are too loud and unpleasant. *Please stop making so much noise!* ■ The opposite is **silence**.
noisily *adverb*, **noisy** *adjective*.

noodle noodles *noun*
a long, thin strip of pasta. *Domenic loves to eat a big bowl of noodles.*

noon *noun*
twelve o'clock in the middle of the day.
■ The opposite is **midnight**.

noose nooses *noun*
a loop made in rope with a special knot so that when you pull on the rope the noose gets smaller.

normal *adjective*
ordinary, the same as usual. *Cold weather is normal in winter.* ■ The opposite is **abnormal**.
normally *adverb*.
I normally go to bed at 10 o'clock.

north *noun*
a direction that is to your left if you face the sun as it is rising in the morning. ■ The opposite is **south**.
north *adjective*, **northern** *adjective*.
a north wind. ◆ *a northern accent.*

nose noses *noun*
your nose is the part sticking out in the middle of your face that you use for breathing and smelling. At the end of your nose there are two holes called nostrils.
❖ ***Look opposite***

Different types of noses

Elephant seal
Elephant
Probiscus monkey
Mandrill
Spear-nosed bat
Snow leopard

note notes *noun*
1 a few words that you write down to remind yourself of something. *I've made a note of your phone number.*
2 a short letter. *I'll send a note to the school to explain that you have to go to the dentist.*
3 a single sound in music or a symbol written to show a sound.
4 a piece of paper money. *He paid with a ₹10 note.*

notice notices noticing noticed *verb*
if you notice something, you start to see it or hear it or smell it. *I suddenly noticed that there were lots of people in the garden.*

notice notices *noun*
a written message that is put in a public place so that many people can read it.

nought *noun*
the number 0. ▲ Say ***nort***.

noun nouns *noun*
a word that gives the name of a thing, a state, a feeling, an idea, a person or a place. *Table, talent, happiness, sadness, Ben and London are all nouns.*

nourishment *noun*
food that is good for you and makes you strong and healthy. ▲ Say ***nur-ish-ment***.
nourishing *adjective*.

novel novels *noun*
a long written story that has been made up by somebody about people and events that do not really exist.
novelist *noun*.

nude *adjective*
without any clothes, naked.

nudge nudges nudging nudged *verb*
if you nudge somebody, you push them with your elbow to make them notice something.

nuisance nuisances *noun*
a person or something that annoys you. ▲ Say ***new-sense***.

numb *adjective*
unable to feel anything in a part of your body. *It was so cold my feet went numb.* ▲ Say ***num***.

number numbers *noun*
a word or sign that shows you how many of something there are.

numerous *adjective*
very many. *Numerous people were invited.*
■ The opposite is **few**.

nun nuns *noun*
nuns are a group of women who obey rules and live and pray together in a building called a convent because of the religion they believe in.

Spelling tip:
Some words that begin with an "n" sound are spelt with "gn" or "kn" such as gnat, gnome, knee.

nurse nurses *noun*
a person whose job is to look after people who are ill or injured.

nursery nurseries *noun*
1 a place where young children can go during the day when they are too young to start school.
2 a place where plants and flowers are grown to be sold.

nut nuts *noun*
the fruit of a tree that has a seed inside a hard shell.

a b c d e f g h i j k l m n o p q r s t u v w x y z

O o

oak oaks *noun*
1 a large tree that acorns grow on.
2 the wood from this tree.

oar oars *noun*
a long pole with one flat end that you use to row a boat. ▲ Say ***or***.

oasis oases *noun*
a place in a desert with water, plants and trees.
▲ Say *oh-**ay**-sis*.

oats *noun*
oats are plants that farmers grow for their seeds called grain.

obey obeys obeying obeyed *verb*
if you obey somebody, you do what they tell you to do. ■ The opposite is **disobey**.
obedient *adjective*.

object objects *noun*
1 a thing that you can see and touch. *The box was full of objects of all shapes and sizes.*
2 the purpose or thing that you are trying to achieve. *Her object was to win the contest.*
3 in the sentence, *"Jim hit the ball"*, the object of the sentence is "the ball".
▲ Say ***ob**-jekt*.

object objects objecting objected *verb*
if somebody objects to something, they do not like it or agree with it. *The teacher objects to noisy children.*
▲ Say *ob-**jekt***.

oblong oblongs *noun*
a shape with two long, opposite sides and two short, opposite sides.
oblong *adjective*. *The pages of this dictionary are oblong.*

observe observes observing observed *verb*
when you observe somebody or something, you watch them carefully. *We observed a bird feeding its babies.*

obstacle obstacles *noun*
something that is in your way and stops you from doing something. *The fallen tree was an obstacle in the road.*

obstinate *adjective*
an obstinate person does not like to change what they think, or do what other people want them to do. *Oliver is so obstinate that he will only do what he wants to do.*

obvious *adjective*
if something is obvious, it is easy to see or understand. *The answers to the quiz were obvious.*

occasion occasions *noun*
a time when something happens. *A wedding is an important occasion.*
◆ *We've been to Canada on many occasions.*

occasionally *adverb*
if something happens occasionally, it happens but not very often. *I usually walk to school, but occasionally I go by bicycle.*

occupant occupants *noun*
somebody who lives or works in a place.

occupy occupies occupying occupied *verb*
1 if you occupy a house, you live in it.
2 if somebody or something occupies a space, they are in it. *All the parking spaces were occupied.*
3 if you are occupied, you are busy. *I was occupied with my computer.*

occupation occupations *noun*
a job. *'What's your occupation?' 'I'm a vet.'*

occur occurs occurring occurred *verb*
1 when something occurs, it happens. *The storm occurred last night.*
2 if something occurs to you, you suddenly think about it. *It occurred to me that I had been rude to my aunt.*

ocean oceans *noun*
any of the very large areas of sea. *the Atlantic Ocean.*

octagon octagons *noun*
a shape with eight straight sides.

octopus octopuses *noun*
an animal that lives in the sea. It has eight long arms called tentacles.

odd odder oddest *adjective*
1 strange or unusual. *She was wearing a very odd hat.*
2 odd things do not belong together in a pair or a set. *I'm wearing odd socks, one is red and the other is brown.*
3 an odd number is any number that ends in 1, 3, 5, 7, or 9. You cannot divide these numbers by two without leaving something over.
■ The opposite is **even**.
4 the **odd one out** is something that is different from the rest. *Out of apple, orange, potato and banana, potato is the odd one out because it is a vegetable. All the others are fruits.*

odour odours *noun*
a strong smell. *Domenic's socks have a strong odour!*

offend offends offending offended *verb*
if you offend somebody, you upset them and hurt their feelings. *She offended me because she said I was fat.* **offence** *noun*, **offensive** *adjective. offensive behaviour.*

offer offers offering offered *verb*
1 if you offer somebody something, you ask them if they would like it. *She offered me a biscuit.*
2 if you offer to do something, you say you are willing to do it. *He offered to do the washing up.*

office offices *noun*
1 a place where people go to work. Offices have things such as desks, chairs, computers and telephones.
2 a place where you can buy something or get information. *the post office.*

officer officers *noun*
1 a person in the army, navy or air force who gives orders to other people. *an army officer.*
2 a person who does important work. *a police officer.*

official *adjective*
if something is official, it is important and people must believe it or do it. *an official report from the government.*
▲ Say *o-**fish**-al.*

oil *noun*
1 a smooth, thick liquid that comes from the ground. You can burn oil to make heat or to make machines work.
2 Oil is also a smooth liquid that comes from plants and animals. Some people use it for cooking. *olive oil.* ◆ *vegetable oil.*
oily *adjective.*

ointment *noun*
a cream that you put on a cut or sore skin to heal it.

old older oldest *adjective*
1 somebody who is old has lived for a long time. *My great grandfather is very old – he is ninety!*
2 something that is old was made a long time ago. *This castle is very old – it was built five hundred years ago.*
■ The opposite is **new**.
3 having a certain age. *My mum is thirty-five years old.*
4 something that you had or knew before. *Yesterday I saw an old friend from my old school.*

olive olives *noun*
a small green or black fruit. Olives are used to make olive oil that is used in cooking.

Olympic *adjective*
of the Olympic Games or the Olympics, international sports contests held every four years in a different country.

onion onions *noun*
a round vegetable with a strong taste and smell that grows under the ground.

only *adjective, adverb*
1 with no others. *This is the only photo I have of her.*
2 no more than. *I've only got one brother.* ◆ *It will only take five minutes to prepare the food.*
3 but. *This is a good story, only it's a bit long.*

open *adjective*
1 not closed or covered. *The dog escaped through the open gate.*
2 spread out, with the edges apart. *The book lay open on the desk.*

open opens opening opened *verb*
1 if you open a door, you let people or things go through.
2 to open means to move something so that it is not closed or covered. *Open your eyes!* ◆ *He opened the box and found a present inside.*
3 if you open a shop or office, you make it ready for people to come in. *The museum opens at nine o'clock.*
opening *noun.*

opera operas *noun*
a play where actors sing most of the words. *"The Magic Flute" is an opera by Mozart.*

operate operates operating operated *verb*
1 when surgeons operate, they take away or mend part of a patient's body to make them well again.
2 if you operate a machine, you use it or make it work. *Can you operate this computer?*

operation operations *noun*
when somebody has an operation, a surgeon takes away or mends a part of their body.

opinion opinions *noun*
what you think about something. *In my opinion, people should always be kind to animals.*

opportunity opportunities *noun*
a time or chance that is right for doing something. *On holiday, we had the opportunity to go sailing.*

opposite opposites *noun*
something that is different from another thing in every way. *Bad is the opposite of good.*

A B C D E F G H I J K L M N O P Q R S T U V W X Y Z

opposite *adjective, adverb*
1 different in every way. *North is in the opposite direction to South.*
2 across or on the other side. *The women stood opposite each other.*

optician opticians *noun*
a person who tests your eyes to see if you need glasses.

orbit orbits *noun*
the invisible path that something such as a planet or a spaceship follows as it travels around the Earth, another planet or the Sun.
orbit *verb*.

orchard orchards *noun*
an area of land where fruit trees grow.

orchestra orchestras *noun*
a group of people who play different musical instruments together.
▲ Say ***or**-kes-tra*.

order orders *noun*
1 order means the way that things follow one another. *The letters of the alphabet always come in the same order.*
2 an order is something that you must do because somebody tells you to do it. *The officer gave the soldier an order to march.*

order orders ordering ordered *verb*
1 if you order something, you say you would like to have it. *We ordered bacon, sausages and eggs.*
2 if you order somebody to do something, you say that they must do it. *The doctor ordered Tom to stay in bed for a week.*

ordinary *adjective*
not exciting or special. *Yesterday was my birthday, but today is just an ordinary day.*

organ organs *noun*
1 an organ is a part of your body that does something special. Your heart, liver and kidneys are all organs.
2 a big musical instrument like a piano with pipes that air goes through to make sounds. *a church organ.*

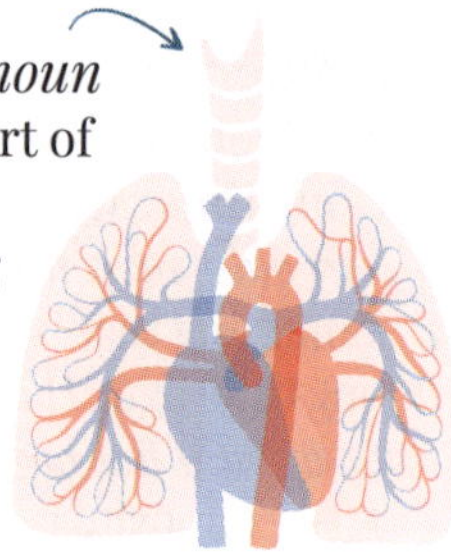

organization organizations *noun*
a group of people who work together.

organize organizes organizing organized *verb*
if you organize something you arrange or plan it. *The school has organized a trip to London.*

origin origins *noun*
1 the beginning of something and how and why it began. *We are learning about the origins of life on Earth.*
2 where somebody or something came from. *a vase of ancient Greek origin.*

original *adjective*
1 something that is original is the first to be made. *This is an original painting. All the others are copies.*
2 different and exciting. *What an original idea!*

ornament ornaments *noun*
an object that you like and use to make a place look pretty. *china ornaments.*

orphan orphans *noun*
a child whose mother and father are dead.

ostrich ostriches *noun*
a very large bird with long legs and a long neck that lives in Africa. Ostriches can run fast, but they cannot fly.

otter otters *noun*
a small animal with brown fur. Otters can swim well and catch fish to eat.

ought *verb*
if you ought to do something, you should do it because it is important. *You ought to clean your teeth before you go to bed.*

outdoors *noun*
the open air or outside a building. *The outdoors is the best place to practise the violin!* ■ The opposite is **indoors**.

outer *adjective*
1 not in the middle of a place. *I live in outer London.*
2 the outside of something. *His outer clothes were covered with mud.*
■ The opposite is **inner**.

outing outings *noun*
a short trip that you go on to enjoy yourself. *We had an outing to the seaside.*

outline outlines *noun*
1 a line around the edge of something that shows its shape. *As it grew dark, we could just see the outline of the house against the sky.*
2 a drawing where you just draw a line to show the shape of something. *Tom drew the outline of a car.*

oval ovals *noun*
an oval is a shape like an egg.
oval *adjective*.
an oval rugby ball.

oven ovens *noun*
the part like a box inside a cooker where you cook food. *Chris baked a chocolate cake in the oven.*

overalls *noun*
clothes that you wear to keep your other clothes clean when you do things such as painting.

overflow overflows overflowing overflowed *verb*
if something like a bath overflows, the water comes over the top of it. *I forgot to turn off the taps and the basin is overflowing!*

overgrown *adjective*
if a garden is overgrown, it is covered with weeds and the plants look untidy.

overhead *adjective, adverb*
above your head. *an overhead light.* ◆ *A plane flew overhead.*

overhear overhears overhearing overheard *verb*
when you overhear something, you hear what somebody says when they are speaking to someone else. *Jessie overheard Rachel and Sarah talking.*

overlap overlaps overlapping overlapped *verb*
when two things overlap, part of one thing covers part of the other thing. *The tiles on the roof overlap.*

overtake overtakes overtaking overtook overtaken *verb*
when drivers overtake, they pass a car, a bus or a lorry that is going slowly. *The car overtook a bus.*

owe owes owing owed *verb*
if you owe money, you have to give the money back to the person who lent it to you. *I owe you ₹50 for the sweets.*

owl owls *noun*
a bird with large eyes that can see well in the dark and hunts small animals, such as mice, at night.

own owns owning owned *verb*
if you own something, you have something that belongs to you. *Do you own that bike or did you borrow it?*

owner owners *noun*
a person who has or owns something. *Who is the owner of this pencil case?*

ox oxen *noun*
a bull that is used in some countries for pulling carts.

oxygen *noun*
a gas in the air we breathe. People, animals and plants need oxygen to live and things cannot burn without it.

oyster oysters *noun*
a sea animal that lives inside a pair of shells. A few oysters produce a pearl inside their shells.

ozone *noun*
a gas in the air. The ozone layer around the Earth protects us from the harmful rays of the sun.
ozone friendly not harmful to the ozone layer. *We buy only ozone friendly aerosols.*

P p

pace *noun*
the speed at which something happens or moves. *They started off at a fast pace.*

pack packs packing packed *verb*
when you pack, you put clothes and other things you need in a case or container to take away with you.

package packages *noun*
a parcel.

packet packets **noun**
a box, bag or envelope containing things. *a packet of cornflakes.* ◆ *a seed packet.*

pad pads *noun*
1 a thick piece of soft material that can be used to protect something.
2 a lot of pieces of paper to write or draw on that are fixed together at one edge.
3 the soft part on the underneath of an animal's paw.

paddle paddles paddling paddled *verb*
1 if you paddle, you walk in the shallow water at the edge of the sea or a lake.
2 when you paddle a canoe, you move it through the water.

paddle paddles *noun*
a short, flat oar for a boat or canoe. *Hold the paddle in both hands.*

padlock padlocks *noun*
a small, metal block with a bar in the shape of a U at the top which you can use to lock things such as gates and bicycles.

page pages *noun*
one side of a piece of paper in a book or newspaper. *This dictionary has lots of pages.*

paid past of pay.

pain *noun*
the feeling that you have in a part of your body when it hurts. *I have a bad headache and a stomach pain as well.*
● A word that sounds like **pain** is **pane**.

painful *adjective*
when something is painful, it hurts a lot. *I fell over and my knee is quite painful.*
painfully *adverb.*

paint paints *noun*
a liquid that you use to make coloured pictures or to give a new colour to the walls and ceilings in a house.
paint *verb.*
I am going to paint a picture.

painter painters *noun*
1 a person whose job is to put paint on walls, doors and window frames.
2 an artist who paints pictures. *Monet was a French painter.*

painting paintings *noun*
a picture made using paint. *She was painting in the garden.*

pair pairs *noun*
1 two things that go together or that you use together. *a pair of gloves.*
2 we also talk about pairs of things such as trousers, scissors or binoculars that have two identical parts joined together. ● A word that sounds like **pair** is **pear**.

palace palaces *noun*
a large building for somebody very important to live in. *The king lives in Buckingham Palace.*

pale paler palest *adjective*
something that is pale is almost white. *pale blue.* ■ The opposite is **dark**.

palm palms *noun*
1 a tree with no branches but that has long leaves that grow from the top of the trunk. *Palm trees grow where the weather is hot.*
2 the flat part inside your hand between your wrist and your fingers.
▲ Say ***parm***.

Coconut palm

European fan palm

Date palm

pan pans *noun*
a container with a handle that you use for cooking food in. *a frying-pan.*

pancake pancakes *noun*
a thin, flat cake made from flour, eggs and milk that is fried in a pan in hot oil.

panda pandas *noun*
a large animal that looks like a black and white bear. *Pandas live in China and are very rare.*

Panda

Red Panda

pane panes *noun*
a flat piece of glass. *a window pane.* ● A word that sounds like **pane** is **pain**.

panel panels *noun*
a long, flat piece of wood or glass that is part of a door or fence.

panic panics panicking panicked *verb*
if you panic, you feel so worried or afraid that you do not know what to do and you cannot act or think in a sensible or calm way. **panic** *noun*.

pant pants panting panted *verb*
if a person or animal pants, they breathe quickly with their mouth open. *Dogs pant to cool themselves when they get hot.*

panther panthers *noun*
a black leopard.

pantomime pantomimes *noun*
a traditional Christmas show for children, with songs, jokes and dancing. The stories for pantomimes are taken from fairy tales.

pants *noun*
a piece of clothing joined at the top that covers the lower part of the body from the waist to the foot. Pants have two holes for your legs.

paper *noun*
1 thin material that you use for writing on or wrapping things in, and that books and newspapers are printed on.
2 a newspaper.

parable parables *noun*
a story that teaches people something.

parachute parachutes *noun*
a large piece of cloth fixed to a person, with ropes that open up like an umbrella so that a person can jump from a plane and float safely to the ground. ▲ Say ***par**-a-shoot.*

parade parades *noun*
a lot of people marching along, often with decorated vehicles and music to celebrate something special. *The Indian Republic Day parade is a spectacle to watch.*

paragraph paragraphs *noun*
several sentences about the same idea that are written or printed together. The first sentence of a paragraph starts on a new line. ▲ Say ***par**-a-grarf* or ***par**-a-graf.*

parallel *adjective*
parallel lines are straight and always the same distance from each other. *Railway lines are parallel.*

paralysed *adjective*
if part of somebody's body is paralysed, they cannot move it or feel anything in it. *She is paralysed from the waist down and moves around in a wheelchair.*

parcel parcels *noun*
something that is wrapped in paper so that it can be sent through the post.

parchment *noun*
a material made from the skin of a sheep or goat that was used for writing on in the past.

pardon pardons pardoning pardoned *verb*
if you pardon somebody, you forgive them. *The judge pardoned the criminal.*

parent parents *noun*
a mother or a father.

park parks *noun*
an area of land, usually in a town, with grass and plants where people can go to walk and children can play.

park parks parking parked *verb*
when you park a car, you leave it somewhere until you need it again.

parliament parliaments *noun*
a group of elected people who meet to discuss or make new laws for a country.
▲ Say ***par**-li-ment*.

parrot parrots *noun*
a tropical bird with brightly coloured feathers and a curved beak. Parrots can be taught to copy human speech.

part parts *noun*
1 one piece or bit of something.
2 if you have a part in a play, you act as one of the characters in the play.

part parts parting parted *verb*
1 to divide. *hair parted in the middle.*
2 to separate. *We parted at the crossroads.*

particular *adjective*
a particular thing or person is the one that you specially mean and not anything or anybody else. *I don't want any old kitten, I want that particular one over there.*

partner partners *noun*
a partner is somebody who does something with another person. *She's my partner when we go dancing.*

party parties *noun*
1 a group of people who get together to have fun. *a birthday party.*
2 a group of people who have the same ideas about politics. *The Democratic Party.* ◆ *The Socialist Party.*

pass passes passing passed *verb*
1 if you pass something, you go by it without stopping.
2 if you pass an exam, you do it well enough to succeed.
3 if you pass something to somebody, you give or hand it to them. *Pass me that pair of scissors, please.*
● A word that sounds like **passed** is **past**.

pass passes *noun*
a ticket or card that allows you to do something, such as travel free or enter a building.

passage passages *noun*
a narrow place with walls on each side like a corridor.

passenger passengers *noun*
a person who is travelling in a vehicle but not driving it.

passport passports *noun*
a small book or document that you take when you travel to another country, that shows who you are and what country you come from.

password passwords *noun*
a secret word that you have to know to get into a place or, sometimes, to be able to work on a computer.

past *noun*
the time up until now. *In the past there were no televisions and computers.* ■ The opposite is **future**.
● A word that sounds like **past** is **passed**.

past *preposition*
farther on than something, or after it. *Go past the church and then turn left.*
● A word that sounds like **past** is **passed**.

pasta *noun*
a food made from flour that is formed into different shapes. Spaghetti and macaroni are kinds of pasta.

paste *noun*
1 a thick, soft glue.
2 a thick, soft mixture of food.

pastel pastels *noun*
a stick of coloured pigment that you use for drawing.

pastime pastimes *noun*
a hobby or sport that you do when you are not working.

pastry *noun*
a mixture of flour, fat and water that is rolled, cooked and used for making pies.

pasture pastures *noun*
a field with grass for animals such as cows and sheep to eat.

pat pats patting patted *verb*
if you pat something, you hit it gently with your hand. *He patted the dog.*

patch patches *noun*
1 a piece of material that you put over a hole to mend it. *His jeans have patches on the knee.*
2 a small area that is different from the rest. *a patch of white fur.*

path paths *noun*
a narrow piece of ground where people can walk to get somewhere. *There's a path across the field.*

patience *noun*
if you have patience, you stay calm when something takes a long time or is very difficult. ▲ Say ***pay**-shens*.

patient *adjective*
if you are patient, you stay calm and do not complain when something takes a long time.
▲ Say ***pay**-shent*. ■ The opposite is **impatient**.
patiently *adverb*.

patient patients *noun*
a person who is being treated by a doctor or a dentist. ▲ Say ***pay**-shent*.

patrol patrols *noun*
a group of soldiers, guards or police officers who regularly go round an area to protect it and make sure there is no trouble or danger.

pattern patterns *noun*
a design or arrangement of colours and shapes on something. *It is fun to make patterns using different colours and shapes.*

pause pauses pausing paused *verb*
if you pause, you stop what you are doing for a short time before you go on with it.
pause *noun*.
● A word that sounds like **pause** is **paws**.

pavement pavements *noun*
the part with the hard surface at the side of the road where people walk and cars are not allowed to go.

paw paws *noun*
an animal's foot. ● A word that sounds like **paws** is **pause**.

pay pays paying paid *verb*
when you pay somebody, you give them money for something you have bought or for work they have done. *How much will you pay me to wash your car?*

pea peas *noun*
a small, round, green vegetable that grows in a pod.

peace *noun*
1 a time when people are not fighting. ■ The opposite is **war**.
2 a time when there is no noise or no worry.
peaceful *adjective*.

peach peaches *noun*
a soft, round fruit with a pale, furry orange skin and a large stone inside.

peacock peacocks *noun*
a large, male bird with a tail made of blue and green feathers that it can spread out like a fan. The female is called a peahen.

peak peaks *noun*
1 the pointed top of a mountain.
2 the part of a cap that sticks out in front above your eyes.

peanut peanuts *noun*
a small nut that grows under the ground in a covering called a pod.

pear pears *noun*
a sweet fruit that is round at the bottom but narrower at the top where the stalk is. ● A word that sounds like **pear** is **pair**.

pearl pearls *noun*
a small, hard, round, white ball that is used as jewellery and that grows inside the shell of an oyster.
▲ Rhymes with ***curl***.

pebble pebbles *noun*
a small, smooth stone.

peck pecks pecking pecked *verb*
when a bird pecks, it pushes its beak at something and picks it up. *The hens were pecking at their food scattered on the ground.*

peculiar *adjective*
strange or odd. *This flower has a peculiar smell.*

pedal pedals *noun*
a part on a machine that you push with your foot. You push the pedals round on a bicycle to make it move. You push the pedals down in a car to make the car go faster or slower.

pedestrian pedestrians *noun*
a person who is walking across or along a street.

peel peels peeling peeled *verb*
if you peel a fruit or vegetable you take off the skin. *Sarah is peeling a pomegranate.*

peel *noun*
the outside skin of a fruit or vegetable. *orange peel.*

peep peeps peeping peeped *verb*
if you peep, you look quickly at something. *The film was so frightening, he just peeped at it through his fingers.*

peer peers peering peered *verb*
you peer at something when it is difficult to see, so you have to look hard to see it. ● A word that sounds like **peer** is **pier**.

peg pegs *noun*
a piece of wood, plastic or metal that is used to hold something down or to hang something up. *a tent peg.* ◆ *a clothes peg.* ◆ *a peg to hang your coat on.*

pelican pelicans *noun*
a large water bird with a long, narrow beak with a pouch under it that it uses for holding fish.

pen pens *noun*
a long, narrow object with a point at one end that you use for writing with ink. *I have lost my pen, can I borrow yours?*

penalty penalties *noun*
a punishment given if you do not obey a rule or do something wrong.

pencil pencils *noun*
a long, thin stick made of wood with a substance called graphite in the middle that you use for writing or drawing.

pendulum pendulums *noun*
a weight on the end of a rod inside some clocks. It swings from side to side to make the clock work.

penfriend penfriends *noun*
a penfriend is a person who lives far away that you get to know by exchanging letters with them.

penguin penguins *noun*
a large, black and white bird that swims but cannot fly. Penguins mostly live in the Antarctic, the very cold land and sea in the far south of the world. Penguins feed on fish.

penis penises *noun*
the part of a man's or boy's body between their legs. Boys and men use it to get rid of waste liquid, when they go to the toilet. Men also use it to have sex and make babies with. ▲ Say ***pee**-nus*.

penknife penknives *noun*
a knife with blades that fold back into the handle.

pension pensions *noun*
money that people receive regularly to live on when they have retired and have stopped working.

pentagon pentagons *noun*
a shape with five sides.

people *noun*
men, women and children. *A lot of people were waiting at the bus stop.*

pepper peppers *noun*
1 a spice with a hot taste that is ground to a powder and put in food. *black pepper.*
2 a green, red or yellow vegetable that is hollow inside.

per cent *noun*
a number of parts of something in every hundred. *8 per cent of people or eight people in every hundred travel to work by bike.* The sign for per cent is *% (8%)* ▲ Say *per **sent***.

perch perches *noun*
1 a place for a bird to stand or sit.
2 a fish that lives in fresh water.
perch *verb.*
The birds perched on the fence.

percussion *noun*
all the different musical instruments such as drums and tambourines that you play by hitting them. ❖ ***Look at page 105***

perfect *adjective*
a perfect thing has no mistakes or faults.
perfection *noun*, **perfectly** *adverb.*

perform performs performing performed *verb*
1 if actors perform, they act, sing, dance or tell jokes in front of an audience.
2 to do or carry out. *The surgeon performed an operation.*
performer *noun.*

perfume perfumes *noun*
a liquid with a pleasant smell that you put on your skin to make you smell nice. *a bottle of perfume.*

perimeter perimeters *noun*
the outside edge of something. *the perimeter of a circle.* ▲ Say *per-**im**-it-er*.

period periods *noun*
1 an amount of time. *She'll be away for a period of two weeks.*
2 a particular time in history. *the Tudor period.*

periscope periscopes *noun*
a tube with mirrors inside that are arranged so that when you look in one end of the tube you can see things through the top that you would not be able to see normally. Periscopes are used in submarines to see what is happening above the surface of the water.

permanent *adjective*
lasting forever or for a very long time. ■ The opposite is **temporary**.

permission *noun*
if somebody gives you permission to do something, they say you are allowed to do it. *My teacher gave me permission to go home early.*

permit permits permitting permitted *verb*
if somebody permits you to do something, they allow you to do it. *I'm permitted to stay up late on the weekend.* ■ The opposite is **forbid**.

person *noun*
a man, woman or child.

personal *adjective*
belonging to one person. *This is my personal CD player.*

persuade persuades persuading persuaded *verb*
if you persuade somebody to do something, you manage to make them do it, even if they did not want to. ▲ Say *per-**swade***.

a b c d e f g h i j k l m n o p q r s t u v w x y z

pest pests *noun*
1 an insect or animal that damages plants or is harmful to people.
2 a person who is annoying or causes trouble.

pet pets *noun*
a tame animal that you keep in the house and look after.

petal petals *noun*
one of the white or coloured parts that make the outside of a flower.

petrol *noun*
a liquid made from oil that is used as a fuel in motor vehicles to make them go.

phantom phantoms *noun*
a ghost. ▲ Say ***fan**-tum*.

pharmacy pharmacies *noun*
the part of a chemist's shop that sells medicines. ▲ Say ***far**-ma-see*.

phone phones *noun*
a telephone. ▲ Say ***fone***.

photo photos *noun*
a photograph or picture that you make by using a camera.
▲ Say ***foh**-toh*.

photocopy photocopies *noun*
a copy of a document made by a machine called a photocopier.

physical *adjective*
to do with people's bodies rather than their minds. ▲ Say ***fiz**-ik-al*.
physically *adverb*.
My grandmother is physically fit but she keeps forgetting things.

piano pianos *noun*
a large musical instrument with a row of black and white keys. When you press a key, a small hammer inside the piano hits a string to make a sound.
pianist *noun*.

pick picks picking picked *verb*
1 when you pick something, you take it from a group of things because it is the one that you want. *Pick your favourite tape and we'll buy it.*
2 if you pick a fruit or a flower, you take it off the plant. *We're going to the farm tomorrow to pick strawberries.*
3 when you pick something up, you lift it up from where it is lying. *Can you pick those bags up and bring them into the house?*
4 if you pick at something, you eat a little bit of it. *He picked at his food.*

pickle pickles *noun*
a mixture of vegetables or fruit kept in vinegar to preserve them. *Winston loves pickles on his sandwiches.*

picnic picnics *noun*
a meal that you take somewhere with you and eat outside.

picture pictures *noun*
a drawing, painting or photograph.

pie pies *noun*
a piece of pastry with meat, fruit, fish or vegetables cooked inside it.

piece pieces *noun*
1 a part or bit that is cut off something bigger. *Cut the pie into four equal pieces.*
2 a single thing. *a piece of paper.*

piece

Some words you can use instead of piece:

May I have a piece of cake?
slice, portion

She tore the paper into pieces
bits, scraps

There were huge pieces of meat in the soup.
lumps

On this piece of land we grow roses.
part, section

pier piers *noun*
a long platform built out over the sea where people can walk or where boats can be tied up. ● A word that sounds like **pier** is **peer**.

pierce pierces piercing pierced *verb*
when a sharp object pierces something, it makes a hole in it. *Have you had your ears pierced?*

pig pigs *noun*
a farm animal with a flat nose, short legs and a curly tail. Male pigs are called boars and female pigs are called sows. The meat of pigs is eaten as pork, bacon and ham.

pigeon pigeons *noun*
a grey bird with a fat body. Some pigeons have been trained to carry messages and some are used for racing.

pile piles *noun*
a lot of things that have been put one on top of the other. *a pile of books.*

pill pills *noun*
a pill is a medicine that has been made into a small, round object that you swallow.

pillar pillars *noun*
a tall, round column made of stone or brick that holds up part of a building.

pillow pillows *noun*
a soft cushion that you put your head on when you are in bed.

pilot pilots *noun*
a person who flies an aircraft.

pin pins *noun*
a small, thin, metal stick with a sharp point at one end that you use for holding two pieces of cloth or paper in place.
pin *verb*.
She pinned the badge to her dress.

pinch pinches pinching pinched *verb*
1 if you pinch somebody, you squeeze a little bit of their skin with your thumb and finger.
2 If you pinch something, you steal it.

pine pines *noun*
a tall, evergreen tree that has narrow, pointed leaves called needles and has its seeds held in cones.

pineapple pineapples *noun*
a large, sweet fruit that is yellow inside and has a thick, prickly skin and leaves growing out of the top. Pineapples grow in hot countries.

pip pips *noun*
a seed inside a fruit. *an orange pip.*

pipe pipes *noun*
a tube, usually made of metal or plastic, that carries things like water and gas.

pirate pirates *noun*
a person (especially in the past) who attacked and robbed ships.

pistol pistols *noun*
a small gun that is held in the hand.

pit pits *noun*
1 a large hole in the ground.
2 a coal mine.

pitch pitches *noun*
1 an area of ground for playing games such as football or cricket.
2 the pitch of a sound is how low or high the sound is. *As she got angrier, her voice rose in pitch.*

pity *noun*
if you feel pity for somebody, you feel sorry for them. *He feels pity for children who do not have enough to eat.*
pity *verb.*

pixie pixies *noun*
a small fairy.

pizza pizzas *noun*
a round piece of flat dough with things on top such as tomatoes and cheese, that is baked in the oven. ▲ Say ***peet-sa.***

place places *noun*
1 an area or building. *Show me the place on your leg that hurts.*
2 a position in a race. *He was in third place.*

plague plagues *noun*
a serious disease that spreads quickly. Plague can be spread by rats and fleas.

plain plainer plainest *adjective*
1 something that is plain has no pattern or marks on it. *Take a piece of plain paper and write the essay on it.* ◆ *He wore a plain red tie.*
2 ordinary and not beautiful. *She had a plain face but she was very kind.*
3 if something is plain to you, it is clear and easy to understand. *She made it plain that she expected good behaviour at all times.* ● A word that sounds like **plain** is **plane**.

plait plaits *noun*
hair divided into three pieces that are twisted over each other to make a tidy line like a piece of rope. *She wore her hair in two plaits.* ▲ Rhymes with ***cat***.
plait *verb.*

plan plans *noun*
a set of ideas that show how you are going to do something.

plan plans planning planned *verb*
when you plan something, you work out what you are going to do and how you are going to do it.

plane planes *noun*
an aeroplane or flying machine that takes people to places by air. ● A word that sounds like **plane** is **plain**.

planet planets *noun*
a very big, round object in space, such as Venus, Mars or the Earth, that moves around a star such as the Sun.
❖ ***Look at page 154***

plank planks *noun*
a long, flat piece of wood. *The floors are made of planks.*

plant plants *noun*
a tree, flower, bush or other living thing that grows in one place and has roots and a stem and leaves.
❖ ***Look at page 120***

plant plants planting planted *verb*
when you plant things such as flowers or trees, you put them into the ground where you want them to grow. *The council has planted trees on both sides of the road.*

plaster plasters *noun*
1 a small piece of sticky material that you can put over a cut to stop dirt getting into it.
2 a soft, wet mixture that you use to cover walls and ceilings inside a house and that becomes hard and smooth so that you can put paint or wallpaper on it.

plastic *noun*
a material that is made in a factory for a lot of different uses. It is light in weight and does not break easily.

plate plates *noun*
a flat dish that you put food on.

A B C D E F G H I J K L M N O P Q R S T U V W X Y Z

Plants

Vocabulary

annual
a plant that lives for one season only.

anther
the part of the stamen that contains pollen.

carpel or pistil
the female part of a flowering plant containing the stigma, style and ovary.

chlorophyll
a green substance that plants use to help make food and which makes their leaves look green.

stamen
the male part of a flowering plant containing the anther.

stigma
the tip of the carpel which receives the pollen.

Pitcher plant

Broad bean

Potato

Fly agaric

Barrel cactus

Stone plant

Wheat

Barley

Rushes

Daffodil

Grasses

Tulip

Wood lily

platform platforms *noun*
1 the part of a railway station where you get on and off the train.
2 a flat area that is built higher than the floor so that the people on it can be seen more easily.
3 a flat structure that is higher than the ground or built over water. *an oil platform.*

play plays playing played *verb*
1 when you play, you do things that you enjoy doing, such as games.
2 if you play a musical instrument, you use it to make music. *He plays the clarinet.*

play plays *noun*
a story that is performed in the theatre, on television or on the radio. *a play by Shakespeare.*

playful *adjective*
liking to play and have fun.

playground playgrounds *noun*
an area of land where children can play. *Freddie plays in the school playground.*

plead pleads pleading pleaded *verb*
if you plead with somebody, you strongly ask them to do something. *She pleaded to be allowed to go home.*

pleasant pleasanter pleasantest *adjective*
a pleasant thing is something you enjoy or like. *We had a pleasant afternoon on the beach.*

please *interjection*
you say "please" to be polite when you are asking for something. *Would you pass me that magazine, please?*

pleasure *noun*
the feeling you get when you are happy and enjoying something. ▲ Say ***plesh**-er.*

plenty *noun*
a large amount of something and more than is needed. *There's plenty of cake, so you can all have a piece.*

plot plots *noun*
1 a secret plan by a group of people to do something, usually wrong.
2 the story in a book, film or TV programme.
3 a small area of ground. *a vegetable plot.* ◆ *a building plot.*

plough ploughs *noun*
a tool that is used for turning over the soil to make it ready for planting seeds. It is pulled along by a tractor or an animal. ▲ Rhymes with ***cow***.
plough *verb*.

pluck plucks plucking plucked *verb*
1 when you pluck a musical instrument such as a guitar or a violin, you pull on the strings to make the notes sound.
2 when you pluck a flower or fruit, you pick it from the place where it was growing.

plug plugs *noun*
1 a round object that you put into the hole of a bath or basin to stop the water running out.
2 a thing at the end of a wire on a machine that fits into a socket on the wall so that the machine can be connected to the electricity supply.

plum plums *noun*
a soft, dark red, purple or yellow fruit with a thin skin and a stone in the centre.

plumber plumbers *noun*
a person whose job is to put in water pipes in a house and to mend them when they go wrong. *The plumber has come to mend the tap.* ▲ Say ***plum**-er.*

plump plumper plumpest *noun*
nicely fat. *The baby had plump cheeks.*
■ The opposite is **slim**.

plural plurals *noun*
the form of a word that you use when you are talking about two or more things instead of just one. The plural of "desk" is "desks" and the plural of "mouse" is "mice". ▲ Say ***ploo**-ral.*
■ The opposite is **singular**.

plus *preposition*
you use the word plus to talk about adding numbers together. In arithmetic, you can use the sign + to mean plus. *Six plus five equals eleven is the same as 6 + 5 = 11.*

pocket pockets *noun*
a part like a flat bag in your clothes that you can put things in.

pocket money *noun*
money that is given each week to a child to spend.

pod pods *noun*
a long, narrow part of some plants that seeds grow inside. Peas and beans grow in pods.

poem poems *noun*
a piece of writing arranged in short lines. The words in the lines make a rhythm and sometimes the words at the ends of the lines rhyme.

poet poets *noun*
a person who writes poetry.

poetry *noun*
poems are poetry.

A B C D E F G H I J K L M N O P Q R S T U V W X Y Z

point points *noun*
1 the end of something sharp like a needle or a pencil.
2 a particular place or time. *At this point, she suddenly saw that everybody had left the room.*
3 a mark that somebody gets in a game or competition.
4 the purpose for doing something. *What's the point in taking your coat off if you're going straight out again?*

point points pointing pointed *verb*
if you point, you show where something is by using your finger.

pointed *adjective*
a pointed thing has a point at one end.

poison *noun*
a substance that will make you ill or kill you if it gets into your body.
poisonous *adjective*.

poke pokes poking poked *verb*
to poke somebody is to push something into them. *She poked me in my back with her finger.*

polar bear polar bears *noun*
a large, white bear that lives near the North Pole.

pole poles *noun*
1 a long, narrow, round piece of wood or metal. *a telegraph pole.* ◆ *a flag pole.*
2 a point at each end of the Earth that is farthest from the Equator. *the North Pole and the South Pole.*

police *noun*
those whose job is to protect people and make sure that everybody obeys the law.
policeman *noun*, **policewoman** *noun*, **police officer** *noun*.

polish polishes polishing polished *verb*
if you polish something, you rub it to make it shine. *David polishes his shoes.*
polish *noun*.

polite politer politest *adjective*
if you are polite, you behave well towards other people and think about how to make them feel comfortable. *It is polite to say "thank you" and "please".*
■ The opposite is **rude**.
politely *adverb*.

politics *noun*
all the activities to do with the government of a country.
political *adjective*.

pollen *noun*
a fine powder inside flowers that the wind or insects take to other flowers of the same kind so that they can produce seeds.

pollution *noun*
poisonous chemicals and other forms of dangerous dirt that cause damage to the air, water and environment.

pond ponds *noun*
a small area of water.

pony ponies *noun*
a small kind of horse.

pool pools *noun*
1 a small area of water.
2 a swimming pool.

poor poorer poorest *adjective*
1 a person who is poor has very little money. ■ The opposite is **rich**.
2 not good enough. *My spelling is very poor.*
3 unlucky or in a bad situation. *Poor John failed his driving test.* ● A word that sounds like **poor** is **pour**.

pop pops *noun*
1 modern, popular music.
2 a short, sharp sound like a small explosion.

poppy poppies *noun*
a plant with a large, bright flower.

popular *adjective*
liked by a lot of people. *a popular film.* ◆ *a popular girl.*
popularly *adverb*.

population populations *noun*
all the people who live in a particular area or country.

porcupine porcupines *noun*
an animal that has stiff hairs on its back, called quills.

pork *noun*
meat from a pig.

port ports *noun*
a place or town beside a large river or the sea where ships can stay and load and unload.

portable *adjective*
something that is portable is small enough or light enough to be carried around easily. *a portable computer.*

portion portions *noun*
an amount of food for one person. *a portion of chips.*

portrait portraits *noun*
a picture of a person.

position positions *noun*
1 the place where something is. *Can you check our position on the map?*
2 the way you are sitting, standing or lying down. *Get into a comfortable position.*

positive *adjective*
1 certain about something. *I'm positive I saw him.*
2 a positive number is higher than zero. ■ The opposite is **negative**.

possess possesses possessing possessed *verb*
if you possess something, you own it and it belongs to you. *Do you possess a TV?*

possible *adjective*
if something is possible, it can be done or it can happen. *Come as soon as possible.* ■ The opposite is **impossible**.
possibility *noun*, **possibly** *adverb*.
Is there the possibility of rain today?

post posts *noun*
1 a long, thick, strong pole or piece of wood fixed in the ground. *a fence post.*
2 the system of sending letters and parcels from one place to another and delivering them to people's doors.

post posts posting posted *verb*
when you post a letter or a parcel, you send it through the post.

postcard postcards *noun*
a small piece of card, usually with a picture on one side, that you can use to send a short message to somebody. *They sent me a postcard with a cross drawn on it to show where their hotel is.*

postcode postcodes *noun*
a set of letters and numbers at the end of your address that tells the post office where you live. *My postcode is 110008.*

poster posters *noun*
a large picture, notice or advertisement that is put up on a wall.

post office post offices *noun*
1 a place where you can send letters and parcels and buy stamps.
2 the organization or group of people who collect, sort and deliver people's letters and parcels.

postpone postpones postponing postponed *verb*
if you postpone something, you put it off until later. *The race was postponed because of bad weather.*

pot pots *noun*
1 a round container. *a pot of tea.* ◆ *a paint pot.*
2 a container for plants to grow in made of plastic or clay.

potato potatoes *noun*
a white vegetable with a thin, brown skin that grows under the ground.

pottery *noun*
dishes and other objects made out of clay and then baked hard in a special oven called a kiln.

pouch pouches *noun*
1 a small bag.
2 a bag of skin that female kangaroos and some other female animals have on their stomach and which they use for carrying their babies in.

pounce pounces pouncing pounced *verb*
to pounce is to jump forward suddenly and catch hold of something. *The kitten pounced on the ball of wool.* ◆ *He pounced on the disk saying, "I thought I'd lost this!"*

pour pours pouring poured *verb*
when you pour a liquid, you tip a container such as a jug or bottle so that the liquid flows out. *Can you pour Granny another cup of tea?*

poverty *noun*
people who live in poverty are very poor.

powder *noun*
tiny, dry grains that you get when you crush or grind something well.
powder *verb*.

power *noun*
1 the ability to do something. *Human beings have the power of speech.*
2 the force or strength of something. *The power of the wind brought the trees down.*
3 a person who has power can control what happens to a lot of people.

powerful *adjective*
a powerful person or thing has a lot of power. *a powerful king.* ◆ *a powerful engine.* ■ The opposite is **weak**.

practical *adjective*
1 to do with actually working or doing something rather than knowing or having ideas about it. *Do you have practical training in using computers?*
2 sensible, useful and likely to work, *a practical suggestion.* ◆ *He is a very practical man.*
practically *adverb*.
almost. *I've practically finished eating.*

practice *noun*
doing something again and again until you can do it well. *guitar practice.*

practise practises practising practised *verb*
if you practise something, you keep doing it until you can do it well. *Rachel practises her guitar playing for three hours everyday.*

praise praises praising praised *verb*
when you praise somebody, you say how well they have done something. *Everybody praised the brave firefighters.* ■ The opposite is **criticize**.

pram prams *noun*
a kind of cot on wheels that people use to push a baby in.

pray prays praying prayed *verb*
if you pray, you talk to God. ● A word that sounds like **pray** is **prey**.

prayer prayers *noun*
the words somebody says when they are talking to God.

precious *adjective*
very valuable or very important to you. ▲ Say ***presh****-us.*

predict predicts predicting predicted *verb*
if you predict something, you say that you think it is going to happen. *The weather forecast predicts rain over the weekend.*
prediction *noun.*

prefer prefers preferred *verb*
if you prefer one thing to another thing, you like it better. *Would you prefer an apple or a peach?*
preference noun.

pregnant *adjective*
when a woman is pregnant, she is going to have a baby and the baby is growing inside her womb.

prehistoric *adjective*
belonging to a very long time ago before history was remembered and written down. *Dinosaurs lived in prehistoric times.* ❖ ***Look at page 125***

prepare prepares preparing prepared *verb*
when you prepare something, you make it ready. *Jackson helped prepare lunch.*
preparation *noun.*

preposition prepositions *noun*
a word you use for such things as where and how. "Down", "on" and "in" are prepositions used in the following sentences. "He ran down the hill." "The phone was on the table." "The milk is in the jug." Prepositions show how the word before and after it are related.

prescription prescriptions *noun*
the piece of paper that a doctor uses to write down the medicines or pills you need to get from the chemist.

present *adjective*
1 being in a place or being there. *Many people were present at the concert.* ■ The opposite is **absent**.
2 happening now. *the present time.*

present presents *noun*
1 a thing that you give to somebody. *What presents did you get?*
2 the time now. *We've had no trouble up to the present.*

preserve preserves preserving preserved *verb*
1 if you preserve something, you keep it the way it is without changing it. *These foods are all preserved in different ways.*
2 if you preserve food, you do something to it so that it will not go bad.

president presidents *noun*
a person who is chosen to lead a country that does not have a king or queen.

press presses pressing pressed *verb*
if you press something, you push hard on it. *You press a button and the door slides open.*

pressure *noun*
the force of one thing pressing or pushing on another. *If you put pressure on that cut, it will stop bleeding.* ▲ *Say* ***presh****-er.*

pretend pretends pretending pretended *verb*
if you pretend, you try to make other people believe something that is not true. *He's pretending to be a tree!*

pretty prettier prettiest *adjective*
attractive and nice to look at. *Flowers are pretty.* ▲ Say ***prit****-ee.*

prevent prevents preventing prevented *verb*
if you prevent something, you stop it happening. *Shut the gate to prevent the horse from running away.*

previous *adjective*
the previous thing is the thing that came before or earlier. *I went round to Jane's house on Wednesday as we had arranged on the phone the previous day.* ▲ Say ***pree****-vee-us.*
previously *adverb.*

prey *noun*
any animal that is hunted for food. *Mice are the owl's natural prey.*
▲ Rhymes with ***may***. ● A word that sounds like **prey** is **pray**.

price prices *noun*
the amount of money you have to pay to buy something. *What's the price of that pair of trainers?*

prick pricks pricking pricked *verb*
if you prick something, you make a small hole in it with something sharp. *Mark said he'd prick the balloon with a pin.*

prickle prickles *noun*
a sharp point or thorn. *Mind this bush, it's covered with prickles.*
prickly *adjective.*

pride *noun*
1 the good feeling you get when you are proud and have done something well or somebody you love has done something well.
2 a group of lions that live together.

Prehistoric animals

Vocabulary

ankylosaurs
a group of dinosaurs that had body armour of bony spines.

carnosaurs
large meat-eating dinosaurs.

dinosaur
a word meaning "terrible lizard" – though not all dinosaurs were reptiles.

hadrosaurs
dinosaurs with mouths shaped like duck's bills.

ichthyosaurs
big, swimming reptiles that looked like dolphins.

ornithopod
plant-eating dinosaurs that stood on their hind legs like birds.

pterosaurs
flying reptiles with wings of skin.

stegosaurs
dinosaurs that had a body armour of large triangular bony plates.

Stegosaurus

Thalassodromeus

Spinosaurus

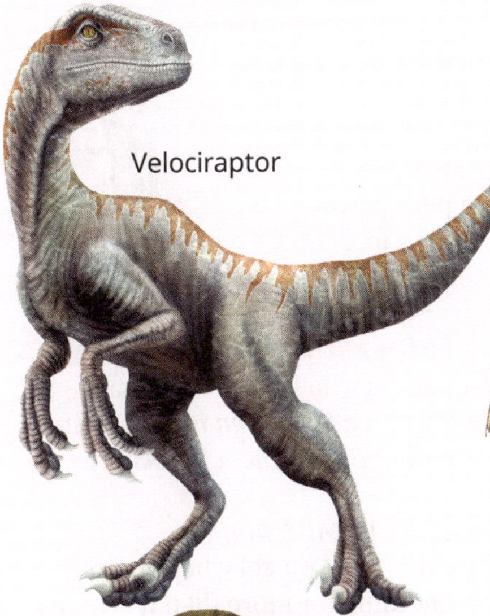

Velociraptor

Oviraptor

Tyrannosaurus

Parasaurolophus

Dimetrodon

Brachiosaurus

Kelenken

Triceratops

priest priests *noun*
a person in the Christian religion who leads people in service. ▲ Say ***preest***.

primary *adjective*
1 first and most important. *Our primary need is to make sure everybody has enough to eat.*
2 to do with teaching children between the ages of 5 and 11. *primary education.*

prime *adjective*
first and most important. *A matter of prime importance.*

prime number *noun*
a number that can only be divided exactly by itself or one. *Seven and seventeen are prime numbers.*

Prime Numbers 1-100
2, 3, 5, 7, 11, 13, 17, 19, 23, 29, 31, 37, 41, 43, 47, 53, 59, 61, 67, 71, 73, 79, 83, 89, 97

prime minister prime ministers *noun*
the person chosen to lead a government.

prince princes *noun*
the son of a king or queen, or a man or boy who is a member of a royal family.

princess princesses *noun*
the daughter of a king or queen, or a woman or girl who is a member of a royal family.

principle principles *noun*
an important rule that you have about what is right and wrong. *It's against my principles to take drugs.*

print prints printing printed *verb*
1 when somebody prints a book, magazine or newspaper, they make copies of it on paper using a machine called a printer.
2 if you print something out from a computer, you use a machine called a printer to put information in the computer on paper.
3 if you print words, you write using letters that are not joined up.
printer *noun*.

prison prisons *noun*
a building where people who have broken the law are kept locked up.
prisoner *noun*.

private *adjective*
something that is private is for only one person or one small group of people and not for everybody. *You can't see my letter, it's private.* ▲ Say ***pry-vit***. ■ The opposite is **public**.
privately *adverb*.

prize prizes *noun*
a thing that you are given for winning a competition or for doing good work.

probably *adverb*
something will be true or likely to happen if you think it is probably true or will probably happen.

problem problems *noun*
a problem is something that is difficult to work out, understand or do.

procession processions *noun*
a number of people walking or driving in a public place as part of a ceremony. *A brass band led the procession*

prod prods prodding prodded *verb*
if you prod something, you push at it with something such as a stick or a finger. *I prodded him in the ribs.*

produce produces producing produced *verb*
1 to produce something is to make it. *The factory produces hundreds of new cars a week.*
2 if you produce something, you take it out and show it. *She peered in her bag and produced a clean handkerchief.*
3 to produce a play, film or TV programme is to organize the people making it and get it ready to show to the public. ▲ Say ***prod-yoos***.

product products *noun*
a thing that is made to be sold. *Timber is a product of Canada.*

profession professions *noun*
a job that needs special knowledge and training, such as being a doctor or a teacher.

professional *noun*
a person who works in a profession. *A doctor is a professional.*

professor professors *noun*
a person who is a teacher at a university. *My cousin is a professor of Greek at Birmingham University.*

profit profits *noun*
money that you get when you sell something for more than it cost to buy or make.

program programs *noun*
a list of instructions that makes a computer work.

programme programmes *noun*
1 a television or radio show.
2 a printed piece of paper that gives you information about things such as a play, a concert or a football match.

progress progresses *noun*
the way something or someone moves forward or gets better. *She is making good progress learning French.*

project projects *noun*
a piece of work you do in which you find out as much as you can about a subject. *We're doing a project on the Second World War at school.*

promise promises promising promised *verb*
when you promise you will do something, you say you will do it and you really mean it. *Pam promised not to make a noise.*

prompt *adjective*
when you are prompt, you do something quickly or immediately, without delay.

pronoun pronouns *noun*
a word like "you", "her", or "one" that you use when you already know the person or thing that is being talked about. "Her" and "one" are pronouns in these sentences. *Sam tossed me the ball and I threw it back to her.* ◆ *I don't want the red pen, I want the green one.*

pronounce pronounces pronouncing pronounced *verb*
when you pronounce a word right, you say the sound of the word in the correct way. *Some English words are hard for French people to pronounce correctly.*
pronunciation *noun.*

proof *noun*
to have proof of something is to have all the facts that show that it is true.

prop props propping propped *verb*
if you prop something, you put it or lay it against something. *She propped her bike against the wall.*

propeller propellers *noun*
a set of blades that spin round to make a ship, plane or helicopter move.

proper *adjective*
the proper way to do something is the right or correct way to do it.
properly *adverb.*

property properties *noun*
1 things that you own. *Those books don't belong to the school, they're my property.*
2 a building and the land around it.

prosecute prosecutes prosecuting prosecuted *verb*
to prosecute somebody is to accuse them of a crime and make them go to court. *Trespassers will be prosecuted.*

protect protects protecting protected *verb*
if you protect somebody or something, you try to keep them from being hurt or damaged.
protection *noun.*

protest protests protesting protested *verb*
if you protest, you say that you think something is wrong and should be changed.

proud *adjective*
the good feeling of pleasure you get when you or someone else has done something very well. *I got better marks than I ever had before and I was really proud of myself.*
proudly *adverb.*

prove proves proving proved *verb*
when you prove something, you show that it is true. ▲ Rhymes with ***move***.

provide provides providing provided *verb*
if you provide something, you get it and make sure that you give it when it is needed. *I'll provide the sandwiches if you bring something to drink.*

prune prunes pruning pruned *verb*
when you prune a tree or bush, you cut back its branches to keep it healthy or keep it from getting too big.

pub pubs *noun*
a place where adults can go to buy drinks and meet friends.

public *adjective*
for everybody to go to, or use, or see. *a public phone box.* ◆ *public transport.*
■ The opposite is **private**.

publish publishes publishing published *verb*
to publish a book, magazine or newspaper is to have it printed and ready for people to buy a copy.

pudding puddings *noun*
sweet food that you eat at the end of a meal. *Christmas pudding.*

puddle puddles *noun*
a pool or small area of water left on the ground after it has rained.

puff puffs *noun*
a small amount of moving air, smoke or wind. *a puff of smoke.*

puffin puffins *noun*
a black and white sea bird that has a big brightly coloured beak.

pull pulls pulling pulled *verb*
when you pull something, you hold it and move it towards you.

pulp *noun*
the soft part inside a fruit or vegetable.

pulse *noun*
the regular beat or throbbing that your blood makes as it goes through your body. You can feel your pulse by putting your fingers on your wrist.

pump pumps *noun*
a machine that is used to push air, liquid, or gas into or out of something.

pump pumps pumping pumped *verb*
to force air or liquid with a pump. *Jordan pumps up the tyre.*

pumpkin pumpkins *noun*
a large, round orange vegetable that grows on the ground.

pun puns *noun*
a joke that works because a word has two meanings. *Two pears make one pair.*

punch punches punching punched *verb*
1 if you punch somebody, you hit them with your fist.
2 if you punch something, you make a hole in it. *The guard inspected everybody's tickets and punched them.*

punctual *adjective*
arriving on time.
punctually *adverb.*

punctuation *noun*
marks such as commas, full stops and quotation marks that you use when you are writing.

puncture punctures *noun*
a hole in a bicycle tyre or a car tyre.
▲ Say ***punk**-cher.*

punish punishes punishing punished *verb*
to punish somebody is to make them hurt or suffer because they have done something wrong.
punishment *noun.*

pupa pupae *noun*
a stage in an insect's life after it is a larva but before it is an adult insect with wings. ▲ Say ***pyoo**-pa.*

pupil pupils *noun*
1 a person who is studying at school.
2 the small, round, black part at the centre of the eye.

puppet puppets *noun*
a kind of doll that you can make move by pulling strings that are fixed to the different parts of the puppet, or by putting your hand inside the puppet and moving it with your fingers.

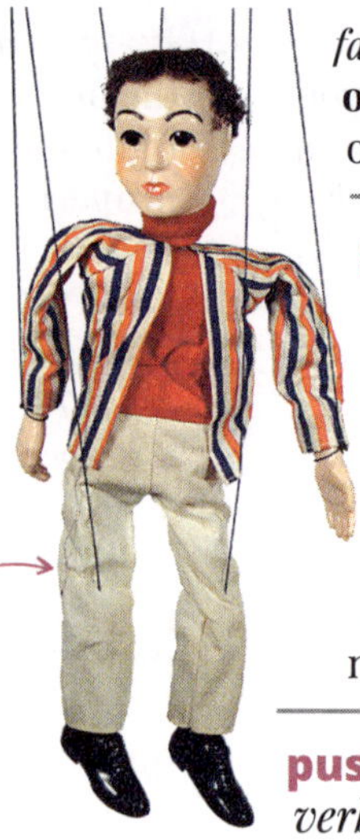

puppy puppies *noun*
a young dog.

purchase purchases purchasing purchased *verb*
if you purchase something, you buy it.

pure purer purest *adjective*
something that is pure is not mixed with anything else. *pure apple juice.*
▲ Say ***pyoor**.*

purpose purposes *noun*
the reason that something is being done or what it is meant to do. *The purpose of the trip is to see some famous paintings.*
on purpose if you do something on purpose, you mean to do it.

purr purrs purring purred *verb*
when a cat purrs, it makes a low sound to show that it is pleased.

purse purses *noun*
a small bag that you keep money in.

push pushes pushing pushed *verb*
if you push something, you move it away from you. *When the car broke down, all the family had to get out and push it.*

puzzle puzzles *noun*
a question, problem, or game that is hard to work out the answer to. *a crossword puzzle.*

pyjamas *noun*
trousers and a jacket that you wear in bed. ▲ Say *pa-**jah**-maz.*

pyramid pyramids *noun*
1 a solid shape with triangular sides that meet in a point at the top.
2 a building with four triangular sides that meet at the top. *There are pyramids in Egypt and Mexico and the ancient Egyptians buried their dead kings and queens, called Pharaohs, in them.*

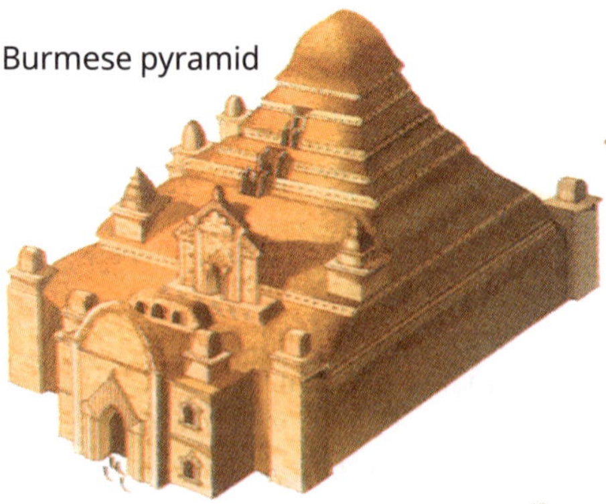

Burmese pyramid

Sumerian pyramid

Egyptian pyramid

Q q

Spelling tip:

Most words that begin with a "qu" sound as in "queen" are spelt with a "c" or "k" as in cat, kangaroo.

quack quacks quacking quacked *verb*
to quack is to make the sound that a duck makes.
quack *noun*.

quaint quainter quaintest *adjective*
pretty and unusual. *a quaint old cottage.*

qualify qualifies qualifying qualified *verb*
1 if you qualify, you pass an exam that allows you to do a job or study at a college. *She qualified as a teacher.*
2 you qualify if you win part of a competition and are able to go on to the next part. *Our team qualified for the football final.*
qualification *noun*.

quality *noun*
1 how good or bad something is. *a dress made from material of good quality.*
2 what makes something what it is. *The quality of lemons is that they are sour.*

quantity quantities *noun*
an amount of something. *Birds need a large quantity of twigs to make a nest.*

quarrel quarrels quarrelling quarrelled *verb*
if you quarrel with somebody, you have an angry argument with them. *My two younger brothers are always quarrelling over their toys.*

quarry quarries *noun*
a place where things such as stone, chalk or slate are dug out of the ground.

quarter quarters *noun*
one of four equal parts of something. Four quarters make a whole. *We cut the apple into quarters.*

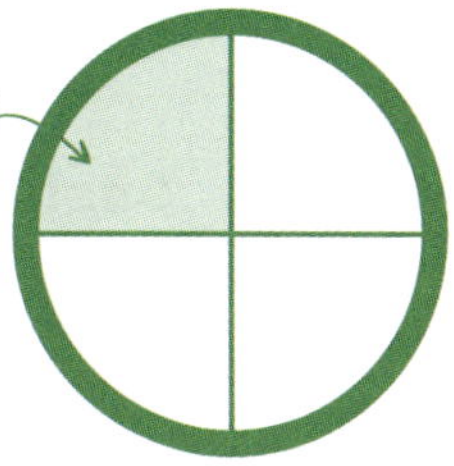

quay quays
a place in a harbour where boats are tied up to be loaded or unloaded.
▲ Say ***kee***.

queen queens *noun*
a woman who leads her people or who is the wife of a king and a member of a royal family.

queer *adjective*
odd or very strange. *There's a queer smell in here.*

query queries *noun*
a question. *Does anyone have any queries?*

quest quests *noun*
a long and difficult search for something important. *a quest for a cure for cancer.*

question questions *noun*
you ask a question when you want to find out about something. *I asked my teacher a question about the computer.*
■ The opposite is **answer**.

question mark question marks *noun*
a mark (?) that you use in writing. You put a question mark at the end of a sentence to show that somebody has asked a question. *What did you say?*

queue queues *noun*
a line of people who are waiting for something. *There is a long queue outside the cinema.* ▲ Say ***kyoo***.
queue *verb*.
We queued up for hours for tickets.

quick quicker quickest *adjective*
1 fast. *Be quick or we'll miss the bus.*
2 done in a short time. *We had a quick breakfast before we went out.*
quickly *adverb*.
Go as quickly as you can.

quiet quieter quietest *adjective*
no noise or very little noise. *She played quiet music.* ■ The opposite is **loud**.

quilt quilts *noun*
a soft, light cover for a bed.

quit quits quitting quit or quitted *verb*
if you quit, you leave or stop doing something. *We quit when we started to lose the game.*

quite *adverb*
1 more than a little but not very much. *He's quite tall.*
2 completely. *You're quite right.*

quiz quizzes *noun*
a kind of game when somebody asks a lot of questions to see how much you know. *Our team won the quiz because we knew all the answers.*

quotation quotations *noun*
words that you say or write that somebody else has said before. *"To be or not to be" is a quotation from one of William Shakespeare's famous play,* Hamlet.

quotation mark quotation marks *noun*
marks (" ") that you use in writing. You put quotation marks before and after the words that somebody has said. *"What did you say?" he asked.*

quote quotes quoting quoted *verb*
1 if you quote something, you say or write something that somebody else has said before. *She quoted some lines from the poem.*
2 to name a price.

R r

Spelling tip:
Some words that begin with an "r" sound are spelt "wr" such as wrong, wriggle, wrestle.

rabbi rabbis *noun*
a teacher of the Jewish religion.

rabbit rabbits *noun*
a small, wild animal with soft fur and long ears. Rabbits live in holes in the ground called burrows.

raccoon raccoons *noun*
a small animal that has black marks on its face and black-coloured rings around its tail.
❖ ***Look at page 99***

race races *noun*
1 a competition to see who is the fastest. *a cycle race.*
2 a large number of human beings whose ancestors all came from the same area and who look alike in some way, for example in skin colour.

race races racing raced *verb*
if you race, you go very fast. *She was racing along the path, trying to catch her dog.*

rack racks *noun*
a frame or set of shelves that you can put things on or hang things on. *a plate rack.* ◆ *a wine rack.* ◆ *a shoe rack.*

racket rackets *noun*
a bat with an oval frame for hitting a ball in tennis, badminton or squash.

radar *noun*
a way of showing on a screen the exact position and speed of a plane or ship that cannot be seen.

radiator radiators *noun*
a flat, metal object against a wall that steam or hot water runs through to heat a room. ▲ Say ***ray**-dee-ay-ter.*

radio radios *noun*
a machine that receives sounds sent through the air so that you can hear them. You turn on a radio to listen to music, news and other programmes.

radius radiuses *noun*
a straight line from the centre of a circle to the edge. ❖ ***Look at page 38***

raft rafts *noun*
a flat boat made of rubber or wood.

rag rags *noun*
an old piece of material that you can use to clean things.

rage *noun*
very great anger. *Benjamin was scarlet with rage.*

raid raids *noun*
a sudden attack on a place. *There was a bank raid in the centre of town today.*

rail rails *noun*
1 a bar for people to hold on to or to stop them from falling. *She held the rail as she climbed the stairs.*
2 the long, parallel metal bars (lines) that trains run on.
3 a railway system. *We travelled all round Europe by rail.*
railings *noun.*

railway railways *noun*
the system of trains, stations and track that is used when people travel by train.

rain *noun*
water that falls to the ground from clouds in small drops.
rainy *adjective*, **rain** *verb.*
rainy weather.

rainbow rainbows *noun*
an arc or curve of light of different colours that you can sometimes see in the sky when there is rain and sunshine at the same time.

rainforest rainforests *noun*
an area of thick, tropical forest where a lot of rain falls.

raise raises raising raised *verb*
if you raise something, you lift it up or move it so that it is higher. *Raise your hand if you know the answer.*
■ The opposite is **lower**.

A B C D E F G H I J K L M N O P Q R S T U V W X Y Z

raisin raisins *noun*
a dried grape.

rake rakes *noun*
a garden tool with a long handle and a row of metal teeth like a comb that you use to make the earth level or to gather leaves into a pile.
rake *verb*.

rally rallies *noun*
1 a large public meeting.
2 a car or motorcycle race that takes place over a long distance.

ram rams *noun*
a male sheep.

ran past of run.

ranch ranches *noun*
a very large farm in North America for cattle, horses or sheep.

rang past of ring.

range ranges *noun*
1 a choice of things of the same kind. *The shop stocks a wide range of trainers and sports shoes.*
2 a long line of mountains.
3 the area or distance over which something can be used.

ransom ransoms *noun*
money that is demanded in return for letting a person who has been kidnapped go free.

rap raps *noun*
1 a short, sharp sound like a single knock on a door.
2 a kind of music where the words are spoken in rhythm, not sung.

rapid *adjective*
very quick. *a rapid heartbeat.*
rapidly *adverb*.

rare rarer rarest *adjective*
not often seen or done. *This flower is very rare.* ■ The opposite is **common**.

rash rashes *noun*
a lot of small, red spots that you get on your skin if you have an illness like measles.

raspberry raspberries *noun*
a small, sweet, red fruit that grows on a bush. ❖ ***Look at page 22***

rat rats *noun*
an animal that is like a very large mouse with a long tail.

rate rates *noun*
1 the speed at which something happens. *Scientists are worried by the rate at which rainforests are being cut down and destroyed.*
2 the amount of money that you pay for a service. *You pay a cheaper rate for phone calls in the evenings and at weekends.*

rattle rattles rattling rattled *verb*
when something rattles, it makes the noise of things knocking together. *The coins rattled when Penelope shook her money box.*

rattle rattles *noun*
a baby's toy that makes a noise when you shake it.

raw *adjective*
food that is raw has not been cooked. *raw cabbage.* ◆ *Rose puts the raw ingredients for making vegetable soup into the pan.*

ray rays *noun*
a line of light. *the Sun's rays.*

razor razors *noun*
a tool with a very sharp blade for shaving.

reach reaches reaching reached *verb*
1 when you reach a place, you get there. *When we reach London, we'll stop and have lunch.*
2 when you reach for something, you stretch out your arm towards it. *I'm not tall enough to reach the books on the top shelf.*

react reacts reacting reacted *verb*
when you react to something, you behave in a certain way because of that thing and as a kind of answer to it. *Rose taps Freddie's knee to see if his leg reacts.*
reaction *noun*.

read reads reading read *verb*
when you read something, you look at written words and understand what they mean. ● A word that sounds like **read** is **reed**.

ready *adjective*
when you are ready, you are prepared and can do something straight away. *Are you ready to go yet?* ▲ Say **red**-ee.

real *adjective*
1 really existing and not made up. *Do you think that dinosaurs were real?*
2 not a copy. *real leather.*
■ The opposite is **fake**. ● A word that sounds like **real** is **reel**.

realize realizes realizing realized *verb*
when you realize something, you start to know or understand it. *I realize I can't have everything I want.*

reap reaps reaping reaped *verb*
when you reap crops such as wheat, you cut them and gather them up.

rear *noun*
the back of something. *There's a large garden at the rear of the house.* ■ The opposite is **front**.

A B C D E F G H I J K L M N O P Q R S T U V W X Y Z

reason reasons *noun*
a fact that explains why something happens. *The reason I'm afraid of geese is that I was once bitten by one.*

rebel rebels rebelling rebelled *verb*
when a person rebels, they refuse to obey the people who are in charge.
▲ Say *ree-**bell**.*

receipt receipts *noun*
a piece of paper that shows how much money you paid for something.
▲ Say *ree-**seet**.*

receive receives receiving received *verb*
if you receive something, you get it when it has been given or sent to you. *They received a cup for winning the contest.* ▲ Say *ree-**seeve**.* ■ The opposite is **give**.

recent *adjective*
a short time ago. *a recent photo of my brother and mother.*
recently *adverb.*

reception receptions *noun*
the place in a building, like a hotel or hospital, where visitors go first. *Tell the nurse at reception which doctor you are going to see and then sit down.*

recipe recipes *noun*
a list of things you need to cook something and the instructions on how to cook it. ▲ Say ***res**-i-pee.*

reckon reckons reckoning reckoned *verb*
if you reckon something, you think it is probably true. *I reckon our team will win on Saturday.*

recognize recognizes recognizing recognized *verb*
if you recognize somebody, you know who they are because you have seen them before. *You look so different I didn't recognize you at first.*

recommend recommends recommending recommended *verb*
if you recommend something, you say that you think it is good. *I recommend the apple pie and cream.*

record records recording recorded *verb*
1 if you record something, you write down what happened. *He recorded the day's events in his diary.*
2 to record something is to store it on film, tape, a compact disc, or a record so that it can be played or shown again. ▲ Say *ree-**kord**.*

record records *noun*
1 a written list of what has happened. *I kept a record of everything I spent while we were on holiday.*
2 a round, black piece of plastic that has music or other sounds recorded on it.
3 the best performance so far. *She holds the record for the high jump.* ▲ Say ***rek**-ord.*

recorder recorders *noun*
a musical instrument that you play by blowing into it at one end.

recover recovers recovering recovered *verb*
1 when you recover from an illness, you get better. *He's recovering from flu.*
2 if you recover something, you get it back after it has been lost or stolen.

rectangle rectangles *noun*
a shape with four sides and four corners. Each side of a rectangle is the same length as the side opposite to it.
rectangular *adjective.*

recycle recycles recycling recycled *verb*
to recycle things is to make them into something new after they have already been used instead of throwing them away. *Daniella's book was printed on recycled paper.*

reduce reduces reducing reduced *verb*
to reduce is to make something smaller or less. *I'm trying to reduce the amount of chocolate I eat.*

reed reeds *noun*
a plant with long, hollow stems that grows near water. ● A word that sounds like **reed** is **read**.

reef reefs *noun*
a long line of rocks, sand or coral in the sea. *In very bad weather, ships sometimes hit the reef and sink.*

reel reels *noun*
a round object that you wrap film, tape or thread around. ● A word that sounds like **reel** is **real**.

referee referees *noun*
a person who makes sure that everybody playing in a game such as football obeys the rules. *My friend's dad is usually the referee when we play hockey.*
referee *verb.*

reference book reference books *noun*
a book with facts and information in it. *A dictionary is a reference book.*

reflect reflects reflecting reflected *verb*
1 if a surface reflects light, the light hits the surface and bounces back, rather than passing through it.
2 a mirror reflects something in front of it and shows what it looks like.
reflection *noun.*

refrigerator refrigerators *noun*
a metal cupboard where you can put food to keep it cold and fresh. A refrigerator is called a fridge for short. ▲ Say *ree-**frij**-er-ay-ter.*

refund refunds *noun*
money that you are given back if you have paid too much.

refuse refuses refusing refused *verb*
if you refuse to do something, you will not do it. *Dad refused to wash the dishes.* ■ The opposite is **accept**.

regard regards regarding regarded *verb*
if you regard something in a certain way, that is what you think about it. *She regarded the uniform as old-fashioned.*

region regions *noun*
an area of land or part of a country. *a mountain region.* ▲ Say **ree**-*jun*.

register registers *noun*
a book containing a list of names or important information. *The teacher called the register at the beginning of the class.*

regret regrets regretting regretted *verb*
if you regret something, you are sorry about it and wish that you had not done it or that it had not happened.

regular *adjective*
regular things have exactly the same amount of time between them. *When you exercise, your pulse gets faster but it stays regular.*
regularly *adverb*.

rehearse rehearses rehearsing rehearsed *verb*
if you rehearse, you practise something before doing it for an audience. *We rehearsed the play every night for a week.* ▲ Say *ree*-**hurse**.
rehearsal *noun*.

reign reigns reigning reigned *verb*
to reign is to be the king or queen of a country. ▲ Rhymes with ***pain***.
● A word that sounds like **reign** is **rain**.

reindeer *noun*
a large deer with very large antlers that lives in northern countries where it is very cold. ▲ Say **rain**-*deer*.

rein reins *noun*
reins are long leather straps that you use to guide a horse. ▲ Say **rains**.

reject rejects rejecting rejected *verb*
if you reject something, you will not accept it. *He rejected my advice.*

related *adjective*
if you are related to somebody, you are in the same family as them.

relation relations *noun*
a person who is in the same family. *I've got a lot of relations.*

relative relatives *noun*
a person who is in your family.

relax relaxes relaxing relaxed *verb*
when you relax, your body becomes less tense and you feel calm and less worried.
relaxation *noun*.

relay relays *noun*
a race between teams of runners. A special stick called a baton is passed to the person whose turn it is to run. Each member of the team takes it in turn to run a part of the race.

release releases releasing released *verb*
when you release somebody or an animal that has been held in some way, you set them free. *Robert released the bird that was caught in a bush.*

reliable *adjective*
if somebody is reliable, you can trust them and depend on them. ▲ Say *ree*-**lie**-*a*-*bul*.

relief *noun*
the good feeling that you get when you can stop worrying. *It was such a great relief when I was told that I'd passed my exams.* ▲ Say **ree**-*leef*.

religion religions *noun*
believing in God or gods and a way of worshipping.
religious *adjective*.

rely relies relying relied *verb*
if you can rely on somebody, you know you can trust them and depend on them. ▲ Say *ree*-**lie**.

remain remains remaining remained *verb*
1 if somebody remains in a place, they stay there. *He did not go out to play but remained in the house all day.*
2 if something remains, it is still there. *The roof had gone but the rest of the temple remains.*

remark remarks *noun*
a thing that you say about someone or something. *She made a nasty remark about my hat.*

remedy remedies *noun*
1 an answer to a problem.
2 a way of curing an illness or making something better.
remedy *verb*.

remember remembers remembering remembered *verb*
when you remember something, you have it in your mind or bring it into your mind again. *Can you remember where you went on holiday last year?*

remind reminds reminding reminded *verb*
1 if you remind somebody, you tell them something again in case they have forgotten. *Can you remind me to phone David?*
2 if something reminds you, it makes you remember something.
3 if somebody reminds you of somebody else, they are like the other person in some way.

a b c d e f g h i j k l m n o p q r s t u v w x y z

remote remoter remotest *adjective*
very far away. ■ The opposite is **close.**
remoteness *noun.*

remove removes removing removed *verb*
when you remove something, you take it away. *Please remove the dishes from the table.*
removal *noun.*

rendezvous *noun*
an arranged time and place for a meeting. ▲ Say ***rond**-ay-oo.*

renew renews renewing renewed *verb*
1 when you renew something, you arrange for it to go on longer.
2 when you renew something, you start doing it again.
3 to renew is to replace something old with something new.

rent rents *noun*
money that you pay to live in a place or to use something that you do not own yourself. *The rent for this house is ₹5,000 a week.*
rent *verb.*

repair repairs repairing repaired *verb*
if you repair something that is broken or does not work, you mend it.

repeat repeats repeating repeated *verb*
if you repeat something, you say it or do it again. *Can you repeat the question?*
repetition *noun.*

replace replaces replacing replaced *verb*
1 if you replace something, you put it back where it came from. *She replaced the book on the shelf.*
2 when you replace something, you get a new one instead of the old one. *The school is replacing its computers with more modern ones.*

reply replies replying replied *verb*
when you reply, you give an answer. *"Must I reply to this letter?" "I don't know," he replied.*

report reports *noun*
1 something that someone says or writes that tells you about something that has happened.
2 a piece of paper that teachers write to say how well a pupil has worked at school.

represent represents representing represented *verb*
if one thing represents another thing, it is a picture or symbol of it. *On the map, crosses represent churches.*

reproduction reproductions *noun*
1 a copy of something, especially a famous painting or old kind of furniture.
2 making new, young animals or plants.

reptile reptiles *noun*
an animal with cold blood that has scales on its skin. Female reptiles lay eggs. Snakes, crocodiles, tortoises and lizards are reptiles.
❖ ***Look at page 135***

request requests requesting requested *verb*
if you request something, you ask for it politely. *People using the library are requested not to talk.*

require requires requiring required *verb*
if you require something, you need it.

rescue rescues rescuing rescued *verb*
if you rescue somebody, you save them from danger. *The helicopters came to rescue animals from the forest fire.*

research researches researching researched *verb*
if you research a subject, you find out all the information you can about it.

resent resents resenting resented *verb*
to feel injured, annoyed or insulted by.

reserve reserves reserving reserved *verb*
to reserve is to ask for something to be kept for you to use later. *Tom reserved a table for six at the restaurant.*
reservation *noun.*

reservoir reservoirs *noun*
a lake used to hold water that is sent through pipes to people's houses.
▲ Say ***rez**-er-vwar.*

resign resigns resigning resigned *verb*
if you resign, you give up your job and leave. ▲ Say *ree-**zine.***

resist resists resisting resisted *verb*
if you resist something, you fight against it or try to stop it from happening.

Reptiles

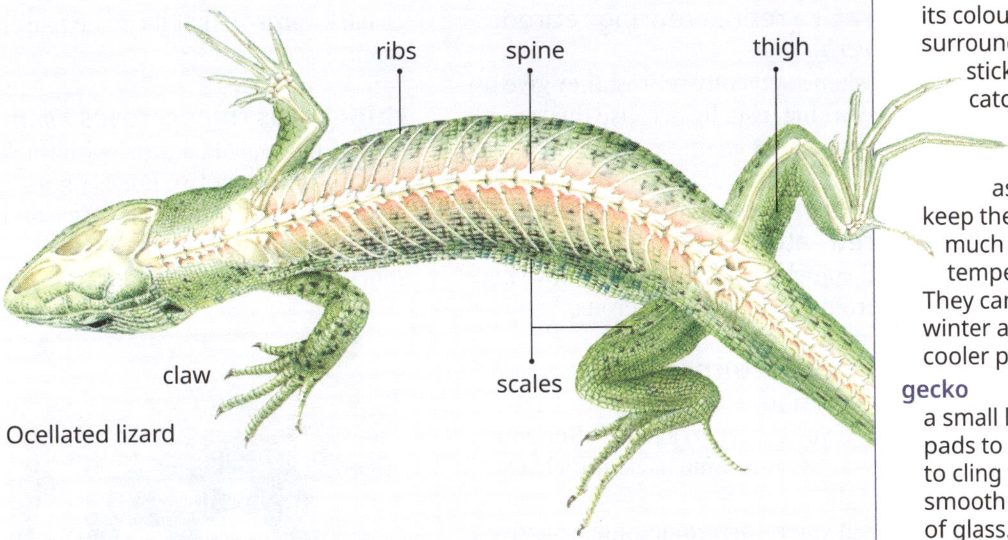

Ocellated lizard

Vocabulary

chameleon
a lizard that can change its colour to match its surroundings. It has a long sticky tongue that it uses to catch its prey.

cold-blooded
describes animals such as reptiles that cannot keep their blood temperature much above or below the temperature around them. They cannot stay active in winter and so are not found in cooler parts of the earth.

gecko
a small lizard that has "sticky" pads to its feet that enables it to cling to surfaces that seem smooth such as an upright pane of glass.

Komodo dragon
is the largest of all lizards. it survives only on some small islands of Indonesia.

Rattlesnake

Red-eared terrapin

Chameleon

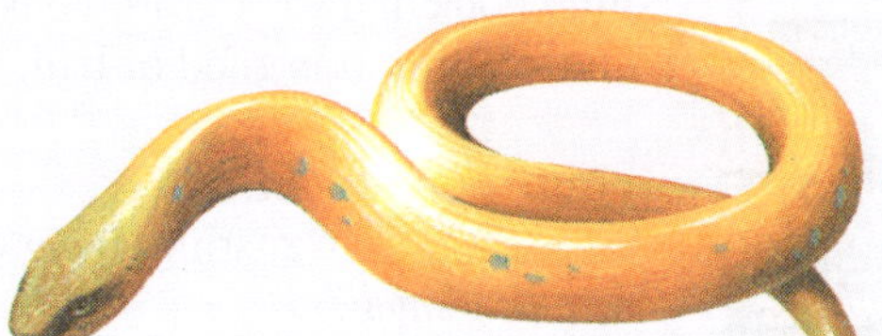

Slow worm

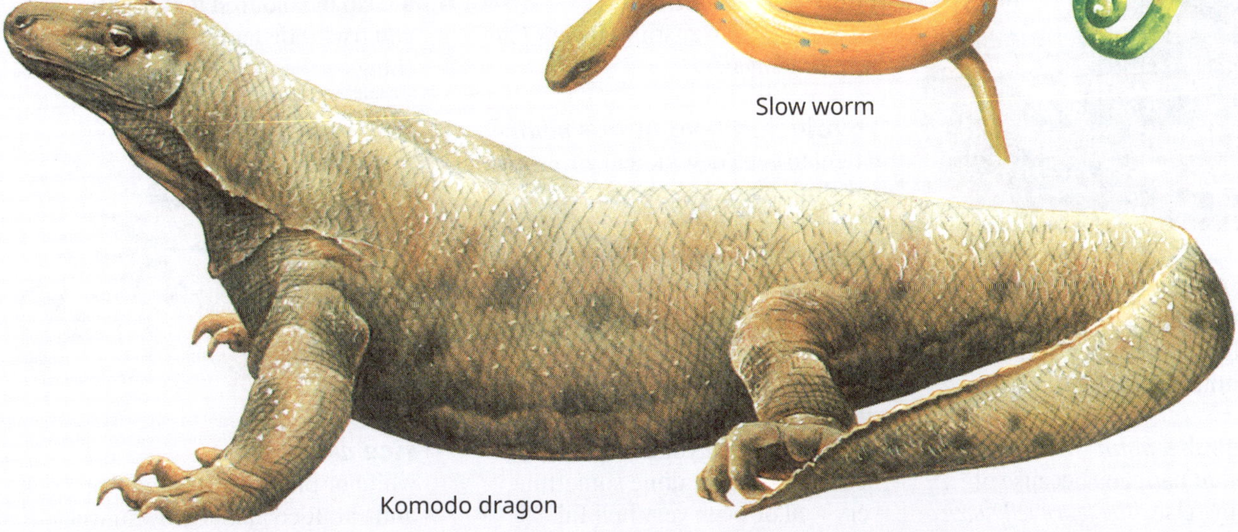

Komodo dragon

a b c d e f g h i j k l m n o p q r s t u v w x y z

A B C D E F G H I J K L M N O P Q R S T U V W X Y Z

resources *noun*
things that are found naturally in a country, such as gas or oil, that can make the country richer.

---

respect *noun*
the feeling that you have for somebody you like and admire because they are a good person or know a lot or are clever.

---

respond responds responding responded *verb*
if you respond to somebody, you answer them.
response *noun*.

---

responsible *adjective*
1 a responsible person is sensible and can be trusted.
2 if you are responsible for somebody or something, you are in charge of them.

---

rest *noun*
1 a time when you are quiet and do not work or do anything energetic. *Jordan was having a rest reading a book.*
2 everything or everybody that is left over. *Jim and his friends went home but the rest went swimming.* ◆ *What shall we do for the rest of the day?*

---

restaurant restaurants *noun*
a place where you can pay to eat a meal. ▲ Say ***rest**-er-ont*.

---

restrict restricts restricting restricted *verb*
if you restrict something, you keep it within a limit so it is not too large.

---

result results *noun*
1 a thing that happens because of something else. *The fence fell down as a result of the storm.*
2 the score at the end of a match. *the rugby results.*

---

retire retires retiring retired *verb*
when somebody retires, they give up working, usually because they are old.
retirement *noun*.

---

retreat retreats retreating retreated *verb*
if somebody retreats, they move back from something dangerous.

---

return returns returning returned *verb*
1 if you return to a place after going away, you come back or go back there.
2 if you return something, you give it back. *James returned his library books after he had read them.*

---

revenge *noun*
a thing that you do to hurt somebody for being horrible to you. *Tina took revenge on Tim for laughing at her.*

---

reverse reverses reversing reversed *verb*
if you reverse, you go backwards. *I've reversed my car into a tree!*

---

review reviews *noun*
something that somebody says or writes in a newspaper or on radio or television telling people what a new film, book or TV programme is like and whether it is good or bad.

---

revolting *adjective*
horrible and disgusting. *What's that revolting smell?*

---

revolution revolutions *noun*
a fight to get a new kind of government.
revolutionary *noun*.

---

revolver revolvers *noun*
a small gun that can be fired several times before it needs to be loaded again.

---

reward rewards *noun*
a nice thing that you are given because you have done something very well or been very helpful.
reward *verb*.

---

rewind rewinds rewinding rewound *verb*
to rewind a tape or video is to make it go backwards so that it can be played again.

---

rhinoceros rhinoceroses *noun*
a large, heavy, wild animal with thick skin. It has one or two horns on its nose. Rhinoceroses live in Africa and Asia. They are called rhinos for short. ▲ Say *rye-**noss**-er-us*.

---

rhyme rhymes *noun*
a word that sounds the same as another word except for the first letter. "Batter" and "fatter" are rhymes. ▲ Say ***rime***.

---

rhythm rhythms *noun*
a pattern of repeated sounds which is regular. Music and poetry have rhythm. ▲ Say ***rith**-um*.

---

rib ribs *noun*
your ribs are the bones that curve around your chest to protect your heart and lungs.

---

ribbon ribbons *noun*
a strip of coloured material that you can use to tie hair or for decorating things.

---

rice *noun*
white or brown grains that you cook and eat. Rice plants grow in wet ground in hot regions.

rich richer richest *adjective*
a person who is rich has a lot of money. ■ The opposite is **poor.**
rich in containing a lot of. *Fruit is rich in vitamin C.*

rid rids ridding rid *verb*
to free somebody from something harmful or annoying.
get rid of to throw something away. *Get rid of those old comics.*

riddle riddles *noun*
a question that is a puzzle and has a clever or funny answer. *"What goes up when the rain comes down?" Answer: "An umbrella."*

ride rides *noun*
a journey on a horse, bicycle, bus or train. *I went for a ride on my horse.*

ride rides riding rode ridden *verb*
1 when you ride a horse or a motorbike, you sit on it and travel along.
2 when you ride in something such as a car or bus, you travel in it.

ridiculous *adjective*
very silly. *What a ridiculous hat!*

right *adjective*
1 when you write the word "right", the "i" is to the right of the "r". *I write with my right hand.* ■ The opposite is **left.**
2 if something is right, it is correct. *Congratulations, that's the right answer!* ■ The opposite is **wrong.**
● A word that sounds like **right** is **write.**

right *adverb*
correctly. *Did I guess right?* ● A word that sounds like **right** is **write.** ■ The opposite is **wrong.**

right angle right angles *noun*
an angle of 90 degrees like the corners of a square where two lines meet.

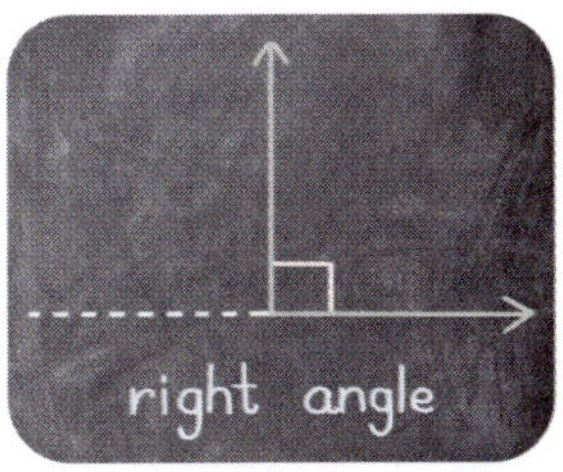

rigid *adjective*
if something is rigid, you cannot bend or stretch it. *You can't bend a rigid metal bar.*

rim rims *noun*
the edge around the top of such things as a glass, a jar or cup. *the rim of a wheel.*

ring rings *noun*
1 a round piece of metal that you wear on your finger.
2 a circle with an empty centre.
3 the noise of a bell.

ring rings ringing rang rung *verb*
1 when something rings, it makes the sound of a bell.
2 if you ring somebody, you call them on the phone.

rinse rinses rinsing rinsed *verb*
to wash in clean water, not using soap.

rip rips ripping ripped *verb*
if you rip something, you tear it. *He ripped his shirt on a nail.*

ripe riper ripest *adjective*
when a fruit is ripe, it is ready to eat. *The banana isn't ripe yet – it's green.*

ripple ripples *noun*
a very small wave or movement on the surface of water.

rise rises rising rose risen *verb*
to rise is to move upwards. *The bread dough has risen.* ■ The opposite is **dip** or **fall.**

risk risks *noun*
a danger that something bad or harmful will happen. *She took a risk when she rushed into the burning house.*
risk *verb,* **risky** *adjective.*

rival rivals *noun*
someone who is trying to win the same thing as you are.

river rivers *noun*
a large amount of water flowing across the land towards the sea or a lake.

road roads *noun*
a long piece of hard ground that cars, bicycles and lorries can travel on.
● A word that sounds like **road** is **rode.**

roam roams roaming roamed *verb*
to roam is to wander about without trying to go anywhere. *He roamed the streets at night.*

roar roars roaring roared *verb*
to roar is to make a very loud noise. *The lion roared.* ◆ *The car engine roared.*

roast roasts roasting roasted *verb*
when you roast food, you cook it in an oven or over a fire. *roast chicken.*

rob robs robbing robbed *verb*
to rob somebody is to steal from them.
robber *noun,* **robbery** *noun.*

robe robes *noun*
a long, loose piece of clothing.

robin robins *noun*
a small brown bird with red feathers on the front of its body.

robot robots *noun*
a machine controlled by a computer that can do jobs that people would otherwise do. *In factories, robots now do a lot of work.* ▲ Say **roe-bot**.

rock rocks *noun*
1 the very hard material that mountains and the hardest ground are made of.
2 a large piece of stone.
3 pop music with a very strong rhythm.

rock rocks rocking rocked *verb*
when you rock, you move or move something gently from side to side or backwards and forwards. *She was rocking the baby in her arms.*

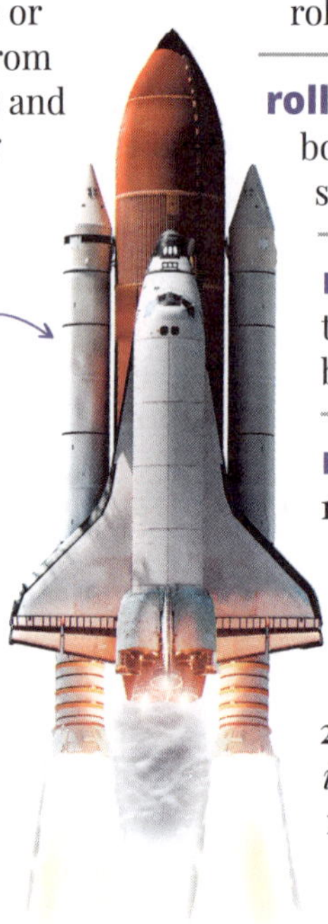

rocket rockets *noun*
1 an engine in a tall metal tube that is used to send spacecraft into space or to carry bombs.
2 a firework that is sent high up into the air and then explodes in different colours.

rod rods *noun*
a long, thin, round piece of wood or metal. *a fishing rod.*

rode past of ride.
● A word that sounds like **rode** is **road**.

rodent rodents *noun*
a small animal with sharp front teeth that gnaws things. Mice, rats and squirrels are all rodents.

roll rolls *noun*
1 a very small, round loaf of bread.
2 a long, thin tube made by rolling a piece of paper or material round and round. *a roll of wallpaper.*

roll rolls rolling rolled *verb*
1 when something rolls, it goes along the ground turning over and over. *The ball rolled slowly down the hill.*
2 To roll something is to wrap it around itself several times in the shape of a long, thin tube.
3 To roll pastry is to make it flat by pushing a wooden tube called a rolling pin over it.

roller skate roller skates *noun*
boots with wheels for skating on smooth, hard surfaces.

roof roofs *noun*
the part that covers the top of a building or the top of a car.

room rooms *noun*
1 a part inside a building that is separated from the other parts inside the building by walls. Bathrooms and kitchens are rooms.
2 space. *There's not enough room in our car for ten people!*
roomy *adjective*.
a roomy house with plenty of space.

root roots *noun*
1 part of a plant that grows underground and takes in water and food from the soil.
2 the part of a tooth or hair growing under the gum or skin that you cannot see. ● A word that sounds like **root** is **route**.

rope ropes *noun*
very thick, strong string that is used for tying things. *Tie the boat up with rope.*

rose roses *noun*
a plant that grows on thorny bushes.

rose past of rise.

rot rots rotting rotted *verb*
when something rots, it goes bad or starts to get soft and weak. *The tomatoes were rotting on the ground.* ◆ *Wood rots in water.*

rotate rotates rotating rotated *verb*
if something rotates, it turns round and round like a wheel. *The Earth rotates as it goes around the Sun.*

rotten *adjective*
if something is rotten, it has rotted and is so bad that it cannot be used. *That fruit is rotten.*

rough rougher roughest *adjective*
1 bumpy or uneven, not smooth. *A cat's tongue is very rough.*
2 not exact. *a rough guess.*
3 using a lot of force. *Rugby is a rough game.* ■ The opposite is **gentle**.
▲ Say ***ruff***.
roughly *adverb*, **roughness** *noun*.

round *adjective*
shaped like a circle or a ball. *Most coins are round.*

roundabout roundabouts *noun*
1 a round place where roads meet and where traffic goes around in a clockwise circle.
2 a machine in a playground for children to ride on that turns around and around in circles.

route routes *noun*
the way you go from one place to another place on a journey. *Please work out the best route on the map before we leave.* ▲ Rhymes with ***boot***. ● A word that sounds like **route** is **root**.

row rows *noun*
1 a quarrel or angry argument.
▲ Rhymes with ***cow***.
2 a number of things or people that are in a line. *a row of jars.*
▲ Rhymes with ***low***.

row rows rowing rowed *verb*
when you row a boat, you make it move by pushing against the water with oars. ▲ Rhymes with ***low***.

royal *adjective*
belonging to a king or queen. *the royal family.* ◆ *a royal palace.*

rub rubs rubbing rubbed *verb*
1 if you rub something, you move your hand up and down it. *She yawned and rubbed her eyes.*
2 to rub is to press one thing backwards and forwards against another. *People say that you can make a fire by rubbing two sticks together but I've never been able to do it.*

rubber *noun*
1 a strong, waterproof material that stretches and bounces. Tyres are made of black rubber.
2 a small piece of rubber that you use to make pencil marks disappear.

rubbish *noun*
things that you do not want that you throw away.

ruby rubies *noun*
a valuable red jewel.▲ Say ***roo-bee***.

rucksack rucksacks *noun*
a bag for carrying things in that you wear on your back. *We need tents and rucksacks to take on our walking holiday.*

rude ruder rudest *adjective*
if somebody is rude, they behave in a bad way and are not polite.

rug rugs *noun*
a small piece of thick, heavy material that you put on the floor.

rugby *noun*
a game played between two teams using an oval ball. Players score points by trying to carry the ball over a line or kicking it over a bar.

ruin ruins ruining ruined *verb*
to ruin something is to completely spoil it. *The rain ruined our picnic.*
▲ Say ***roo-in***.

ruins *noun*
the parts of a building that are left after the rest of it has fallen down or been destroyed. *the ruins of a castle.*
▲ Say ***roo-ins***.

rule rules ruling ruled *verb*
to rule a country is to be in charge of it.

rule rules *noun*
something that says what you are allowed to do and what you are not allowed to do. *the rules of rugby.*

ruler rulers *noun*
1 a long, narrow piece of wood, metal or plastic that you use for drawing straight lines and for measuring.
2 a person who rules a country.

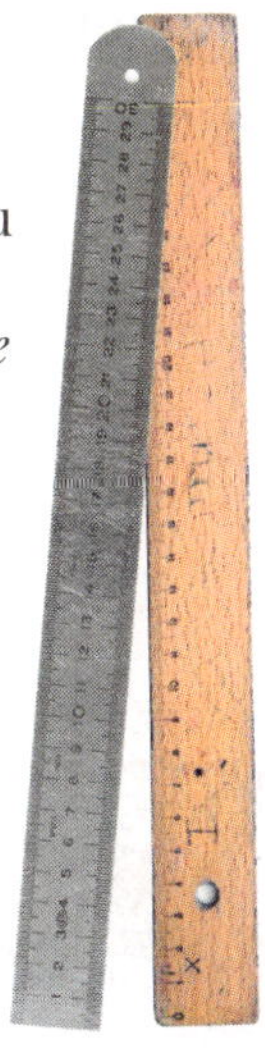

rumble rumbles rumbling rumbled *verb*
when something rumbles, it makes a long, low sound like thunder. *The lorries rumbled past.*

run runs running ran run *verb*
1 when a person or animal runs, they go on their feet much faster than when they walk.
2 if you run something, you are in charge of it and you make sure that it works properly.
3 when liquid runs, it flows. *Tears were running down her face.*

rung past of ring.

runway runways *noun*
the long, hard, level strip of land at an airport on which aeroplanes take off and land.

rush rushes rushing rushed *verb*
if you rush, you go somewhere or do something very quickly. *He was rushing to get to the bus stop before the bus.*

rust *noun*
a red-brown substance that covers iron or steel when they get wet.
rusty *adjective*.

rustle rustles rustling rustled *verb*
to rustle is to make the soft sound that leaves make as they move together in the wind. ▲ Say ***russ-ul***.

A B C D E F G H I J K L M N O P Q R S T U V W X Y Z

S s

sack sacks *noun*
a large, strong bag that you put things such as coal, potatoes or rubbish in.

sack sacks sacking sacked *verb*
if somebody is sacked from their job, they are told to leave.

sad sadder saddest *adjective*
unhappy. *Cecile was very sad when her hamster died.* ■ The opposite is **happy**.

saddle saddles *noun*
1 a seat for a rider on a horse.
2 a seat on a bicycle.

safe *adjective*
1 if you are safe, you are unharmed. *The lost kitten was found safe and well.*
2 if something is safe, it is not dangerous. *Is this ladder safe?*
safety *noun*.

safe safes *noun*
a strong box or cupboard with a lock that you keep money or jewels in.

said past of say.

sail sails *noun*
a sail is a big piece of cloth on a boat. When the wind blows against the sail, the boat moves along.

sail sails sailing sailed *verb*
to sail means to move along in a boat using its sails. *Sam went sailing on the river.*

sailor sailors *noun*
a person who works on a ship or boat.

salad salads *noun*
a cold food made of raw vegetables such as lettuce, beetroot and cucumbers.

salary salaries *noun*
the money that somebody is paid for the work that they do. *Teachers' salaries are paid regularly every month.*

sale sales *noun*
a time when a shop sells things at a cheaper price than usual. *Mum bought some shoes in the sale.*

saliva *noun*
the liquid in your mouth.

salmon salmon *noun*
a fish with silver skin and pink flesh that you can eat. ▲ Say ***sam-un***.
❖ ***Look at page 65***

salt *noun*
a white powder that you put on food to give it a stronger taste. Sea water has salt in it.
salty *adjective*.
The soup that I made was too salty.

salute salutes saluting saluted *verb*
when soldiers salute, they make a sign by lifting their right hand to their forehead as a greeting or to show respect to somebody. *She saluted when the General walked by.*

sample samples *noun*
a small amount of something that shows what the rest of it is like.

sand *noun*
a white or yellow substance that is made from lots of tiny pieces of rock. You can see sand by the sea or in deserts.

sandal sandals *noun*
a light shoe made of a sole with straps that go over your foot.

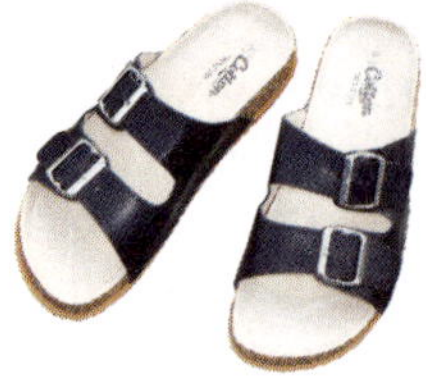

sandwich sandwiches *noun*
two slices of bread with food in between them. *an egg and tomato sandwich.*

sang past of sing.

sank past of sink.

sap *noun*
the sticky liquid inside the stems of plants and the trunks of trees. Sap carries food to all parts of the plant.

sapphire sapphires *noun*
a bright blue jewel.

sari saris *noun*
a long piece of material that many Indian women and girls wrap around their body like a dress.

sat past of sit.

satellite satellites *noun*
1 a natural object in space, like a moon, that moves around a larger object, like a planet.
2 a satellite is also a machine that is sent into space to pick up and send back signals and information. Satellite television comes to us by satellite. ▲ Say ***sat-ul-ite***.

satisfy satisfies satisfying satisfied *verb*
if you satisfy somebody, you please them and give them what they want or need. *Nothing I ever do satisfies you.*

sauce *noun*
a thick liquid that you pour over food to add to its flavour. *Do you like tomato sauce on your chips?*

saucepan saucepans *noun*
a metal pot with a handle and a lid for cooking food.

saucer saucers *noun*
a saucer is a kind of small plate for putting a cup on.

sausage sausages *noun*
meat that is cut up into very small pieces and made into a long, thin shape like a tube.

save saves saving saved *verb*
1 if you save somebody, you take them away from danger. *The man saved the child from drowning.*
2 if you save money or something else, you keep it somewhere to use later. *I'm saving for a new computer game.*

savoury *adjective*
a savoury food tastes salty instead of sweet. Cheese and crisps are savoury foods.

saw past of see.

saw saws *noun*
a tool for cutting wood. It has a metal blade with sharp points called teeth along one edge.
saw *verb*.

saxophone saxophones *noun*
a musical instrument made of brass that you play by blowing into it.
saxophonist *noun*.

say says saying said *verb*
if you say something you speak words. *My uncle said that he didn't like eating meat very often.*

scab scabs *noun*
a piece of dried blood that forms over a cut in your skin when it is healing.

scald scalds scalding scalded *verb*
if you scald yourself, you burn yourself with very hot liquid or steam.

scale scales *noun*
1 a row of marks on something such as a ruler that is used to measure things.
2 a way of showing distances between places on a map. *This map has a scale of one centimetre to one kilometre.*
3 one of the small, hard pieces of skin that cover the body of a fish or reptile.
4 a scale is also a series of musical notes. *You play or sing the notes of a scale one after the other.*

map scale

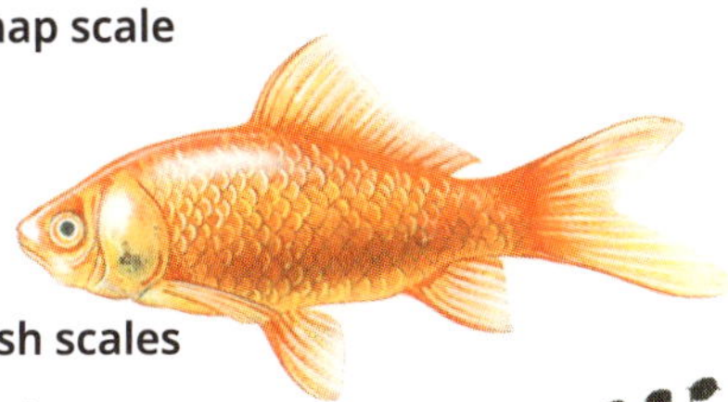
fish scales

musical scale in C

scales *noun*
you use scales to find out how heavy you are, or to weigh things such as fruits and vegetables.

scar scars *noun*
a mark on your skin left by a cut that has healed.

scarce scarcer scarcest *adjective*
if things are scarce, they are difficult to find because there are only a few of them. *Flowers are scarce in winter.*
scarcely *adverb*.
I was so happy I could scarcely speak.

say

Some words you can use instead of say:

I heard her say that she has read the book.
remark, comment, mention

How do you say 'last'?
pronounce

She said I would have to work much harder.
explained, announced

Other ways of saying things:
chat, exclaim, have a conversation, murmur, mutter, scream, shout, shriek, talk, tell, whisper

scare scares scaring scared *verb*
if something scares you, it frightens you. *That ghost story really scared me.*

scarecrow scarecrows *noun*
a thing that looks like a person dressed in old clothes. Farmers put scarecrows in their fields when crops are growing to frighten off birds.

scarf scarves *noun*
a long piece of material or knitted wool that you wear around your neck.

scatter scatters scattering scattered *verb*
1 if animals or things scatter, they move quickly in different directions. *The loud noise frightened the squirrels and they scattered in many different directions.*
2 if you scatter things, you throw them about in different directions. *Ben scattered some bread for the ducks.*

scene scenes *noun*
1 what you see in the countryside around you. *a mountain scene.*
2 a place where something happens. *the scene of the murder.*
3 a part of a play. *Does the hero get killed in the last scene?*

scenery *noun*
1 what you see around you in the countryside, such as mountains, forests, rivers and lakes. *What beautiful scenery!*
2 the things on the stage of a theatre that make a play more real to the audience.

scent scents *noun*
1 a nice smell. *a beautiful scent.*
2 a liquid that you can put on your skin to make you smell nice. ● A word that sounds like **scent** is **sent**.

A B C D E F G H I J K L M N O P Q R S T U V W X Y Z

scheme schemes *noun*
a plan for doing something. *There are many schemes for helping the environment.* ▲ Say ***skeem***.

school schools *noun*
a place where children go to learn. ▲ Say ***skule***.

science sciences *noun*
finding out about things such as animals, plants and natural materials. **scientific** *adjective.*

scientist scientists *noun*
a person who finds out about animals, plants and other things in the world by looking at them closely, writing down information about them, and doing experiments.

scissors *noun*
a small tool for cutting paper and other things. A pair of scissors has two sharp blades that are joined together.

scoop scoops scooping scooped *verb*
to scoop is to lift something up using your hands or with a kind of spoon called a scoop. *Nicky scooped some ice-cream out of the bowl.*

scooter scooters *noun*
1 a motorbike with a small engine.
2 a toy with wheels and a handlebar for a child to ride on. You stand on it with one foot and push along with the other.

scorch scorches scorching scorched *verb*
if you scorch something like a piece of material, you burn it a little, leaving a brown mark. *I scorched my shirt because the iron was too hot.*

score scores *noun*
in a game, the score is how many points each side has. *At the end of the match the score was 4-2.*

score scores scoring scored *verb*
to score means to get a point in a game. *Andy scored the winning goal in the football match.*

scowl scowls scowling scowled *verb*
if you scowl, you have an angry, bad-tempered look on your face. *She scowled at the pile of dirty clothes.* **scowl** *noun.*

scramble scrambles scrambling scrambled *verb*
if you scramble over rocks or rough ground, you use your hands and feet to help you move quickly.

scrap scraps *noun*
a small piece of something such as paper or material.

scrapbook scrapbooks *noun*
a book with blank pages that you can stick pictures, postcards or pieces of writing in.

scrape scrapes scraping scraped *verb*
1 if you scrape your knee, you hurt it by rubbing it against something hard or rough.
2 if you scrape mud off your shoes, you get it off with a thing such as a knife.

scratch scratches scratching scratched *verb*
1 if you scratch your skin, you make thin cuts on it by rubbing something sharp against it. *Sarah scratched her hand on the thorns.*
2 if you scratch yourself, you rub your nails across your skin because it itches.
scratch *noun.*

scream screams screaming screamed *verb*
if you scream, you shout in a very loud, high voice because you are excited or frightened. *Sophie screamed when she went on the big wheel at the fair.*

screen screens *noun*
1 the flat part of a TV or computer where you see the pictures or words.
2 the place on the wall where the film is shown in a cinema.

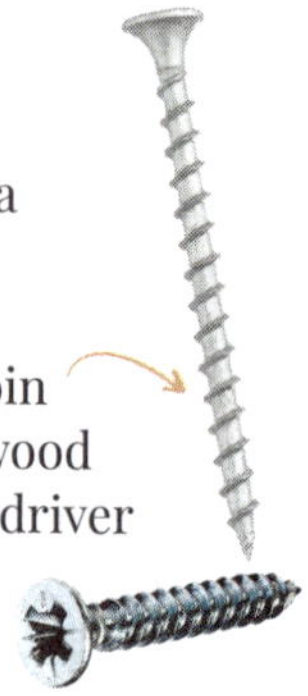

screw screws *noun*
a thin piece of metal like a nail with a sharp point at one end and a slot in the top. Screws are used to join things such as pieces of wood together. You use a screwdriver to turn the screw into a piece of wood.

screw screws screwing screwed *verb*
1 to join things together using screws. *He screwed the shelf to the wall.*
2 if you screw things up, you squeeze them into a ball. *She screwed up the paper and threw it into the bin.*

scribble scribbles scribbling scribbled *verb*
to write quickly and without care.

script scripts *noun*
all the words that have been written for the actors to say in a play or film.

scrub scrubs scrubbing scrubbed *verb*
if you scrub something, you rub it hard to clean it. *Paul scrubbed the floor with a stiff brush.*

scruffy *adjective*
untidy and dirty. *scruffy clothes.*

sculpture sculptures *noun*
1 a person, an animal or a shape that has been made of stone, wood or metal by an artist called a sculptor.
2 sculpture is the art of carving or modelling things.

scythe scythes *noun*
a tool with a long handle and a sharp, curved blade that you use to cut long grass. ▲ Say ***sithe***.

sea seas *noun*
a large area of salt water. *We went swimming in the sea.*

sea-horse sea-horses *noun*
a tiny fish with a head shaped like a horse's head and a long curling tail.

seal seals *noun*
an animal with short, grey fur that lives near the sea. Seals spend a lot of time in the sea and catch fish to eat.

seam seams *noun*
a line made where two pieces of material are sewn together. *These two pieces of material are joined with a seam.*

search searches searching searched *verb*
if you search for somebody or something, you look very carefully for them. *We searched everywhere for the lost kitten.*

season seasons *noun*
one of the four parts of the year. They are spring, summer, autumn and winter.
seasonal *adjective.*
seasonal vegetables.

seat seats *noun*
a thing you sit on. Buses and cars have seats. *We sat in the front seats at the cinema.*

seaweed *noun*
a red, green or brown plant that grows in the sea.

second seconds *noun*
a very short measure of time. There are 60 seconds in a minute.

second *adjective*
second means next after the first. *Tom won the race and Ron came second.*

secret secrets *noun*
something that only a few people know about. *I'm not telling you what you're getting for your birthday – it's a secret!*

secretary secretaries *noun*
a person who works in an office. Secretaries answer the phone, make appointments and type letters.

section sections *noun*
one of the separate parts of something. *Rob was trying to fit together the sections of the model aeroplane.*

security *noun*
feeling safe or trying to keep things safe. *She locked the door for extra security.*

see sees seeing saw seen *verb*
1 when you see somebody or something, you look at them with your eyes.
2 to see also means to understand something. *You see what I mean?*

seed seeds *noun*
a tiny, hard part inside the flower or fruit of a plant. If you put seeds into the ground they will grow into new plants.

seek seeks seeking sought *verb*
to seek means to look for somebody or something. *The police are seeking a woman who was seen near the bank at midnight.*

seem seems seeming seemed *verb*
to seem means to look or feel like something. *Ben is tall so he seems older than he really is.*

seen past of see.

seesaw seesaws *noun*
a thing that you ride on in a playground. One person sits at each end of a long piece of wood and they take it in turns to go up and down.

seize seizes seizing seized *verb*
if you seize something, you take hold of it firmly and suddenly. *The thief seized the bag.* ▲ Say ***seez***. ● A word that sounds like **seize** is **sees.**
seize-up to become stuck.

seldom *adverb*
not very often. *I seldom see my aunt because she lives a long way from us.*

select selects selecting selected *verb*
when you select someone or something, you choose them. *We selected the best painting to go on the wall.*
selection *noun.*
a selection of chocolates.

selfish *adjective*
a selfish person does not like to help or share things with other people and only thinks of themself. *It was selfish of you to eat all the sweets yourself.*

sell sells selling sold *verb*
if somebody sells something to you, they give it to you and you pay them money.

semicircle semicircles *noun*
1 half a circle.
2 the shape of half a circle. *We put the chairs in a semicircle.*

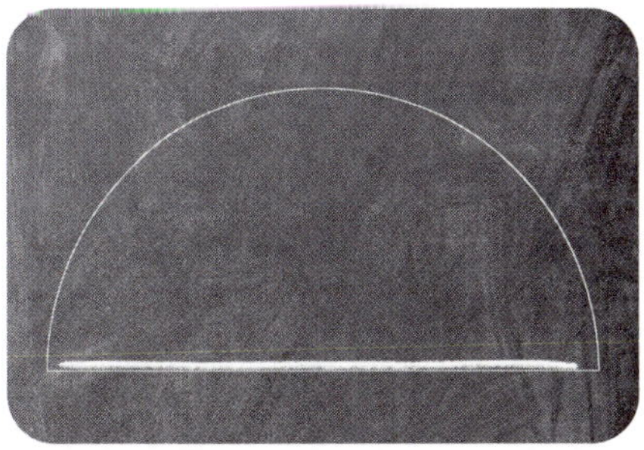

semi-final semi-finals *noun*
in a sport, the person or team that wins each semi-final will play in the final and decide who will win the whole competition.

send sends sending sent *verb*
to send is to make somebody or something go to another place. *I am going to send a postcard to Katie.*
◆ *Mum sent me to the shops.*

senior *adjective*
older in years or more important. *the senior school.* ◆ *a senior minister in the government.* ■ The opposite is **junior**.

sense senses *noun*
1 the ability that most people have to see, hear, touch, taste and smell.
2 knowing and being careful to do the right thing. *If you had any sense, you wouldn't play with matches.*

sensible *adjective*
a sensible person thinks carefully about what they are doing and does not do anything silly or foolish. *Gita won't get lost, she's very sensible.*

sensitive *adjective*
1 a sensitive person cares about other people's feelings.
2 if your skin is sensitive, it is sore or it gets sore very easily.

sent past of send.
● A word that sounds like **sent** is **scent**.

sentence sentences *noun*
a group of words that make sense together. A written sentence begins with a capital letter and ends with a full stop. 'Jamie stroked the cat.' and 'Joan is late today.' are both sentences.

separate *adjective*
if two things are separate they are not joined together. ▲ Say *sep-er-ut.*

separate separates separating separated *verb*
to set or keep apart. *He separates the white from the yolk.* ▲ Say *sep-er-ate.*

serial serials *noun*
a story that is told in parts on television or in a magazine. ● A word that sounds like **serial** is **cereal**.

series *noun*
1 a set of things of the same kind that follow each other.
2 a number of programmes on radio or television on the same subject, that follow each other. *I am watching a series on dinosaurs.*

serious *adjective*
1 important or very bad. *a serious accident.*
2 a serious person is quiet and does not laugh or joke very often.

servant servants *noun*
a servant is a person who works in somebody else's house, doing such things as cooking and cleaning.

serve serves serving served *verb*
1 if somebody serves you in a restaurant, they bring you food and drink.
2 if somebody serves you in a shop, they help you to look at things you want to buy. *Are you being served?*

service services *noun*
1 something useful that a person or a company does for other people. *a train service.* ◆ *the postal service.*
2 a service is also a meeting in a church where people pray and sing.

session sessions *noun*
a time when people meet to do something. *a football training session.*

set sets *noun*
a group of things that belong together, *a china tea set.* ◆ *a chess set.*

set sets setting set *verb*
1 when something liquid like cement sets, it goes hard.
2 when the sun sets, it goes down below the horizon and then the sky gets dark.
3 when you set a table, you put all the things on it you need for a meal such as cups, plates, knives and forks.
4 when you set a clock or a watch, you move the hands to a certain time. *I set my alarm clock for 7.30 p.m.*
5 to set also means to give somebody work to do. *The teacher set a test for her pupils.*

settee settees *noun*
a long, comfortable seat for two or more people, also called a sofa.

settle settles settling settled *verb*
if you settle, you go to a place and stay there. *A ladybird settled on my hand.* ◆ *Nita and Bill have settled in Australia.*

several *adjective*
more than two but not very many.

severe *adjective*
very bad. *a severe headache.*

sew sews sewing sewed sewn *verb*
when you sew, you join pieces of material together or join something to the material using a needle and thread. *Can you sew this button back on my shirt, please?* ▲ Say **so**.

sewer sewers *noun*
a large pipe under the ground that takes waste away from houses and other buildings.
▲ Say *soo-er.*

sex sexes *noun*
1 the two groups that people and animals belong to. The two sexes are males and females.
2 sex is the way that people and animals produce young ones.

shade *noun*
1 a place where the sun cannot reach. *We sat in the shade of an oak tree.*
2 a cover for a lamp.
3 a variety of a colour. *a dark shade of blue.*
shady *adjective.*

shadow shadows *noun*
a dark shape that you see near somebody or something that is under or in front of the light. *When you place your hands in front of a light, you can have fun by making hand shadows.*

shake shakes shaking shook shaken *verb*
1 when you shake something, you move it up and down or backwards and forwards. *I shook the bottle of tomato sauce.*
2 if your body shakes because you are cold or frightened, it wobbles about.
shaky *adjective*, **shakily** *adverb*.

shallow *adjective*
not very deep. *This water is shallow, it only just covers my feet.*

shame *noun*
the guilty feeling that you have if you have done something wrong.
shameful *adjective*. *shameful behaviour*.

shampoo shampoos *noun*
a liquid that you use to wash your hair.

shape shapes *noun*
what you see if you draw a line around the outside of something. Circles, squares, triangles and rectangles are all different shapes.
❖ ***Look at page 146***

share shares sharing shared *verb*
1 if you share something, you give some of it to somebody else. *I shared my birthday cake with my friends.*
2 to share also means to use something together with another person. *I share a bedroom with my sister.*
share *noun*.

shark sharks *noun*
a big, sea fish that has lots of very sharp teeth and a big mouth.

White shark

sharp sharper sharpest *adjective*
1 something that is sharp has an edge or a point that is good for cutting. *Knives and scissors are usually sharp.*
2 sudden and severe. *a sharp pain.*
sharply *adverb*.

shatter shatters shattering shattered *verb*
if something such as glass shatters, it breaks into lots of little pieces.

shave shaves shaving shaved *verb*
to shave is to cut hair off the skin with a razor.

shawl shawls *noun*
a wide scarf that you wear around your shoulders or wrap a baby in.

shed sheds *noun*
a small building made of wood. *a tool-shed.* ◆ *a cow-shed.*

shed sheds shedding shed *verb*
1 if an animal sheds hair, some of its hair falls out.
2 when trees shed their leaves, the leaves fall off because it is autumn.

sheep sheep *noun*
an animal that farmers keep for their wool and for their meat. A male sheep is called a ram and a female sheep is called a ewe.

Soay sheep

Oxford downs

Merino

Different types of sheep

sheet sheets *noun*
1 a large piece of material for putting on a bed.
2 a thin, flat piece of paper, glass or metal. *a sheet of headed notepaper.* ◆ *The road was like a sheet of ice.*

shelf shelves *noun*
a long, flat piece of wood or glass fixed on a wall or in a cupboard where you can put things. *a bookshelf.*

shell shells *noun*
1 the hard outside part of some living things. Eggs, nuts, snails and crabs have shells.
2 a very large kind of bullet.

shelter shelters *noun*
a covered place where you are safe from bad weather or danger. *We stood in the bus shelter while it rained.*
shelter *verb*.

shield shields *noun*
a large piece of wood or metal that soldiers used to carry to protect their bodies from enemy weapons.

shin shins *noun*
your shin is the front part of your leg between your knee and your ankle.

shine shines shining shone *verb*
when something shines, it gives out light, or is bright like silver. *The sun is shining.* ◆ *She polished the silver bowl until it shone.*
shiny *adjective*. *a shiny new coin.*

Shapes

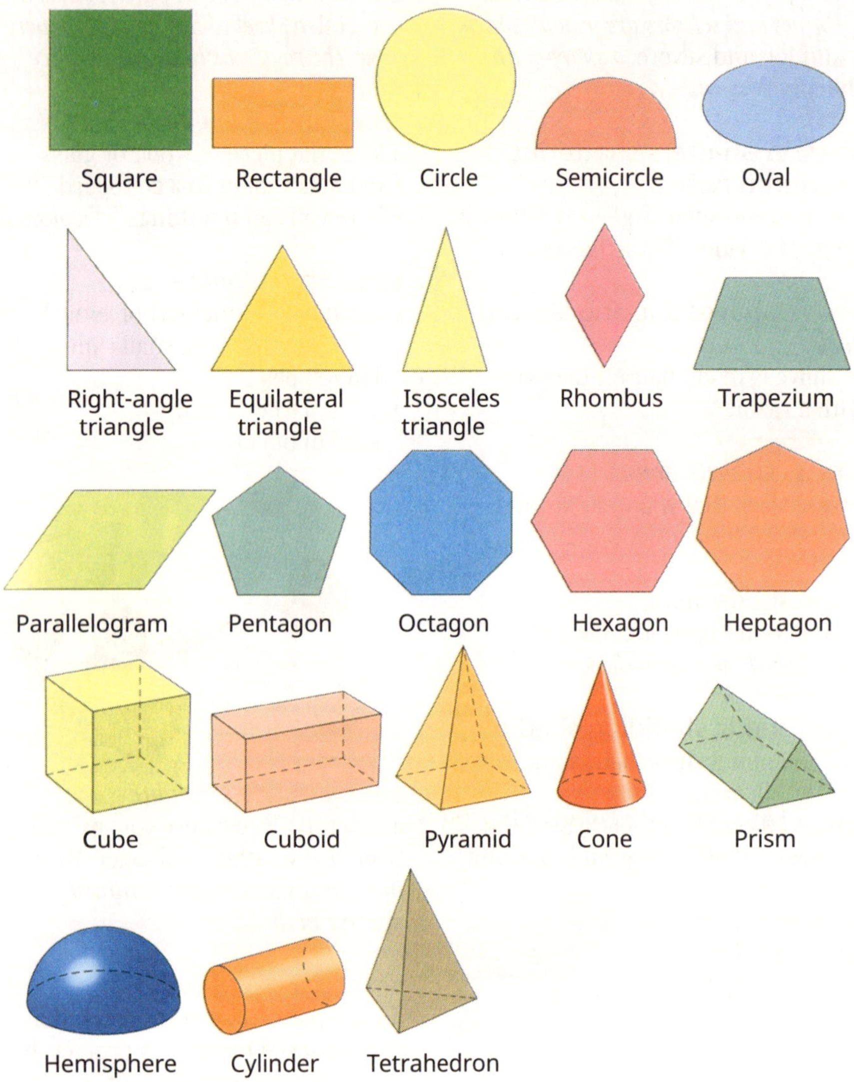

Vocabulary

hemisphere
half of a sphere or ball-shape.

heptagon
a flat figure with seven sides.

parallelogram
a quadrilateral with two equal sides parallel in one direction and the other two equal sides parallel in another direction.

polygon
any figure with many sides such as a heptagon (7 sides), hexagon (6), octagon (8) and pentagon (5).

quadrilateral
a flat figure that has four sides.

rhombus
a diamond-shaped parallelogram with four equal sides.

spiral (not shown).
a shape of a line that coils around the same spot like a spring in smaller and smaller or bigger and bigger circles.

trapezoid (not shown)
a quadrilateral having no sides parallel.

trapezium
a quadrilateral having two sides parallel (lying in the same direction but never meeting), and two sides not parallel.

Colours

Primary colours

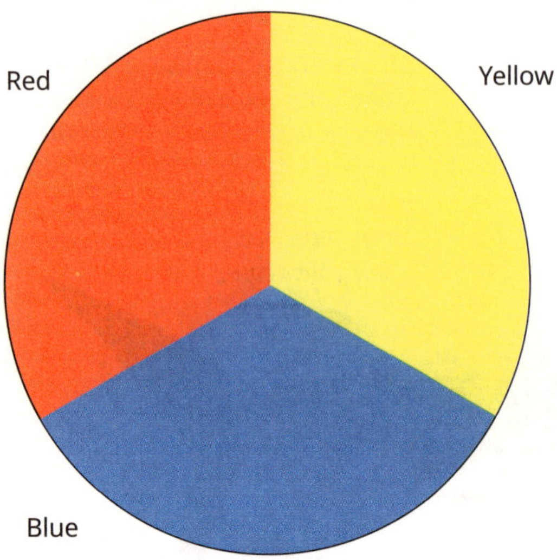

Secondary colours

ship ships *noun*
a big boat for carrying people and things across the sea. ❖ ***Look at page 148***

shipwreck shipwrecks *noun*
a bad accident when a ship is broken up by rocks or a rough sea.

shirt shirts *noun*
a piece of clothing that you wear on the top part of your body. Shirts have a collar, sleeves and buttons down the front.

shiver shivers shivering shivered *verb*
when you shiver, you shake because you are cold or frightened. *The rabbit was shivering with fright.*

shock shocks *noun*
1 a sudden and bad thing that happens to you. *The news of the car accident gave us all a shock.*
2 an electric shock is a sharp pain that you get if electricity goes through your body.

shoe shoes *noun*
things that you wear on your feet. Shoes are usually made of leather or plastic.

shone past of shine.
▲ Say ***shon***.

shook past of shake.

shoot shoots shooting shot *verb*
1 to shoot means to fire bullets from a gun or to use a bow and arrow.
2 to shoot also means to kick or throw a ball at a goal in sports like football or netball.
3 to shoot can also mean to move somewhere very fast. *The kitten shot under the sofa.*

shop shops *noun*
a place where you go to buy things. *a shoe shop.*

shop shops shopping shopped *verb*
when you shop, you go to the shops to buy things. *We went shopping for food in the supermarket.*
shopper *noun*.

shore shores *noun*
the land along the edge of the sea or a lake. *We walked along the sandy shore.*

short shorter shortest *adjective*
1 not tall. *Vincent is tall and Jennifer is short, but Joe is the shortest.*
2 not long. *Gerald has short hair.*
3 not lasting long. *The queen made a short speech.*
4 **short for** a short way of writing or saying something. *Phone is short for telephone.*

shorts *noun*
short trousers that usually do not cover your knees. *Rose and Freddie are wearing football shorts.*

shot past of shoot.

shoulder shoulders *noun*
Your shoulder joins your arm to the rest of your body.

shout shouts shouting shouted *verb*
if you shout, you say something in a very loud voice. *Jill had to shout so we could hear her.*

show shows showing showed shown *verb*
1 when you show somebody something, you let them see it or you point it out to them. *Show me your photos.* ◆ *Show me the girl who hit you.*
2 when you show somebody how to do something, you explain to them how to do it. *Can you show me how to use the computer?*

show shows *noun*
1 something you see at the theatre or on television. Shows often have singing and dancing in them.
2 things arranged so that people can look at them. *a dog show.*

shower showers *noun*
1 a place where you can wash by standing under water that sprays down on you.
2 a shower is also rain that falls for only a short time.

shrank past of shrink.

shred shreds *noun*
a small, thin piece that has been cut or torn from something larger. *He tore the paper to shreds.* ◆ *We decorated the cake with shreds of orange peel.*

shriek shrieks shrieking shrieked *verb*
if you shriek, you shout in a high voice. *He shrieked when he saw the spider.* ▲ Say ***shreek***.

shrink shrinks shrinking shrank shrunk *verb*
when something shrinks, it gets smaller. *Jordan's T-shirt shrank in the wash.*
shrunken *adjective*.

shut shuts shutting shut *verb*
1 if you shut something, you move a door, window, lid or book so that it is no longer open.
2 to shut something like a shop means that people cannot go into it until it opens again. *What time do the shops shut?* ■ The opposite is **open**.

Ships and Boats

Yacht

Vintage sailing ship

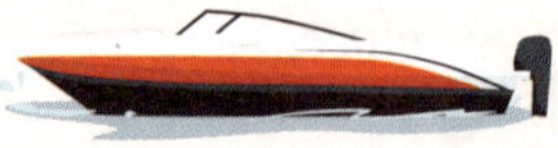

Motor boat

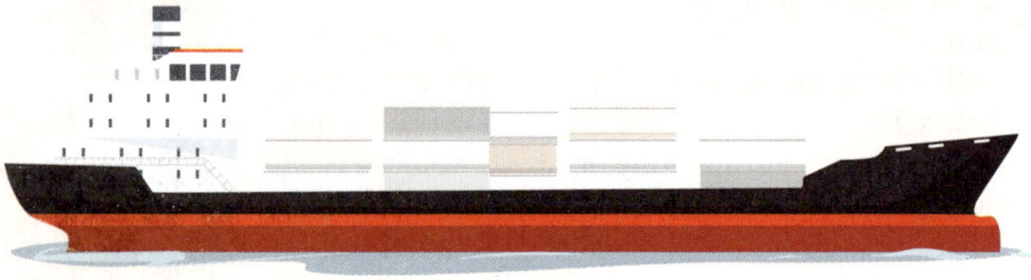

Cargo ship

Vocabulary

bow
the front of a vessel.

galley
a ship's kitchen.

hull
the body or framework of a ship.

keel
the piece of a ship's frame that runs lengthways along the bottom of the hull.

port
the left side of a ship as you look forward.

rudder
a flat part at the stern (back) of a ship. It moves to make the ship go left or right.

starboard
the right side of a ship as you look to the bow (front).

stern
the rear (back) of a vessel.

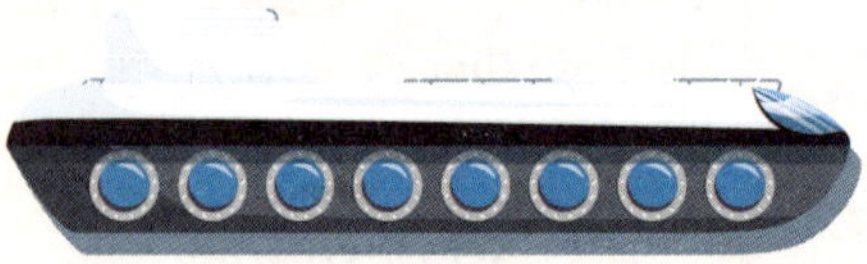

Sea scope

Liquified Natural Gas (LNG) Tanker

Mini submarine

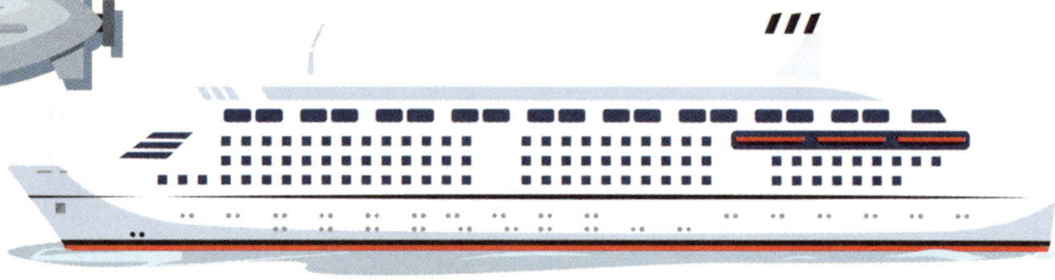

Cruise

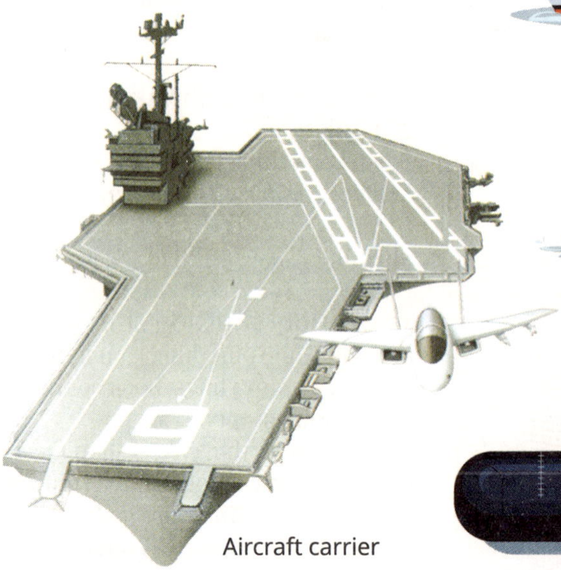

Aircraft carrier

Tugboat

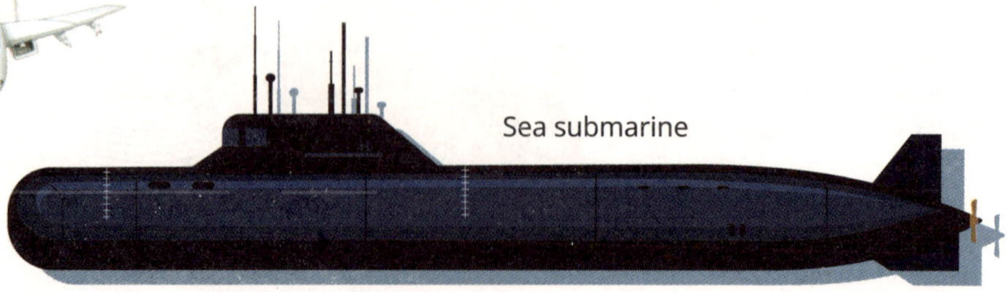

Sea submarine

shuttle shuttles *noun*
1 an aeroplane or bus that goes backwards and forwards between two places. *the Edinburgh shuttle.*
2 A shuttle is also a kind of spaceship. *the space shuttle.*

shy shyer shyest *adjective*
if somebody is shy, they do not feel happy or comfortable with people they do not know very well. *She doesn't talk much because she is shy.*

sick sicker sickest *adjective*
1 when you are sick, you are ill and do not feel well.
2 if you are sick, you bring food up from your stomach through your mouth.
sickness *noun.*

side sides *noun*
1 the left or right of something. *She drew a margin down the side of the page.*
2 the flat surfaces of something. *This box has six sides.*
3 the edges of something. *A square has four sides.*
4 the two teams that are playing against each other in a game.

sieve sieves *noun*
a kitchen container or bowl with lots of tiny holes in it. You use a sieve to separate small pieces from larger pieces or a liquid from something solid. ▲ Say ***siv***.

sigh sighs sighing sighed *verb*
when you sigh, you breathe out loudly because you are tired, sad or bored.

sight sights *noun*
1 the ability to see things with your eyes. *Owls have good sight in the dark.*
2 things such as interesting old buildings that people go to see are also sights. *Buckingham Palace is one of the most famous sights of London.*

sign signs *noun*
1 a notice that tells you something or where to find something. *Can you see a sign to the castle?*

2 a movement you make to tell somebody something. *His sister made a sign to him to keep quiet.*
3 a mark that means something special. In maths, a sign like this + means add.

sign signs signing signed *verb*
1 when you sign your name, you write it. *He signed the cheque.*
2 **sign on** to agree to work or stay. *Uncle Jack signed on for work at the factory yesterday.*

signal signals *noun*
a sound, a light or a movement that tells you something. *The referee blew a whistle as a signal to start the game.*

signature signatures *noun*
your name written in your own writing.

Sikh Sikhs *noun*
a person who follows the religion called Sikhism.

silent *adjective*
not making any noise. *The house was silent and empty.*
silence *noun*, **silently** *adverb.*

silk silks *noun*
a smooth, shiny material made from threads produced by an insect called a silkworm. *a silk scarf.*
silky *adjective.*

silly sillier silliest *adjective*
stupid and not sensible or clever. *You were very silly to run across the road.*

silver *noun*
a grey, shiny metal. Rings, bracelets and necklaces are often made of silver.
silver *adjective.*
a silver moon.

similar *adjective*
if two things are similar they are almost the same. *A mule, zebra and donkey are similar animals.*

simple simpler simplest *adjective*
easy to do or understand. *These questions are simple!* ■ The opposite is **difficult.**
simply *adverb.*
She works simply for the money.

sing sings singing sang sung *verb*
when you sing, you make music with your voice. *Sing that song again.* ◆ *The birds started singing early in the morning.*
singer *noun.*
Who's your favourite singer?

single *adjective*
1 one. *I can't find a single sock anywhere!*
2 a person who is single is not married.
3 a single ticket on a train or a bus only takes you one way, but not back again.

singular *noun*
one person or thing. *The singular of geese is goose.* ■ The opposite is **plural.**

sink sinks sinking sank sunk *verb*
if something like a ship sinks, it goes under water. *The ship sank in the storm.*

sink sinks *noun*
a basin with taps in the kitchen where you can wash dishes.

sip sips sipping sipped *verb*
if you sip a drink, you drink it slowly, taking a little bit at a time. *She sipped her tea slowly because it was hot.*

sister sisters *noun*
a person's sister is a girl or woman who has the same mother and father.

sit sits sitting sat *verb*
1 when you sit somewhere you rest your bottom there. *We sat in a circle.*
2 when a bird sits on its nest, it stays there to cover its eggs.

situation situations *noun*
1 something that is happening in a place at a particular time. *the political situation in China.*
2 the place where something is. *The hospital is in a beautiful situation by the lake.*

size sizes *noun*
the size of something is how big it is. *What size shoes do you wear?*

skate skates *noun*
1 roller skates are special boots with wheels on the bottom that you wear for moving about on smooth ground.
2 ice-skates are boots with sharp blades on the bottom that you wear for moving about on ice.
skate *verb*.

skateboard skateboards *noun*
a long piece of wood or plastic with wheels that you stand on to move along fast and to do clever jumps and turns.

skeleton skeletons *noun*
all the bones that are joined together inside the body of a person or an animal.

sketch sketches *noun*
a picture that you draw quickly.

ski skis *noun*
long, flat pieces of plastic, wood or metal that are fixed to boots for moving over snow. ▲ Say ***skee***.
ski *verb*.

skid skids skidding skidded *verb*
when something like a car skids, it slides sideways on the road. *The van skidded on the icy road.*

skill skills *noun*
if you have a skill, you have the ability to do something very well. *Playing the piano is a skill you have to learn.*
skilful *adjective*.

skin *noun*
1 the natural outside covering of the bodies of people and many animals. *Goat's skin is sometime used for making coats.*
2 the outside covering of many fruits and vegetables. *a banana skin.*

skip skips skipping skipped *verb*
when you skip, you move with little jumps from one foot to the other. *Jonah and Ali were skipping down the street.*

skirt skirts *noun*
a piece of clothing that women and girls wear. A skirt hangs down from the waist.

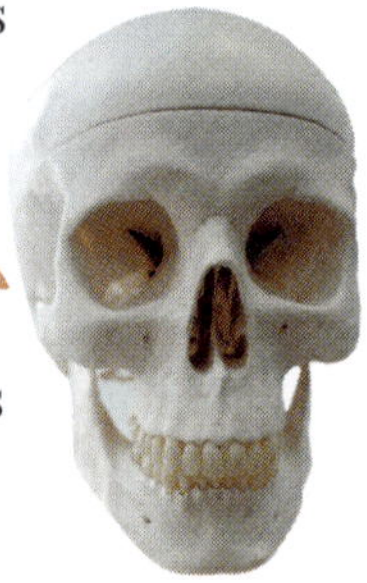

skull skulls *noun*
your skull is the round, bony part of your head. Your brain is inside your skull.

sky skies *noun*
the space above the Earth. You can see the sun and clouds in the sky in the daytime. You can often see the moon and the stars in the sky at night.

skyscraper skyscrapers *noun*
a very tall building.

slam slams slamming slammed *verb*
when a door slams, it closes with a bang. *She slammed the door.*

slang *noun*
words that you use in conversation, especially with people of your own age, but not when you are writing or being polite. *'Quid' is slang for 'pound'.*

slanted *adjective*
something that is slanted is not straight but leans in one direction.

slap slaps slapping slapped *verb*
if you slap somebody, you hit them with the palm of your hand. *My sister slapped me on the arm.*

slate slates *noun*
a grey rock that can be split into thin flat pieces and used to cover roofs.

slave slaves *noun*
a person who is owned by somebody else and is forced to work for them without being paid. Slavery has now been abolished in many countries, including India.
slavery *noun*.

sleep sleeps sleeping slept *verb*
when you sleep, you close your eyes and rest your body as you do in bed at night. *I slept for eight hours last night.*
sleep *noun*.

sleepy sleepier sleepiest *adjective*
when you are sleepy, you feel tired and it is hard to keep your eyes open.

sleeve sleeves *noun*
the part of a shirt, a coat or a dress that covers your arm.

sleigh sleighs *noun*
a vehicle that you sit on to move over snow. Sleighs are usually pulled by animals such as horses or reindeer.
▲ Say ***slay***.

slept past of sleep.

slice slices *noun*
a thin, flat piece that has been cut from something. *a slice of cake.*

slide slides sliding slid *verb*
when something slides, it moves smoothly over a surface. *The children were sliding on the ice.*

slide slides *noun*
something that you play on. You climb up the steps on one side and slide down the other side.

slight *adjective*
small or not very important. *I've got a slight earache.*
slightly *adverb.*

slim slimmer slimmest *adjective*
if you are slim, you are thin, but not too thin. ■ The opposite is **plump**.

slimy slimier slimiest *adjective*
dirty and slippery. *The rocks were covered with slimy seaweed.*

slip slips slipping slipped *verb*
if you slip, you slide by mistake and fall down. *I slipped on the wet floor.*

slipper slippers *noun*
a soft, comfortable shoe that you wear in the house.

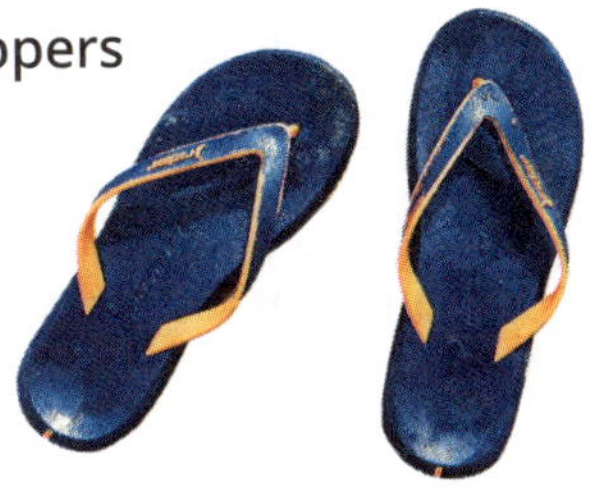

slippery *adjective*
something that is slippery is very smooth and difficult to hold, or to stand on without sliding and falling over. *a slippery floor.* ◆ *a slippery, wet fish.*

slit slits *noun*
a long, thin cut in something. *They cut a slit in the material.*

slope slopes *noun*
ground that goes upwards or downwards. *We walked down the mountain slope.*

slot slots *noun*
a short, thin hole in something. *You put a coin in the slot to use the telephone.*

slow slower slowest *adjective*
somebody or something that is slow does not move quickly. *Snails and tortoises are very slow animals.*
■ The opposite is **fast**.
slowly *adverb.*
We walked home slowly.

slug slugs *noun*
a small, slimy animal like a snail without a shell. Gardeners do not like slugs because they eat plants.

sly slyer slyest *adjective*
if somebody is sly, they are clever in a secret and not very nice way. *That was a very sly trick.*

small smaller smallest *adjective*
not very big. *Ants are small insects.*
◆ *My brother is smaller than me.*
■ The opposite is **big** or **large**.

small

Some words you can use instead of small:

All small animals look sweet.
baby, young

The writing is so small you need a magnifying glass to read it.
minute, tiny

Don't worry. It's only a small mistake.
unimportant, slight, minor

Centipedes have lots of small legs.
short

smart smarter smartest *adjective*
1 neat and tidy. *Dad wears a smart suit for work.*
2 clever. *You're too smart for this quiz!*

smash smashes smashing smashed *verb*
if something smashes, it breaks into a lot of pieces. *I dropped the plate and it smashed on the floor.*

smell smells smelling smelt or smelled *verb*
1 when you smell something, you use your nose to find out about it. *I can smell food cooking in the kitchen.*
2 when something smells, you notice it with your nose. *She smells of soap.*
smelly *adjective.*
smelly old socks.

smile smiles smiling smiled *verb*
when you smile, the corners of your mouth turn up to show that you are happy.
smile *noun.*

smoke smokes smoking smoked *verb*
when somebody smokes, they have a cigarette or a pipe in their mouth, and breathe the smoke in and out.

smoke smokes *noun*
the white, grey or black stuff that you see going up in the air when something is burning. *Smoke was pouring out of the chimney.*

smooth smoother smoothest *adjective*
if something is smooth, you cannot feel lumps or any rough parts when you touch it. *These vases have smooth surfaces.*
smoothly *adverb.*

smudge smudges *noun*
a dirty mark on something.

smuggle smuggles smuggling smuggled *verb*
to smuggle means to take things such as alcohol, drugs or cigarettes into or out of a country when it is illegal.
smuggler *noun.*

snack snacks *noun*
a small amount of food that you eat when you are in a hurry. *We had a quick snack of cheese on toast.*

snail snails *noun*
a small creature with a hard shell on its back. Snails move along very slowly.

snake snakes *noun*
a long, thin kind of animal called a reptile. Snakes have no legs and move by sliding along the ground. *Some snakes can give a poisonous bite.*
❖ ***Look at page 135***

snap snaps snapping snapped *verb*
1 when something snaps, it breaks and makes a sudden sharp sound. *The pencil snapped when I stepped on it.*
2 when a dog snaps, it tries to bite somebody or something. *The dog snapped at us when we walked by.*
3 when a person snaps, they speak in an angry way. *'Be quiet!' she snapped.*

snatch snatches snatching snatched *verb*
if you snatch something, you take it quickly and roughly. *The thief snatched her purse.*

sneak sneaks sneaking sneaked *verb*
if you sneak somewhere, you move in a quiet and secret way. *No one saw him sneak out of the room.*

sneeze sneezes sneezing sneezed *verb*
when you sneeze, you blow air out of your nose and mouth with a sudden, loud noise. *You sometimes sneeze when you have a cold.*

sniff sniffs sniffing sniffed *verb*
when you sniff, you breathe air in through your nose in a quick and noisy way. You often sniff when you are crying or when you have a cold.

snore snores snoring snored *verb*
when somebody snores, they breathe noisily when they are asleep.

snout snouts *noun*
the nose and mouth of an animal such as a pig or a badger.

snow *noun*
small, white pieces of frozen water that fall from the sky when it is very cold. **snow** *verb*, **snowy** *adjective*.

snowboarding *noun*
a sport where you move down snowy hills on a piece of wood or metal that looks like a skateboard without wheels.

snowflake snowflakes *noun*
a small piece of falling snow. Snowflakes are star-shaped ice crystals.

soak soaks soaking soaked *verb*
1 when you soak something, you put it in water and leave it for a long time.
2 if you get soaked, you get very wet. *We got soaked in the rain.*

soap *noun*
a substance that can be solid, liquid or powder that you use with water for washing. *This bar of soap smells nice.*

sob sobs sobbing sobbed *verb*
when you sob, you cry loudly.

soccer *noun*
a game of football, played by two teams of 11 players. The teams try to score goals by kicking a ball into a net at each end of a field called a pitch.

society societies *noun*
1 all the people who live in the same country or area and have the same laws and customs.
2 a kind of club for people who like the same things. *a drama society.*

sock socks *noun*
a thing that you wear on your foot inside your shoe.

socket sockets *noun*
a thing in a wall with holes where you can push in an electric plug.

sofa sofas *noun*
a long, comfortable seat for two or more people, also called a settee.

soft softer softest *adjective*
1 not hard or rough. *Cats have soft fur.*
2 not firm or stiff. *soft snow.*
3 not loud, quiet and gentle. *He has a soft voice.*
4 too kind. *The teacher is too soft, so her class is always noisy.*
softly *adverb*, **soften** *verb*.
The butter is very hard because it has been in the refrigerator, we should leave it out to soften.

software *noun*
the part inside a computer or on a computer disk that has the instructions that make a computer work.

soil *noun*
the brown stuff, also called earth, that plants grow in.

solar *adjective*
to do with the Sun. *the Solar System.*

sold past of sell.
My mum sold our old car and bought a new one.

soldier soldiers *noun*
a person in an army. ▲ Say ***sole-jer***.

sole soles *noun*
the bottom of your foot or your shoe.

solid solids *noun*
an object that is hard and not a liquid or a gas. *Water is a liquid, but ice is a solid.*

solid *adjective*
1 hard. *a solid rock.*
2 with no space inside. *a solid brick wall.* ■ The opposite is **hollow**.

solution solutions *noun*
1 an answer to a sum or a problem. *I can't find the solution to this puzzle.*
2 a liquid that has some substance completely mixed into it. *This solution is made of sugar and water.*

solve solves solving solved *verb*
1 if you solve a problem, you find the answer to it.
2 if you solve a mystery, you find out why it happened. *The detective was trying to solve the mystery of the stolen necklace.*

somersault somersaults *noun*
when you do a somersault, you roll your body in a circle so that your feet go over your head.

son sons *noun*
somebody's son is a boy or man who is their child. ● A word that sounds like **son** is **sun**.

song songs *noun*
a short piece of music with words that you sing.

soot *noun*
black powder that comes from smoke after a fire.
sooty *adjective*.

sore *adjective*
if a part of your body is sore, it hurts. *I've got a sore throat.*

sorrow *noun*
the feeling that you have when you are very sad. *He felt great sorrow when his mother died.* ■ The opposite is **joy**.

sort sorts sorting sorted *verb*
if you sort things, you put them into different groups. *He sorts the blocks into plain, coloured and patterned ones.*

sort sorts *noun*
a kind. *What sort of animal is it? It's a lizard.*

sought past of seek.

sound sounds *noun*
something that you can hear. *I can hear the sound of somebody playing a guitar.*

soup soups *noun*
a hot, liquid food that you make by boiling vegetables or meat in water. *tomato soup.* ◆ *chicken soup.*

sour sourer sourest *adjective*
1 something that tastes sour is not sweet. *Lemons are sour.*
2 when milk is sour, it is not fresh.

source sources *noun*
1 the place, person or thing that something comes from. *The library is a good source of information.*
2 the place where a river starts. *The source of the river is in the mountains.*

south *noun*
the direction that is on your right if you face the Sun as it rises in the morning. ■ The opposite is **north**.
south *adjective*, **southern** *adjective*.
I have a south-facing garden.
◆ *Bournemouth is in southern England.*
south *adverb*.
The Arctic tern flies south from the Arctic to the Antarctic every winter.

souvenir souvenirs *noun*
something that you keep to remember a place or something that happened. *My friend bought me a Dutch doll as a souvenir of Holland.*

sow sows sowing sown *verb*
when you sow seeds, you put them in the soil so that they will grow into plants. ▲ Rhymes with ***low***.

space spaces *noun*
1 an empty place with nothing in it. *There is space in this cupboard for your clothes.* ◆ *Mum couldn't find a space to park the car.*
2 the place above the Earth where the Sun, stars and planets are.
❖ ***Look at page 154***

spacecraft *noun*
a vehicle that travels in space.

spade spades *noun*
a tool with a long handle and a wide, flat blade that you use for digging.

span spans spanning spanned *verb*
when something like a bridge spans a river, it goes across it.

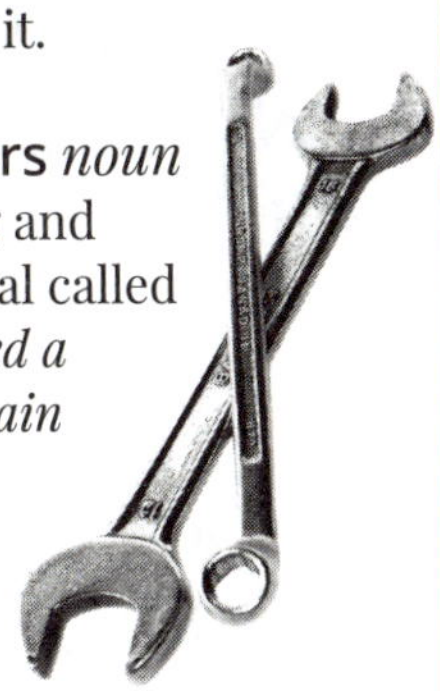

spanner spanners *noun*
a tool for tightening and undoing bits of metal called nuts and bolts. *I need a spanner to fix the chain on my bike.*

spare *adjective*
something that is spare is not being used now, but you can use it when you need. *When my friend stayed, he slept in the spare room.*

spark sparks *noun*
a tiny piece of fire. Sparks can be made by electricity. *Sparks from the fire flew up the chimney.*

sparkle sparkles sparkling sparkled *verb*
when something sparkles, it shines with little flashes of light. *sparkling objects.*

spat past of spit.

speak speaks speaking spoke spoken *verb*
when you speak, you say words. *Philippa was speaking to her friend on the telephone.* ◆ *Can you speak Spanish?*

spear spears *noun*
a weapon made from a long stick with a sharp point at one end.

special *adjective*
1 if something is special, it is not ordinary but better or more important than other things. *Today is a special day because it's my birthday.*
2 special also means for a particular person or thing, or to do a particular job. *An ambulance is a special van for taking people to the hospital.*
specially *adverb*.
I bought a present specially for you.

SPACE

Vocabulary

capsule
a section of a spacecraft that returns to Earth, containing astronauts and instruments.

docking
joining craft to a space station or to another craft in space.

module
any section of a spacecraft that can be detached.

probe
a spacecraft that travels deep into space, to the moon and planets.

shuttle
a space plane that can fly into space and back many times.

weightlessness
the condition astronauts have in space when their bodies have no weight.

Compton Gamma Ray Observatory

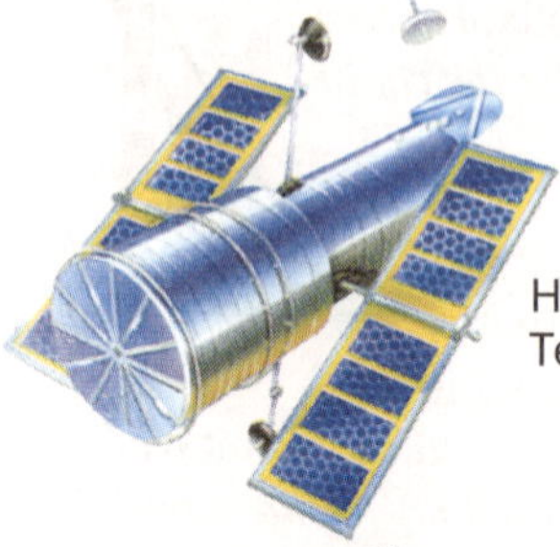
Hubble Space Telescope

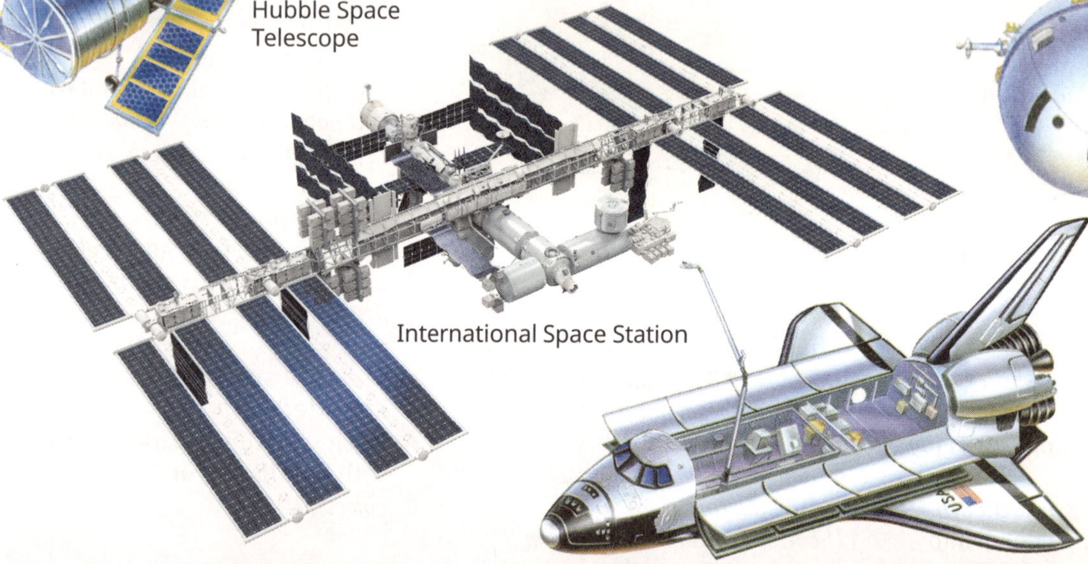
International Space Station

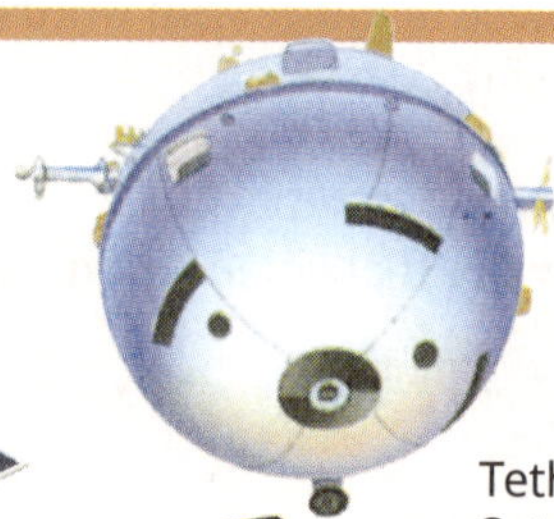
Tethered Satellite System

Space Shuttle

species *noun*
a group of animals or plants that are the same in some way.

spectator spectators *noun*
a person who watches something. *There were lots of spectators at the football match.*

speech speeches *noun*
1 the ability to talk. Speech is one of the main ways of communicating.
2 a special talk that you give to a group of people.

speed *noun*
how fast something goes or happens. *The car was travelling at a speed of 60 kilometres an hour.*

speedometer speedometers *noun*
an instrument that shows how fast a vehicle is travelling.

spell spells spelling spelt or spelled *verb*
when you spell a word, you say or write the letters in the right order. *'How do you spell tiger?' 'T-i-g-e-r.'*
spelling *noun.*

spend spends spending spent *verb*
1 when you spend money, you use it to buy something. *I must stop spending so much money on sweets.*
2 when you spend time with somebody, you stay with them. *I spent a week with my aunt and uncle.*

sphere spheres *noun*
a solid shape like a ball. *The Earth is a sphere.*
spherical *adjective.*

spice spices *noun*
powder or seeds from a plant that you put in food to give it a stronger taste. *Cinnamon, ginger and nutmeg are spices.*
spicy *adjective.*

spider spiders *noun*
a small creature with eight legs and no wings. *Spiders spin webs to catch insects.*

spike spikes *noun*
a piece of metal or wood with a sharp point at one end. *The fence has spikes along the top.*

spill spills spilling spilt or spilled *verb*
if you spill a liquid, you let it flow out of a container by mistake. *I spilt my drink on the carpet.*

spin spins spinning span spun *verb*
1 when something spins, it turns around and around very fast. *The ball spun through the air.*
2 to spin also means to pull cotton or wool into long, thin pieces and twist them together to make thread.

spine spines *noun*
1 your spine is the row of bones down your back.
2 one of the sharp points that cover some animals and plants. *Hedgehogs and cactuses have spines.*
3 the spine of the book is the part of the cover between the front and the back.

spiral spirals *noun*
a shape that goes round and round in circles like a spring.

spirit spirits *noun*
1 your spirit is the part of you that some people believe does not die when the body dies.
2 a ghost.

spit spits spitting spat *verb*
if you spit, you send food or liquid out of your mouth. *We spat out the cherry stones.*

splash splashes splashing splashed *verb*
if you splash someone or something, you make them wet with drops of water or some other liquid.

split splits splitting split *verb*
1 when something splits, it breaks open. *The bag split and all the things fell out.*
2 to split also means to share something. *We split the sweets between us.*

spoil spoils spoiling spoilt or spoiled *verb*
1 if somebody spoils something, they make it less good than it was before. *I spoilt my shirt when I spilt paint all over it.*
2 if somebody spoils a child, they give it everything that it wants.

spoke spoken past of speak
Clive spoke very good French.

sponge sponges *noun*
1 a soft thing that is full of holes. You use a sponge to wash yourself or to clean things. *Wendy washed the car with a sponge.*

2 a sponge is also a sea creature with a soft part inside that is full of holes.
3 a kind of light cake. *a chocolate sponge.*

sponsor sponsors *noun*
a person or a company that gives money to somebody or a group of people for doing something special such as walking for a charity. *A famous chocolate company is a sponsor for the rugby competition.*

spooky spookier spookiest *adjective*
something that is spooky is frightening. *I read a spooky ghost story.*

spoon spoons *noun*
a metal tool that you use for eating things such as soup and cereals.
spoonful *noun.*
six spoonfuls of sugar.

sport sports *noun*
something that you do to keep your body strong and well and to have fun. *Football, tennis, cricket and swimming are all sports.*

spot spots *noun*
1 a small, round mark. *Leopards have yellow fur with dark spots.*
2 a small red mark on your skin.
3 a place. *This is the spot where I fell off my horse.*
spotted *adjective.*
a spotted scarf.
spotty *adjective.*
a spotty face.

spout spouts *noun*
a part of a container such as a teapot where the liquid comes out.

sprain sprains spraining sprained *verb*
when you sprain something such as your ankle or your wrist, you hurt it by twisting it suddenly.

sprang past of spring.

spray sprays spraying sprayed *verb*
when you spray something, you make lots of small drops of liquid fall on it. *Parul sprayed the flowers with water.*

spread spreads spreading spread *verb*
1 if you spread something such as butter, you cover something else with it. *Freddie spread syrup on the cake.*
2 when something spreads, it moves all over a place. *The rain has spread to all parts of the country.*
3 when you spread your arms, you stretch them out. *The bird spread its wings.*

spring springs *noun*
1 the season of the year between winter and summer. *Plants start to grow in spring.*
2 a spring is a piece of wire that is twisted around in circles. A spring will jump back into the same shape if you press or pull it and then let it go.

spring springs springing sprang sprung *verb*
to spring is to jump. *The cat sprang on to the wall.*

sprinkle sprinkles sprinkling sprinkled *verb*
if you sprinkle something, you throw small drops or pieces of something on to it. *Angelina sprinkled the flowers with some water.*

sprung past of spring.

spun past of spin.

spy spies *noun*
a person who tries to find out secret information about another person or a country.

square squares *noun*
a flat shape with four straight sides that are the same length.
square *adjective.*
a square table.

squash squashes squashing squashed *verb*
if you squash something, you press it hard and make it flat. *He sat on my hat and squashed it.*

squeak squeaks squeaking squeaked *verb*
to squeak is to make the small, high sound that a mouse makes. *The door squeaks when you open it.*

squeeze squeezes squeezing squeezed *verb*
if you squeeze something, you press it hard on the sides. *I squeezed the lemon for lemon juice.*

squirrel squirrels *noun*
a small, grey or red animal with a big, thick tail. *Squirrels can climb well and live in trees.*

squirt squirts squirting squirted *verb*
when something squirts, liquid comes out very fast. *I opened the bottle and lemonade squirted everywhere.*

stab stabs stabbing stabbed *verb*
to stab is to stick a knife or weapon into somebody or something.

stable stables *noun*
a building where horses are kept.

stadium stadiums or stadia *noun*
a large area for sports such as football or athletics. There are usually seats around the edge so that people can watch the games. *an ancient stadium.*

stage stages *noun*
1 a stage is the part of the theatre where the actors perform.
2 if you do something in stages, you do it in parts. *It will take a long time to build the tree house, so we'll have to do it in stages.*

stain stains *noun*
a dirty mark on something that is very difficult to get rid of. *Sushant's football shorts were covered in grass stains.*

stair stairs *noun*
one of a set of steps for going up or down inside a building.

staircase staircases *noun*
a set of stairs inside a building.

stale staler stalest *adjective*
not fresh. *Sheri threw away the last piece of cake because it was stale.*

stalk stalks *noun*
the stem or long, thin part of a plant that flowers, leaves and fruit grow on.

stall stalls *noun*
1 a stall is a kind of open shop where things for sale are put on a big table. *a fruit and vegetable stall.*
2 a stall is also a place in a shed for one cow or in a stable for one horse.

stamp stamps *noun*
a small piece of paper with a picture and a price on it. *You have to stick a stamp on a letter before you post it.*

stamp stamps stamping stamped *verb*
1 if you stamp your foot, you put it down hard on the floor. *My sister stamps her foot when she is angry.*
2 if you stamp a passport, you make a mark on it with a special tool to show that you have come into a country or a place. Some stamps show that you have paid for something or that you have returned it.

stand stands standing stood *verb*
when you stand somewhere, you are on your feet.

standard standards *noun*
1 a measure of how good or bad something is. *Your drawing is of a very high standard.*
2 a flag.

stank past of stink.

star stars *noun*
1 a small, bright light that you can see in the sky on a clear night.
2 a shape with five or six points.
3 a famous person who sings, acts or plays a sport. *a film star.*

stare stares staring stared *verb*
if you stare at somebody or something, you look at them for a long time. *Freddie and James stared at each other.*

start starts starting started *verb*
1 when something starts, it begins. *What time does the film start?* ■ The opposite is **end** or **finish**.
2 when you start something like a car, you make it move.

start *noun*
the beginning. *the start of the play.*

startle startles startling startled *verb*
if somebody or something startles you, they surprise you in a frightening way. *You startled me when you jumped out from behind the curtain.*

starve starves starving starved *verb*
if a person or an animal starves, they become ill and can die because they do not have enough to eat. *Many birds starve during the winter months.* **starvation** *noun*.

state states *noun*
1 a country and its government. *Many schools are run by the state.*
2 a part of a country. *California is one of the states of the United States of America.*
3 a state is also how somebody or something looks or is. *Your clothes are in a terrible state!*

station stations *noun*
1 a place where trains and buses stop and pick up passengers. *a railway station.*
2 a building that is used for something special. *a police station.*

statue statues *noun*
a sculpture or model of a person or an animal that is made of stone or metal. *This is a statue of Niccolo Machiavelli.*

stay stays staying stayed *verb*
1 if you stay somewhere, you do not move from that place. *I told the puppy to stay in the garden.*
2 if you stay with somebody, you live in their house for a short time. *I'm staying with my friend Janet tonight.*

steady steadier steadiest *adjective*
somebody or something that is steady is not moving about or shaking. *Hold the ladder steady while I climb it.*
■ The opposite is **unsteady.**

steal steals stealing stole stolen *verb*
to steal is to take something that does not belong to you and keep it. *Somebody stole my purse.*

a b c d e f g h i j k l m n o p q r s t u v w x y z

steam *noun*
steam is the gas that water turns into when it boils. *Steam was coming out of the kettle.*

steel *noun*
a strong metal that is used for making such things as knives, tools and machines.

steep steeper steepest *adjective*
if something such as a hill is steep, it goes up or down sharply. *This hill is too steep to climb up.*

steer steers steering steered *verb*
when you steer a car, you turn the wheel so that it goes in the direction you want.

stem stems *noun*
the long, thin part of a plant that grows above the ground.

step steps *noun*
1 what you do when you lift your foot and put it down in a different place. *Try to follow these dance steps.*
2 the flat part of stairs where you put your foot for going up or down.

step steps stepping stepped *verb*
to step is to lift your foot and put it down in another place as you walk. *You stepped on my foot!*

stereo *noun*
music or sound that comes from two different loudspeakers at the same time. *Music sounds much better in stereo.*

stick sticks *noun*
a long, thin piece of wood. *The old man walked with a stick.*

stick sticks sticking stuck *verb*
1 when you stick two things together, you join them with glue. *Camilla stuck a picture in her book.*
2 if something sticks, it cannot be moved. *The car is stuck in the mud.*
3 when you stick a pointed thing into something else, you push it in. *If you stick a pin into a balloon, it will burst.*
sticky *adjective.*
Her fingers are sticky with jam!

sticker stickers *noun*
a small piece of paper with a picture or words on it that you can fix on to something.
My bag is covered in stickers.

stiff stiffer stiffest *adjective*
1 if something is stiff, it does not bend easily. *a stiff piece of cardboard.*
2 not moving easily. *a stiff neck.*

still *adjective, adverb*
1 not moving. *Please stand still while I take your photo.*
2 going on and on. *It's still raining.*

sting stings stinging stung *verb*
if an insect or a plant stings you, a small sharp point goes into your skin and hurts you. *Bees, wasps and nettles can sting you.*
sting *noun.*

stink stinks stinking stank or stunk *verb*
if something stinks, it smells very bad. *That fish stinks!*

stir stirs stirring stirred *verb*
when you stir a liquid, you move a spoon around to mix it. *Ritu stirred the soup.*

stitch stitches *noun*
a loop that you make when you put a needle and thread through a piece of material and bring it out again a little farther along.

stock stocks *noun*
all the things that a shop keeps ready to sell. *This shop has a large stock of children's shoes.*

stocking stockings *noun*
a piece of clothing like a long, thin sock that women and girls wear over their legs and feet.

stole stolen past of steal.

stomach stomachs *noun*
your stomach is the place in the middle of your body where food goes after you have eaten it.

stone stones *noun*
1 a small piece of rock.
2 a large mass of rock that is used for building. *a stone wall.*
3 a stone is also the hard, round seed in the middle of some fruits. Cherries, plums and peaches have stones.

stood past of stand.

stool stools *noun*
a kind of chair without a back or arms.

stop stops stopping stopped *verb*
1 if you stop what you are doing, you do not do it any more. *Stop talking and listen for a moment.*
2 when something that was moving stops, it stands still. *The bus stopped.*
3 if you stop somebody from doing something, you do not allow them to do it. *I tried to stop the dog from sitting on the sofa.*
4 when a machine stops, it does not work any more. *My watch has stopped.*

store stores *noun*
1 a large shop that sells lots of different kinds of things.
2 a number of things that you are keeping to use later. *We had a good store of food in the tent.*

store stores storing stored *verb*
if you store something somewhere, you put it there so that you can use it later. *The tins of food were stored in the cupboard.*

storey storeys *noun*
all the rooms on one floor of a building. *This office block has ten storeys.*

stork storks *noun*
a big, white bird with long legs and a large beak. *Storks live near water.*

storm storms *noun*
very bad weather with strong winds and a lot of rain or snow. *Many storms also have thunder and lightning.* **stormy** *adjective.*

story stories *noun*
a story tells you about things that have happened. Some stories are about real things and others are made up. *I read a story about a boy who made friends with a ghost.*

stout stouter stoutest *adjective*
rather fat. *a stout woman.*

stove stoves *noun*
something you can use for heating a room or for cooking. *a gas stove.*

straight straighter straightest *adjective*
if something is straight, it does not bend, curl or turn to the side. *You can use a ruler to draw a straight line.* ◆ *Ben's hair is curly, but mine is straight.*

strain strains straining strained *verb*
1 if you strain a part of your body, you hurt it by stretching a muscle too much.
2 if you strain food, you put it through a tool called a sieve to separate the solid part from the liquid. *James strained the tomatoes.*

strand strands *noun*
a long, thin piece of something. *strands of long, yellow hair.*

strange stranger strangest *adjective*
1 odd or unusual. *I read a story about a strange animal that could talk.*
2 not known or seen before. *a strange house.* ■ The opposite is **familiar**.

stranger strangers *noun*
a person that you do not know. *a complete stranger waved at me.*

strap straps *noun*
a long, thin piece of material that you use for fastening things, carrying things or for holding things. *How many kinds of straps can you see?*

straw straws *noun*
1 the dried stems of plants like wheat. Straw is used for animals such as horses and pet rabbits to lie on. You can make hats out of straw.
2 a long, thin tube made of paper or plastic for drinking through.

strawberry strawberries *noun*
a small, soft, red fruit that grows near the ground.

streak streaks *noun*
a long, thin line of something. *There are streaks of paint on the floor.*

stream streams *noun*
1 a small, narrow river.
2 a long line of things going in one direction. *a stream of traffic.*

street streets *noun*
a road in a town or village, with houses and other buildings along each side.

strength *noun*
how strong somebody or something is. *Do you have the strength to move the table?*

stress *noun*
too much worry or work. *Stress has caused his headaches.*

stretch stretches stretching stretched *verb*
1 if you stretch something, you make it longer or wider by pulling it. *Jordan's jumper is being stretched.*
2 if you stretch your body, you push your arms and legs out and make yourself as tall as you can.

strict stricter strictest *adjective*
a strict person expects people to do what they say and to obey rules. **strictly** *adverb.*

stride strides striding strode *verb*
to walk or run with long steps. *He strode out of the room in a bad temper.*

strike strikes striking struck *verb*
1 if you strike somebody or something, you hit them. *The ball struck me on the back of the head.*
2 when lightning strikes, it hits and goes through somebody or something. *The tree was struck by lightning.*
3 when a clock strikes, it rings a bell to show the time. *The clock struck ten.*
4 when you strike a match, you rub it on something rough to make a flame.
5 when people strike, they stop work because they want more money or because they want to protest about something.

strike strikes *noun*
a time when people stop work because they want more money or because they want to protest about something.

string *noun*

1 very thin rope. You use string to tie up things such as parcels.
2 musical instruments such as guitars and violins have thin wires called strings that you touch to make sounds. ❖ ***Look at page 105***

strip strips *noun*
a long, thin piece of something such as paper or material.

stripe stripes *noun*
a coloured line on something. *My football shirt has red and white stripes.*
striped *adjective.*
a striped dress.

stroke strokes stroking stroked *verb*
when you stroke an animal such as a cat, you move your hand gently over its body.
stroke *noun.*

strong stronger strongest *adjective*
1 if you are strong, you have a lot of power in your muscles. *Are you strong enough to lift these heavy bags?*
2 not easy to break. *These toys are made of strong plastic.*
3 if a taste or a smell is strong, you can notice it easily. *This cheese has a very strong smell.*

struck past of strike.

struggle struggles struggling struggled *verb*
1 to struggle means to fight to get away from somebody or something. *The thief struggled with the policeman.*
2 if you struggle to do something that is difficult, you try hard to do it. *Connie and Joe had to struggle to get into the same pair of trousers!*

stubborn *adjective*
a stubborn person does not change their mind easily and does not like doing what other people tell them to do.

stuck past of stick.

student students *noun*
a person who is learning something at a university or a college.

studio studios *noun*
1 a room where an artist or a photographer works.
2 a place where films, television or radio programmes, or records are made.

study studies studying studied *verb*
1 if you study something, you spend time learning about it. *I am studying history at school.*
2 to study something is to look at it very carefully. *David was studying the stars through his telescope.*
studious *adjective.*
somebody who is studious spends a lot of time studying. *a studious boy.*

stuff *noun*
a word we use for something when we do not know what else to call it. *What's this stuff on the floor?*
◆ *Please tidy up all the stuff in your room.*

stumble stumbles stumbling stumbled *verb*
if you stumble over something, you nearly fall over it. *I stumbled over a pair of shoes on the floor.*

stung past of sting.

stunk past of stink.

stupid stupider stupidest *adjective*
silly, not clever, bright or sensible. *Don't ask stupid questions.*
stupidity *noun.*

style styles *noun*
the way something is done or made, or how it looks. *a new style of shoe.*

subject subjects *noun*
1 something you learn about. *My best subjects at school are English and History.*
2 what something such as a story is all about. *Animals are the subject of this book.*
3 the subject of a sentence is the person or thing that does the action. *In the sentence, 'Katie climbed a tree', 'Katie' is the subject.*

submarine submarines *noun*
a boat that can travel under water.

substance substances *noun*
something that you can see, touch or use for making things. *This vegetable contains a very sticky substance.*

subtract subtracts subtracting subtracted *verb*
to subtract is to take one number away from another number. *If you subtract four from six, you are left with two.* ■ The opposite is **add**.
subtraction *noun.*
Subtraction is harder than addition.

subway subways *noun*
a path that goes under a busy road so that you can get to the other side safely.

succeed succeeds succeeding succeeded *verb*
if you succeed, you do or get the thing that you wanted. *Ben succeeded in passing the swimming test.*

success successes *noun*
doing something well or getting what you wanted. *We wish you success in the race.* ◆ *The party was a great success.*
successful *adjective,* **successfully** *adverb.*

---

suck sucks sucking sucked *verb*
1 when you suck, you pull liquid into your mouth from something. *The baby is sucking milk from a bottle.*
2 when you suck a sweet, you keep it in your mouth and lick it without chewing it.

---

sudden *adjective*
happening quickly when you are not expecting it. *We ran inside to get out of the sudden rain.*
suddenly *adverb.*

---

suffer suffers suffering suffered *verb*
if you suffer, you feel pain because you are ill or because you are unhappy. *Tom suffers a lot from colds.*

---

suffocate suffocates suffocating suffocated *verb*
if a person or an animal suffocates, they die because they have no air to breathe.

---

sugar *noun*
something that you put in food and drinks to make them sweet. Sugar comes from sugar cane or sugar beet.

---

suggest suggests suggesting suggested *verb*
if you suggest something to somebody, you tell them about an idea that you have for doing something. *Sophie suggested that we go to the beach.*
suggestion *noun.*

---

suicide *noun*
suicide means killing yourself on purpose.

---

suit suits *noun*
a set of clothes made out of the same material and that you wear together. A suit can be a jacket and trousers, or a jacket and a skirt.

---

suit suits suited *verb*
1 if clothes suit you, they look good on you. *Does this dress suit me?*
2 if something suits you, it is right for what you want or need. *This bedroom would suit me.*

---

suitable *adjective*
right for somebody or something. *This coat is suitable for rainy weather.*

---

suitcase suitcases *noun*
a large bag or box with a handle that you carry your clothes in when you travel.

---

sulk sulks sulking sulked *verb*
if you sulk, you refuse to talk to anybody because you are angry about something. *Joe is sulking because he's not allowed to watch any more TV.*

---

sum sums *noun*
a problem in arithmetic. *Three plus two is an easy sum.* ● A word that sounds like **sum** is **some.**

---

summer *noun*
the season of the year between spring and autumn. Summer is the hottest part of the year.

---

summit summits *noun*
the top of a mountain.

---

summon summons summoning summoned *verb*
if you summon somebody, you call them and tell them to come. *We were summoned to the headmaster's office.*

---

sun suns *noun*
the bright star that you can see in the sky during the day. The sun gives us light and heat. ● A word that sounds like **sun** is **son.**

---

sunbathe sunbathes sunbathing sunbathed *verb*
to sunbathe is to sit in the Sun and let it make your skin go darker.

---

sung past of sing.

---

sunglasses *noun*
special dark glasses that you wear to protect your eyes from the bright light of the Sun.

---

sunk past of sink.

---

sunny sunnier sunniest *adjective*
with the sun shining brightly. *It's a sunny day – let's have a picnic!*

---

sunrise *noun*
the time when the sun comes up (rises) in the morning.

---

sunset *noun*
the time when the sun goes down (sets) at night.

---

sunshine *noun*
the light and heat from the sun.

---

super *adjective*
very good and great fun. *a super party.*

---

superb *adjective*
wonderful. *We had a superb holiday in America last year.*

---

superior *adjective*
better than somebody or something else. *Suzanne's drawing is superior to mine.*

---

supermarket supermarkets *noun*
a big shop where you can buy food and lots of other things. You take what you want as you go round and pay for everything on your way out.

supersonic *adjective*
if an aircraft, rocket or bullet is supersonic, it goes faster than the speed of sound. *Concorde is a supersonic aeroplane.*

superstitious *adjective*
a superstitious person believes they will have bad luck if they do or do not do certain things. *Superstitious people think it is bad luck to walk under ladders.*
superstition *noun.*

supervise supervises supervising supervised *verb*
if you supervise somebody or something, you watch them to make sure they are doing things in the right way.
supervision *noun.*

supper suppers *noun*
a meal that people eat in the evening.

supply supplies *noun*
an amount of something that you need. *We took a large supply of food on the camping trip.*

support supports supporting supported *verb*
1 to support is to hold somebody or something up. *Joe supported Connie when she twisted her ankle.*
2 if you support a club, a team or some other group, you try to help and encourage them. *Which team do you support?*
support *noun,* **supporter** *noun.*

suppose supposes supposing supposed *verb*
if you suppose that something is true, you think that it is probably true. *I suppose you are right.*

sure surer surest *adjective*
1 if you are sure about something, you know it is true. *I'm sure I packed my raincoat.*
2 if you are sure that something will happen, you know it will. *I'm sure it will snow tomorrow.*

surf *noun*
the foam or white part on top of the waves on the sea.

surf surfs surfing surfed *verb*
to surf is to ride on top of the waves by standing on a long piece of wood or plastic called a surfboard.

surface surfaces *noun*
the outside part of something.

surgeon surgeons *noun*
a doctor whose job is to do operations on people in a hospital.

surgery *noun*
1 a place where you go to see a doctor or a dentist. *a dental surgery.*
2 cutting somebody's body to take out or mend a part inside. *heart surgery.*

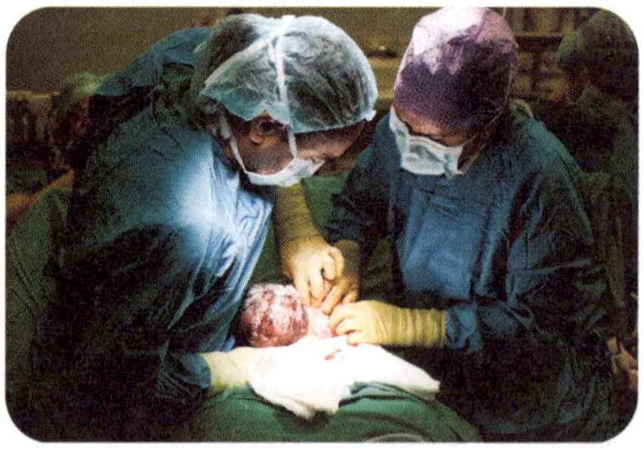

surname surnames *noun*
your last name that shows which family you belong to. *My first name is Ben and my surname is Smith.*

surprise surprises surprising surprised *verb*
if you surprise somebody, you do something that they do not expect. *You surprised me when you came home early.*
surprise *noun.*
Don't tell Chris about the party – it's a surprise!
surprising *adjective.*

surrender surrenders surrendering surrendered *verb*
when an army surrenders, it stops fighting and gives in to the enemy.
surrender *noun.*

surround surrounds surrounding surrounded *verb*
to surround means to be or go all around something. *An island is surrounded by water.* ◆ *The police surrounded the office building.*

survive survives surviving survived *verb*
to stay alive after something very bad or dangerous has happened. *Our cat was lucky to survive after being hit by a car.*

suspect suspects suspecting suspected *verb*
if you suspect somebody of doing something wrong, you think they did it. *The police suspected her of stealing the money and gold.*
suspect *noun.*

suspense *noun*
a feeling of fear or excitement that you have when you do not know what is going to happen. *We waited with suspense for the results of the competition.*

suspicious *adjective*
if you are suspicious, you think that something is wrong, or you do not believe somebody. *I was suspicious when he said he had lost my money.*

swallow swallows swallowing swallowed *verb*
when you swallow food or drink, it goes down your throat.

swam past of swim.

swamp swamps *noun*
a marsh or an area of wet ground. There are many swamps in the southeast of the United States.

swan swans *noun*
a big, white bird with a long neck that lives on water. Young swans are grey and are called cygnets. *We saw swans swimming on the lakes in Cumbria.*

swap swaps swapping swapped *verb*
to swap means to change something for something else. *Can I swap my book for your camera?*
swap *noun*.

sway sways swaying swayed *verb*
when somebody or something sways, they move slowly from side to side for some time. *The daffodils were swaying on their long stems in the wind.*

swear swears swearing swore sworn *verb*
1 if somebody swears, they say bad or rude words.
2 if you swear, you promise something in a very serious way. *I swear I didn't break the window.*

sweat sweats sweating sweated *verb*
when you sweat, you lose liquid from your body through your skin. *Everybody was sweating because it was so hot.*
sweat *noun*.

sweep sweeps sweeping swept *verb*
when you sweep something, you clean it with a brush. *Would you please sweep the kitchen floor?*

sweet sweeter sweetest *adjective*
1 sweet foods and drinks have a taste like sugar. *Honey is sweet.*
2 a sweet person is gentle and kind. *It was very sweet of you to help me.*

sweet *noun*
1 a small piece of sweet food made with sugar or chocolate. *a packet of sweets.*
2 a pudding or sweet food that you eat at the end of a meal. *You can have ice cream or fruit for sweet.*

swell swells swelling swelled swollen *verb*
when something swells, it gets bigger and thicker. *My ankle swelled up when I twisted it.* ◆ *The insect bite made her fingers swell up.*
swelling *noun*.

swept past of sweep.
Gerry swept the snow from the path.

swerve swerves swerving swerved *verb*
when something that is moving swerves, it goes quickly to one side. *The cyclist swerved to avoid the car.*

swim swims swimming swam swum *verb*
when you swim, you use your arms and legs to move along in water. *We are going swimming in the sea.* ◆ *We watched the fish swimming in the pond.*
swim *noun*.

swimming pool swimming pools *noun*
a large indoor or outdoor water-filled tank for swimming and diving in.

swing swings swinging swung *verb*
when something swings, it moves backwards and forwards through the air. *The soldiers were swinging their arms as they marched.*

swing swings *noun*
a seat for swinging that hangs from two strong ropes or chains. People sit in swings and move backwards and forwards.

switch switches *noun*
a thing that you press or turn to stop or start something working. *You press this switch to turn the computer on.*

switch switches switching switched *verb*
1 to switch is to change one thing for another thing. *My friend and I switched places.*
2 when you switch something on, you press a switch to make it work. *Can I switch the TV on?*
3 when you switch something off, you press a switch to make it stop working. *How do you switch the computer off?*

swivel swivels swiveling swivelled *verb*
to swivel is to twist or turn around on the same spot.

swollen past of swell.

swoop swoops swooping swooped *verb*
to rush or fly downwards suddenly. *The bird swooped down to catch the worm.*

a b c d e f g h i j k l m n o p q r s t u v w x y z

A B C D E F G H I J K L M N O P Q R S T U V W X Y Z

sword swords *noun*
a weapon with a handle and a long metal blade with a sharp point at the end. Soldiers used to fight with swords. ▲ Say ***sord***.

swore sworn past of swear.

swum past of swim.

swung past of swing.

syllable syllables *noun*
a word or part of a word that has one sound. The word 'but' has one syllable, the word 'butter' has two syllables and the word 'America' has four syllables.

symbol symbols *noun*
1 a sign or mark that means something. The symbol + means add in maths.
2 a symbol is also a thing that stands for something else. *A dove is a symbol of peace.*

Do you know what these symbols mean? Look at page 190 for the answers.

Spelling tip:
Some words that start with the sound 's' as in 'simple', are spelt with a 'c', such as certain, city, cycle.

symmetrical *adjective*
if a shape is symmetrical, both sides are the same. If you draw a line through the middle of a circle, you will see that both sides are symmetrical.
symmetry *noun*.

sympathy *now*
if you feel or show sympathy to somebody, you are very kind to them because they are hurt or sad.
sympathetic *adjective*, **sympathize** *verb*.
Richard's friends were very sympathetic when he broke his arm.

symphony symphonies *noun*
a long piece of music written for a large orchestra.
symphonic *adjective*.

symptom symptoms *noun*
something that is wrong with you and shows that you are ill. *A sore throat and a temperature are symptoms of a cold.*

synagogue synagogues *noun*
a building where Jewish people go to pray. ▲ Say ***sin-a-gog***.

synonym synonyms *noun*
a word that means nearly the same as another word. Little and small are synonyms. A word that means opposite is an **antonym** - big and small, for example.

synthetic *adjective*
created artificially using chemicals. Nylon is a synthetic fabric.
▲ Say *sin-**thet**-ik*.

syringe syringes *noun*
a special needle that doctors can push into your skin when they give you an injection of medicine or when they take blood out of your body.

syrup *noun*
a sweet, sticky food made from the juice of fruit boiled with sugar.

system systems *noun*
1 an organized way of doing something. *We have changed the system for taking books from the library.*
2 a group of machines or other things that work together. *a computer system.*

T t

table tables *noun*
1 a piece of furniture with a flat top that you can put things on.
2 a set of numbers or words arranged in columns.
3 a list of all the multiplications of all the numbers, especially between 1 and 12.

tablet tablets *noun*
a small, round piece of medicine that you swallow.

table tennis *noun*
a game for two or four people who stand at each end of a table with a net across the middle and hit a very small ball to each other, bouncing it off the table, with small bats.

tackle tackles tackling tackled *verb*
1 when you tackle something, you do whatever is needed, even if it is difficult.
2 if you tackle somebody when playing a game such as rugby, you try to get the ball away from them.

tactful *adjective*
careful not to say anything that would hurt somebody's feelings.
tactfully *adverb*.

tadpole tadpoles *noun*
a tiny animal that lives in water and that will grow into a frog or toad. Tadpoles have tails.

tail tails *noun*
the part at the back end of an animal, bird or fish. *The dog wagged its tail.* ◆ *Aeroplanes have tails.* ● A word that sounds like **tail** is **tale**.

tailor tailors *noun*
a person who makes suits, jackets and coats.

take takes taking took taken *verb*
1 if you take something, you get hold of it or carry it. *Can you take these books to the library?*
2 if somebody takes you, they drive you or you go with them. *Dan took me to school on his way to work.*
3 if you take something, you remove it. *She took her purse out of her bag.* ◆ *Have you taken my bag?*
take off When a plane takes off, it leaves the runway and moves into the air. ■ The opposite is **land**.

tale tales *noun*
a story. *a tale of love and adventure.* ● A word that sounds like **tale** is **tail**.

talent talents *noun*
if you have a talent for something you have a natural ability for it and can do it well. *Clive's got a real talent for acting.*
talented *adjective*.

talk talks talking talked *verb*
when you talk, you say words. *We talked on the phone for hours.* ▲ Say ***tawk***.

tall taller tallest *adjective*
1 higher than usual. *She's very tall.* ◆ *a tall building.* ■ The opposite is **short**.
2 having a certain height. *He's just over a metre tall.*

tambourine tambourines *noun*
a small, round musical instrument that you shake or tap with your fingers. ▲ Say *tam-ber-**een***.
❖ ***Look at page 105***

tame tamer tamest *adjective*
a tame animal or bird has become used to living with people and is not afraid of them. ■ The opposite is **wild**.

tan *noun*
if you have a tan, your skin is a darker colour than usual because you have been in the sun.

tandem tandems *noun*
a special bicycle for two people.

tangled *adjective*
twisted together in knots or muddled up together untidily. *The wool is a tangled mess.*

tank tanks *noun*
1 a big container that holds liquid or gas.
2 a big, heavy vehicle with a gun in it that is used in a war. ❖ ***Look below***

tanker tankers *noun*
1 a very big, long ship that carries oil.
2 a big lorry that carries petrol or some other liquid.

tap taps *noun*
a thing that you turn on to make water or gas flow out of a pipe and turn off to stop the flow.

tap taps tapping tapped *verb*
if you tap somebody or something, you hit them gently. *He tapped a few keys and information came up on the screen.*

A battle tank

tape tapes *noun*
1 a long, narrow piece of material. *a piece of sticky tape.*
2 a long strip of plastic that you can record sounds or pictures on and then play back on a tape-recorder or by using a video and television.
tape *verb*.

tape-recorder tape-recorders *noun*
a machine that you use to play a tape or to record sounds on to a tape.

tapestry tapestries *noun*
a piece of material that has a picture on it made from coloured threads.

tar *noun*
a thick, black, sticky substance that is used mainly for making roads.

target targets *noun*
an object that people aim at or try to hit when they are shooting.

tart tarts *noun*
a piece of pastry with jam or fruit on it.

task tasks *noun*
a job that must be done.

taste tastes tasting tasted *verb*
1 when you taste something, you try a bit of it to see if you like the flavour. *Taste this fish and tell me if you like the sauce.*
2 if something tastes nice or nasty, you think the flavour is nice or nasty. *I like that ice-cream, it tastes lovely.* ◆ *This milk tastes a bit funny.*

taste tastes *noun*
1 the ability to recognize the flavour of something by touching it with your tongue. *Sugar has a sweet taste.*
2 the way something tastes. *This bread has no taste at all.*

A B C D E F G H I J K L M N O P Q R S T U V W X Y Z

tattoo tattoos *noun*
a permanent pattern on a person's skin made by putting coloured dyes under the skin using a needle.

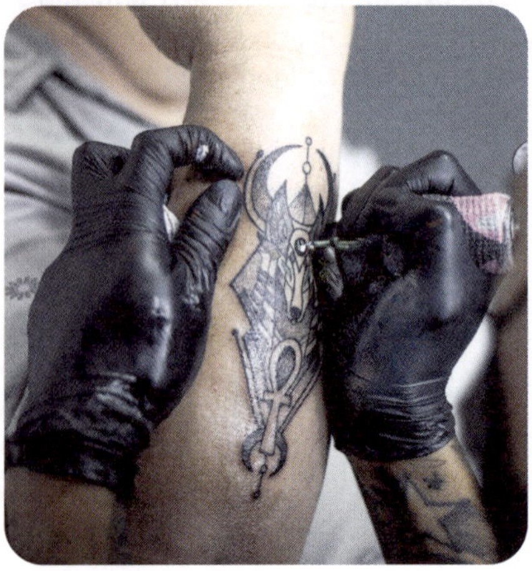

taught past of teach.
▲ Say ***tort***.

tax taxes *noun*
money that people have to pay to the government so that it can pay for running the country. *income tax*.

taxi taxis *noun*
a car that will take you where you want to go if you pay the driver.

tea *noun*
a drink that you make by pouring boiling water on to the dried leaves of the tea plant.

teach teaches teaching taught *verb*
1 when somebody teaches you, they tell you about a subject and help you learn about it. *Mrs Jones teaches History*.
2 to teach also means to show somebody how to do something. *I'm trying to teach my sister how to ride a bicycle*.
teacher *noun*.

team teams *noun*
a group of people who work together or play a sport together. *the football team*.

teapot teapots *noun*
a container for making tea in with a spout for pouring it out.

tear tears *noun*
one of the drops of liquid that comes from your eyes when you cry.
▲ Rhymes with ***here***. ● A word that sounds like **tear** is **tier**.

tear tears tearing tore torn *verb*
when you tear something, you pull one part away from the rest. *If you tear paper in a special way, you can make different shapes and patterns*.
▲ Rhymes with ***chair***.

tease teases teasing teased *verb*
when you tease somebody, you laugh at them or make jokes about them.
▲ Say ***teez***.

technology technologies *noun*
machines or systems that have been invented because of discoveries by scientists. ▲ Say *tek*-***nol***-*o*-*jee*.

teenage *adjective*
between 13 and 19 years old.
teenager *noun*.

teeth plural of tooth.

telephone telephones *noun*
an instrument that you use to speak to another person who is not in the same place as you.
▲ Say ***tel***-*e*-*fone*.

telescope telescopes *noun*
an instrument in the shape of a tube with a lens at each end that makes things that are far away look clearer and closer when you look through it.

television televisions *noun*
an instrument in the shape of a box that receives programmes that are broadcast and shows them in sound and pictures.

tell tells telling told *verb*
1 if you tell somebody something, you give them information in words about it. *I told him how to mend a puncture*. ◆ *She told me a very funny joke*.
2 if you tell somebody to do something, you say that they must do it.

temper *noun*
1 if you have a bad temper you get cross or angry easily. *Bill is always in a bad temper when he loses*.
2 if you lose your temper, you get very angry.

temperature *noun*
1 how hot or cold something is. *Water boils at a temperature of 100 degrees Celsius*.
2 if you have a temperature, your body is hotter than it should be.
▲ Say ***temp***-*re*-*cher*.

temple temples *noun*
a building where people go to pray. *The Golden Temple is famous in India*.

temporary *adjective*
lasting for a short time. *He's got a temporary job*. ■ The opposite is **permanent**.
temporarily *adverb*.

tempt tempts tempting tempted *verb*
if something tempts you, you really want it even if you know you should not have it. *I was really tempted by those shoes but they were too expensive*.
temptation *noun*.

tend tends tending tended *verb*
if something tends to happen, it usually happens or happens often. *I tend to miss the bus if I leave after 8 o'clock*. ◆ *He tends to get angry when he is tired or unhappy*.

tender tenderer tenderest *adjective*
1 easy to chew. *This is very tender meat*. ■ The opposite is **tough**.
2 a bit sore. *My ankle is still tender from when I fell over*.
3 gentle and loving. *He gave her a tender look*.
tenderly *adverb*.
She spoke tenderly to the little girl.
tenderness *noun*.

tennis *noun*
a game for two or four players. The players hit a soft ball with rackets backwards and forwards to each other over a net that is stretched across the middle of an area called a court.

tense tenser tensest *adjective*
1 nervous and anxious about something. *I always get tense when I have to go to the dentist.*
2 if your muscles are tense, they are stiff and tight. *After running the marathon my legs were very stiff and tense.* ■ The opposite is **relaxed**.
tensely *adverb.*
He waited tensely for the results of his medical tests.

tent tents *noun*
a shelter made of strong cloth that is held up by poles and ropes.

tepid *adjective*
slightly warm. *Babies have tepid baths so that they do not burn themselves.*

term terms *noun*
1 one of the periods of a school or university year when students are being taught.
2 a word or phrase. *'Adagio' and 'forte' are musical terms.*

terminal terminals *noun*
a building at an airport where passengers leave and arrive.

terrible *adjective*
very bad or unpleasant. *What a terrible noise.*
terribly *adverb.*

terrific *adjective*
very good indeed. *The video is terrific - I've seen it five times.*

terrify terrifies terrifying terrified *verb*
if you terrify somebody, you make them feel very frightened. *The explosion terrified the horses.* ◆ *Many dogs are terrified of thunder.*

territory territories *noun*
1 land that belongs to or is controlled by a country, army or ruler.
2 an area where an animal lives that it will fight for if another animal tries to come and live there.

terror *noun*
very great fear. *He screamed with terror when he thought he'd seen a ghost.*

test tests *noun*
1 a way of finding out what you know about something by asking you a set of questions or getting you to show what you can do. *a driving test.* ◆ *a spelling test.*
2 a check to see if part of your body is working properly. *an eye test.*

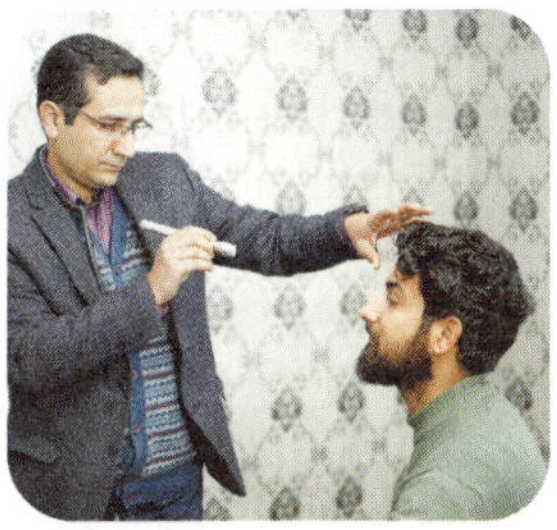

test tests testing tested *verb*
1 when you test something, you use or examine it to see if it works well. *I'm testing the brakes to make sure they're working properly.*
2 when you test somebody, you try to find out how much they know by using a test.

text texts *noun*
written words. *Books for very young children have lots of pictures and not much text.*

texture textures *noun*
the way that something feels. *This wool has a smooth texture almost like silk.*

thank thanks thanking thanked *verb*
when you thank somebody, you tell them how nice it was of them to do something for you or give you something. *Thank you very much for taking us all to the theme park.*

thaw thaws thawing thawed *verb*
when something frozen thaws, it becomes warm enough to melt. *The sun's out and the snow has started to thaw.*

theatre theatres *noun*
a building where people go to see plays. ▲ Say ***thee**-a-ter*.

theft thefts *noun*
the crime of stealing. *He was sent to jail for the crime of theft.*

theme park theme parks *noun*
a place you go to have fun where all the games and activities are to do with the same subject, for example, space.

thermometer thermometers *noun*
an instrument that shows how hot or cold it is.

thick thicker thickest *adjective*
1 something that is thick measures a lot from one side to the other or from top to bottom. *The castle wall was a metre thick.* ■ The opposite is **thin**.
2 a thick liquid does not flow easily. *Honey is thick.* ■ The opposite is **thin**.
3 something that is thick is not easy to get through or to see through. *The airport was closing because of thick fog.* ◆ *a thick forest.*
thicken *verb.*
The fog thickened.
thickly *adverb.*

thief thieves *noun*
a person who steals something. *Thieves broke into the shop and stole all the silver and jewellery.* ▲ Say ***theef***.

thigh thighs *noun*
your thigh is the part of your leg above your knee. *Your thighs are the fattest part of your legs.* ▲ Rhymes with ***by***.

thin thinner thinnest *adjective*
1 narrow from side to side or from top to bottom. *a thin slice of cake.* ◆ *There was a thin layer of ice on the pond.* ■ The opposite is **thick**.
2 a thin person does not have much flesh covering their bones and weighs less than most people. ■ The opposite is **fat**.
3 a thin liquid flows easily. *This soup is too thin.* ■ The opposite is **thick**.
thinly *adverb*.

think thinks thinking thought *verb*
1 when you think, you have ideas or words in your mind. *What are you thinking about?*
2 when you think something is true, you believe it. *I think Monty's plans for the party are super.*

thirsty thirstier thirstiest *adjective*
if you are thirsty, you need something to drink. *Exercise can make you thirsty.*

thistle thistles *noun*
a wild plant with very prickly leaves and purple or white flowers.

thorn thorns *noun*
a little, sharp point on the stem of a plant such as a rose.
thorny *adjective*.

thorough *adjective*
complete or careful. *a thorough investigation.* ▲ Say ***thur-o***.
thoroughly *adverb*.

thought thoughts *noun*
an idea or something that you think. *Any thoughts about what you'd like for your birthday?* ▲ Say ***thort***.

thought past of think.
▲ Say ***thort***.

thoughtful *adjective*
1 quiet and serious while you are thinking about something carefully.
2 if you are thoughtful, you think about what other people want and try to behave in a way that makes them more comfortable or happy. ▲ Say ***thort-ful***.

thoughtfully, **thoughtless** *adverbs*.
thoughtless behaviour.

thread threads *noun*
a long, thin piece of cotton, wool or nylon that you use for sewing or for weaving. ▲ Say ***thred***.
thread *verb*.

threat threats *noun*
a warning that something nasty may happen. ▲ Say ***thret***.

threaten threatens threatening threatened *verb*
if somebody threatens you, they say that they will do something nasty if you do not do what they want. *She threatened to hit me.* ▲ Say ***thret-en***.

three-dimensional *adjective*
something that is three-dimensional is like a real thing with height, width and depth, and not like a flat picture. A sculpture is three-dimensional.

threw past of throw.
● A word that sounds like **threw** is **through**.

thrill thrills *noun*
a sudden feeling of excitement or pleasure.
thrilling *adjective*.

throat throats *noun*
your throat is the front part of your neck and the tube that goes down from inside your mouth taking food and air into your body.

throb throbs throbbing throbbed *verb*
1 if part of your body throbs, it hurts a lot and beats with pain. *My head is throbbing.*
2 to throb is to beat in a regular way like your heart pumping blood.

throne thrones *noun*
a special chair for a king or queen.

through *preposition*
from one side to the other. *The train went through a tunnel.* ◆ *Water is coming through a hole in the ceiling.* ▲ Say ***throo***. ● A word that sounds like **through** is **threw**.

throw throws throwing threw thrown *verb*
when you throw something, you send it through the air from your hand. *Throw the ball up into the air and then hit it with your racket.*

thumb thumbs *noun*
your thumb is the short, thick finger at the side of your hand. ▲ Say ***thum***.

thump thumps thumping thumped *verb*
if you thump somebody or something, you hit them with your fist. *He thumped the door.*

thunder *noun*
the loud noise that you hear after a flash of lightning during a storm called a thunderstorm.

tick ticks *noun*
the mark (✓) used to show that something is correct.

ticket tickets *noun*
a small piece of paper that shows you have paid for something. *Have you bought the cinema tickets yet?* ◆ *a railway ticket.*

tickle tickles tickling tickled *verb*
when you tickle somebody, you touch them very softly in a place where it makes them laugh and wriggle away.

tide tides *noun*
the every day movement of the sea coming towards land and then moving away. *The tide is coming in.* ◆ *The tide is going out.*

tidy tidier tidiest *adjective*
with everything in its proper place. *a tidy room.* ◆ *tidy hair.*
tidy *verb*, **tidily** *adverb*.

tie ties tying tied *verb*
1 when you tie something, you fasten it using string or something similar. *The parcel was tied with red and white ribbons.* ◆ *She tied the dog to a tree.*
2 when two people or teams tie in a race or competition, they finish in an equal position. *They tied in second place.*
tie up *Ships were tied up at the dock.*

tie ties *noun*
a long, thin piece of material that you wear around the neck of a shirt with a knot at the front.

tier tiers *noun*
one of a series of rows or layers that are placed one above the other. *There are several tiers of seats in the theatre.* ◆ *a wedding cake with three tiers.* ▲ Rhymes with ***here***. ● A word that sounds like **tier** is **tear**.

tiger tigers *noun*
a large, wild animal in the cat family which has orange fur with dark stripes. Tigers live in Asia.

tight tighter tightest *adjective*
1 fitting very close to your body. *Connie's shoes are very tight – Joe is trying to pull them off.*
2 when something is tight, it is firmly fastened so that it will not move. *Make sure the lid is tight.* ▲ Say ***tite***. ■ The opposite is **loose**.
tightly *adverb*.

tighten tightens tightening tightened *verb*
if you tighten something, you make it tighter. If something tightens, it gets tighter. ▲ Say ***tite****-en*.

tightrope tightropes *noun*
a rope high up in the air that acrobats walk along in the circus. ▲ Say ***tite****-rope*.

tights *noun*
a piece of clothing made of thin material that tightly covers your legs, feet and bottom. ▲ Say ***tites***.

tile tiles *noun*
a thin piece of hard material that you use to cover a wall, floor or a roof. *The bathroom tiles have pictures of flowers and birds on them.*

till *preposition*
until. *We had to wait two weeks till we heard the exam results.*

time *noun*
1 what we measure in units such as minutes, hours, days, weeks and years.
2 a particular point in time. *What's the time?*
3 a period of time. *Did you enjoy your time in San Francisco?*

timetable timetables *noun*
a list that shows when things are going to happen. *a train timetable.* ◆ *a school timetable.*

timid *adjective*
shy and not very brave. *A mouse is a timid creature.*
timidly *adverb*.

tin tins *noun*
1 a kind of silver-coloured metal.
2 a can or metal container to store food in. *a tin of beans.* ◆ *a biscuit tin.*

tiny tinier tiniest *adjective*
very small. *Bacteria are so tiny that you can only see them through a microscope.* ■ The opposite is **huge** or **enormous**.

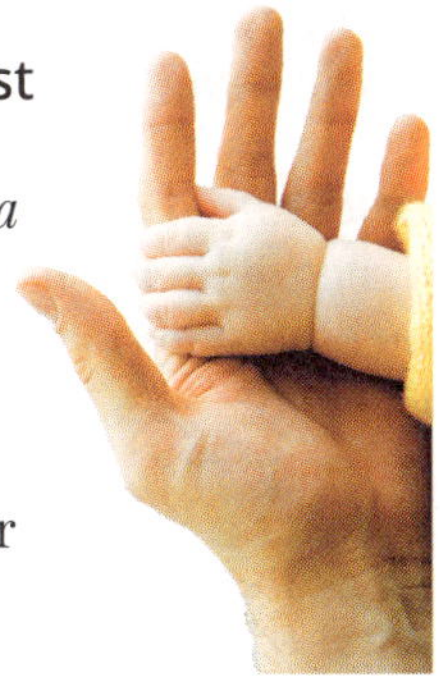

tip tips *noun*
1 the end of something long and thin. *the tips of your fingers.*
2 an extra amount of money that you give to somebody such as a waiter for helping you.
3 a place you can leave rubbish that you cannot get into the rubbish bin. *Take all these old boxes to the tip.*

tiptoe tiptoes tiptoeing tiptoed *verb*
if you tiptoe, you walk on your toes so that you do not make a noise.

tired *adjective*
if you are tired, you want to go to sleep or you want to rest.

tissue tissues *noun*
1 a thin piece of soft paper that you can use as a handkerchief.
2 thin, soft paper for wrapping things in to protect them from damage.
3 a lot of tiny cells of the same kind that make up part of the body. *muscle tissue.*

title titles *noun*
1 the name of something such as a book, film or picture.
2 a word such as Lord, Professor, Dr, Mrs or Princess that a person can have in front of their name.

toad toads *noun*
an animal like a big frog. It lives on land but lays its eggs in water.

Fire-bellied toad
Giant toad

toadstool toadstools *noun*
a poisonous fungus that looks like a mushroom.

toast *noun*
a slice of bread that has been grilled on both sides to make it brown and crunchy.

tobacco *noun*
the cut and dried leaves of the tobacco plant that are used in cigarettes, cigars and pipes.

toboggan toboggans *noun*
a vehicle like a long seat fixed to two long strips of wood or metal called runners that you use to slide downhill on snow.

toddler toddlers *noun*
a very young child who is just learning to walk.

toe toes *noun*
your toes are the five parts at the end of your foot. ● A word that sounds like **toe** is **tow**.

toilet toilets *noun*
1 a large bowl with a seat that you use to get rid of liquid and solid waste from your body.
2 the room where the toilet is.

token tokens *noun*
a card or piece of paper that you can use instead of money to buy something. *a record token.* ◆ *a book token.*

told past of tell.

tomato tomatoes *noun*
a soft, round, red fruit that you eat in salads or that can be used to make soup or ketchup.

tomb tombs *noun*
a grave or place where somebody is buried. ▲ Say ***toom***.

tongue tongues *noun*
the long, pink part inside your mouth that you use to lick something and that helps you to taste things and to speak. ▲ Say ***tung***.

tonsil tonsils *noun*
your tonsils are the two small, soft lumps at the back of your throat. They sometimes swell and get painful in an illness called tonsillitis.

took past of take.

tool tools *noun*
anything that you use to help you to do a particular job. Hammers and saws are tools. Here are lots of different tools.

tooth teeth *noun*
1 one of the hard, white parts inside your mouth that you use to bite and to chew.
2 one of the thin parts that stick out in a row on such things as a comb, saw or zip.

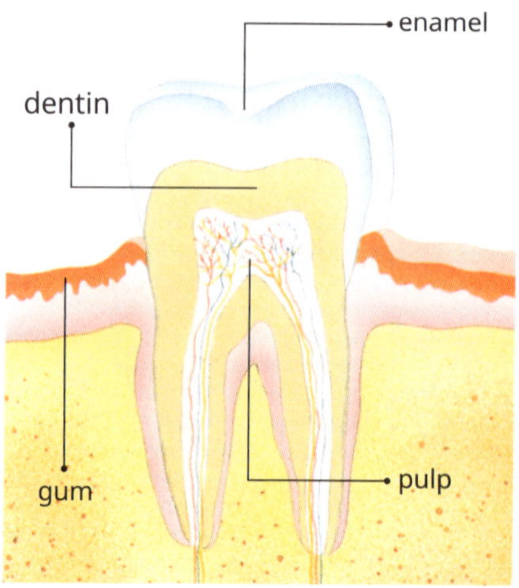

toothbrush toothbrushes *noun*
a small brush with a handle that you use to clean your teeth with.

toothpaste *noun*
a paste that you put on your toothbrush to clean your teeth with.

top tops *noun*
1 the highest part of something. *We walked to the top of the hill.* ■ The opposite is **bottom**.
2 a lid or cover for something. *a milk bottle top.*

topic topics *noun*
something that is being talked about or written about. *The weather is his only topic of conversation.*

topple topples toppling toppled *verb*
if something topples, it falls over because it is too heavy at the top. *The tree toppled over in the wind.*

torch torches *noun*
a small, electric light that you can hold in your hand.

tore torn past of tear.

tornado tornadoes *noun*
a very strong wind that travels in circles and that can do a lot of damage to buildings. ▲ Say *tor-**nay**-doh*.

tortoise tortoises *noun*
a small animal that has a hard shell over its back and that moves very slowly. Tortoises are reptiles. ▲ Say ***tor**-tus*.

Giant Galapagos tortoise

torture tortures torturing tortured *verb*
to make somebody feel great pain on purpose, as a punishment or to get information from them. ▲ Say ***tor**-cher*.
torturer *noun*.

toss tosses tossing tossed *verb*
1 if you toss something, you throw it upwards in a careless way. *She tossed me a pen and said 'Write down this number.'*
2 if something tosses, it moves about from side to side. *The boat tossed in the storm.*

total *adjective*
complete. *a total disaster.*
totally *adverb.*

total totals *noun*
the amount that you get when you add everything together. *If you add 12, 17, and 8, you get a total of 37.*

touch touches touching touched *verb*
1 when you touch something, you feel it with your hand or another part of you. *Don't touch the iron – it's very hot.*
2 if two things touch, there is no space between them.
▲ Say *tuch*.

tough tougher toughest *adjective*
1 strong and hard to break or damage. *Plastic is a tough material.*
2 difficult. *a tough decision.*
3 difficult to chew. *This meat is tough.*
■ The opposite is **tender**. ▲ Say *tuff*.

tour tours *noun*
a journey to different interesting places. *a tour of Paris.* ▲ Say *toor*.

tourist tourists *noun*
a person who is visiting interesting places on holiday. ▲ Say *toor-ist*.

tournament tournaments *noun*
a competition in which a lot of matches are played until one person wins over all the others. ▲ Say *toor-na-ment*.

tow tows towing towed *verb*
to tow a vehicle is to pull it along behind another vehicle. *The car is towing a caravan.* ● A word that sounds like **tow** is **toe**.

towel towels *noun*
a large piece of soft, thick material that you use to dry yourself.

tower towers *noun*
a very tall, narrow building or part of a building. *the Eiffel Tower.* ◆ *the Leaning Tower of Pisa.*

town towns *noun*
a place with streets, houses, shops and other buildings where a lot of people live and work.

toy toys *noun*
a thing for a child to play with.

trace traces tracing traced *verb*
1 when you trace a picture, you put a thin piece of paper over it and draw over the lines that show through.
2 if you trace somebody or something, you find them after looking for them. *He is trying to trace an uncle whom nobody in the family has heard from for years.*

trace traces *noun*
a tiny amount. *Traces of poison were found in the soup.*

track tracks *noun*
1 footprints or other marks left by a person or animal that show where they have been.
2 a narrow path. *a mountain track.*
3 an area of ground where races take place.
4 the rails that a train runs on.
5 one of the songs or pieces of music on a record or tape.

tractor tractors *noun*
a powerful vehicle with very large back wheels used on a farm for pulling heavy machinery.

trade *noun*
buying and selling things. *Ireland does a lot of trade with Britain.*

tradition traditions *noun*
a way of doing something that has been the same for a very long time.
traditional *adjective.*
traditional songs.
traditionally *adverb.*

traffic *noun*
cars, lorries, buses and other vehicles that are moving along the roads. *A lot of traffic goes through the village.*

tragedy tragedies *noun*
1 a very sad event. *Two of his brothers and a sister died in the tragedy.*
2 a serious play with a sad ending.
▲ Say *traj-e-dee.*
tragic *adjective.*
a tragic accident.

trail trails *noun*
1 a track or path for people to follow or go along in the country.
2 marks or other signs left behind where a person or animal has been. *He left a trail of muddy footprints on the floor.*

trailer trailers *noun*
1 a vehicle that is towed behind a car or lorry to carry very large or heavy things, such as a boat.
2 an advertisement that shows short scenes from a film or TV programme.

train trains *noun*
a set of carriages that move along rails pulled by an engine. Some trains carry passengers and some trains carry freight.

train trains training trained *verb*
1 when you train, you practise a sport or do exercises to get fitter. *He's training for the Olympics.*
2 to train a person or animal is to teach them how to do something. *She's training the dog to shake a paw.*
3 if you train, you learn the skills you need to do a job. *Sue's training to be a doctor.*
trainer *noun.*

trainers *noun*
shoes with thick soles that can be worn for running and exercising.

trample tramples trampling trampled *verb*
if you trample on something, you walk on it and crush it. *They trampled the flowers.*

trampoline trampolines *noun*
a piece of very strong material fixed to a metal frame with springs that is used for jumping up and down in gymnastics. ▲ Say ***tramp**-o-leen.*

transfer transfers transferring transferred *verb*
to transfer a person or thing is to move them to a different place.

transform transforms transforming transformed *verb*
if you transform something, you change it completely. *With make up, a wig and good acting, he transformed himself into an old man.*

translate translates translating translated *verb*
if you translate something, you change the same words in to a different language. *Richard translated the novel from English into French.*

transparent *adjective*
if something is transparent, you can see through it. *This plastic is transparent.*

transplant transplants *noun*
an operation in which a surgeon takes out a damaged part of the body and replaces it with one that is not damaged. *a heart transplant.*

transport *noun*
buses, trains and other vehicles that take people or goods from one place to another.

transport transports transporting transported *verb*
to transport people or goods is to take them from one place to another in a vehicle. *The parcels were transported by air.*

trap traps *noun*
a thing to catch an animal or bird. *a mouse trap.*
trap *verb.*

trapeze trapezes *noun*
a bar hanging from ropes high up in the air that acrobats swing from in a circus.

travel travels travelling travelled *verb*
when you travel, you go from one place to another. *We'll be travelling back to Scotland on Wednesday.*
travel *noun,* **traveller** *noun.*

trawler trawlers *noun*
a boat for catching fish by pulling a wide net behind it in the sea.

tray trays *noun*
a flat piece of wood, metal or plastic that you carry things on. *He put the cups and saucers on a tray.*

treacle *noun*
a thick, black liquid made from sugar.

tread treads treading trod trodden *verb*
when you tread on something, you put your foot down on it. *Ouch! You trod on my toe.* ▲ Say ***tred**.*

treasure treasures *noun*
a collection of very valuable objects such as gold, silver or jewels. *The pirates hid the treasure in a cave.* ▲ Say ***tresh**-er.*

treat treats treating treated *verb*
1 when you treat somebody in a particular way, you behave towards them like that. *He always treats me kindly.*
2 to treat somebody is to give them medicine or to look after them in a way that will make them well. *The doctor treated her for an earache.*

treatment treatments *noun*
1 how a doctor treats somebody who is ill. *What's the right treatment?*
2 how somebody behaves towards a person, animal or thing. *cruel treatment.*

tree trees *noun*
a big plant that has a thick, hard stem of wood called a trunk and branches and leaves. ❖ ***Look at page 174***

tremble trembles trembling trembled *verb*
if you tremble, you shake a little because you are frightened, cold or excited.

trend trends *noun*
the way things seem to be changing. *The trend is for people to save their money and spend less.*

trespass trespasses trespassing trespassed *verb*
if you trespass, you go on somebody's land without asking them if you can.

trial trials *noun*
1 a period of time in a law court when lawyers, judge and jury try to find out whether somebody is guilty or innocent of a crime.
2 a test to find out how good a thing is.

triangle triangles *noun*
1 a shape with three straight sides.
2 a small musical instrument with three metal sides that you play by hitting with a short metal rod.
▲ Say ***try**-ang-gul.*
triangular *adjective. a triangular shape.*

tribe tribes *noun*
a group of people of the same race that speak the same language and live in the same area.

trick tricks *noun*
1 something that is done to cheat somebody or to try to make them believe something that is not true.
2 something that looks as if it could not be done. *a magic trick.*

trick tricks tricking tricked *verb*
to trick somebody is to cheat them or try to make them believe something that is not true. *We changed the time on the clock and tricked our teacher into sending us home early.*

trickle trickles trickling trickled *verb*
when liquid trickles, a small amount of it flows slowly. *Tears slowly trickled down his cheeks.*

tricycle tricycles *noun*
a vehicle like a bicycle with three wheels. ▲ Say ***try**-sik-ul.*

trim trims trimming trimmed *verb*
if you trim something, you cut small pieces off it so that it has a better shape and looks tidy. *The hairdresser is trimming Manish's hair.*

trip trips *noun*
a journey to a place and back again. *We went on a school trip to the museum.*

trip trips tripping tripped *verb*
if you trip, you knock your foot on something and fall over. *She tripped over the cat.*

triple *adjective*
having three parts or done three times. *He's a triple winner.* ◆ *A triple chocolate milkshake.*

triplet triplets *noun*
one of three people or animals who have the same mother and were born at the same time.

triumph triumphs *noun*
a great success at something you have had to try hard to do. ▲ Say ***try**-umf.*

trod trodden past of tread.

trolley trolleys *noun*
an open container on wheels that you use to carry heavy things. *a supermarket trolley.*

trombone trombones *noun*
a large, brass musical instrument that you play by blowing into and moving one tube in and out of another tube to change the notes.
trombonist *noun.*

trophy trophies *noun*
a prize such as a silver cup that is given to a person who has won a competition or tournament. *My baseball team got a huge silver trophy for winning the contest.*
▲ Say ***troh**-fee.*

tropical *adjective*
to do with the tropics, the very hot parts of the world near the Equator. *a tropical rainforest.*

trot trots trotting trotted *verb*
when a horse trots, it moves quite quickly.
trot *noun.*

trouble troubles *noun*
a problem or a difficulty or worrying situation.
in trouble if you are in trouble, you have done something wrong and made somebody angry who might punish you. *If you break the window with that ball, you'll be in big trouble.*
▲ Say ***trub**-ul.*

Trees

Hornbeam

Douglas fir

Cedar of Lebanon

Vocabulary

broadleaf
trees with broad, flat leaves are deciduous. The leaves fall in the autumn.

deciduous
trees that shed their leaves in the autumn.

evergreen
conifers that keep their needle-like leaves in the winter.

hardwood
the wood of slow-growing, broadleaf or deciduous trees. The wood is strong and used for making furniture.

heartwood
the oldest, hardest wood at the centre of the trunk.

softwood
the wood of evergreen trees. The word is misleading as some 'softwoods' are 'hard'.

Common juniper

Golden weeping willow

Hybrid black-poplar

Sea buckthorn

Red oak

Spindle

Box

Pedunculate oak

Common jujube

Guelder rose

Dragon tree

Petticoat palm

trough troughs *noun*
a long, narrow container to keep food or water in for animals. ▲ Say *troff*.

trousers *noun*
a piece of clothing that covers the lower half of your body with separate parts for each leg. *a pair of trousers.*

trowel trowels *noun*
a tool like a very small spade with a curved blade and a short handle.

truck trucks *noun*
1 a lorry.
2 a railway carriage for carrying goods in rather than people.

trudge trudges trudging trudged *verb*
if you trudge somewhere, you walk slowly because you are tired or cross. *We trudged home through the mud.*
▲ Say *trudj*.

true truer truest *adjective*
if something is true, it is based on known facts and accurate, not made up or guessed at. *a true joke.* ■ The opposite is **false**.
truly *adverb*.
very. *It was a truly funny story.*

trumpet trumpets *noun*
a brass musical instrument that you play by blowing into it.
trumpeter *noun*.

trunk trunks *noun*
1 the round, hard stem of a tree that the branches grow from.
2 the long nose of an elephant.
3 the main part of your body from the top of your legs to your shoulders.
4 a large, strong box for carrying things in on a long journey or for storing things in.

trust trusts trusting trusted *verb*
if you trust somebody, you believe that they are good and honest and will not do anything to hurt you.
trust *noun*.

truth *noun*
what is true, accurate and correct. *I'm sure she's telling the truth.*

try tries trying tried *verb*
1 if you try to do something, you do your best to do it.
2 if you try something, you test it to see what it is like. *Try this soup and tell me if it needs more salt.*

T-shirt T-shirts *noun*
a shirt made of cotton with short sleeves and no collar or buttons, that you pull over your head.

tub tubs *noun*
a container for food. *a tub of ice-cream.*

tube tubes *noun*
1 a long, round, hollow thing, like a pipe.
2 a long, thin container that you squeeze to get the contents out. *a tube of toothpaste.*

tuck tucks tucking tucked *verb*
if you tuck something, you push the end of it under something or in something else. *He tucked his shirt into his trousers.*

tuft tufts *noun*
a clump of hair or grass.

tug tugs tugging tugged *verb*
if you tug something, you pull hard at it. *The baby kept tugging at her hair.*

tulip tulips *noun*
a plant that grows from a bulb and has a long stem and a bright flower in the shape of a cup.

tumble tumbles tumbling tumbled *verb*
if you tumble, you fall suddenly, rolling over and over. *The child tumbled down the stairs.*

tune tunes *noun*
a series of musical notes that are nice to listen to.

tunic tunics *noun*
a loose piece of clothing with no sleeves or collar.

tunnel tunnels *noun*
a long hole under the ground or through a hill. *the Channel Tunnel.*
tunnel *verb*.
The moles have tunnelled under the lawn in the back garden.

turban turbans *noun*
a long strip of material wound around the head and especially worn by Sikh men.

turf *noun*
short, thick grass.

turkey turkeys *noun*
a large bird that does not fly and that is usually kept on a farm for its meat.

Ocellated turkey

Common turkey

turn turns turning turned *verb*
1 when something turns, it moves around so that it faces a different direction or goes in a different direction. *The car turned right at the traffic lights.* ◆ *He turned round and looked behind him.*
2 when something turns, it goes round. *The wheel turned.*
3 when you turn something, you turn it round. *She turned the handle.*
4 when something turns into something else, it changes to become that thing. *A caterpillar turns into a butterfly.*

a b c d e f g h i j k l m n o p q r s t u v w x y z

turn turns *noun*
a time when you do something that other people have done before you and that other people will do after you. *It's my turn to use the computer.*

turtle turtles *noun*
a large reptile with a hard shell that lives in the sea.

tusk tusks *noun*
a long, pointed tooth that comes right outside the mouth of an animal such as an elephant.

TV TVs *noun*
short for television. *She's upstairs watching TV.*

twice *adverb*
two times. *I've been to see the film twice now. How many times have you seen it?*

twig twigs *noun*
a small branch of a tree.

twilight *noun*
a time after sunset before it gets completely dark. ▲ Say ***twy**-lite.*

twin twins *noun*
one of two people or animals who have the same mother and were born at the same time.

twinkle twinkles twinkling twinkled *verb*
when something twinkles, it shines with little flashes of light. *The stars were twinkling.*

twirl twirls twirling twirled *verb*
to turn or spin round and round. *She twirled her hair around her fingers.* **twirl** *noun.*

twist twists twisting twisted *verb*
1 if you twist something, you turn it around and around. *She twisted the screwdriver to tighten the screw.*
2 when you twist something, you bend it or turn it around. *He twisted the wires together.*

twitch twitches twitching twitched *verb*
to twitch is to make a small, quick movement.

twitter *noun*
the high sounds made by small birds.

tycoon tycoons *verb*
a tycoon is a rich and powerful businessman or businesswoman.

type types typing typed *verb*
when you type, you press the keys on a keyboard to write something. ▲ Say ***tipe***.

type types *noun*
1 a kind of thing. *What type of apple is that?*
2 the size and style of printed letters and numbers.
▲ Say ***tipe***.

typewriter typewriters *noun*
a machine with keys that you press to print letters and numbers on paper.

typhoon typhoons *noun*
a violent tropical storm of wind and rain. ▲ Say *tye-**foon***.

typical *adjective*
a typical thing is the most usual of that kind of thing. *a typical English village.* ▲ Say ***tip**-i-cal*

tyrant tyrants *noun*
a cruel and unfair ruler.

tyre tyres *noun*
a circle of rubber around the outside or rim of a bicycle or car wheel.
▲ Rhymes with ***fire***.

tyrannosaurus *noun*
a very large dinosaur with small front legs, a large head and sharp teeth.
❖ ***Look at page 125***

U u

udder udders *noun*
the part of a cow, goat or sheep that hangs under its body, near the back legs, and that produces milk.

ugly uglier ugliest *adjective*
not nice to look at. *a monster's ugly face.* ■ The opposite is **beautiful**.

umbrella umbrellas *noun*
a thing that you hold over your head to stay dry when it rains. The frame of an umbrella is covered with a round piece of material and joined to a long handle.

uncle uncles *noun*
your uncle is the brother of your mother or your father, or the husband of your aunt.

unconscious *adjective*
1 if you are unconscious, you are in a kind of sleep and you do not know what is happening. *When she fell downstairs and hit her head, she was unconscious for an hour.*
2 if you are unconscious of something, you do not know about it. *Rachel was unconscious that she had been rude.*

uncover uncovers uncovering uncovered *verb*
1 when you uncover something, you take off the thing or things that cover it. *He uncovered the box and looked inside.*
2 to uncover also means to find something that was hidden or not known about. *A skeleton was uncovered by a farmer digging in a field.* ◆ *The plot to blow up the building was uncovered.*

underground *adjective, adverb*
under the ground. *Rabbits build their burrows underground below the surface of the earth.*

undergrowth *noun*
all the bushes and other plants that grow under trees. *They cleared a path through the thick undergrowth.*

underline underlines underlining underlined *verb*
if you underline something, you draw a line under it to make people notice it. *Please write the date and underline it with a ruler.*

underneath *preposition, adverb*
below or under something. *I found my shoes underneath the bed.* ◆ *He laughed, but underneath he was sad.*

understand understands understanding understood *verb*
if you understand something, you know what it means, how it works or why it happens. *I didn't understand what the teacher said.* ◆ *Mark can now understand computers.*

underwear *noun*
underwear is clothes such as vests and pants that you wear under your other clothes.

undo undoes undoing undid undone *verb*
if you undo something like a parcel, you open it. *Can you undo this knot?*

undress undresses undressing undressed *verb*
when you undress, you take off your clothes. *It's time to undress and go to bed.* ■ The opposite is **dress**.

unemployed *adjective*
a person who is unemployed does not have a job and is not working. *She has been unemployed for six months.*
unemployment *noun*.

unfold unfolds unfolding unfolded *verb*
when you unfold something like a piece of paper or material, you open it out so that it lies flat. *I unfolded the map and put it on the table.* ■ The opposite is **fold**.

uniform uniforms *noun*
a special set of clothes that people wear to show that they belong to the same group. *Pilots, nurses and security guards wear uniforms.*

union unions *noun*
a group of workers that come together to talk to their managers about any problems at work. *the National Union of Teachers.*

unique *adjective*
different from anybody or anything else and the only one of its kind. *Each person's voice is unique.* ▲ Say *yoo-**neek**.*

unit units *noun*
1 one part of something. *A kitchen unit.*
2 an amount used in measuring or counting. *A metre is a unit of length, a kilogram is a unit of weight and a minute is a unit of time.*
▲ Say ***yoo**-nit.*

unite unites uniting united *verb*
if things or people unite, they join together or do something together. *Children in the school are united in wanting to win the cup.* ▲ Say *yoo-**nite**.*
united *adjective.*
the United States of America.

universe *noun*
the Earth, the Sun, the Moon and all the other planets and stars in space. *The Earth is a tiny spot in the universe.*
▲ Say ***yoo**-ni-verse.*

university universities *noun*
a place where people can go to study things when they have left school. *My sister is studying biology at university.*
▲ Say *yoo-ni-**ver**-sit-ee.*

unload unloads, unloading, unloaded *verb*
to unload is to take goods off a ship or vehicle. ■ The opposite is **load**.

unlock unlocks unlocking unlocked *verb*
when you unlock something, you turn a key to open it. *I unlocked the door and went inside.* ■ The opposite is **lock**.

untidy *adjective*
in a mess and nothing in the proper place. *untidy hair.*

untie untie**s**
untying untied *verb*
if you untie something, you undo the knots that fasten it. *I untied my shoelaces.*

until *preposition*
up to a certain time or day. *Dad is in his office until six o'clock every evening.* ◆ *I can't come until tomorrow.*

unusual *adjective*
something that is unusual is not ordinary, normal or usual. *It is unusual to see snow in summer.*

upper *adjective*
above or higher than another thing.

upright *adjective, adverb*
if something like a bottle is upright, it is standing up, with the top facing upwards. *Connie is standing upright and Joe is lying down.*

upset upsets upsetting upset *verb*
1 if you upset somebody, you make them unhappy. *She upset me when she said I was fat.*
2 if you upset something like a drink, you knock it over and spill it.

upside-down *adjective, adverb*
if something is upside-down, the bottom is at the top and the top is at the bottom. *This sloth is hanging upside-down.*

upstairs *adjective, adverb*
on or to an upper floor. *My bedroom is upstairs.*

up-to-date *adjective*
new and modern. *News is information that is up-to-date.*

upward, upwards *adverb*
from lower to higher.

urgent *adjective*
so very important that it must be done immediately. *She made an urgent phone call to the doctor.*
urgency *noun.*

use uses using used *verb*
1 if you use something, you do a job with it. *You use scissors to cut things with.*
2 to use also means to take something. *Don't use all the glue.*
▲ Say ***yooz***.
used to *verb.*
1 if you used to do something, you did it before, but you do not do it now. *I used to go swimming every Tuesday, but now I play tennis.*
2 used to can also mean knowing somebody or something well. *We are all used to her jokes.* ▲ Say ***yoost**-too.*

use uses *noun*
what you can do with something. *This bag has many uses.* ▲ Say ***yooss***.

useful *adjective*
if somebody or something is useful, they help you in some way. *Ben was very useful because he helped with the baby.* ■ The opposite is **useless**.

useless *adjective*
if something is useless, it is no good for anything and you cannot use it. *This bag is useless because the handle has broken.* ■ The opposite is **useful**.

usual *adjective*
if something is usual, it happens often or most of the time. *Seven o'clock is our usual time for breakfast.*
usually *adverb.*
I usually go to school by bike.

utensil utensils *noun*
a tool or container, especially one used for cooking.

utter utters uttering uttered *verb*
to make a sound or to say something. *He uttered a cry of pain.*

V v

vacant *adjective*
empty and not being used. *Do you have any vacant rooms in the hotel?*
▲ Say ***vay**-kant.*
vacancy *noun.*

vaccination vaccinations *noun*
an injection that stops you from getting an illness. *Joey had his vaccination against measels today.* ▲ Say *vak-si-**nay**-shun.*
vaccinate *verb.*

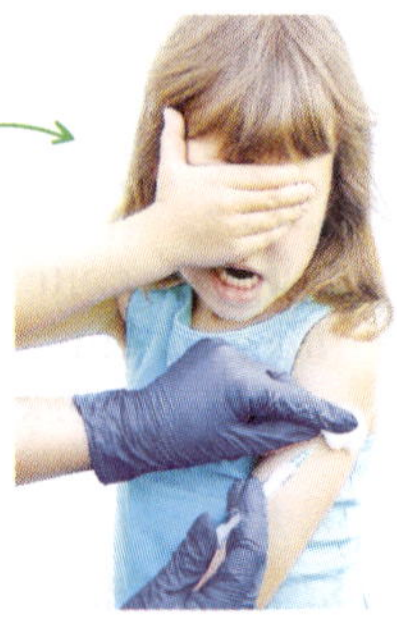

vacuum cleaner vacuum cleaners *noun*
a machine that sucks up dirt from floors and carpets.

vagina vaginas *noun*
the vagina is a part of a woman's body that leads to the womb.

vague vaguer vaguest *adjective*
not clear or definite. *I could*

see a vague shape in the mist. ▲ Say ***vayg***.
vaguely *adverb*.

vain vainer vainest *adjective*
vain people are too proud of themselves, especially of how they look.

valley valleys *noun*
low land between hills or mountains.

valuable *adjective*
1 worth a lot of money. *a valuable necklace*.
2 useful and helpful. *He gave me some valuable advice*.

value *noun*
1 the amount of money that something is worth. *What is the value of your house?*
2 how useful and helpful something is. *The instructions you gave were of great value in helping me to make the machine work*.

vampire vampires *noun*
in stories, a dead person who sucks people's blood.

van vans *noun*
a small, covered lorry with doors at the back that is used for carrying goods.

vandal vandals *noun*
a person who breaks or damages property on purpose. *Vandals have smashed the telephone box*.

vanilla *noun*
a flavour that comes from the pod of a tropical plant and is used in sweet foods. *vanilla ice-cream*.

vanish vanishes vanishing vanished *verb*
if something vanishes, it suddenly disappears.

vanity *noun*
being vain and very proud of what you look like.

variety varieties *noun*
1 a number of different kinds of thing. *They had a variety of skirts and dresses in the sale*.
2 a kind or sort of thing. *There are lots of different varieties of breakfast cereal*.

3 a lot of different things happening. *I like a lot of variety in my life*.
▲ Say *var-**eye**-i-tee*.

various *adjective*
several different things. *You can buy these towels in various colours*. ▲ Say ***vair**-ee-us*.

varnish *noun*
a clear liquid that you paint on wood to protect it and make it look shiny.

vary varies varying varied *verb*
if something varies, it keeps changing. *I take sandwiches to school every day but what goes in them varies*. ▲ Say ***vair**-ee*.

vase vases *noun*
a jar or container for putting flowers in.
▲ Say ***varz***.

vast vaster vastest *adjective*
very, very large. *The Sahara is a vast desert*.

vegetable vegetables *noun*
a plant that people eat. Cabbages, carrots and potatoes are vegetables.
▲ Say ***vejte**- bul*.

vegetarian vegetarians *noun*
a person who does not eat meat or fish. ▲ Say *vej-e-**tair**-ee-an*.

vehicle vehicles *noun*
a thing that takes people or goods from one place to another. Buses, cars, lorries, planes and trains are all vehicles. ▲ Say ***vee**-ik-ul*.

veil veils *noun*
a piece of very thin material that some women wear over their face or head.

vein veins *noun*
a vein is one of the tubes in your body that carries blood back to your heart.

velvet *noun*
cloth that is thick and soft on one side.

verb verbs *noun*
a word that tells you what somebody or something does or what is happening. 'Think', 'run' and 'cut' are all verbs. *What are you thinking?*

verdict verdicts *noun*
what the judge and jury decide at the end of a trial in a law court.

verse verses *noun*
a part of a poem or song made of several lines.

version versions *noun*
1 a changed form of something. *We bought a new version of the computer game*.
2 one person's way of telling a story or what happened that is a little different from other people's. *In Harry's version of the story, the bull didn't chase her to the gate, she just ran because she was scared*.

vertical *adjective*
standing straight up. *a vertical post*.
■ The opposite is **horizontal**.

vessel vessels *noun*
1 a ship or large boat.
2 a container for liquid.

vest vests *noun*
a piece of clothing that you wear under a shirt or blouse.

vet vets *noun*
a person whose job is to treat animals and help them to get well when they get ill or hurt.

via *preposition*
if you go somewhere via another place, you go to the other place first. *We went to the supermarket via the library.*

viaduct viaducts *noun*
a long bridge that carries a road or railway over a valley. ▲ Say ***vye**-a-dukt.*

vibrate vibrates vibrating vibrated *verb*
when something vibrates, it shakes very quickly. *The floor vibrated every time a train went past.* ▲ Say *vye-**brate**.*
vibration *noun.*

vicious *adjective*
cruel and violent. a vicious attack. ▲ Say ***vish**-us.*
viciously *adverb.*

victim victims *noun*
a person who has been attacked, hurt, robbed or killed.

victory victories *noun*
a success in winning a battle or game. ■ The opposite is **defeat**.

video videos *noun*
1 a machine that you use to record a television programme so that you can watch it later.
2 a tape that is used to record a film or television programme.

view views *noun*
1 what you can see from one place. *We had a good view of the mountains.*
2 a person's opinion or what they think about something. *In my view, he fell over because he wasn't looking where he was going.* ▲ Say ***vyoo**.*

vile viler vilest *adjective*
horrible. *This cheese has a vile taste.*

village villages *noun*
a group of houses and other buildings in the country. *Villages are smaller than towns.*

villain villains *noun*
a very bad person, especially in a film, story or play. *The villain was killed at the end of the film.* ▲ Say ***vil**-en.*

vine vines *noun*
a climbing plant that grapes grow on.

vinegar *noun*
a sour liquid that is used to add flavor to food.

vineyard vineyards *noun*
a place where grape vines are grown for making wine. ▲ Say ***vin**-yard.*

violent *adjective*
1 a violent person uses force or weapons to hurt somebody.
2 very strong or rough. *a violent storm.*

violet violets *noun*
a small plant with small white or purple flowers.

violin violins *noun*
a musical instrument with strings stretched across a wooden frame. You play a violin by holding it under your chin and moving a stick called a bow across the strings.
violinist *noun.*

virtual reality *noun*
an image made by a computer that surrounds you and that looks real.

virtue noun
a kind of goodness. *Honesty is a virtue.*

virus viruses *noun*
1 a tiny germ that causes a disease. *Colds and flu are caused by viruses.*
2 a computer program that damages the data in a computer system.

visible *adjective*
if something is visible, you can see it. ▲ Say ***viz**-i-bul.* ■ The opposite is **invisible**.

vision *noun*
a person's ability to see. *He has excellent vision.* ▲ Say ***vish**-un.*

visit visits visiting visited *verb*
if you visit somebody or somewhere, you go to see them. *Matt visited his friend Tom in hospital.*
visitor *noun.*

vitamin vitamins *noun*
one of the substances that are in food naturally that you need to keep healthy.

vocabulary vocabularies *noun*
1 all the words somebody knows.
2 a list of words and what they mean.

voice voices *noun*
the sound that you make when you speak or sing.

volcano volcanoes *noun*
a mountain with an opening called a crater in the top from which very hot melted rock called lava and gases sometimes pour out.

volume volumes *noun*
1 the amount of space inside something or the amount of space that something takes up. *What's the volume of that petrol can?*
2 a book in a set of books. *Sanya has the first volume of a 20-volume encyclopaedia.*
3 how loud a sound is. *Can you turn the volume of your radio down?*

volunteer volunteers *noun*
a person who does something without being paid and without being made to do it. *This work is done by volunteers.*
voluntary *adjective.*
I do voluntary work for the homeless.

vote votes voting voted *verb*
if you vote for somebody or something you choose them by putting your hand up or by making a mark on a piece of paper. *Have you voted yet?*
vote *noun.*
There were ten votes for my plan and eight votes against.

vowel vowels *noun*
the letters a, e, i, o and u are vowels and sometimes y has a vowel sound.

voyage voyages *noun*
a long journey by sea or in space.
▲ Say *voy-ij*.

vulture
vultures *noun*
a large, tropical bird that eats dead animals.

Ww

wade wades wading waded *verb*
to wade is to walk through deep water. *He waded across the stream.*

wag wags wagging wagged *verb*
when a dog wags its tail, it moves it quickly from side to side and up and down.

wages *noun*
the money that people are paid for the work they do.

wagon wagons *noun*
a cart that is used to carry people and things from one place to another. It has four wheels and is usually pulled along by horses.

wail wails wailing wailed *verb*
if somebody wails, they shout or make a sad cry because they are hurt or sad. *'You kicked me!' he wailed.*

waist waists *noun*
your waist is the narrow, middle part of your body. *Jack is wearing a belt round his waist.*

waistcoat waistcoats *noun*
a short jacket with no sleeves or collar.

wait waits waiting waited *verb*
if you wait, you stay where you are because you are expecting something to happen. *We waited half an hour for the bus.*

waiter waiters *noun*
a person who brings you food in a café or a restaurant.

wake wakes waking woke woken *verb*
1 when you wake, you stop sleeping. *I woke up at seven o'clock this morning.*
2 when you wake someone, you make them stop sleeping.

walk walks walking walked *verb*
when you walk, you move along on your feet. *I walk to the park every day.*
walk *noun.*
We took the dog for a walk.

wall walls *noun*
1 one of the sides of a building or a room. *I helped to paint my bedroom walls.*
2 a wall is also something made of bricks or stones that you can see around some fields and gardens. *We climbed over the wall into the secret garden.*

wallet wallets *noun*
a small, flat purse for keeping paper money in. *Dad had a ₹20 note in his wallet.*

wand wands *noun*
a stick that fairies and magicians wave when they do magic.

wander wanders wandering wandered *verb*
when you wander, you walk around slowly without going in any particular direction. *We wandered around in the woods looking for mushrooms.*

want wants wanting wanted *verb*
when you want something, you need it or you would like to have it. *Do you want an apple or an orange?*

war wars *noun*
a time when armies of different countries are fighting. ■ The opposite is **peace**.

ward wards *noun*
a big room in a hospital with beds in it for patients.

wardrobe wardrobes *noun*
a large cupboard where you can keep your clothes. *She hung her dress in the wardrobe.*

warehouse warehouses *noun*
a big building where goods are stored before they are taken to shops or other places. *a furniture warehouse.*

A B C D E F G H I J K L M N O P Q R S T U V W X Y Z

warm warmer warmest *adjective*
quite hot but not too hot. *The cat sat by the fire to keep warm.* ■ The opposite is **cool**.
warmth *noun.*
I felt the warmth of the sun on my skin.

warn warns warning warned *verb*
if you warn somebody, you tell them about something dangerous or bad that may happen. *He warned us not to swim in the river because it was very deep.* ◆ *Dad warned us not to be late or he'd get cross.*

warning warnings *noun*
something that tells you about a danger that may happen. *The sign on the gate said: 'Warning! Keep out – dangerous bull in field'.*

wart warts *noun*
a hard lump on your skin. ▲ Rhymes with ***sort***.

wash washes washing washed *verb*
when you wash something, you use soap and water to clean it. *He washed his face before going to bed.*

washing *noun*
clothes that you need to wash or that you have washed. *I put the clothes in the washing machine.*

washing-up *noun*
when you do the washing-up, you clean the knives, forks, plates and cups after a meal. *I'll help you do the washing-up.*

wasp wasps *noun*
a flying insect with yellow and black stripes on its body. Wasps can sting.

waste *noun*
1 things that people throw away because they are old, broken, used up or not wanted.
2 what is left after you have digested your food and that is sent out of your body.
3 something is a waste when you use too much of it, or do not use it carefully. *It's a waste to throw food away.*

waste wastes wasting wasted *verb*
1 if you waste something, you use more than you need. *Don't waste water.*
2 to waste also means not to make good use of something. *Don't waste time.*

watch watches watching watched *verb*
if you watch something, you look at it for a long time. *We watched the football match.* ◆ *Watch how I do this trick.*

watch watches *noun*
a small clock that you wear around your wrist

water *noun*
the clear liquid that is in seas, lakes and rivers. *All living things need water.*

water waters watering watered *verb*
when you water plants, you pour water over them to help them grow.

waterfall waterfalls *noun*
a place on a river where a lot of water falls over high rocks or down a mountain. *Niagara Falls is a famous waterfall in North America.*

waterproof *adjective*
if something is waterproof, it does not let water go through it. *a waterproof jacket.*

wave waves *noun*
1 a curved line of water moving across a sea. *The waves crashed upon the shore.*
2 a vibrating movement like a wave on the sea that carries sound or light. *sound waves.*
3 a curving shape in your hair.
4 a movement with your hand that you make when you say 'hello' or 'goodbye' to somebody.

wave waves waving waved *verb*
when you wave, you move your hand up and down to say 'hello' or 'goodbye' to somebody. *Gran waved me goodbye as she got on the bus.*

wax *noun*
material that candles are made out of. Wax is hard when it is cold but it goes soft and melts when you heat it.

weak weaker weakest *adjective*
1 a weak person or thing has little power or strength. *She felt weak after her illness.* ◆ *weak knees.*
2 likely to break very easily. *That branch is too weak to support your weight.*
3 a weak drink has a lot of water or milk in it. *weak tea.* ● A word that sounds like **weak** is **week**. ■ The opposite is **strong** or **powerful**.

wealthy wealthier wealthiest *adjective*
rich and with a lot of money.

weapon weapons *noun*
something such as a gun, spear, a sword or a bow and arrow that people use to fight with.

wear wears wearing wore worn *verb*
1 when you wear clothes, you have them on your body. *Lindsay is wearing a blue dress.* ◆ *Steve wore jeans.*
2 when something wears out, you cannot use it anymore because it is broken or too old. *These socks are worn out – they have holes in them.*
3 when something wears you out, it makes you very tired. *After running all the way to school, I was worn out.*

weather *noun*
the weather is how hot, cold, windy, rainy or dry it is outside. *The weather forecast tells you what the weather will be like for the next few days.*

weave weaves weaving wove woven *noun*
1 when you weave, you make a piece of cloth using a machine called a loom. *The loom has rows of thread fixed at each end and you move another thread in and out of these.*
2 to weave also means to make something like a basket or a mat by twisting thin strips of wood or straw in and out of each other.

web webs *noun*
a round net that a spider makes to catch flies in.
web-footed *adjective.*
having feet with a piece of skin between the toes, such as geese and ducks have.

wedding weddings *noun*
when two people get married, they have a wedding.

weed weeds *noun*
a wild plant that grows in the garden and that you do not want. *Dandelions are weeds.*

week weeks *noun*
a measure of time. There are seven days in a week – Sunday, Monday, Tuesday, Wednesday, Thursday, Friday and Saturday. There are 52 weeks in a year. ● A word that sounds like **week** is **weak**.

weekend weekends *noun*
the end of the week: Saturday and Sunday.

weep weeps weeping wept *verb*
if somebody weeps, they cry. *She wept because her cat had died.*

weigh weighs weighing weighed *verb*
1 you weigh something on scales to find out how heavy it is.
2 weigh also means how heavy you are. *How much do you weigh?*

weight weights *noun*
1 how heavy somebody or something is. *What's the weight of these apples?*
2 a piece of metal weighing a certain amount that you use on scales to find out how heavy something is.
weighty *adjective*
a weighty problem.

weird weirder weirdest *adjective*
very strange. *I heard a weird noise last night.*

welcome welcomes welcoming welcomed *verb*
if you welcome somebody, you show that you are happy to see them. *She came to the door to welcome us.*

well better best *adjective, adverb*
1 when you do something well, you do it in a good way. *Gerry plays the guitar very well.*
2 if you are well, you feel healthy.

well wells *noun*
a well is a deep hole in the ground with water or oil at the bottom.

wellingtons *noun*
long boots made of rubber or plastic that you wear to keep your feet dry.

went past of go.

wept past of weep.

west *noun*
the direction in which the sun sets in the evening.
west *adjective*, **western** *adjective.*
Senegal is in West Africa.
west *adverb.*
The boat was sailing west.

wet wetter wettest *adjective*
something that is wet is covered with or full of water or other liquid. *You will get wet if you go out in the rain.*
■ The opposite is **dry**.

whale whales *noun*
a very large mammal that lives in the sea. Whales need air to breathe. A young whale is called a calf.
❖ ***Look below***

wheat *noun*
a plant that farmers grow. We use its seeds, called grain, to make flour.

wheel wheels *noun*
a wheel is a round thing on something like a car, lorry or bicycle. Wheels turn around and around to move things along the ground.

wheelchair wheelchairs *noun*
a special chair with wheels for somebody who cannot walk very well.

whether *conjunction*
if. *I don't know whether I can come tonight.*

whine whines whining whined *verb*
to whine is to make a long, miserable sound because you want something.

whip whips whipping whipped *verb*
1 if you whip a person or an animal you hit them with a long piece of rope or leather called a whip.
2 to whip also means to stir cream or eggs very fast until they become stiff.

whisk whisks whisking whisked *verb*
when you whisk things such as eggs or cream, you beat them very quickly.
whisk *noun*.

whisker whiskers *noun*
one of the long hairs that cats, mice and some other animals have on their faces.

whisper whispers whispering whispered *verb*
when you whisper, you speak very quietly so that other people cannot hear you. *She whispered in his ear.*

whistle whistles *noun*
1 an instrument that you blow into to make very high sounds. *He blew a whistle to end the football match.*
2 a high sound that you make when you blow through your lips.
whistle *verb*.

whole *adjective*
all of something. *He ate the whole cake.* ● A word that sounds like **whole** is **hole**.
whole *noun*.
Two halves make a whole.

wick wicks *noun*
a piece of string that goes through the middle of a candle. When you light the wick, the candle burns.

wicked wickeder wickedest *adjective*
very bad or cruel. *That was a very wicked thing to do.*

wide wider widest *adjective*
1 something that is wide measures a lot from one side to the other. *Motorways are very wide roads.* ■ The opposite is **narrow**.
2 wide also means how much something measures. *The window is one metre wide.*

widow widows *noun*
a woman whose husband is dead.

widower widowers *noun*
a man whose wife is dead.

width *noun*
how wide something is. *He measured from side to side to find the width of the box.*

wife wives *noun*
one's wife is the woman they are married to.

wig wigs *noun*
a thing made of hair that covers your head. Actors and bald people sometimes wear wigs.

wild wilder wildest *adjective*
1 wild animals are animals that are not kept by people for food or as pets. Foxes and badgers are wild animals. ■ The opposite is **tame**.
2 wild flowers and plants are not planted by people.

will wills *noun*
the part of your mind that makes you want to do things or decide what you want to do. *She has the will to win the race.* ◆ *He tidied his bedroom against his will.*

willing *adjective*
if you are willing, you are ready and happy to do what is wanted. *Are you willing to go to the shops for me?*

willow willows *noun*
a tree with long, narrow leaves that grows near water. Weeping willows have thin branches that hang downwards. ❖ ***Look at page 174***

wilt wilts wilting wilted *verb*
if a plant wilts, it droops because it needs water.

win wins winning won *verb*
when you win a race or game you come first and do better than everybody else. *Kamran won the 100-metre race.*

wind winds *noun*
air that is moving very fast. *The wind blew the sailing boat along.* ▲ Rhymes with ***tinned***.
windy *adjective*.
windy weather.

wind winds winding wound *verb*
1 when you wind a clock or a watch, you turn a key or a knob so that it starts working.
2 when you wind something like string around another thing, you twist it round and round. *They wound the wool into a ball.*
3 when a road or a river winds, it has lots of bends in it.
4 when you wind a film or a tape, you move it backwards or forwards. *Remember to wind the film on before you take the next picture.* ▲ Rhymes with ***find***.

windmill windmills *noun*
a tall building with large pieces of wood, called sails, on top that turn around in the wind. As the sails turn, they make machines inside work to grind corn into flour.

window windows *noun*
a hole covered by glass in a wall of a building that lets in light and air.

windscreen windscreens *noun*
the window at the front of a car.

windsurf windsurfs windsurfing windsurfed *verb*
to windsurf is to ride over water on a special board with a sail.
windsurfer *noun.*

wine wines *noun*
wine is an alcoholic drink usually made from grapes.

wing wings *noun*
1 birds, bats and some insects, like bees, have wings which they flap when they fly.
2 the wings of an aeroplane are the two flat parts on each side that help it move through the air.

wink winks winking winked *verb*
if you wink at somebody, you close and open one eye very quickly. *She winked at me to show that it was a joke.*

winter *noun*
the season of the year between autumn and spring. Winter is the coldest part of the year.

wipe wipes wiping wiped *verb*
when you wipe something, you move a cloth over it to clean or dry it. *Freddie wiped the mess off the table.*

wire wires *noun*
a long, thin piece of metal that bends easily. Copper wire is used to carry electricity. Some fences are made of wire.

wise wiser wisest *adjective*
a person who is wise knows and understands a lot about many things. *Mum says you get wiser as you get older.*
wisdom *noun.*

wish wishes wishing wished *verb*
if you wish for something, you want to have it or you want it to happen very much. *I wish I was good at sport.*
wish *noun.*

witch witches *noun*
a woman in fairy stories who has magic powers. *The prince rescued the princess from the wicked witch.*

wither withers withering withered *verb*
when a plant withers, it becomes dry and dies. *The flowers withered in the hot sun and died.*

witness witnesses *noun*
a person who sees something important happen and can tell other people about it later. *The police are looking for a witness to the accident.*

wives plural of wife.

wizard wizards *noun*
a man in fairy stories who has magical powers.

wobble wobbles wobbling wobbled *verb*
when something wobbles, it shakes a little from side to side. *The jelly wobbled on the plate.*
wobbly *adjective.*

woke woken past of wake.

wolf wolves *noun*
a wild animal that looks like a big dog, with a pointed nose and pointed ears. Wolves hunt in groups called packs. A young wolf is called a cub.

woman women *noun*
a grown-up female person.

womb wombs *noun*
the womb is the part of a woman or a female animal where a baby grows before it is born. ▲ Say ***woom***.

won past of win.

wonder wonders wondering wondered *verb*
to wonder is to think about something that you do not know the answer to. *I wonder why snails move so slowly.*
wonder *noun.*
They gazed with wonder at the fireworks.

wonderful *adjective*
very beautiful or very good. *We had a wonderful holiday.*

wood woods *noun*
1 the material that trees are made of. Tables and chairs are usually made of wood. You can also use wood to make paper.
2 a wood is a place where there are a lot of trees growing near each other.
wooden *adjective.*
a wooden table.

wool wools *noun*
the soft, thick hair that grows on sheep. Wool is used for making cloth and for knitting. Jumpers and scarves are often made of wool.
woollen *adjective.*
woollen gloves.
woolly *adjective.*
a woolly hat.

word words *noun*
we use words when we speak or write. Words are made of letters of the alphabet and each word means something. *Angela looked up the meaning of a word in the dictionary.*

wore past of wear.

work works working worked *verb*
1 when you work, you do or make something as a job. *I work in a bank.*
2 to work also means to do something that takes a lot of time and effort. *I worked hard to finish the essay.*
3 when a machine works, it does what it should do. *The computer isn't working.*
work *noun.*

world *noun*
1 the planet that we live on, and all its countries and people.
2 the universe.

worm worms *noun*
a small creature with a long, thin body and no legs. Many worms live in the earth in gardens.

worn past of wear.
worn socks.

worry worries worrying worried *verb*
if you worry, you keep thinking of bad things that might happen. *Dad worries if I'm late home from school.*

worship worships worshipping worshipped *verb*
to worship is to pray to God.

worth *adjective*
having a certain value. If something is worth ₹20, you could sell it for ₹20. *This candy is worth ₹20.*

wound wounds wounding wounded *verb*
to wound is to hurt or injure somebody. *He was shot and wounded in the leg.* ▲ Say ***woond***.
wound *noun.*

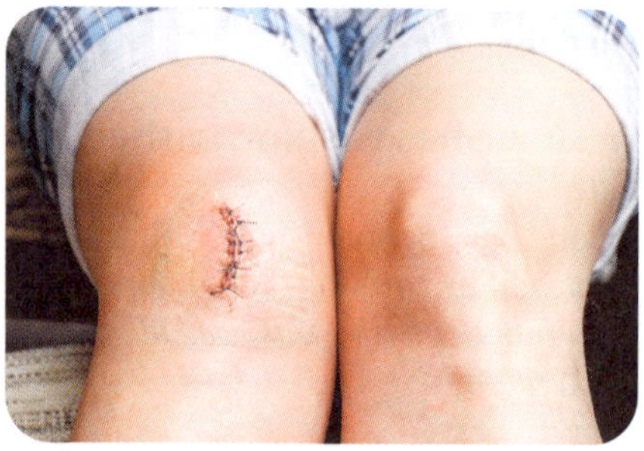

wound past of wind.
▲ Ryhmes with **found**.

wove woven past of weave.

wrap wraps wrapping wrapped *verb*
if you wrap something, you cover it in paper or cloth. *He wrapped up the birthday present.*

wreck wrecks wrecking wrecked *verb*
to wreck is to break or destroy something completely so that you cannot use it. *The fire wrecked the house.*

wreck wrecks *noun*
a boat or an aircraft that has been badly damaged in an accident.

wreckage wreckages *noun*
the broken parts of something that has been badly damaged. *They found the wreckage of a plane.*

wrestle wrestles wrestling wrestled *verb*
to wrestle is to fight with somebody and try to push them on to the ground.

wriggle wriggles wriggling wriggled *verb*
if you wriggle, you keep twisting and moving about because you feel excited or uncomfortable. *The worm wriggled through the grass.*

wring wrings wringing wrung *verb*
if you wring something that is wet, you twist and squeeze it to get water out of it. *He wrung out clothes and hung them out to dry.*

wrinkle wrinkles *noun*
a crease or line in your skin. *The old man's face was full of wrinkles.*
wrinkle *verb.*
He wrinkled his forehead.
wrinkled *adjective.*
wrinkled skin.

wrist wrists *noun*
your wrist is the thin part of your arm just above your hand.

write writes writing wrote written *verb*
when you write, you make words with a pen or pencil. *Tom wrote his name at the top of the paper.* ● A word that sounds like **write** is **right**.
writer *noun.*

writing *noun*
the words that you make on paper with a pen or pencil. *Primrose has very neat writing.*

wrong *adjective*
1 if something is wrong, it is incorrect. *The answer to that sum is wrong.* ■ The opposite is **right**.
2 bad. *Being unkind to animals is wrong.*

wrung past of wring.

X x

X-ray X-rays *noun*
a picture of part of your body that shows the bones and other parts inside so that doctors can see if anything is broken or damaged.

xylophone xylophones *noun*
a musical instrument that has a row of wooden or metal bars of different lengths that you hit to give different notes. ▲ Say *zye-lo-fone*.

Y y

yacht yachts *noun*
a large boat with sails or an engine. Some yachts are used for racing.
▲ Say *yot*.

yawn yawns yawning yawned *verb*
when you yawn, you open your mouth wide and breathe in as you do when you are very tired.

year years *noun*
a measure of time. There are 12 months in a year.
yearly *adjective, adverb.*
a yearly visit.

yeast *noun*
a substance that is used to make bread rise.

yell yells yelling yelled *verb*
if you yell, you shout very loudly.

yoghurt *noun*
a thick, slightly sour liquid made from milk. ▲ Say *yog-ert*.

yoke yokes *noun*
a wooden frame that goes across the back of two oxen pulling a plough or cart to make them stay together.
● A word that sounds like **yoke** is **yolk**.

yolk yolks *noun*
the yellow part inside an egg. ▲ Say *yoke*.

young younger youngest *adjective*
not having lived for many years or for as many years as somebody else. *I'm younger than my granddad.* ▲ Say **yung**. ■ The opposite is **old**.

youth youths *noun*
1 a time when a person is young. *He spent his youth in Australia.* ■ The opposite is **old age.**
2 a young man.
3 all young people. *the youth of today.* ◆ *a youth hostel.* ▲ Say *yooth*.

Z z

zap zaps zapping zapped *verb*
1 to zap is to shoot somebody or destroy something in a computer game.
2 to zap also means to keep changing quickly from one TV programme to another or from one section of a videotape to another.

zebra zebras *noun*
an animal like a horse with black and white stripes on its body. Zebras live in Africa.

zero zeros *noun*
the number 0. You write ten with a one and a zero – 10.

zest *noun*
orange, lemon or lime peel.

zigzag zigzags *noun*
a line that keeps changing direction and that bends sharply up and down.

zinc *noun*
a hard, blue-white metal.

zip zips *noun*
a long metal or plastic thing with two rows of teeth that fit together and that holds together two edges of material. *Trousers and bags often have zips.*
zip *verb.*

zombie zombies *noun*
in stories, a dead body brought back to life by witchcraft.

zone zones *noun*
an area in a town or a country used for a special purpose. *a danger zone.* ◆ *a no-parking zone.*

zoo zoos *noun*
a place where wild animals are kept so that people can look at them.
❖ ***Look at page 188***

zoology *noun*
the scientific study of animals. ▲ Say *zoo-ol-ogee*.
zoological *adjective,* **zoologist** *noun.*
zoological gardens.

zoom zooms zooming zoomed *verb*
if something zooms, it moves very fast. *The rocket zoomed into space.*

A B C D E F G H I J K L M N O P Q R S T U V W X Y Z

Zoos and National Parks

Vocabulary

captive breeding
a project operated by zoos to help increase the population of endangered species by encouraging them to reproduce in zoos. Many of these animals are then released back into their natural environments.

conservation
the careful management and protection of wildlife and natural resources.

deforestation
clearing land of trees. Huge areas of rainforests in South America are being cleared away, destroying animals' natural environment.

enclosure
a fenced off natural-looking area where animals are kept.

endangered species
a species of animal or plant that is threatened with extinction.

national park
an area of countryside, usually important for its natural beauty or wildlife, under the care of the nation.

pesticide
a chemical which kills insects and pests; it can also pollute soil and rivers.

poacher
a person who hunts or fishes without permission on private or protected land such as wildlife parks and game reserves.

zoo keeper
a person who looks after all the animals in a zoo.

Spellcheck

Words we use all the time and how to spell them. The words in **heavy black type** are some words which are difficult to spell.

a
about
ache
address
advertisement
after
ago
all
already
also
always
am
an
and
any
anybody
anyone
anything
anyway
anywhere
are
aren't = are not
as
at
away

b
be
became
because
become
been
being
best
better
business
but
by
bye

c
calendar
came
can
cannot = can not
can't = can not
career
ceiling
come
could
couldn't = could not

d
did
didn't = did not
do
does
doesn't = does not
doing
done
don't = do not
down
Dr = Doctor
during

e
each
either
else
ever
every
everybody
everyone
everywhere

f
few
first
for
friend
from

g
gave
get
getting
give
go
goes
going
gone
gorilla
got

h
had
hadn't = had not
handkerchief
has
have
haven't = have not
he
he'll = he will
her
here
hers
herself
he's = he is
him
himself
his
how
hurrah

i
I
I'd = I had
if
I'll = I shall, I will
I'm = I am
in
into
is
isn't = is not
it
its
it's = it is
itself
I've = I have

j
jewellery
just

k
kilogram
kilometre

l
last
least
less
let's = let us
lot

m
made
make
many
may
me
might
mile
mine
more
most
Mr = Mister
Mrs = Missus
Ms = Miss
much
mum
must
mustn't = must not
my
myself

n
needn't = need not
neither
nephew
next
niece
nobody
none
nonsense
no one
nothing
now
nowhere

o
o'clock
of
off
okay
on
once
only
or
other
our
ours
ourselves
out
over

p
perhaps
probably
put
putting

s
same
shall
shan't
she
she'll = she will
she's = she is
should
shouldn't = should not
since
sir
so
some
somebody
someone
something
sometime
somewhere
soon
sorry
success
such

t
than
that
the
their
theirs
them
themselves
then
there
these
they
they'd =they had
they'll = they will
they're = they are
they've = they have
this
those
to
today
tomorrow
tongue
tonight
too

u
up
upon
us

v
very

w
was
wasn't = was not
way
we
we'd = we had
we'll = we shall, we will
went
were
we're = we are
weren't = were not
what
when
where
which
while
who
who'll = who will
whom
who's = who is
whose
why
will
with
won't = will not
worst
would
wouldn't = would not

y
yet
you
you'd = you had
you'll = you will
your
you're = you are
yours
yourself
you've = you have

Useful information

Days of the week
Monday
Tuesday
Wednesday
Thursday
Friday
Saturday
Sunday

Monday's child is fair of face.
Tuesday's child is full of grace.
Wednesday's child is full of woe.
Thursday's child has far to go.
Friday's child is loving and giving.
Saturday's child works hard for a living.
But the child that is born on the Sabbath day,
Is bonny and blithe, good and gay.

Months of the year
January
February
March
April
May
June
July
August
September
October
November
December

Mnemonics
A mnemonic (▲say nem-on-ik) is a little rhyme or 'catch-phrase' that helps us to remember something. For instance there is an old spelling rule 'i before e except after c'. For example *field, ceiling.* And this rhyme:
'Thirty days hath September,
April, June and November.
All the rest have thirty-one.
Excepting February alone
which has 28 days and 29 days each leap year.'

Symbols
Here are some everyday symbols:

%	per cent
₹	rupee
$	dollar
@	at. Flowers @ ₹10 a bunch.

Seasons
Spring, Summer, Autumn, Winter

Numbers

1	one	first
2	two	second
3	three	third
4	four	fourth
5	five	fifth
6	six	sixth
7	seven	seventh
8	eight	eighth
9	nine	ninth
10	ten	tenth
11	eleven	eleventh
12	twelve	twelfth
13	thirteen	thirteenth
14	fourteen	fourteenth
15	fifteen	fifteenth
16	sixteen	sixteenth
17	seventeen	seventeenth
18	eighteen	eighteenth
19	nineteen	nineteenth
20	twenty	twentieth
21	twenty-one	twenty-first
30	thirty	thirtieth
40	forty	fortieth
50	fifty	fiftieth
60	sixty	sixtieth
70	seventy	seventieth
80	eighty	eightieth
90	ninety	ninetieth
100	a hundred	hundredth
101	one hundred and one	
1000	thousand	thousandth
1,000,000	million	millionth
1,000,000,000	billion	billionth

(sometimes a billion is counted as a million multiplied by a million: 1,000,000,000,000)

Time

60	seconds in one minute
60	minutes in one hour
24	hours in one day
7	days in one week
4	weeks in one month
12	months in one year
10	years in one decade
100	years in a century
1000	years in a millennium

Measurement

1 centimetre	=	10 millimetres
1 metre	=	100 centimetres
1 kilometre	=	1,000 metres
1 gram	=	1,000 milligrams
1 kilogram	=	1,000 grams
1 litre	=	1,000 millilitres

Answers to word games on page 9

Guess what
1 bacteria. **2** ballet. **3** ditch.

The plural for more than one
sheep, deer, children, geese, calves, mice, men, feet, cities, loaves.

What's the word?
bulb, cone, horn

Match the opposites

deep/shallow	late/early
hot/cold	careful/careless
above/below	forget/remember
happy/sad	tall/short
wide/narrow	begin/end

Complete the words
butterfly, kingfisher, keyboard, portable, roundabout, seaweed, season, tightrope, toadstool.

Odd ones out
dot (the other words are spelt with an a)
fastest (the other adjectives are comparatives)
ring (the other words are noises animals make)
toboggan (all the other vehicles have wheels)

Secret message
Meet me in the restaurant at midday.

Similar meaning
harmful/damaging; bit/piece; even/smooth; talk/chat; go/leave; discover/find; feel/touch; start/begin; cross/angry; afraid/frightened

Did you know what the symbols were on page 164?

Countries and People

Some countries and the people or adjective that go with them.

Belgium

Canada

Finland

Indonesia

Ireland

Jamaica

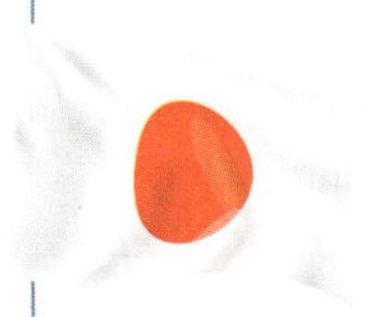
Japan

Afghanistan	Afghan
Albania	Albanian
Algeria	Algerian
Angola	Angolan
Argentina	Argentine/Argentinian
Australia	Australian
Austria	Austrian
Bangladesh	Bangladeshi
Belarus	Belarusian
Belgium	Belgian
Benin	Beninese
Bhutan	Bhutanese
Bolivia	Bolivian
Brazil	Brazilian
Cambodia	Cambodian
Cameroon	Cameroonian
Canada	Canadian
Chad	Chadian
Chile	Chilean
China	Chinese
Colombia	Colombian
Congo	Congolese
Costa Rica	Costa Rican
Cuba	Cuban
Cyprus	Cypriot
Czech Republic/Czechia	Czech
Denmark	Dane/Danish
Ecuador	Ecuadorean
Egypt	Egyptian
England	English
Ethiopia	Ethiopian
Fiji	Fijian
Finland	Finn/Finnish
France	French
Gambia, The	Gambian
Greece	Greek
Guatemala	Guatemalan
Guinea	Guinean
Guyana	Guyanese
Haiti	Haitian
Honduras	Honduran
Hungary	Hungarian
Iceland	Icelander/Icelandic
India	Indian
Indonesia	Indonesian
Iran	Iranian
Iraq	Iraqi
Ireland	Irish
Israel	Israeli
Italy	Italian
Jamaica	Jamaican
Japan	Japanese
Jordan	Jordanian
Kenya	Kenyan
Korea	Korean
Kuwait	Kuwaiti
Lebanon	Lebanese
Liberia	Liberian
Libya	Libyan
Luxembourg	Luxembourger
Malawi	Malawian
Malaysia	Malaysian
Mali	Malian
Mauritania	Mauritanian
Mexico	Mexican
Mongolia	Mongolian
Morocco	Moroccan
Namibia	Namibian
Nepal	Nepalese/Nepali
Netherlands	Dutch
New Zealand	New Zealander
Nicaragua	Nicaraguan
Niger	Nigerien
Nigeria	Nigerian
Norway	Norwegian
Oman	Omani
Pakistan	Pakistani
Panama	Panamanian
Paraguay	Paraguayan
Peru	Peruvian
Philippines	Filipino/Philippine
Poland	Pole/Polish
Portugal	Portuguese
Qatar	Qatari
Romania	Romanian
Russia	Russian
Saudi Arabia	Saudi Arabian/Saudi
Scotland	Scot/Scottish
Senegal	Senegalese
Singapore	Singaporean
Slovakia	Slovak/Slovakian
South Africa	South African
Spain	Spanish/Spaniard
Sri Lanka	Sri Lankan
Sudan	Sudanese
Sweden	Swede/Swedish
Switzerland	Swiss
Syria	Syrian
Tanzania	Tanzanian
Thailand	Thai
Tunisia	Tunisian
Türkiye	Turk/Turkish
Uganda	Ugandan
The USA	American
Uruguay	Uruguayan
Venezuela	Venezuelan
Vietnam	Vietnamese
Wales	Welsh
Yemen	Yemeni
Zambia	Zambian
Zimbabwe	Zimbabwean

Netherlands

Norway

Poland

Russia

Sweden

Thailand

United States of America

Image Copyright Information

Pexels.com

Accident; Address; Advertisement; Aerosol; Aim; Aisle; Ants; Astronaut; Audience; Award; Bacon; Bag; Bench; Biscuit; Block; Blow; Boat; Bouquet; Bow – bowing down; Bow – gift bow; Bow – violin bow; Buckle; Bullet; Camp; Carnival; Cassette; Cello; Centipede; Chariot; Chef; Chess; Chocolate; Circuit; Cliff; Climb; Cobweb; Coffee; Collar – cat; Collar – shirt; Comb; Compass; Computer; Concert; Cone – ice cream cone; Cone – pine; Coral; Corridor; Cow; Crane – bird; Crane – machine; Crayon; Crime; Crow; Cup; Cup – victory; Cushion; Dance; Desert; Diary; Directions; Dolphin; Door; Dress; Drum; Egg; Embroidery; Emerald; Engine; Envelope; Erupt; Even – floor; Even – numbers; Experiment; Eye; Factory; Fair; Fan; Fang; Farm; Finish; Fire; Fire Engine; Flask; Floppy Disk; Fly; Football; Fork; Frog; Fungus; Gadget; Geese; Generation; Glove; Gnome; Go-kart; Goldfish; Graffiti; Grate; Grill; Gymnastics; Half; Hamburger; Hare; Hawk; Hedgehog; Hen; Hieroglyphics; Hive; Hump – Bactrian Camel; Hump – Dromedary Camel; Iceberg; Inflate; Ingredient; Injection; Interior; Invitation; Jam; Jam – traffic; Jellyfish; Jug; Key; Kingfisher; Kite; Lamp; Laptop; Lasso; Leopard; Library; Lick; Lighthouse; Lion; Loaf; Lock; Loudspeaker; Magnifying Glass; Make-up; Marbles; Mast; Meal; Medal; Menu; Milk; Mirror; Monkey; Mug; Narrow; Negative; Nib; Nocturnal; Noodle; Nose – Mandrill; Nose – Snow leopard; Oak; Oil; Old; Open; Orchestra; Pad; Painting; Parrot; Pasta; Pattern; Peel; Pendulum; Penguin; Pepper; Phone; Pie; Pizza; Platform; Plug; Pocket; Pod; Pointed; Pollen; Poppy; Powder; Present; Press; Propeller; Pudding; Puddle; Queue; Rabbit; Radio; Ram; Ray; Record; Recycle; Referee; Reindeer; Remain; Repair; Rescue; Reservoir; Ribbon; Ripple; Rodent; Roundabout; Ruby; Saddle; Salad; Sandal; Scissors; Scooter; Screw; Seahorse; Set; Sew; Shadow; Shell; Shower; Sign; Skull; Skyscraper; Slipper; Slug; Snout; Solid; Stadium; Staircase; Statue; Stem; Stork; Submarine; Sugar; Suitcase; Sunglasses; Surf; Surround; Swim; Table tennis; Tail; Tandem; Tent; Test; Theatre; Thorn; Tiny; Tomato; Tractor; Train; Treasure; Tricycle; Trough; Tulip; Turtle; Typewriter; Utensil; Veil; Violin; Vulture; Wagon; Wand; Watch; Waterfall; Wax; Web; Wheel; Whisker; Windsurf; Wolf; Worm; Wrinkle; Xylophone

Shutterstock.com

Alike; Aircraft; Apparatus; Bee; Bicycle; Birds; Boomerang; Bug; Cats; Cocoa; Decimal; Dinosaur; Dogs; Fever; Fish; Human Body; Infant; Insects; Magazine: Delpixel; Musical Instruments; Organ; Prehistoric Animals; Rocket; Scratch; Sculpture; Ships and Boats; Solar System; Spider; Sweat; Tank; Tickle; Tiger; Vaccine; Wire; Wound; Zoos and National Parks

Wikimedia commons

Angles: Public Domain – Pearson Scott Foresman; Right Angle – Public Domain; Igloo: Creative Commons Attribution 3.0 Unported/Maurizio Ceol/ https://commons.wikimedia.org/wiki/File:Un_igloo_ma_non_siamo_in_alaska_ma_nei_pressi_della_Pala_di_Santa_-_panoramio.jpg; Illusion: Creative Commons Attribution 3.0 Unported/ SABO123/https://commons.wikimedia.org/wiki/File:5_Optical_Illusion.jpg; Nose – Elephant seal: Public Domain/ NOAA; Nose – Probiscus Monkey: Creative Commons Attribution – Share Alike 4.0 International/Charles J. Sharp/ https://commons.wikimedia.org/wiki/File:Proboscis_monkey_(Nasalis_larvatus)_male_head.jpg; Nose – Spear-nosed Bat: Creative Commons Attribution 3.0 Unported/Karin Schneeberger alias Felineora/https://commons.wikimedia.org/wiki/File:Phyllostomus_hastatus.jpg; Shark: Creative Commons Attribution 2.0 Generic/NOAA Photo Library/ https://commons.wikimedia.org/wiki/File:Corl0207_(28225976491).jpg;

Pixabay.com

Beach; Bread; Bus; Camel; Clock; Cottage; Crab; Cub; Crown; Daisy; Dart; Demolish; Den; Desk; Diet; Disaster; Earth; Elephant; Exam; Exit; Forest; Fox; Fridge; Furniture; Garlic; Gift; Glasses; Globe; Grasshopper; Grind; Guard; Guinea pig; Guitar; Hail; Headphones; Helicopter; Hut; Incubator; Iron; Jaguar; Jockey; Jog; Juggle; Jump; Kick; Lemon; Lorry; Luggage; Melon; Meter; Microscope; Money; Motorbike; Nun; Nut; Oats; Onion; Ostrich; Panda; Panda – Red Panda; Pasture; Pear; Peppercorn; Perch; Pile; Pipe; Plank; Porcupine; Pour; Prickle; Procession; Professional; Puffin; Puppet; Puppy; Racket; Razor; Reap; Restaurant; Rhinoceros; Ring; Rugby; Ruler; Runway; Rust; Saxophone; Scarecrow; Scooter; Screw; Seed; Shirt; Shop; Silver; Sing; Skateboard; Spear; Sofa; Soup; Spanner; Sun; Sky; Squeeze; Stamp; Sticker; Stool; Stove; Straw; Stretch; String; Study; Supermarket; Supersonic; Surgery; Tattoo; Teapot; Telescope; Thoughtful; Throne; Tile; Tourist; Trapeze; Tribe; Trolley; Trot; Umbrella; Undergrowth; Uniform; Unit; Universe; Untidy; Variety; Vase; Viaduct; Vineyard; Wasp; Well; Wig; Windmill; Wither

Designed by Freepik

Feather; Flags; Produce; Word Snake

by courtesy of Shubhali Chopra

Prime Numbers; Quarter; Right Angle; Semicircle; Square

All other images, illustrations and artwork from old edition

Illustrators: Rachel Fuller, Ron Hayward, Karen Hiscock, Ruth Lindsay, Jerry Malone, Patrick Mulrey, Rob Perry, Jm Robins, David Russell, Sue Sharpies, Rob Shone, Guy Smith (Mainline), Harry Titcombe. ***Artwork:*** Fred Anderson, Arcana, Liz Butler, Joanne Cowne, Angelika Elsebach, Michael Fisher (Garden Studio), Lee Gibbons, Peter Goodfellow, Ray Grinaway, Geoff Hamilton, David Holmes (Garden Studio), Richard Hook, John James, Terry Lambert, Alan Male, Andrew Macdonald, Janos Marffy, Josephine Martin, William Olliver, Bruce Pearson, Eric Rowe (Linden Artists), Roger Stewart, Ian Thompson, Guy Troughton, Phil Weare (Linden Artists).
Additional: Hannah Landis, St Bartholomew's Hospital for the physiotherapy equipment. Nice Irma's, London. Footes Musical Instruments, London. GK Locksmiths, London. Advisory Services, London, ('Roger' Clutton, Ray Coventry, William Greaves, Kil Hamilton, Jon Meakin, John Pearson, Roger and Linda Stong and Peter Footman).